Contents

Introduction	1
Population	9
Health	26
Social protection	59
Household and families	80
e-Society	101
Lifestyles and social participation	131
International comparisons	165
Labour market	192
Income and wealth	215
Housing	236
Expenditure	266
Transport	281
Education and training	315
Crime and justice	344
Environment	372

Introduction

In the editorial for the first edition of *Social Trends* in 1970 Muriel Nissel explained the new publication as follows:

'The growing realisation in Parliament, the Press and elsewhere that economic progress must be measured, in part at least, in terms of social benefits makes it the more important that the available key figures about our society should be readily accessible..... There is, of course already a wealth of information in the separate statistical publications of the various government departments. *Social Trends* … sets out to bring together from these widespread sources a set of comprehensive, and at the same time, selective statistics designed to highlight the most important aspects of social conditions in the United Kingdom.'

In an introductory chapter to the same edition, Professor (now Lord) Claus Moser, then the head of the Government Statistical Service, confirmed that the aim was to bring together 'a number of significant statistical series relating to social policies and conditions…[so that] the combination and confrontation of tables bearing on different aspects of social life may produce a more rounded picture of the social scene…. If it is successful then *Social Trends* will help public understanding and discussion of social policy.'

Since then, *Social Trends* has continued to try to fulfil these aims and, indeed, to interpret them as widely as possible. In particular, statistics about the environment are included along with social and economic statistics, reflecting increased interest in how all three are inter-related.

There is now an Office for National Statistics programme to deliver accepted and trusted National Statistics to help understanding of national well-being, which is how we now describe the rounded picture of 'how the UK is doing' envisioned by the founders of *Social Trends*. *Social Trends* will evolve as we report on national well-being and identify new requirements for coverage and presentation of these statistics.

In 2010 the fortieth edition of *Social Trends* was published; the last to be made available by the Office for National Statistics in printed format as the office became a web-only publisher. It looked back at the historical data and described the social scene in the each of the decades during which *Social Trends* has been published.

For *Social Trends 41* we have used an entirely web-based format and this has meant some changes in what we have reported and how it is presented. The rest of this chapter gives more information about what has been included and summarises it into some emerging themes.

Jen Beaumont
Editor, Social Trends
Office for National Statistics, August 2011

Contributors and acknowledgements

The editor would like to thank colleagues in contributing Departments and other organisations for their generous support and helpful comments, without which this edition of *Social Trends* would not have been possible.

Editor:	Jen Beaumont
Authors:	Grace Anyaegbu
	Louise Barnes
	Jen Beaumont
	Sonia Carrera
	Louise Clarke
	Anna Donabie
	Ian Macrory
	Chris Randall
	Carla Seddon
	Alison Spence
	David Sweet
	Allan Baird
Production Managers:	Anna Donabie
	Carla Seddon
Production Team:	Ann Corp
	Tony James
	Rittah Njeru
	Tammy Powell
	Karen Whittaker
Lead reviewers:	Paul Allin
	Stephen Hicks

Overview

Social Trends provides a unique overview of the state of the nation. In this year's edition, there are new chapters on international comparisons and e-Society. In this overview the updated statistics in each of the chapters have been grouped under four major themes, showing that in the United Kingdom the population is ageing, more digitally orientated, affected by the recent recession and concerned with well-being.

An ageing population living in smaller households

The **Population** chapter examines the long and short term changes in the population of the UK. The population continued to grow with an estimated 61.8 million people resident in 2009, an increase of 23.6 million since the start of the twentieth century. For every 1,000 residents, births and deaths added 3.5 people and net migration and other changes 2.9 people between 2008 and 2009. Natural change (2004-2009) was greater in the UK than the European average (EU-27) but migration was similar to the European average (EU-27) from a higher base of foreign citizens in the UK.

Overall, in the second half of the twentieth century, growth in the UK population was slower than across the world (see **International Comparisons** chapter). Provisional conception rates in 2009 for England and Wales increased from 2008, most markedly to women aged 30 and over whilst the number of conceptions resulting in legal abortions decreased in all age groups during the same period (see **Households and families** chapter).

Improvements to medical treatments, housing and living standards have resulted in an increase over time in the proportion of the population in older age groups. It is projected that by 2018 the number of UK residents aged 65 and over will be larger than the number aged under 16. The estimated number of UK residents aged 90 and over increased by 12 per cent from 388,200 in 2002 to 436,500 in 2009.

The health of the population has improved considerably since the start of the twentieth century and the **Health** chapter analyses these changes. The chapter highlights increases in life expectancy at birth in the UK to 77.6 years for males and 81.7 years for females in 2008 coupled with the lowest recorded levels of infant and neonatal mortality rates since 1930. Total spending on health as a percentage of GDP in the UK was the second lowest of the G7 countries but the UK had the highest proportion from public sources. Public satisfaction with healthcare in the UK was markedly above the European average (see **International Comparisons** chapter).

There has been a fall in mortality rates in the UK compared with 1971. Cancer is now the most common cause of death with rates of 2,081 per million males and 1,497 per million females in 2009. The death rates for cancer in 2007 for men, however, were below the EU average, for the 25 countries for which data are available, and above the EU average for women (see **International Comparisons** chapter). The **Health** chapter highlights incidence and mortality rates of specific cancers in the UK and improvements in five-year age-standardised survival rates in England since the early 1970s. The chapter also describes excess winter mortality trends in Great Britain over the last 60 years and how the recent 'Swine Flu' epidemic impacted on GP consultations across the UK.

The **Social Protection** chapter shows that in 2009/10, 183 million hours of home care was provided by local authorities in England to households compared with just over 151 million hours in 2003/04, an increase of 21 per cent. In 2003/04 the independent sector provided 68 per cent of home care, by 2009/10 this had increased to 84 per cent. In England during 2009/10 nearly 1.7 million adults received caring services: of these almost 1.5 million received community-based services. The largest users of services, around two-thirds of the total, were the 1.1 million clients aged 65 and over.

As the population has increased and aged, the number of households has also grown as shown in the **Households and families** chapter. There were an estimated 25.3 million households in 2010, an increase of 1.4 million from 2001. The number of dwellings in Great Britain reached 26.2 million in 2008 (see **Housing** chapter). Average household size reduced from 3.1 people in 1961 to 2.4 people in 2010 as the number of households increased faster than population. The decrease in household size was caused by the combination of a rise in the number of people living alone, a reduction in the proportion of families with children and a decrease in the number of children within those families.

Digital Lifestyles

The **e-Society** chapter shows how new technology plays a crucial part in daily life for most people. In 2010, 73 per cent of households in the UK had Internet access and, in 2009, 63 per cent had broadband Internet access. The most common use of the Internet was to send or receive emails. The increased popularity of modern technologies has changed the way we communicate with each other, such as video calls via webcams, social networking sites and telephone calls over the Internet. Also 27 per cent of children aged 5 to 15 who owned a mobile phone in 2009 first acquired one by the time they were eight years old.

The way in which transactions are carried out in the UK has also changed dramatically over the last decade with an increase in the use of electronic payment methods leading to a decline in the use of cheques. There were 1.8 billion transactions by cheque in 1985 compared with 0.6 billion in 2009 (see **Expenditure** chapter).

The **Lifestyles and social participation** chapter also discusses use of technology. In 2009/10, UK adults aged 16 and over spent an average of 3.5 hours a day watching television, 2.5 hours using a computer and 1 hour listening to the radio. Also, almost all single music tracks (98 per cent) were purchased digitally in 2009. The chapter also shows that holiday visits abroad by UK residents decreased by 15 per cent from 45.5 million visits in 2008 to 38.5 million in 2009, whilst domestic tourism grew by 12 per cent from 75 million trips within the UK in 2008 to 84 million in 2009. This change coincided with the recent recession.

Recession

The **International Comparisons** chapter places the UK in an international context and, by analysing GDP data, suggests that the UK had followed the US into recession in 2008 ahead of the

European Union (EU-27) and that growth between 2000 and 2009 was lower in the UK than the European average.

Recessions in the 1970s, 1980s, 1990s and the recent recession in 2008–09 have had different effects on the labour market in the UK and the **Labour market** chapter discusses these in some detail. During and after the 2008–09 recession unemployment rates were lower than earlier recessions having increased from 5.2 per cent in the first quarter of 2008 to a peak of 8.0 per cent in the first quarter of 2010 and falling slightly to 7.7 per cent in the first quarter of 2011.

While there was a decrease in employment as a result of the 2008–09 recession, the effect has not been equal across types of employment: there was a decrease in full-time and an increase in part-time employment. The impact of unemployment rates during the most recent recession has been different for men and women. For men the unemployment rate increased from a pre-recession level of 5.6 per cent in the first quarter of 2008 to a high of 9.1 per cent in the first quarter of 2010 before falling again to 8.4 per cent in the first quarter of 2011. The unemployment rate for women rose from 4.8 per cent in the first quarter of 2008 to 7.1 per cent in the fourth quarter of 2010, falling slightly to 7.0 per cent in the first quarter of 2011.

The labour market is a key part of the economy and long-term trends have major implications not only for the economy but also society more generally. Some of the changes in the UK labour market over recent decades include: growth in the size of the labour force as the population has increased, an increase in the proportion of women in the labour market and a reduction in the size of the manufacturing sector. The employment rate for women increased from 53 per cent in the second quarter of 1971 to 66 per cent in the first quarter of 2011. In the first quarter of 1979, 26.1 per cent of jobs were in the 'Manufacturing' industry; by the first quarter of 2010 this proportion had fallen to 8.9 per cent, a fall of 17.2 percentage points. These longer term trends have continued through the recessions.

The **Income and wealth** chapter shows that GDP per head decreased by 5.5 per cent during the recent period of recession (2008 to 2009) while real household disposable income per head increased by 1.2 per cent. The chapter also analyses the long and short-term trends in economic circumstances and income distribution. The main source of household income in the UK (73 per cent) from 2006/07 to 2008/09 was derived from wages, salaries and self-employed earnings. Household net wealth in real terms in 2009 was more than double net wealth in 1987.

Changes in house prices and mortgage availability during the most recent recession are considered in the **Housing** chapter. Thirty seven per cent of households in Great Britain were buying their homes with a mortgage in 2009 with the average price paid for a dwelling in the UK being £194,235, a decrease of 8.1 per cent since 2008. The decline in house prices was accompanied by reduced mortgage availability and stricter lending criteria. In the last 12 years the seasonally adjusted number of loans approved for house purchase in the UK peaked in March 2002 at 92,912 but by November 2008 approvals fell to a low of 17,421.

Some of the effects of the economic recession in the UK can also be seen in the **Expenditure** chapter. The number of individual insolvencies in England and Wales was 34,743 in the second quarter of 2010, of which 14,982 were bankruptcies. Between 1997 and 2009 total household debt in the UK as a percentage of household disposable income, rose from 103 per cent to 161 per cent slightly lower than the peak of 173 per cent in 2007. In 2009 the volume of consumption of goods and services by UK households was more than two-and-a-half times the consumption in 1971 (£810 million compared with £312 million at 2006 prices). Averaged over the period 2006–2008, the total average weekly household expenditure in the UK was £459.70; London had the highest average weekly household expenditure at £544.70 while the North East had the lowest at £386.10. There have also been changes in the way in which households allocate expenditure between different goods and services.

The **Social Protection** chapter shows that social security benefit expenditure in the UK increased by 128 per cent from £72 billion in 1979/80 to £165 billion in 2009/10, after allowing for inflation. In 1981/82 and in 1991/92 the annual increase in social security benefits expenditure was 10 per cent, reflecting increases in the number of people who were unemployed or economically inactive during the economic recessions in the early 1980s and 1990s. Between 2008/09 and 2009/10, at the time of the most recent recession, social security benefits expenditure increased by more than 7 per cent.

In the **Transport** chapter we find that trips made by car remained the most popular form of transport in Great Britain for all households in 2009. UK petrol and diesel prices reached an all time high in January 2011. The number of licensed cars on Britain's roads has continued to increase, reaching over 28 million in 2009 (12 per cent increase from 2001). However, the number of new registrations of cars fell by 24 per cent between 2001 and 2009. Also, between 2008 and 2009 total domestic freight lifted within Great Britain decreased by 15 per cent, most likely due to the recession. Sea freight at UK ports decreased by 10.9 per cent over the same period and freight handled at UK airports fell by 10 per cent.

Well-being

As part of the ONS programme of work to measure National Well-being, a national debate was undertaken to ascertain what matters to people and what influences their well-being. The responses during the national debate showed that individuals felt health, good connections with friends and family, job satisfaction, education, personal security, the environment, access to green spaces and equality mattered to the well-being of the nation.

The **Health** chapter shows that we are feeling healthier and remaining healthy and disability free for longer. Life expectancy at birth is 1.6 years longer than the European average for men but 0.3 years less for women; healthy life expectancy at 65 is higher than the EU-27 average for both (see **International Comparisons** chapter). The **Health** chapter also reports that regular smoking prevalence in Great Britain had fallen to 22 per cent of men and 20 per cent of women in 2009. In Great Britain, the proportion of men drinking more than the daily recommended guidelines had fallen over the last decade (39 per cent in 2000/01 to 37 per cent in 2009), while the proportion of women had risen from 23 per cent to 29 per cent over the same period. Physical activity levels in Great Britain also decreased with age while prevalence of obesity in Great Britain peaked among both sexes between the ages of 65 and 74 at 81 per cent of males and 74 per cent of females.

This is corroborated by the **Lifestyles and social participation** chapter, which shows that the proportion of adults aged 16 and over in England who participated in active sport for at least 30 minutes, in the 4 weeks prior to interview in 2009/10, decreased with age from 75 per cent of those aged 16 to 24 to 18 per cent of those aged 75 and over. For UK adults who did not practice sport in 2009, 40 per cent stated a lack of time as their main reason. The **Lifestyles and social participation** chapter also notes that the number of adults aged 16 and over volunteering informally at least once a month in England fell from 35 per cent in 2008/09 to 29 per cent in 2009/10.

The **Households and families** chapter examines connections within families and found that the number of people living alone in the UK increased from 7.0 million to 7.5 million between 2001 and 2010 while an estimated 50.8 million people were living in families, an increase from 48.8 million in 2001. The number of divorces in England and Wales continued a downward trend with a 6.4 per cent decrease between 2008 and 2009. The **Transport** chapter showed that according to the National Travel Survey on average each person made nearly 160 trips per year to visit friends from 2007 to 2009.

The **Labour market** chapter refers to the link researchers have found between people's satisfaction with their job and their satisfaction with life overall and the lasting negative impact on people's well-being unemployment can have.

The **Education and training** chapter shows that UK public expenditure on education and training doubled in real terms over the last 24 years, from £43 billion in 1987/88 to a planned spend of £87 billion in 2010/11. A new item on the value of human capital stock shows the value of human capital stock in 2009 (£16,700 billion) was three times the value of the physical assets of the UK. While many young people are choosing to enter further education and higher education, others opt to work and study at the same time through apprenticeships. Between 2008/09 and 2009/10 the number of apprenticeships started in England increased by 17 per cent from 239,900 to 279,700. In 2008/09 there were approximately 2.6 million students in Higher Education in the UK; nearly 6 in 10 were women. In 2009/10, 4.6 million adult learners in England participated in some form of government-funded further education, a decrease of 4.5 per cent compared with 2008/09. The chapter also discusses changes in the types of school in the UK and appeals against non-admission.

Crime remains a key concern in the UK and a higher proportion of UK prisoners were guilty of violent offences than in most other EU countries (see **International Comparison** chapter). The **Crime and Justice** chapter discusses crimes recorded by the police in the United Kingdom. It also reports on crime levels, types of offence, victims of crime and how residents of England and Wales perceive changes in levels of crime both nationally and locally using information from the British Crime Survey.

In England and Wales in 2009/10, a majority of adults aged 16 and over believed that crime was not going up at the local level, while a majority believed that it was increasing at the national level. However, in 2009/10 in England and Wales, estimated crime levels were at their historically lowest level since the British Crime Survey began in 1981. There was also a fall of 8 per cent in crimes recorded by the police across the UK from 5.2 million offences in 2008/09 to 4.8 million in 2009/10.

The chapter also discusses statistics on offenders, prisons, sentencing and the police. In 2010 in England and Wales, the total number of offenders found guilty of or cautioned for indictable offences had increased by 0.8 per cent for males and decreased by 8.0 per cent for females when compared with 2009. This chapter also discusses Penalty Notices for Disorder (PND), Anti-Social Behaviour Orders and the numbers sentenced to life imprisonment in England and Wales. In 2009/10 in England and Wales, police funding in real terms was at its highest recorded level of £12.6 billion, 44 per cent higher than 1995/96 when it was £8.8 billion.

According to the **Environment** chapter, when adults aged 16 and over in England in 2009 were asked which areas the government should address, the environment was considered the third most important issue after the economy and unemployment. Being environmentally-friendly in most or everything they did was reported by around a third (32 per cent) of adults in England. An example of an environmentally friendly task is recycling waste. In 2009/10, 40 per cent of household waste per person in England was composted or reused compared with less than 1 per cent in 1983/84.

In 2011 feeling proud of people's local environment was important to over 8 in 10 (85 per cent) of adults in England and over 6 in 10 (63 per cent) reported that it was very important to have public gardens, commons and other green space nearby. The **Environment** chapter also covers energy, pollution, climate change, environmental taxes, countryside and wildlife.

Income inequality is discussed in the **Income and Wealth** chapter where it is reported that 18 per cent of individuals in the UK lived in households where the income was below £244 per week (60 per cent of the UK median) in 2008/09.

Population

The population of the UK at both national and regional level is continuously changing. Birth, death, migration and the mobility of residents all affect the size, age and sex structure, and geographical distribution of the population. Changes in demographic patterns influence social structures, and have implications for public policy in a wide range of areas such as the provision of education, transport and health services. Demographic patterns also influence commercial decisions, such as the development of new products and the location of retail outlets and other business premises. This chapter examines the long and short term changes in the population of the UK.

Key Points

UK population

- In 2009 there were an estimated 61.8 million people resident in the UK, an increase of 2.7 million since 2001, and an increase of 23.6 million since the start of the 20th century

Births and deaths

- In 2009 in the UK there were 790,000 live births, a decrease of 0.5 per cent since 2008, and 560,000 deaths, a decrease of 3.5 per cent

Components of population change

- Between 1951 and 2001 and from 2007 onwards the main driver of population increase in the UK is net natural change (the difference between births and deaths)
- For every 1,000 residents in the UK net natural change added 3.5 people and net migration and other changes 2.9 people in the UK between 2008 and 2009

International migration

- Between 2008-09 and 2009-10 provisional estimates are that net migration increased from 166,000 to 226,000 largely because of a decrease in emigration
- The most common country of last residence for long term immigrants to the UK in 2009 was India
- There were 195,100 grants of British citizenship in the UK in 2010, a decrease of 3.9 per cent compared with 2009
- In 2009 an estimated 93 per cent of UK residents were British citizens, and 89 per cent had been born in the UK

Population movement within the UK

- Internal migration resulted in an estimated net loss of 5,700 residents from England to other countries in the UK between 2008 and 2009

- The largest net change for regions within England was a net outward migration of approximately 38,100 residents from London

- The largest net gains from inward migration from other parts of the UK were in the South East and South West

Changes in age structure

- Between 1971 and 2009 the proportion of the UK population aged under 16 years decreased from 25.5 per cent to 18.7 per cent, while the proportion aged 75 and over increased from 4.7 per cent to 7.8 per cent

- It is projected that the number of UK residents aged 65 and over will be larger than the number aged under 16 years by 2018

- It is estimated that the number of residents aged 90 and over increased by 12 per cent between 2002 to 2009, from 388,200 to 436,500

- The average age of the population in the UK has increased from 36 years in 1992 to 40 years in 2009

UK Population

In 2009 there were an estimated 61.8 million people resident in the UK[i], an increase of 2.7 million since 2001, and an increase of 23.6 million since the start of the 20th century (**Table 1**).

Between mid-2001 and mid-2009, the UK population increased by an average of 0.6 per cent per year. Over the same time period growth was highest in Northern Ireland, at 0.7 per cent while the population in England grew by 0.6 per cent, in Scotland by 0.2 per cent and in Wales by 0.4 per cent.

In 2009, 83.8 per cent of the UK population lived in England, 8.4 per cent in Scotland, 4.9 per cent in Wales and 2.9 per cent in Northern Ireland. Despite differences in population growth rates across the UK, these proportions have varied very little since the first edition of Social Trends was published in 1971.

Table 1   **Population[1] of the United Kingdom**

Millions

	United Kingdom	England	Wales	Scotland	Northern Ireland
1901	38.2	30.5	2.0	4.5	1.2
1911	42.1	33.6	2.4	4.8	1.3
1921[2]	44.0	35.2	2.7	4.9	1.3
1931	46.0	37.4	2.6	4.8	1.2
1951	50.2	41.2	2.6	5.1	1.4
1961	52.7	43.5	2.6	5.2	1.4
1971	55.9	46.4	2.7	5.2	1.5
1981	56.4	46.8	2.8	5.2	1.5
1991	57.4	47.9	2.9	5.1	1.6
2001	59.1	49.5	2.9	5.1	1.7
2009	61.8	51.8	3.0	5.2	1.8
2011	62.6	52.6	3.0	5.2	1.8
2016	64.8	54.5	3.1	5.3	1.9
2021	67.0	56.4	3.2	5.4	1.9
2026	69.1	58.3	3.3	5.5	2.0
2031	70.9	60.1	3.3	5.5	2.0

1 Data for 1901 to 1961 are enumerated Census figures, 1971 to 2009 are mid-year estimates, 2011 onward are national projections based on mid-2008 population estimates.

2 Figures for Northern Ireland are estimated. The population at the Census of 1921 was 1,257 thousand (608 thousand males and 649 thousand females).

Source: *Office for National Statistics; General Register Office for Scotland; Northern Ireland Statistics and Research Agency (ONS, 2009a; 2010a; 2010b)*

Births and deaths

The two World Wars had a major impact on births. There was a substantial fall in the number of births during the First World War, followed by a post-war increase with the number of births reaching 1.1 million in 1920, the highest number of births in any one year during the 20th century. Births then decreased and remained low during the 1930s' depression and the Second World War. A second increase occurred after the Second World War and another in the 1960s, peaking in 1964 **(Figure 1)**. The lowest number of births in any year in the 20th Century was in 1977 (at 0.7 million).

Figure 1   **Births[1,2] and deaths[1]**

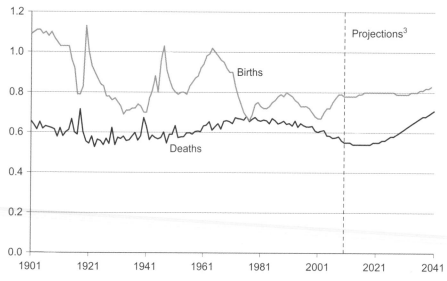

United Kingdom
Millions

1 Data for 1901 to 1921 exclude Ireland which was constitutionally part of the UK during this period.
2 Data from 1981 exclude the non-residents of Northern Ireland.
3 2008-based projections for 2010 to 2041.
Source: Office for National Statistics

In general, the size of net natural change (the difference between births and deaths) has been driven by changes in the numbers of births rather than in the numbers of deaths. While there are obvious increases in deaths related to the two World Wars and to the Spanish influenza outbreak just after the First World War, the numbers do not vary by as much as those for births. In the mid 1970s there were a number of years when the number of births and deaths were very similar. More recently people are living longer and the number of deaths has been decreasing in spite of the increase in population. In 2009 in the UK there were 790,000 live births, a decrease of 0.5 per cent since 2008, and 560,000 deaths, a decrease of 3.5 per cent since 2008.

The number of births in the UK is projected to fall in 2010, with a longer-term rise over the next 30 years. This longer-term projected increase in births, when the total fertility rate is assumed to be constant, is due to an increase in the female population of childbearing age resulting from assumed net inward migration[ii].

The declining trend in the annual number of deaths is projected to continue until about 2019, when an upward trend in the number of deaths is suggested as the large cohorts born immediately after the Second World War and during the 1960s baby boom begin to reach elderly ages.

Components of population change

Historically, net natural change – the difference between births and deaths – was the main driver behind population increase, accounting for 98 per cent of population change in the UK between 1951 and 1961. Over the same time period, the impact of net migration on the change in the UK population was either a very small increase or a decrease when emigration was higher than immigration.

In the decade between 1991 and 2001, the effects of net inward migration and other changes[iii] on overall population change begins to be more noticeable with an average annual increase of 68,000. However, net natural change was a larger part of the increase with an annual average change of 100,000 (**Table 2**).

Table 2   Population change[1]

United Kingdom   Thousands

		Annual averages				
	Population at start of period	Live Births	Deaths	Net natural change	Net migration and other[2]	Overall change
1951–1961	50,287	839	593	246	6	252
1961–1971	52,807	962	638	324	-12	312
1971–1981	55,928	736	666	69	-27	42
1981–1991	56,357	757	655	103	5	108
1991–2001	57,439	731	631	100	68	167
2001–2002	59,113	663	601	62	143	205
2002–2003	59,319	682	605	77	156	233
2003–2004	59,552	707	603	104	186	290
2004–2005	59,842	717	591	127	267	394
2005–2006	60,235	734	575	159	190	349
2006–2007	60,584	758	571	187	214	401
2007–2008[3]	60,986	791	570	220	192	413
2008–2009	61,398	787	570	217	177	394
2009–2010	61,794	780	557	223	206	429
2010–2011	62,222	778	552	226	201	427
2011–2021	62,649	791	544	248	183	431

1 Mid-year estimates for 1951–1961 to 2008-2009; 2008-based projections for 2009–2021.

2 'Other changes' at the UK level includes changes in the population due to changes in the number of armed forces (both foreign and home) and their dependents resident in the UK.

3 Population at start of period for 2008–2009 and overall change will not sum to the population at start of period for 2009-10 due to the transition between population estimates and projections.

Source: Office for National Statistics; General Register Office for Scotland; Northern Ireland Statistics & Research

Agency (ONS, 2010c)

Between mid-2001 and mid-2009, the number of live births in the UK increased and the number of deaths decreased so that net natural change went up from 62,000 between 2001 and 2002 to 217,000 between 2008 and 2009. Over the same time period, the contribution to population change of net migration has varied. Between 2001 and 2007, net migration and other change was larger than net natural change. Over this time period, the largest increase because of net migration and other changes of 267,000 was between 2004 and 2005, coinciding with the Accession countries joining the European Union[iv]. However, net natural change was again larger than net migration and other changes between 2007 to 2008 and 2008 to 2009 and is projected to remain the larger component of change up to 2021.

Between 2008 and 2009, net natural change added 3.5 people and net migration and other changes 2.9 people for every 1,000 residents in the UK.

International migration[v]

The previous section discussed net natural change and net migration and other changes in UK. This section looks at the number of immigrants and emigrants and the difference between them (net migration) for the years between mid 1991 and mid 2010.

Figure 2   Long-term international migration into and out of the UK[1,2]

United Kingdom

Thousands

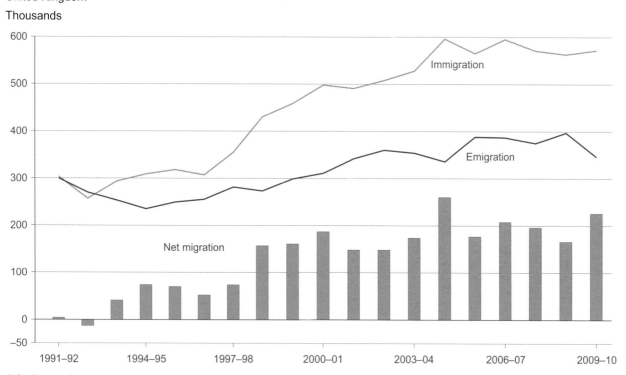

1 An international long-term migrant is defined as a person who moves to a country other than that of his or her usual residence for a period of at least 12 months.

2 The 2001-02 to 2006-07 estimates were revised in February 2010 following changes to source data. Therefore they may not agree with estimates published prior to this date. 2009-10 data are provisional.

Source: Long-Term International Migration (LTIM), (ONS 2010d)

For the first two years shown in **Figure 2** immigration and emigration were about the same. However, between 1993-94 and 2009-10 there has been a bigger inflow to the UK than outflow from it. Between 1993-94 and 1997-98 net migration to the UK varied between 41,000 and 74,000. There was an increase in net migration in 1998-99 to 157,000 resulting from an increase of immigrants to the UK while the number of emigrants fell slightly. From then until 2003-04 there were only small variations in net migration.

The largest net migration over the time period 1991-92 to 2009-10, of 260,000, was in 2004-2005. This was largely because of an increase in immigrants coinciding with the Accession countries joined the European Union. The increase in net migration to 226,000 in 2009-10 from 166,000 in 2008-09 is due largely to a fall in emigration rather than an increase in immigration.

Estimates from the International Passenger Survey show that the last place of residence for the highest number of long-term international immigrants in 2009 was India (63,000). This is a change from the previous four years when the highest number of immigrants stated that their last place of residence was Poland (**Figure 3**).

Figure 3   **Top five[1] countries of last residence of immigrants**

United Kingdom
Thousands

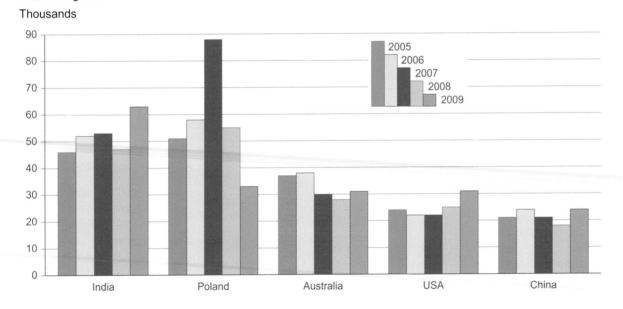

1 Top five countries in 2009.
Source: International Passenger Survey, Office for National Statistics (ONS 2009b)

Apart from changing the total population of the UK, international migration can change the proportion of residents who are British citizens and also of those who were born in the UK.

It can take some time after the arrival of long term immigrants to this country before they are eligible to obtain British Citizenship. In 2010, there were 195,100 grants of British Citizenship in the UK, a 4.2 per cent decrease compared to 2009 when 203,800 grants were made. Nearly half (48 per cent) of these grants of citizenship were made because of qualification by residence,[vi] with approximately a quarter made because of the applicant's children (25 per cent) and a further quarter following marriage or civil partnership (24 per cent) (**Figure 4**).

Figure 4   Grants of British citizenship:[1] by basis of grant

United Kingdom

Thousands

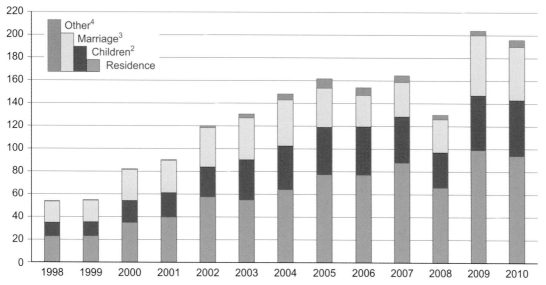

1 Data from November 2001 include grants of British citizenship in the Channel Islands and Isle of Man.

2 Children aged under 18.

3 Includes civil partnerships from 5 December 2005.

4 Includes British Overseas Territories citizens from Gibraltar registered as British citizens under section 5 of the *British Nationality Act 1981*.

Source: Home Office (2009; 2011)

Estimates from the Annual Population Survey[vii] show that the proportions of the UK resident population who are either of British nationality or who were born in the UK have decreased between 2004 and 2009.

An estimated 91 per cent of UK residents in 2004 were born in the UK and this had decreased to 89 per cent by 2009. A larger percentage of UK residents were of British nationality: 95 per cent of the UK population reported that they were of British nationality in 2004 although this had decreased to 93 per cent by 2009.

Of the countries within the UK in 2009, England had the smallest percentage of its resident population who were born in the UK at 88 per cent, followed by Scotland at 94 per cent, Northern Ireland at 94 per cent and Wales at 95 per cent. The pattern is repeated for residents who are British nationals: 92 per cent in England, 95 per cent in Scotland, 96 per cent in Northern Ireland and 97 per cent in Wales.

Population movement within the UK

In addition to births, deaths and international migration, changes in population numbers in areas within the UK occur because residents move from one area to another (internal migration). Population gains and losses due to internal migration have important implications for housing planning as well as for the provision of welfare services and are estimated using information on re-registrations with NHS doctors and other sources.

Between 2008 and 2009, England experienced a net loss to other countries in the UK of around 5,700 people with an outflow of 97,900 people and an inflow of 92,200 people. Over the same time period Scotland and Wales experienced net gains and Northern Ireland a net loss because of internal movement in the UK (ONS, 2010e).

At a regional level within England, London experienced the most population movement overall between 2008 and 2009: around 216,200 people moved from the capital to other parts of the UK while 178,100 people moved into the area, resulting in a net loss of 38,100 residents. The majority of those moving out of London go to the adjacent regions of the South East and the East of England. Four other regions were also estimated to have had net outflows between 2008 and 2009: the North East, the North West, Yorkshire and The Humber and the West Midlands. The largest regional net increases because of internal movements were into the South East (20,600 people) and the South West (18,500 people) (ONS, 2010f).

> If you want to know more about changes in population including birth, deaths, international and internal migration at regional and local authority area level in England and Wales, the Office for National Statistics population analysis tool can be downloaded from our website.[viii]

Changes in age structure

The age structure of the resident population is also very important for planning services in the UK. For example a local area with a high proportion of children will require a very different mix of services when compared to an area with a high proportion of elderly people. Over time the proportions and numbers of residents in different age groups in the UK has changed. In particular there has been an increase in the number and proportion of those in the older age groups as a result of increased survival due to improved medical treatment, housing and living standards.

Table 3   Population:[1] by age

United Kingdom   Percentages

	Under 16	16–24	25–34	35–44	45–54	55–64	65–74	75 and over	All ages (thousands) = 100 per cent
1971	25.5	13.2	12.5	11.6	12.2	11.8	8.5	4.7	55,928
1981	22.3	14.3	14.2	12.0	11.1	11.0	9.2	5.8	56,357
1991	20.3	13.0	15.5	13.8	11.5	10.1	8.8	6.9	57,439
2001	20.1	11.0	14.3	15.0	13.2	10.6	8.4	7.5	59,113
2009	18.7	12.1	12.9	14.6	13.5	11.8	8.5	7.8	61,792
2011	18.6	11.9	13.4	13.8	13.9	11.7	8.8	8.0	62,649
2016	18.5	10.9	14.3	12.5	14.0	11.5	9.8	8.5	64,773
2021	18.7	10.1	14.0	12.8	12.7	12.4	9.8	9.5	66,958
2026	18.4	10.3	13.0	13.6	11.5	12.6	9.7	10.9	69,051
2031	18.0	10.6	12.3	13.5	11.9	11.5	10.6	11.7	70,933

1 Mid-year estimates for 1971 to 2009; 2008-based projections for 2011 to 2031.

Source: Office for National Statistics; General Register Office for Scotland; Northern Ireland Statistics and Research Agency (ONS 2009c; 2010a)

In 1971 just over a quarter (25.5 per cent) of the resident population in the UK were children aged less than 16. In the next three decades this proportion decreased so that by 2001 only about a fifth (20.1 per cent) of the UK population was in this age group. By 2009 the proportion had fallen to 18.7 per cent and it is projected to vary around this level up until 2026 before falling to 18.0 per cent in 2031. At the other end of the age spectrum, the proportion of the population aged 75 and over increased from 4.7 per cent in 1971 to 7.8 per cent in 2009 and then is projected to rise to 11.7 per cent by 2031. Combining the two oldest age groups, the proportion of those aged 65 and over is projected to rise to more than one in five of the population (22.3 per cent) by 2031 **(Table 3)**.

Figure 5   Population[1] aged under 16 and 65 and over

United Kingdom

Millions

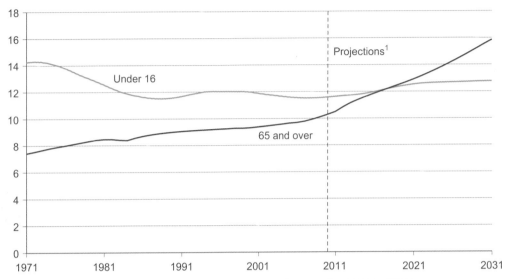

1 Mid-year estimates for 1971 to 2001; 2008-based projections for 2011 to 2031.

Source: Office for National Statistics; General Register Office for Scotland; Northern Ireland Statistics and Research Agency (ONS 2009c; 2010a)

Figure 5 shows the estimated and projected number of residents in the UK in two age groups, under 16 and 65 and over. There was a decrease in the number of children between 1971 and 1991 from 14.2 to 11.7 million followed by relatively stable numbers between 1991 and 2001 and a slight rise to a projected 12.8 million in 2031. For the older age group there is a steady increase in numbers from 7.4 million in 1971 to 9.4 million in 2001, followed by a higher projected rate of growth which leads to an increase from 10.5 to 15.8 million between 2011 and 2031. The number of those aged 65 and over is projected to become larger than the number aged less than 16 in about 2018.

In terms of planning one area of concern is the growth of the numbers in the oldest age groups as it is likely that older people will make more use of health and social care services. Estimates for 2009 were that around one in 13 of the UK resident population were aged 75 and over (4.8 million residents) while projected growth suggests that about one in nine will be in this age group by 2031 (8.3 million) (ONS 2009c; 2010a).

The actual numbers of residents and the growth rates in the 75 and over age group differ by sex: the main cause being that life expectancy for males is increasing at a faster rate than for females[ix]. About 32 per cent of UK residents aged 75 and over were male in 1971; by 2031 this is projected to rise to 44 per cent (ONS 2009c).

Table 4   **Population[1] aged 90 years and over: by sex**

United Kingdom   Numbers

	90–94	95–99	100 and over	Total aged 90 and over
Men				
2002	76,800	11,900	800	89,500
2003	80,100	12,600	800	93,500
2004	83,800	13,500	900	98,200
2005	87,300	14,600	1,000	102,900
2006	89,000	15,400	1,200	105,600
2007	90,000	16,800	1,300	108,100
2008	89,100	17,900	1,500	108,500
2009	96,900	20,200	1,800	118,900
Women				
2002	235,200	56,700	6,900	298,800
2003	239,200	58,600	7,100	304,900
2004	242,700	60,300	7,300	310,300
2005	245,600	62,400	7,900	315,900
2006	244,700	64,400	8,200	317,300
2007	241,100	67,200	8,700	317,000
2008	231,200	68,700	9,200	309,100
2009	235,600	72,400	10,000	318,000

1 2002 to 2008 figures are based on revised mid-year population estimates. Data are to the nearest hundred.
Source: Office for National Statistics (ONS 2009d)

ONS experimental estimates for 2002 to 2009 show that the inequality in the number of males and females continues in the very oldest ages. In 2009 an estimated 27 per cent of UK residents aged 90 and over were male. The proportion of men reduced as age increased: 29 per cent of those aged 90-94, 22 per cent of those aged 95-99 and 16 per cent of those aged 100 or more were male **(Table 4)**. The estimated growth in the number of UK residents aged 90 and over between 2002 and 2009 was 12 per cent (from 388,200 to 436,500 people).

As a result of these structural changes in the UK the average age of the population has risen. In 1992, the median age of the population[x] in the UK was 36 years. By 2009, this had increased by over three years to 39 and a half years and is projected to increase to nearly 42 years by 2031 (ONS, 2010g).

These UK averages mask considerable variation across the UK, differences which have implications for the planning of local services. The median age of residents in individual local authority areas in 1992 varied from 27 years to 48 years, a difference of 21 years. In 2009 the difference between the local authority area with the lowest and highest median age was slightly larger at 23 years, and the difference is projected to increase to 28 years in 2023.

Local authority areas with resident populations with low median ages tend to be urban and have large university populations: in 2009 the lowest median ages in UK local authorities were in Manchester, Oxford, Cambridge and Nottingham, all of which had average ages below 30 years. At the other extreme, local authorities with the highest median ages were largely coastal areas which attract those who have retired: in 2009 the highest median ages were in West Somerset, North Norfolk, Rother and Christchurch, all of which had median ages above 50 years.

> **If you want to explore the differences in age distribution at regional and local authority area level ONS have made these data available through an interactive map[xi].**

References

Home Office (2009). Grants. Available at www.homeoffice.gov.uk/publications/non-personal-data/Passports-immigration/citizenship-statistics-1998-2008/citizenship-stats-2008-excel?view=Binary

Home Office (2011). Control of immigration: Quarterly statistical summary, United Kingdom: Quarter 4 2010 (October – December). Available at www.search.homeoffice.gov.uk/search?q=grants+of+british+citizenship+2010&btnG=Search&entqr=0&output=xml_no_dtd&sort=date%3AD%3AL%3Ad1&client=default_frontend&ud=1&oe=UTF-8&ie=UTF-8&proxystylesheet=default_frontend&site=default_collection

ONS (2009a). Population: national, 1971 onwards: Population Trends. Available at www.statistics.gov.uk/STATBASE/ssdataset.asp?vlnk=9542

ONS (2009b). Migration Statistics 2009: Statistical Bulletin. Available at www.statistics.gov.uk/StatBase/Product.asp?vlnk=507

ONS (2009c). Population Pyramid datasets. Available at www.statistics.gov.uk/populationestimates/flash_pyramid/default.htm

ONS (2009d). United Kingdom 90+ Mid-Year Population Estimates 2002-2009 (revised 2002-2008) (experimental). Available at www.statistics.gov.uk/statbase/Product.asp?vlnk=15003

ONS (2010a). Mid Year Population Estimates 2009: 24/06/10. Available at www.statistics.gov.uk/StatBase/Product.asp?vlnk=15106&Pos=&ColRank=1&Rank=272

ONS (2010b). Annual Abstract 2010. Available at www.statistics.gov.uk/StatBase/Product.asp?vlnk=94&Pos=&ColRank=1&Rank=272

ONS (2010c). Population estimates: Statistical bulletin. Available at www.statistics.gov.uk/STATBASE/Product.asp?vlnk=601

ONS (2010d). Long-Term International Migration (LTIM) tables: 1991 - latest: 2 series (LTIM mid year): Table 2.11. Available at www.statistics.gov.uk/STATBASE/Product.asp?vlnk=15053

ONS (2010e). NHSCR Internal migration time series. Available at www.statistics.gov.uk/downloads/theme_population/tnhscr.xls

ONS(2010f). Internal migration within the UK during the year 2009. Available at www.statistics.gov.uk/StatBase/Product.asp?vlnk=10191&Pos=2&ColRank=2&Rank=192

ONS (2010g). Ageing in the UK datasets. Available at www.statistics.gov.uk/ageingintheuk/default.htm

Notes

[i] The estimated and projected populations are of the resident population of an area, that is all those usually resident there, whatever their nationality. Members of HM Forces stationed outside the UK are excluded; members of foreign forces stationed in the UK are included. Students are taken to be resident at their term-time addresses. Figures for the UK do not include the population of the Channel Islands or the Isle of Man.

[ii] Further information about the assumptions underlying national population projections are available at www.statistics.gov.uk/pdfdir/pproj1009.pdf

[iii] 'Other changes' at the UK level include changes in the number of armed forces (both foreign and home) and their dependents resident in the UK

[iv] Residents of the EU enjoy freedom of movement and work within the UK. On May 1st 2004 Cyprus, the Czech Republic, Estonia, Hungary, Latvia, Lithuania, Malta, Poland, Slovak Republic and Slovenia (known as the 'Accession' countries) became full members of the European Union.

[v] An international migrant is defined as someone who changes his or her country of usual residence for a period of at least a year, so that the country of destination becomes the country of usual residence. The richest source of information on international migrants comes from the International Passenger Survey (IPS), which is a sample survey of passengers arriving at, and departing from, the main UK air and sea ports and the Channel Tunnel. This survey provides migration estimates based on respondents' intended length of stay in the UK or abroad.

Adjustments are made to account for people who do not realise their intended length of stay. An estimate is made for the number of people who initially come to or leave the UK for a short period but subsequently stay for a year or longer ('visitor switchers'). The number of people who intend to be migrants, but who in reality stay in the UK or abroad for less than a year ('migrant switchers') are also estimated.

Data from other sources are used to supplement the IPS migration estimates. Home Office asylum seeker data are used to estimate the number of asylum seekers and their dependants who enter or leave the country without being counted in the IPS. Estimates of migration between the UK and Ireland are made using information from the Irish Central Statistics Office.

[vi] The rules for qualification for British Citizenship include being resident in the UK for a qualifying period of five years, being the spouse or civil partner of a British Citizen, or being the child of a British Citizen. More information can be found at www.ukba.homeoffice.gov.uk/britishcitizenship/eligibility/naturalisation/standardrequirements/

[vii] Data available from 'Population by country of birth and nationality' available at www.statistics.gov.uk/statbase/Product.asp?vlnk=15147

[viii] The mid 2009 population analysis tool can be found at
www.statistics.gov.uk/statbase/Product.asp?vlnk=14060

[ix] More information about period life expectancy by sex is available at
www.statistics.gov.uk/StatBase/Product.asp?vlnk=15354

[x] Median age is the age above and below which the ages of half the population lie

[xi] The interactive map of age statistics can be found at www.statistics.gov.uk/ageingintheuk/agemap.html

Health

The World Health Organisation defines good health as 'a state of complete physical, mental and social well-being and not merely the absence of disease and infirmity'.

People in the UK are healthier and living longer than ever before, with the major advances in life expectancy over the last century due mainly to public health innovations such as improvements in water quality and sewerage, and mass immunisation programmes which have reduced infectious diseases (DH,2010).

This chapter looks not only at these improvements in life expectancy and lifestyles in the population, but changes in the prevalence of chronic sickness and disability and the impact on health services. There is also analysis of mental well-being and the effects of environmental factors such as winter temperature and infections on health.

Key points:

Expenditure on health and life expectancy

- In the UK in 2008 health expenditure per head and life expectancy were ranked 16th and 17th respectively of 32 Organisation for Economic Co-operation and Development (OECD) countries at $3,281 and 79.9 years

- In 2008 in the 32 OECD countries, the highest health expenditure per head was in the United States where life expectancy was ranked 24th and the highest life expectancy was in Japan where health expenditure was ranked 20th

- In 2009 life expectancy at birth in the UK was at the highest level recorded for both males and females at 78.3 years and 82.1 years respectively: both had increased by about 20 years since 1930

- One of the contributors to these changes in life expectancy is the decrease in infant and neonatal mortality rates which, in 2010, were at their lowest recorded level since 1930, falling more than 90 per cent to 4.5 per 1,000 and 3.1 per 1,000 live births respectively

- Not only are life expectancies increasing, but both men and women are staying healthy and free of disability for more of their lives: the most recent estimates are that at age 65 men can expect to live 58 per cent and women 56 per cent of their remaining life in good health

Self-reported health status

- In 2009 around 4 in 5 adults (79 per cent) in Great Britain reported that they were in good or very good health, compared with 75 per cent in 2005

- In Great Britain in 2009, around 1 in 3 adults (30 per cent) reported that they had a long-standing illness or disability, compared with around 1 in 4 adults (21 per cent) in 1972

- The proportion of adults reporting that a long-standing illness or disability limited their daily activities changed very little between 1981 and 2009

- Reported long-standing illness or disability was more than 8 times higher among the very elderly than the very young; two-thirds (66 per cent) aged 75 and over compared with around 1 in 12 (8 per cent) aged between 0 and 4 years

Use of services

- There have been recent decreases in the rates of use of in-patient, outpatient and casualty services in Great Britain, while the proportion of the population consulting with their GP has changed relatively little. Use of online services such as NHS Online increased seven-fold between 2002-03 and 2007-08

Mortality

- In 2009, for the first time, cancer was the most common cause of death for both sexes with 2,081 deaths per million males and 1,497 per million females

- Males accounted for more than a half of all deaths as a result of diseases of the circulatory system (62 per cent), diseases of the respiratory system (59 per cent) and cancer (58 per cent)

Cancer

- In the UK between 2006 and 2008 the highest incidence of cancer in males was of the prostate (100.0 per 100,000 population) and in females was of the breast (123.0 per 100,000), arguably reflecting higher diagnosis rates following improvements in screening programmes for both cancers

- The highest cancer mortality rates for both sexes were for lung cancer at 51.7 per 100,000 males and 31.6 per 100,000 females

- Between 2004 and 2008 in England male survival rates were highest for testicular cancer with more than 97 per cent surviving five years after diagnosis; female survival was highest for melanoma skin cancer with 90 per cent surviving five years after diagnosis

Healthy lifestyles

- Between 2000/01 and 2009 the percentage of men in Great Britain who were regular smokers fell from 29 per cent to 22 per cent; the proportion of women who were smokers fell from 25 per cent to 20 per cent

- Between 2000/01 and 2009 the proportion of men in Great Britain drinking more than daily alcohol guidelines fell from 39 per cent to 37 per cent, but the proportion of women drinking more than daily alcohol guidelines increased from 23 per cent in 2000/01 to 29 per cent in 2009

- In 2009/10 more than a third of adults (35 per cent) in the UK reported using illegal drugs at least once in their lifetime, while around 1 in 20 people (5 per cent) reported using drugs at least once in the last month

- Between 2008 and 2009, 39 per cent of males in Great Britain met physical activity recommendations compared with 29 per cent of females and this activity decreased with age

- In 2008/09 more than a half of males and females in Great Britain were classed as overweight or obese (60 per cent and 52 per cent respectively)

Mental health

- In 2009/10 more than 1 in 10 adults (11 per cent) in England were diagnosed with depression

- Within the UK diagnosis of depression was lowest in Wales with around 1 in 12 adults (8 per cent) diagnosed in 2009/10

- Between 1991 and 2009, suicide rates among males and females fell by more than 10 per cent

- In 2009 suicide rates were highest among males aged 15 to 44 years (18.0 per 100,000) and among females aged 45 to 74 years (5.8 per 100,000)
- Between 1991 and 2009 prescriptions dispensed for antidepressants increased by 334 per cent in England

Health care expenditure per head and life expectancy

While there is some positive relationship between expenditure per head on healthcare and the life expectancy in a country, it is not always the case that those countries with high expenditure have the highest life expectancy, indicating that there are other factors which affect life expectancy. For example within the Organisation for Economic Co-operation and Development (OECD)[i], of the countries where data were available in 2008, health care expenditure was highest in the United States (USA) at $7,720 per head, but the USA had average life expectancy of 78.3 years which was ranked 24th highest **(Figure 1)**.

Figure 1   **Expenditure on health per head and average life expectancy, 2008**

OECD countries

US$, Years

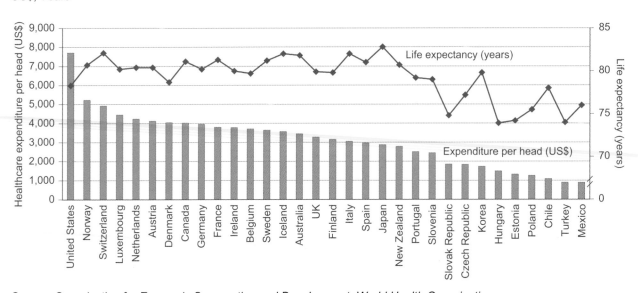

Source: Organisation for Economic Cooperation and Development; World Health Organisation

Life expectancy within the OECD was highest in Japan, at 82.8 years, while expenditure on health care was ranked 20th highest at $2,878 per head. In the UK in 2008 average life expectancy (79.9 years) and health expenditure per head ($3,281) were ranked 16th and 17th highest respectively.

Expenditure on health care was lowest in Mexico at $892; more than 8 times lower than in the United States. Life expectancy was lowest in Hungary at 73.9 years; more than 8 years lower than in Japan.

Potential Years of Life Lost (PYLL)[ii] is an estimate of the average number of years a person would have lived if he or she had not died prematurely. In 1960 PYLL was highest in Portugal for both sexes: 19,910 years lost per 100,000 males aged 0 to 69 and 14,740 years per 100,000 females (OECD, 2010).

In the UK, expenditure[iii] on health services increased by a third (32 per cent) from £82.9 billion in 2004–05 to £110.0 billion in 2008–09. Over the same period, identifiable expenditure on health per head increased by 29 per cent from £1,380 to £1,780. Within the UK identifiable expenditure per head on health services in 2008–09 was highest in Scotland at £1,970, and lowest in England at £1,750 (HMT, 2010).

In 2008 (or the latest available period), PYLL was highest among males in Estonia, 9,870 years per 100,000 and among females in Mexico, 4,950 per 100,000 (2007 data). PYLL was lowest in 2008 in Iceland, 2,800 years per 100,000 males and 1,590 per 100,000 females. It should be noted that 2008 data are not yet available for all countries (OECD, 2010).

Figure 2   **Life expectancy at birth and age 65, and infant[1] and neonatal[2] mortality rates**

United Kingdom

Life expectancy in years; mortality rates per 1,000 live births

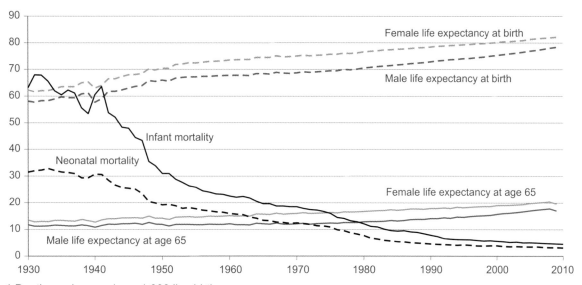

1 Deaths under age 1 per 1,000 live births.

2 Deaths under 28 days per 1,000 live births.

Source: Office for National Statistics; National Records of Scotland; Northern Ireland Statistics and Research Agency

Between 1930 and 2009 life expectancy at birth in the UK increased by around 20 years for both sexes **(Figure 2)**. In 1930 life expectancy at birth was 58.1 years for males and 62.3 years for females, increasing 35 per cent among males to 78.3 years and 32 per cent among females to 82.1 years in 2009.

At age 65 life expectancy increased by 45 per cent for both sexes: from 11.7 years for males and 13.5 years for females in 1930, to 17.0 years and 19.6 years respectively in 2009.

Between 2007 and 2009 in the UK life expectancy at birth was highest in England at 78.0 years for males and 82.1 years for females and lowest in Scotland at 75.3 years and 80.1 years respectively (ONS, 2010b).

An important reason for the increase in life expectancy is the fall in infant mortality rates (deaths under one year old), which decreased by 93 per cent from a rate of 63.1 per 1,000 live births in 1930 to 4.5 per 1,000 in 2010, the lowest on record. Similarly, neonatal mortality rates (deaths under 28 days old) have fallen by 90 per cent to their lowest recorded level, from 31.5 per 1,000 live births in 1930 to 3.1 per 1,000 in 2010.

In 2009 the main cause of infant mortality in Great Britain was 'certain conditions originating in the perinatal period'[iv], accounting for around a quarter of all infant deaths among males (27 per cent) and females (25 per cent) (ONS, 2010c; NRS, 2010a).

With life expectancy increasing for both sexes, consideration should be given to how long people can expect to live free from a limiting illness or disability as one way of assessing the health of the nation in-line with the WHO definition quoted at the start of this chapter.

Table 1   Life expectancy, healthy life expectancy and disability-free life expectancy at birth and age 65: by sex

United Kingdom   Years, percentages

	At birth					At age 65				
	Life expectancy	Healthy life expectancy[1]	Life spent in very good/ good health (%)	Disability- free life expectancy	Life spent disability- free (%)	Life expectancy	Healthy life expectancy[1]	Life spent in very good/ good health (%)	Disability- free life expectancy	Life spent disability- free (%)
Males										
2000–02	75.7	60.7	80.2	60.3	79.7	15.9	9.5	59.6	8.8	55.2
2001–03	75.9	60.6	79.8	60.9	80.2	16.1	9.4	58.4	9.0	56.1
2002–04	76.3	61.0	80.0	61.5	80.6	16.4	9.6	58.9	9.4	57.2
2003–05	76.6	61.5	80.2	62.3	81.3	16.6	9.9	59.5	9.9	59.6
2004–06	76.9	62.0	80.6	62.4	81.2	16.9	10.1	59.9	10.1	59.6
2005–07	77.2	61.4	79.6	62.5	81.0	17.2	9.9	57.5	10.0	58.1
2006–08	77.4	62.5	80.8	63.2	81.7	17.4	10.1	58.2	10.1	58.2
Females										
2000–02	80.4	62.4	77.6	62.8	78.1	19.0	10.8	56.8	10.2	53.8
2001–03	80.5	62.2	77.3	63.0	78.2	19.1	10.7	55.9	10.3	53.9
2002–04	80.7	62.5	77.4	63.3	78.4	19.3	10.9	56.6	10.4	54.1
2003–05	81.0	62.9	77.7	63.9	79.0	19.4	11.1	57.2	10.7	54.8
2004–06	81.3	63.7	78.3	63.9	78.6	19.7	11.4	57.7	10.6	53.8
2005–07	81.5	62.9	77.2	63.7	78.2	19.9	10.9	55.0	10.5	53.0
2006–08	81.6	64.3	78.7	64.2	78.6	20.0	11.3	56.4	10.6	52.9

1 HLE based on five-point response general health question 2005–07 to 2006–08. Estimates for 2000–02 to 2004–06 are simulations based on original survey data.

Source: Office for National Statistics (ONS, 2010d)

Over the period 2000–02 to 2006–08, healthy life expectancy (HLE)[v] for males at birth in the UK increased from 60.7 years to 62.5 years and from 62.4 years to 64.3 years for females. Estimates of HLE for the periods 2000–02 to 2004–06 are simulations based on original survey data. This is due to a discontinuity in the historic time series caused by adoption of an EU-wide general health question from the period 2005–07. In 2006–08 males could expect to spend more than four-fifths (80.8 per cent) of their lives in very good or good health and females 78.7 per cent **(Table 1)**.

Disability-free life expectancy (DFLE) has also risen for both males and females at birth in the UK over the period 2000–02 to 2006–08. In 2006–08 the proportion of life spent free from a disability was 81.7 per cent for males and 78.6 per cent for females.

In 2006–08, men at age 65 could expect to spend a further 10.1 years in very good or good health and an equal length of time free from a disability. This represents 58.2 per cent of life expectancy at this age. Women aged 65, could expect to live for a further 11.3 years in very good or good health and 10.6 years free from a disability, representing 56.4 per cent and 52.9 per cent of life expectancy respectively.

For the constituent countries of the UK in 2006–08 HLE at birth was highest in England, 63.0 years for males and 64.5 years for females, and lowest in Wales; 60.2 years for males and 62.7 years for females. At age 65 HLE for men and women was again highest in England; 10.2 and 11.4 years respectively, but lowest in Northern Ireland for men (9.5 years) and in Wales for women (10.5 years).

In contrast to HLE, the geographical distribution of the highest DFLE at birth differed by sex. While DLFE at birth was highest in England for males (64.1 years), for females it was highest in Wales (64.9 years). The lowest DFLE at birth was in Northern Ireland at 60.3 for males and 61.6 years for females. At age 65 DFLE was also highest in England for men (10.5 years) but highest in Wales for women (11.3 years). The lowest DFLE at age 65 for both sexes was in Northern Ireland, 8.8 years for men and 9.3 years for women (ONS, 2010b).

Self-reported health status

Table 2   **Self perception of general health**[1]

Great Britain   Percentages

	Males					Females				
	Very good	**Good**	**Fair**	**Bad**	**Very bad**	**Very good**	**Good**	**Fair**	**Bad**	**Very bad**
2005[2]	41.2	38.6	14.5	4.8	0.9	37.5	39.5	16.9	4.7	1.4
2006	41.1	39.3	14.2	4.4	1.1	39.0	39.8	14.5	5.0	1.7
2007	43.6	37.7	13.1	4.6	0.9	39.9	39.2	15.9	4.0	1.0
2008	47.7	35.5	12.1	3.7	0.9	45.1	36.0	14.0	4.2	0.8
2009	46.8	35.6	12.6	3.9	1.1	45.4	35.8	13.5	4.4	0.9

1 Those answering the survey question 'how is your/his/her health in general; would you say it was very good, good, fair, bad or very bad?' There are potential exposure and order effects associated with the five-category general health question prior to 2008. Particular care should therefore be taken if drawing conclusions concerning the changes between 2007 and 2008.

2 2005 estimates are based on data collected from April to December. From 2006 estimates are based on the full calendar year.

Source: General Lifestyle Survey, Office for National Statistics

As well as the objective studies which show that more of life is spent free from limiting illness or disability, reports by individuals on their own health also show improvement **(Table 2)**.

In 2005 in Great Britain, more than three-quarters of males (80 per cent) and females (77 per cent) considered themselves to be in 'very good' or 'good' health, while around 6 per cent of males and of females considered themselves to be in ' very bad' or 'bad' health.

By 2009 the perception of general health had improved, with 82 per cent of males and 81 per cent of females in Great Britain considering themselves to be in at least 'good' health and around 5 per cent respectively in 'bad' or 'very bad' health. In 2009 more than half of females in Great Britain considered themselves to be in 'good' or 'very good' health for all age-groups while in males it was those who were between 0 and 74 years.

Within Great Britain in 2009 the proportion of the population in 'good' or 'very good' health was highest for males in Wales at 86 per cent and for females in both England and Wales at 82 per cent.

Improvements in preventive health are seen in immunisation programmes among children and reductions in communicable disease.

In Wales, Scotland and Northern Ireland, between 2000 and 2010 the proportion of children aged two who had completed their primary immunisation against diphtheria, tetanus, polio and whooping cough was fairly stable at 95 per cent and 98 percent respectively, while for England it was slightly lower at 94 percent. In 2000–01 immunisation against measles, mumps and rubella (MMR) in the UK was 88 per cent, falling to 81 per cent in 2003–04. In 2009–10 MMR immunisation had risen to 89 per cent (ONS, 2010b).

Between 1989 and 2009, rates of selected communicable diseases in the UK fell. The biggest falls were seen for rubella (96 per cent lower), whooping cough (91 per cent) and measles (82 per cent). Notifications increased for meningococcal septicaemia/infection (40 per cent), food poisoning (31 per cent), and tuberculosis and typhoid both increased by around a fifth (17 per cent) (ONS, 2010b).

It is estimated that around 172 million working days were lost to sick absence in 2007, at a cost to the economy of over £13 billion (DH, 2010). Although the proportion of the population in good health is increasing, the proportion of the population reporting a long-standing illness or disability[vi] has increased since the 1970s.

Table 3   Trends in self-reported sickness: by sex

Great Britain   Percentages

	1972	1981	1991	2000	2001	2002	2003	2004	2005[1]	2006	2007	2008	2009
Percentage who reported:													
(a) long-standing illness or disability													
Males	20	28	31	33	32	34	31	31	32	33	31	29	30
Females	21	30	32	32	31	35	32	32	33	34	32	30	31
All persons	21	29	31	32	32	35	31	31	33	33	31	29	30
(b) limiting long-standing illness or disability													
Males	..	16	17	18	18	20	17	17	18	17	18	16	17
Females	..	19	18	19	19	22	19	19	20	20	19	18	19
All persons	..	17	18	19	19	21	18	18	19	19	18	17	18
(c) restricted activity in the 14 days before interview due to illness or injury (acute sickness)													
Males	7	11	11	13	13	14	12	12	11	11	11	10	10
Females	8	13	13	15	15	16	15	14	15	14	13	12	12
All persons	8	12	12	14	14	15	14	13	13	13	12	11	11

1 2005 data includes last quarter of 2004/5 data due to survey change from financial year to calendar year.

Source: General Lifestyle Survey, Office for National Statistics (ONS, 2011)

In 1972 more than one in five adults (21 per cent) in Great Britain reported a long-standing illness or disability, rising to more than one in three adults (35 per cent) in 2002. In 2009 this had fallen to 30 per cent. Prevalence of a long-standing illness or disability is similar among males and females, 30 per cent and 31 per cent respectively **(Table 3)**. However, although there has been an increase in the proportion reporting long-standing illness or disability, those also reporting that the condition limited their everyday activities has varied less: in 1981 around 17 per cent reported such limitation, and after rising to 21 per cent in 2002, fell to 18 per cent in 2009.

In 2009 around 1 in 8 females (12 per cent) in Great Britain reported restricted activity due to acute illness or injury in the 14 days prior to interview, an increase from around 1 in 13 (8 per cent) in 1972; 1 in 10 males (10 per cent) reported recent restricted activity in 2009, rising from 1 in 14 (7 per cent) in 1972. However, there have been recent decreases among those reporting restricted activity, from a peak of 14 per cent of males and 16 per cent of females in 2002.

Results from the General Lifestyle Survey (GLF) show that in 2009, two-thirds of adults (66 per cent) in Great Britain aged 75 and over reported a long-standing illness or disability. This is more than 8 times higher than the rate reported for children aged between 0 and 4 years (8 per cent). Adults aged 75 and over were also 3 times more likely than the very young to report restricted activity, 18 per cent and 6 per cent respectively (ONS, 2011).

In Great Britain, on average, there were 23 days per person per year where activity was restricted because of acute illness or injury in 2009. The number of days was higher among females, 25 days per person per year compared with 21 days for males (ONS, 2011).

The older population averaged more than six times as many days where activity was restricted compared with the younger population; 49 days per person per year among those aged 75 and over compared with eight days among those aged between 0 and 4 years.

For the adult population reporting a chronic sickness in 2009, the most common condition for men was disease of the heart and circulatory system, a rate of 114 per 1,000 men; among women, disease of the musculoskeletal system was more common at 159 per 1,000 (ONS, 2011).

In Great Britain in 2009 the most common condition suffered among the youngest adult age-group (aged between 16 and 44 years) was asthma, 28 per 1,000 men and 45 per 1,000 women. With the exception of men aged between 65 and 74 years, where hypertension was more prevalent, the most common condition suffered in all other age groups for both sexes was arthritis and rheumatism (ONS, 2011).

Use of services

While life expectancies are increasing, the age at which individuals become disabled may also increase to such an extent that the overall burden of lifetime illness (the proportion of their lives that people spend with poor health or disability) may actually decline. Declining disability rates would have considerable implications for the provision of health and social care. There is some evidence from the General Lifestyle Survey (ONS, 2011) of recent decreases in the use of in-patient, outpatient and casualty services in Great Britain, while consultations with GPs have changed relatively little.

Figure 3   **In-patient stays,[1] out-patient/casualty attendances[2] and GP consultations[3]**

Great Britain
Percentages

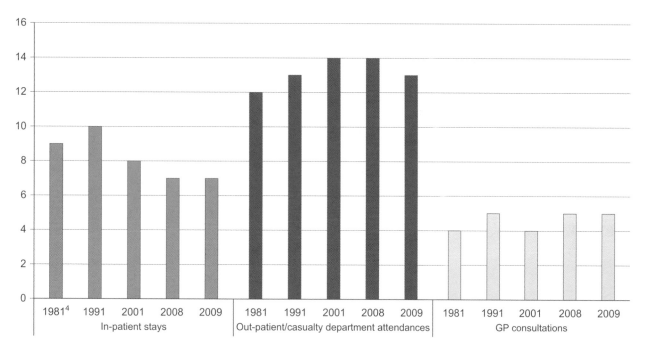

1 In-patient stays in the 12 months before interview.
2 Persons who reported attending an out-patient or casualty department in the 3 months before interview.
3 Consultations with an NHS GP in the 14 days before interview.
4 Earliest in-patient data available are for 1982.
Source: General Lifestyle Survey, Office for National Statistics (ONS, 2011)

Between 1982 and 2009, the proportion of the population in Great Britain reporting an in-patient stay in the 12 months prior to interview fell from around 1 in 11 (9 per cent) to 1 in 14 (7 per cent) **(Figure 3)**. In-patient stays have fallen among all age groups under 65 years, but have increased slightly among adults aged 65 to 74 years (10 per cent in 1982 to 11 per cent in 2009) and those aged 75 and over (13 per cent to 15 per cent) (ONS, 2011). In 2009, in-patient stays among those aged 75 and over were more than double the rate for all ages groups under 65 years. In 2009 in-patient attendance was slightly higher among females, 7 per cent compared with 6 per cent of males, although female attendances had shown the larger fall between 1982 and 2009.

Between 1981 and 2009, attendances at out-patient or casualty departments in the 3 months prior to interview increased from 12 per cent to around 13 per cent. However, in 2009 there had been a slight decrease from 14 per cent in 2008. Attendances by the elderly population rose by more than 50 per cent; among 65 to 74-year-olds attendances rose from 15 per cent in 1981 to 21 per cent in 2009 and among those aged 75 and over from 15 per cent to 25 per cent (ONS, 2011). In 2009 out-patient or casualty attendances were highest among females than males between the ages of 45 and 74 years, although attendances among the very young and the very old were highest for males.

In 2009 around 1 in 20 people (5 per cent) consulted a GP in the 14 days prior to interview. Adults aged 75 and over were 4 times more likely to have a GP consultation than those aged between 5 and 15 years, 8 per cent and 2 per cent respectively (ONS, 2011). In 2009 around 1 in 16 females (6 per cent) attended a GP consultation compared with 1 in 25 males (4 per cent).

Since it was launched in 1998, NHS Online has reported an increasing number of people using telephone or online services. Between 2002/03 and 2007/08 the number of website 'hits' in England increased seven-fold from around four million to 31 million (NHS online 2008). In England in 2009/10 it was estimated that 2.4 million unnecessary GP appointments and 1.2 unnecessary ambulance journeys or visits to an Accident and Emergency department were avoided due to contact with NHS Online services (NHS online 2010).

Mortality

Combined with falls in infant mortality and increases in general health levels, decreases in mortality rates have also contributed to extended life expectancy **(Figure 4)**.

In 2009 the leading cause of death for both sexes was cancer, at 2,081 deaths per million males and 1,497 per million females, despite mortality rates for cancer falling 26 per cent and 14 per cent respectively since 1971.

Figure 4   Mortality: by sex and leading cause group

United Kingdom
Rates per million population

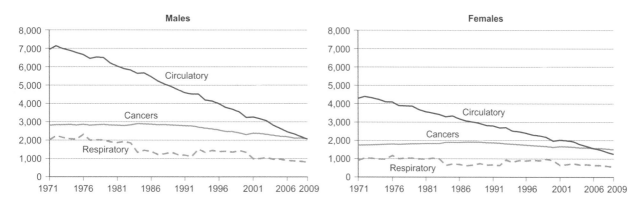

Source: Office for National Statistics; National Records of Scotland; Northern Ireland Statistics and Research Agency

Between 1971 and 2009 in the UK, mortality rates for diseases of the circulatory system and diseases of the respiratory system also fell among both sexes. According to the British Heart Foundation these are due to improvements such as legislative measures and tobacco control strategies to reduce exposure to second hand smoke, restrictions on marketing of foods high in sugar, fat and salt, national frameworks to drive up standards of treatment and care and advances in stem cell research and regenerative medicine (BHF 2010). In 2009, for males the mortality rate for diseases of the circulatory system was 70 per cent lower than in 1971, at 2,061 per million and the mortality rate for respiratory disease was 801 per million, a fall of over 60 per cent since 1971.

Among females, the mortality rate for disease of the circulatory system had fallen more than 71 per cent since 1971 to 1,252 per million in 2009 and mortality from disease of the respiratory system was 39 per cent lower, falling from 909 per million in 1971 to 552 per million in 2009.

In 2009 mortality rates from cancer were highest among those aged between 70 and 74 years; 334.2 per million males and 229.2 per million females. Mortality rates for both diseases of the circulatory system and diseases of the respiratory system were highest among those aged 90 and over; 529.7 per million males and 446.2 per million females and 266.6 per million males and 180.9 per million females respectively.

Cancer

As discussed in the last section, cancer was the most common cause of mortality among both males and females in 2009. It is estimated that around 1 in 3 people will develop some form of cancer during their lifetime (Cancer Research UK, 2010a).

Table 4   **Directly age-standardised cancer mortality[1] and incidence[2] rates, 2006 to 2008[3]**

United Kingdom   Rates per 100,000 population

ICD-10	Site description	Incidence	Mortality
Males			
C00–C97	All malignancies[4]	420.5	211.8
C18–C20	Colorectal	56.7	22.1
C34	Lung	61.1	51.7
C61	Prostate	100.0	24.5
C67	Bladder	19.2	8.0
C81–C96	Lymphomas and leukaemias	39.7	17.2
Females			
C00–C97	All malignancies[4]	364.8	152.8
C18–C20	Colorectal	36.3	13.7
C34	Lung	38.6	31.6
C50	Breast	123.0	26.9
C54	Uterus	18.3	2.5
C81–C96	Lymphomas and leukaemias	26.5	10.6

1 Mortality rates per 100,000 population, age-standardised to the European Standard Population to allow comparison between populations which may contain different proportions of people of different ages.

2 Registration (Incidence) rates are newly diagnosed cases of cancer per 100,000 population.

3 Three-year average.

4 Excluding nmsc (non-melanoma skin cancer) (C44) in newly diagnosed cases of cancer.

Source: Office for National Statistics (ONS, 2010e)

Between 2006 and 2008, the age-standardised incidence rate[viii] for all cancers was 420.5 per 100,000 males and 364.8 per 100,000 females **(Table 4)**. Incidence was highest for males for prostate cancer, 100.0 per 100,000, and for females for breast cancer at 123.0 per 100,000. These high incidence rates are arguably a result of an extensive breast screening programme[ix] among females and the Prostate Cancer Risk Management[x] programme among males, both of which can lead to higher diagnosis rates.

The age-standardised mortality rate for all cancers was highest among males, 211.8 per 100,000 compared with 152.8 per 100,000 females. Mortality from cancer was highest for lung cancer, 51.7 per 100,000 males and 31.6 per 100,000 females. In 2008, mortality rates for lung cancer were highest among males aged 85 and over, 563.8 per 100,000, and among females aged 80 to 84 years, 291.1 per 100,000 (Cancer Research UK, 2010b).

Studies by the International Agency for Research on Cancer show that worldwide in 2008 there were 12.7 million new cases of cancer (an incidence rate of 181.6 per 100,000 population), and 7.6 million cancer deaths (a mortality rate of 106.1 per 100,000). Among males, both the worldwide incidence and mortality rates were highest for lung cancer, 34.0 per 100,000 and 29.3 per 100,000 respectively. For females, both incidence and mortality rates were highest for breast cancer, 39.0 per 100,000 and 12.5 per 100,000 respectively (International Agency for Research on Cancer, 2010).

In the European Union (EU-27) in 2008, the European age-standardised lung cancer mortality rate for males was highest in Hungary, 106.4 per 100,000 and for females in Denmark, 44.6 per 100,000. The European age-standardised lung cancer mortality rate for UK of 50.3 per 100,000 males was around 17 per cent lower than the EU-27 average of 60.6 per 100,000; the rate for females of 31.7 per 100,000 was more than 70 per cent higher than the EU-27 average of 18.6 per 100,000 (Cancer Research UK, 2010c).

Within the UK, between 2006 and 2008 the incidence rate for all cancers for males was highest in Wales, 467.1 per 100,000, and lowest in England, 414.1 per 100,000; for females, incidence rates were highest in Scotland, 398.0 per 100,000 and lowest in England, 360.2 per 100,000 (ONS, 2010e).

For both sexes mortality rates for all cancers was highest in Scotland, 245.8 per 100,000 males and 175.9 per 100,000 females, and lowest in England, 207.4 per 100,000 and 149.9 per 100,000 respectively (ONS, 2010e).

Figure 5   **Five-year age-standardised relative survival, common cancers: by sex[1]**

England

Percentages

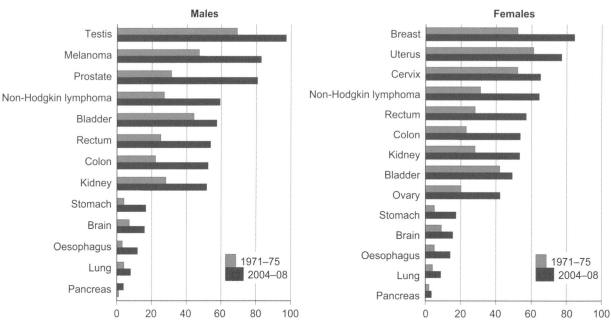

1 Patients diagnosed 2004–2008 and followed up to 2009.

2 Age-standardisation requires the estimation of survival for each age group. Age-standardisation is not possible if there are too few events (deaths) in a given age group. That can happen because survival is very high (there are very few deaths) or because it is very low (most of the patients die early in the five-year period of follow-up). Age-standardised rates are not available for stomach cancer for men in England and lung, stomach and brain cancers for females in England.

Source: Table 4.5 'Cancer Survival Trends in England and Wales, 1971–1995, NHS region and deprivation', Office for National Statistics (ONS 1995, ONS 2010a), London School of Hygiene and Tropical Medicine

Survival from cancer has shown large improvements in England over the last 40 years **(Figure 5)**. Between 1971–75 and 2004–08, five-year age-standardised survival rates improved in all cancers and more than doubled in 8 out of 13 cancers for males and in 7 out of 15 cancers for females.

Between 2004 and 2008, the highest survival rate for males was testicular cancer with more than 97 per cent still alive five years after diagnosis. Among females, between 2004 and 2008 five-year survival rates were highest for melanoma skin cancer at 90 per cent.

The largest improvement in survival rate for both sexes between 1971–75 and 2004–08 was for stomach cancer, increasing 313 per cent for males from a rate of 4.0 per 100,000 to 16.5 per 100,000 and 244 per cent for females from 5.0 per 100,000 to 17.2 per 100,000.The lowest survival rates for both men and women were for cancer of the pancreas, with between 3 per cent and 4 per cent surviving five years after diagnosis.

In the UK, in 2007, incidence of pancreatic cancer was 12.5 per 100,000 males and 12.7 per 100,000 females. Incidence for this cancer was higher among the elderly population, at 92.8 per 100,000 males and 89.3 per 100,000 females aged 85 and over (Cancer Research UK, 2010d). In 2008, mortality rates from pancreatic cancer in the UK were 12.6 per 100,000 males and 12.7 per 100,000 females. Mortality was higher for males aged between 80 and 84 years, 99.8 per 100,000 and among females aged 85 and over, 91.5 per 100,000 (Cancer Research UK, 2010e).

Healthy lifestyles

The causal link between lung cancer and tobacco smoking has been established for over 50 years. Since then, information has been collected on the health consequences of tobacco consumption and the addictive nature of nicotine which makes smoking cessation difficult. In the UK, tobacco consumption is now recognised as the single greatest cause of preventable illness and early death with smoking-related disease responsible for more than 107,000 deaths in 2007. It is estimated that 86 per cent of lung cancer deaths in the UK are caused by smoking (Cancer Research UK, 2010f). Other life style choices, such as drug or alcohol misuse and can also lead to poor health.

Table 5   **Prevalence of smoking, drinking and binge-drinking[1] among adults**

Great Britain   Percentages

	Men			Women		
	Regular smoker	Drank more than 4 units[2]	Drank more than 8 units	Regular smoker	Drank more than 3 units[2]	Drank more than 6 units
2000/01	29	39	21	25	23	10
2001/02	28	40	22	26	23	10
2002/03	27	38	21	25	23	10
2003/04	28	40	23	24	23	9
2004/05 [3]	26	39	22	23	22	9
2005	25	35	19	23	20	8
2006 [4]	23	40	23	21	33	15
2007	22	41	24	20	34	15
2008 [5]	22	37	21	21	29	14
2009	22	37	20	20	29	13

1 Binge-drinking is defined as drinking double the daily recommended consumption.

2 Includes those who drank more than 8 units for men and 6 units for women.
3 2005 data includes last quarter of 2004/5 data due to survey change from financial year to calendar year.

4 Results from 2006 include longitudinal data. From 2006, figures produced using the updated methodology for converting volumes of alcohol to units assuming an average wine glass size.

5 Figures produced from 2008 are using the updated methodology including data on wine glass size, therefore comparisons with earlier data may be misleading.

Source: General Household Survey, Office for National Statistics (ONS, 2011)

In 2009, more than 1 in 5 men (22 per cent) in Great Britain smoked regularly and a similar proportion (20 per cent) had binged on alcohol at least once in the previous week **(Table 5)**.

The proportion of men who were regular smokers fell from 29 per cent in 2000/01 to 22 per cent in 2009. Among women, the proportion of smokers fell from 1 in 4 (25 per cent) in 2000/01 to 1 in 5 (20 per cent) in 2009. Smoking is more prevalent among younger adults, with 27 per cent of men aged 25 to 34 and 28 per cent of women aged 20 to 24 regularly smoking in 2009, compared with 15 per cent of men and 13 per cent of women aged over 60 (ONS, 2011).

In 2009, around 5 per cent of boys aged 11–15 years smoked at least 1 cigarette a week, compared with 7 per cent of girls in the same age group (IC, 2009a). Among 15-year-old boys in England, around 19 per cent smoked compared with 22 per cent of girls. In Great Britain, the proportion of smokers aged between 11 and 16 years was lowest among boys in Wales for all age-groups and lowest in Scotland for girls (ONS, 2010b).

According to the 2008/09 Opinions Survey, around two-thirds (67 per cent) of smokers in Great Britain reported that they would like to stop smoking: the most common reason given was 'at least one health reason', 85 per cent of men and 82 per cent of women, while 6 per cent of men and 7 per cent of women gave the smoking ban introduced in 2007 as the main reason (ONS, 2009).

In 2007 the annual cost to the NHS from alcohol misuse was £2.7 billion (NHS 2009). Alcohol has been identified as a causal factor in more than 60 medical conditions including mouth, throat, stomach, liver and breast cancers; hypertensive disease (high blood pressure); cirrhosis; and depression (IC, 2010).

The proportion of men who drank more than the Department of Health daily alcohol guidelines (3–4 units for men, 2–3 units for females)[xi] fell from 39 per cent in 2000/01 to 37 per cent in 2009. The proportion considered 'binge-drinkers' (drinking double the recommended daily guideline) had fallen slightly from 21 per cent in 2000/01 to 20 per cent in 2009. However, it should be noted that the methodology for calculating alcohol consumption was amended in 2008 and therefore comparisons with data before 2008 may not be valid.

In comparison, the proportion of women in Great Britain who drank more than the recommended daily guidelines had risen from 23 per cent to 29 per cent over the last decade, while the proportion of binge drinkers had increased from 10 per cent to 13 per cent. However, it should be noted that around 1 in 3 men (32 per cent) and nearly a half of women (46 per cent) in Great Britain drank no alcohol in the week prior to interview.

Those considered 'binge-drinkers' decreased with age: men aged 16 to 24 years were nearly 5 times more likely to binge-drink in the previous week compared with those aged 65 and over, 24 per cent and 5 per cent respectively. Similarly, among women, those aged 16 to 24 years were 12 times more likely to binge-drink compared with those aged 65 and over, 24 per cent and 2 per cent respectively (ONS 2011).

In England more than a third of children aged 15 years old reported drinking on a weekly basis in 2010; 39 per cent of boys and 37 per cent of girls (ONS, 2010b). Within Great Britain, drinking prevalence was lowest in Scotland for all age groups between 11 and 16 years.

Between 1991 and 2009 alcohol-related mortality[xii] rates in the UK rose 86 per cent, from a rate of 6.9 per 100,000 to 12.8 per 100,000. In 2009 mortality rates among males were more than double the rates for females; 17.4 per 100,000 males and 8.4 per 100,000 females. In 2009 alcohol-related mortality rates were highest among those aged 55 to 74 years, 41.8 per 100,000 males and 20.1 per 100,000 females (ONS, 2010f).

Table 6   **Percentage of adults[1] reporting lifetime, last year and last month use[2] of individual drugs, 2009[3]**

United Kingdom   Percentages

	Lifetime			Last year			Last month		
	Men	Women	Total	Men	Women	Total	Men	Women	Total
Any drug	40.9	28.3	34.6	12.0	5.4	8.6	7.3	2.7	5.0
Amphetamines	13.7	8.0	10.9	1.4	0.6	1.0	0.5	0.2	0.3
Cannabis	35.3	23.5	29.4	9.5	4.0	6.7	5.8	2.0	3.9
Cocaine	11.2	5.6	8.4	3.9	1.4	2.6	1.8	0.6	1.2
ecstasy	11.4	5.4	8.4	2.6	0.9	1.7	1.1	0.3	0.7
LSD	7.8	3.1	5.4	0.4	0.1	0.3	0.2	0.0	0.1
Magic mushrooms	10.4	3.9	7.1	0.6	0.2	0.4	0.2	0.0	0.1
Opiates	1.3	0.6	1.0	0.3	0.1	0.2	0.2	0.0	0.1

1 Adults aged 16–59 in England and Wales; adults aged 16–64 in Scotland and Northern Ireland.
2 Frequent use was defined in the British Crime Survey as the use of any drug more than once a month in the past year.
3 Data for England and Wales are for 2009/10; data for Scotland and Northern Ireland are for 2008/09.
Source: UK Focal Point on Drugs, 2009, European Monitoring Centre for Drugs and Drug Addiction

In 2009/10, more than a third of people (34.6 per cent) in the UK reported that they had used drugs at least once in their lifetime **(Table 6)**. Cannabis was the most frequently used drug in more than one-quarter (29.4 per cent) of all cases reported by drug users.

Around 1 in 10 people (8.6 per cent) reported using drugs more than once a month in the past year. Prevalence was more than twice as high among men, with around 1 in 8 (12.0 per cent) reporting drug use in the last year compared to around 1 in 20 women (5.4 per cent). In 2009/10, around 1 in 20 people (5.0 per cent) in the UK reported using drugs in the last month.

Between 1993 and 2009, deaths related to drug misuse[xiii] in England and Wales fell among the youngest and oldest adult population. Among those aged under 20 rates have fallen 26 per cent for males – to 29 per 100,000, and 9 per cent for females – to 10 per 100,000; among those aged over 70 rates fell 25 per cent and 43 per cent respectively. In 2009 mortality rates from drug misuse were highest among those aged 30 to 39, 544 per 100,000 males and 97 per 100,000 females (ONS, 2010g).

The latest data for children show that within the UK current drug use was highest in Scotland, where 8.5 per cent reported using drugs in 2009/10, and lowest in Wales at 7.1 per cent (ONS, 2010b).

According to the UK Focal Point on Drugs report[xiv] in 2007/08 there were more than 46,000 first demands for drug treatment in the UK through a structured drug treatment programme such as a hospital inpatient, outpatient or through their GP. Opiates accounted for 41 per cent of the primary drug being treated for (UK Focal Point, 2009).

Studies by National Health Surveys[xv] indicate that in 2008–09, more than 1 in 3 males (39 per cent) and around 1 in 4 females (29 per cent) aged over 16 years in Great Britain met physical activity recommendations of 30 minutes or more vigorous activity on at least 5 days a week[xvi] **(Table 7)**.

Among children, more than two-thirds of boys (68 per cent) and more than a half of girls (57 per cent) aged between 2 and 15 years met physical activity recommendations of 60 minutes activity on all 7 days a week.

Table 7   **Physical activity levels of adults and children and prevalence of BMI classed as 'obese and overweight':[1,2] by sex and age, 2008–09[3]**

Great Britain   Percentages

	Males			Females		
	Meets physical activity recommendations[4]	Low physical activity levels[5]	Obese or overweight	Meets physical activity recommendations[4]	Low physical activity levels[5]	Obese or overweight
2–15[2]	68	21	31	57	28	28
16–24	53	16	35	35	31	39
25–34	50	19	52	36	24	44
35–44	45	23	71	34	27	54
45–54	41	25	79	32	32	63
55–64	33	37	81	28	37	68
65–74	20	47	81	17	52	74
75 and over	10	68	71	6	78	61
All ages	39	30	60	29	37	52

1 Body mass index (BMI) greater than or equal to 25.

2 Data for Wales is based on self-reported weight and height and are not directly comparable with England and Scotland. For Wales, data are for children aged 2–15 with valid height and weight measurements, and based on the 85th (overweight) and 95th (obese) percentiles of the 1990 UK BMI reference curves. For Scotland, data for children whose BMI was more than 3 standard deviations above or below the norm for their age were excluded from the table. Physical activity data are for children aged 2–15 in England and Scotland; children aged 4–15 in Wales.

3 Based on 2009 mid-year population estimates.

4 Those classed as 'meeting recommendations' participated in 30 or more minutes of moderate or vigorous activity on at least 5 days a week.

5 'Low activity' levels indicate less than 30 minutes of moderate or vigorous activity per week.

Source: The NHS Information Centre for Health and Social Care (IC (2010)); Welsh Government (Wales (2010)); Scottish Government (Scot (2010))

Physical activity decreased with age; for those aged 2 to 15, males were more than 7 times as likely and females 9 times more likely to meet physical activity recommendations than those aged 75 and over.

Obesity is associated with chronic conditions such as diabetes, hypertension and hyperlipidaemia (high levels of lipids (fats) in the blood that can lead to blockages and narrowing of blood vessels). Obesity can reduce the quality of a person's life, create a strain on health services and can lead to premature death (IC, 2008). It is estimated that the obesity-related cost to the NHS is around £4.2 billion a year (DH, 2010).

In Great Britain, around two-thirds of males and around a half of females were considered obese or overweight in 2008–09. Obesity was more prevalent among those aged between 65 and 74 years, 81 per cent of males and 74 per cent of females.

Between 1995 and 2009 in England, the proportion of men classed as 'overweight or obese' increased from 59 per cent to 66 per cent, although this was a slight decrease from 67 per cent in 2006. Among women, obesity increased from 50 per cent in 1995 to just over 57 per cent in 2004, subsequently falling to slightly below 57 per cent in 2009 (IC, 2010).

Diet has an important influence on obesity and thus on health. A poor diet can result in a higher risk of disease, and a diet low in fruit and vegetables can result in chronic conditions such as cardiovascular disease, stroke and diabetes, while a diet high in saturated fat can result in raised blood cholesterol and coronary heart disease (IC, 2008).

Since 2005 the Government's food and health action plan has set out a strategy recommending at least 5 portions of fruit and vegetables per day (DH, 2005). In 2008, around a quarter of males (25 per cent) and females (29 per cent) in Great Britain ate at least 5 portions of fruit and vegetables per day (ONS, 2010b).

Excess winter mortality

In 2009/10 there were an estimated 28,200 excess winter deaths[xvii] in Great Britain, a fall of 29 per cent compared with figures for 2008/09, despite Met Office data showing a lower average winter temperature in 2009/10 (2.5°C) than in 2008/09 (3.9°C) (MET) **(Figure 6)**.

Excess winter mortality peaked in 1962/63 with 96,700 deaths, coinciding with the lowest average winter temperature recorded between 1951/52 and 2009/10, 1.1°C.

Figure 6   Excess winter mortality[1] and average winter temperature

Great Britain[2]

Number, temperature (°C)

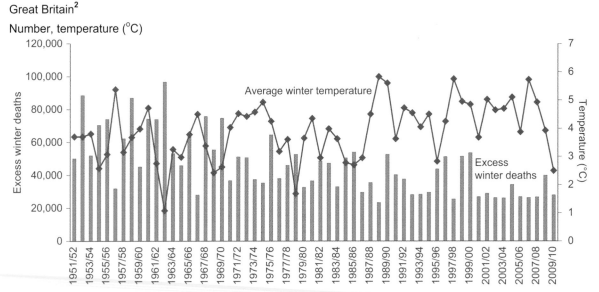

1 Excess winter mortality is defined by the Office for National Statistics as the difference between the number of deaths during the four winter months (December to March) and the average number of deaths during the preceding August to November and the following April to July. Figures are rounded to the nearest 100. Figures for the latest winter period are provisional. Data include deaths of non-residents.

2 Excess winter deaths in Great Britain; average winter temperature in the UK.

Source: Office for National Statistics; National Records of Scotland; Met Office

In England and Wales, females experienced greater excess winter mortality than males, 14,800 compared with 10,600 respectively in 2009/10 (ONS, 2010h).

Of the 28,200 excess winter deaths in Great Britain in 2009/10, more than a half (55 per cent) were among people aged 85 and over, with around 1 in 10 (10 per cent) among people aged under 65 (ONS, 2010h, NRS 2010b).

Deaths from respiratory disease accounted for the majority of excess winter deaths, compared with other causes of death (ONS, 2010h). In the UK between 1999 and 2009, the total number of deaths from respiratory disease fell by around a third (30 per cent) from 109,300 to 76,700, coinciding with lower levels of excess winter mortality. It should be noted that in 1999 there was a flu epidemic which resulted in an increase in the number of respiratory deaths.

In 2009 in the UK, the European age-standardised mortality rate for respiratory diseases among males age 85 and over was 15 times higher than for those aged between 50 and 54 years – 266.6

per million and 17.4 per million respectively; equivalent figures for women were 180.9 per million and 12.5 per million, around 14 times higher among those age 85 and over.

The variation in the number of extra deaths in winter depends not only on temperature but also on the level of disease (particularly influenza) in the population. Influenza is often implicated in winter deaths as it can cause complications such as bronchitis and pneumonia, especially in the elderly. The winter of 2009/10 was the coldest in 14 years but influenza levels were below baseline levels for much of the winter season. The highest excess winter mortality in recent years was seen in 1999/2000, when influenza cases reached epidemic levels, but the average winter temperature was relatively mild. High levels of influenza were also seen in the winters of 1993/94, 1996/97, 1998/99 and 1999/2000, coinciding with years of high excess winter mortality (ONS, 2010h).

In England and Wales, positive influenza specimens detected in laboratories between 1991 and 2009 peaked in 2009 at around 8,100, around 3 times higher than in 1991 when there were around 2,200 positive samples. On average, 21 per cent of positive influenza samples in England and Wales detected between 1991 and 2009 were among those aged over 65, although the proportion of over 65's affected in 2009 was only 4 per cent compared with 17 per cent in 1991 (HPA, 2009).

Figure 7   Weekly GP consultations for influenza:[1,2] 2009 to 2011[3]

England and Wales
Rates per 100,000 population

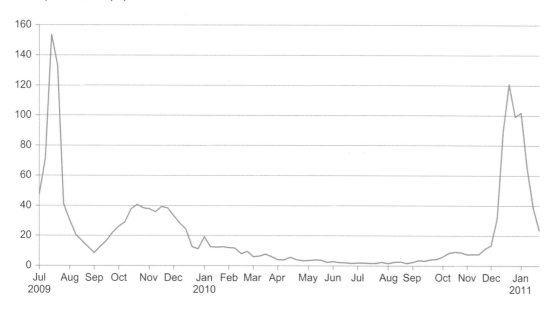

1 In England the definition 'Influenza-like illness' is used; in Wales 'Influenza'.
2 England and Wales include primary consultations only.
3 Weekly consultations between the start of July 2009 and the end of January 2011.
Source: Health Protection Agency; Royal College of General Practitioners; National Public Health Service, Wales

Between July 2009 and January 2011, consultation rates with a GP for influenza / influenza-like illness (ILI) peaked in England and Wales in July 2009, 153.6 per 100,000 population, coinciding with the H1N1 (Swine Flu) outbreak which first appeared in the UK at the end of April 2009 **(Figure**

7). In Scotland and Northern Ireland, rates peaked in January 2011, 77.3 per 100,000 and October 2009, 280.6 per 100,000 respectively, coinciding with the normal influenza season.

During the 2009/10 winter period (December to March), consultation rates peaked in the UK in December. Between the first week of December and the last week of March ILI consultation rates fell 96 per cent in Wales, 82 per cent in England, 79 per cent in Northern Ireland and 33 per cent in Scotland.

During the H1N1 pandemic, people also used the National Pandemic Flu Service which provided advice online or over the telephone. According to NHS Online, between 2009 and 2010 2.7 million people used this service, while 1.8 million people were able to obtain antiviral treatment without the need to visit a GP (NHS online 2010).

Immunising the elderly population against influenza is an important health programme among the UK health authorities. In 2000 immunisation was extended to those aged 65 and over, and in the UK 64 per cent of people aged 65 and over were immunised against influenza. Within five years, the immunisation rate in the UK had risen to over 75 per cent of over 65's, but subsequently fell to around 72 per cent in 2009.

Within the UK, immunisation rates for the elderly in 2009 ranged from 77 per cent in Northern Ireland to 64 per cent in Wales.

Mental health

As with physical health, mental health is an important indicator of the health of the population. It is estimated that mental ill-health represents between 9 and 23 per cent of the total health burden in the UK (DH, 2010).

Common mental disorders (CMDs) are mental conditions that cause marked emotional distress and interfere with daily function, such as different types of depression and anxiety. Symptoms of depressive episodes include low mood, loss of interest and enjoyment. They impair emotional and physical well-being and behaviour. Anxiety disorders include generalised anxiety disorder (GAD), panic disorder, phobias, and obsessive and compulsive disorders (OCD), characterised by a combination of obsessive thoughts and compulsive behaviours (IC, 2009b).

Results from the Adult Psychiatric Morbidity Survey[xviii] showed that in England, in 2007, around 1 in 6 adults (17.6 per cent) met the diagnostic criteria for at least 1 CMD in the week prior to interview **(Table 8)**. Women were more likely than men to have a CMD (21.5 per cent and 13.6 per cent respectively) and rates were higher for women across all CMD categories.

Table 8   Prevalence of a common mental disorder (CMD) in past week [1]: by sex and CMD[2]

England   Percentages

	1993	2000	2007
Men			
Mixed anxiety and depressive disorder	5.3	7.5	7.6
Generalised anxiety disorder	3.7	4.7	3.6
Depressive episode	1.7	2.6	2.2
All phobias	1.1	1.6	1.0
Obsessive compulsive disorder	1.0	1.0	1.1
Panic disorder	0.9	0.6	1.0
Any CMD	**11.9**	**14.6**	**13.6**
Women			
Mixed anxiety and depressive disorder	9.7	11.4	11.8
Generalised anxiety disorder	5.0	4.8	5.8
Depressive episode	2.7	2.9	3.0
All phobias	2.4	2.3	2.4
Obsessive compulsive disorder	1.8	1.5	1.5
Panic disorder	1.0	0.8	1.4
Any CMD	**19.1**	**20.4**	**21.5**
All adults			
Mixed anxiety and depressive disorder	7.5	9.4	9.7
Generalised anxiety disorder	4.4	4.7	4.7
Depressive episode	2.2	2.8	2.6
All phobias	2.2	2.8	2.6
Obsessive compulsive disorder	1.4	1.2	1.3
Panic disorder	1.0	0.7	1.2
Any CMD	**15.5**	**17.5**	**17.6**

1 Adults aged 16–64 and living in England.

2 An individual can have more than one CMD.

Source: The NHS Information Centre for Health and Social Care (IC, 2009)

Prevalence of a CMD in all adults increased from 15.5 per cent in 1993 to 17.5 per cent in 2000, although there was little change between 2000 and 2007.

In England, 1 in 5 adults (20 per cent) in 2007 aged between 45 and 54 years reported suffering with a CMD. Between 1993 and 2007 this age-group saw the largest increase in CMD prevalence, from 16 per cent in 1993 to 20 per cent in 2007, an increase of 4 percentage points (IC, 2009b).

In 2009/10, in England more than 1 in 10 people (10.9 per cent) were diagnosed with depression, with 0.8 per cent diagnosed with a mental illness such as schizophrenia and 0.5 per cent diagnosed with dementia. Within the rest of the UK, depression affected 11.5 per cent of the population of Northern Ireland, 8.6 per cent in Scotland and 7.9 per cent in Wales (ONS, 2010b).

Between 2006/07 and 2008/09, there were an estimated 437,000 cases in Great Britain of self-reported stress, depression or anxiety caused or made worse by a current or recent job. In 2009/10 this resulted in approximately 9.8 million working days lost in Britain. Although those working in 'health and social work' reported more cases (76,000), the industry with the highest prevalence rate was 'public administration and defence; compulsory social security' at 2,300 per 100,000 employees, four times higher than those working in the construction industry, 600 per 100,000 (DH, 2010).

In Great Britain prevalence of work-related stress was highest among females in 2008/09, with 233,000 cases compared with 182,000 for males. Among both sexes, prevalence was greater among the 45- to 54-year-old age-group, 1,700 per 100,000 males and 2,000 per 100,000 females (HSE, 2010).

Around a quarter (24 per cent) of adults with a CMD were receiving treatment for an emotional or mental problem: 14 per cent were taking psychoactive medication, 5 per cent were receiving counselling or therapy and 5 per cent were in receipt of both medication and counselling or therapy. Overall, three-quarters of adults assessed as having a level of neurotic symptoms sufficient to warrant treatment were not in receipt of medication or counselling (IC, 2009b).

In England antidepressant prescriptions have risen by 334 per cent, from 9.0 million in 1991 to 39.1 million in 2009. Within the UK, antidepressant prescriptions have also risen by 88 per cent in Wales between 2000 and 2009, by 54 per cent in Scotland between 2001 and 2010, and by 60 per cent in Northern Ireland between 2000 and 2008.

Mental health problems can ultimately lead people to commit suicide. Between 1991 and 2009, in the UK, suicides have fallen among all adult age-groups and both males and females. In 1991, 4,670 males committed suicide and this decreased by 7.9 per cent to 4,300 in 2009; among females suicides fell 16.7 per cent from 1,650 in 1991 to 1,370 in 2009 (ONS, 2010i).

In 2009 the highest male suicide rates were in the 15 to 44 age group at 18.0 per 100,000 and the highest rate for females was for those aged between 45 and 74 years at 5.8 per 100,000. Suicide rates showed the largest decline for both sexes in those aged over 75 years, falling by 46 per cent from 25.1 per 100,000 males in 1991 to 13.6 per 100,000 in 2009 and 48 per cent among females from 9.0 per 100,000 in 1991 to 4.7 per 100,000 in 2009 (ONS, 2010i).

References

BHF (2010), British Heart Foundation, A prescription for the UK's heart health. Available at
www.bhf.org.uk/publications/publications-search-
results.aspx?m=simple&q=a+prescription+for+the+UKs+heart+health&r=50

Cancer Research UK (2010a). Cancer Stats – Key Facts. Available at
http://info.cancerresearchuk.org/cancerstats/keyfacts/Allcancerscombined/

Cancer Research UK (2010b). Number of deaths and age-specific mortality rates, UK, 2008. Available at
http://info.cancerresearchuk.org/cancerstats/types/lung/mortality/

Cancer Research UK (2010c). Age-standardised (European) cancer mortality rates per 100,000 population, lung cancer, by sex, EU-27, 2008 estimates. Available at http://info.cancerresearchuk.org/cancerstats/types/lung/mortality/

Cancer Research UK (2010d). Pancreatic Cancer (C25), Numbers of new cases and age-specific incidence rates, UK, 2007. Available at http://info.cancerresearchuk.org/cancerstats/types/pancreas/incidence/#age

Cancer Research UK (2010e). Pancreatic Cancer (C025), Number of deaths and age-specific mortality rates, UK, 2008. Available at http://info.cancerresearchuk.org/cancerstats/types/pancreas/mortality/

Cancer Research UK (2010f). Smoking Statistics – Smoking and Cancer.' Available at
http://info.cancerresearchuk.org/cancerstats/types/lung/smoking/

DH (2005). Choosing a Better Diet. Available at
www.dh.gov.uk/en/Publicationsandstatistics/Publications/PublicationsPolicyAndGuidance/DH_4105356

DH (2010). Healthy Lives, Healthy People: Our strategy for public health in England. Available at
www.dh.gov.uk/en/Publicationsandstatistics/Publications/PublicationsPolicyAndGuidance/DH_121941

HMT (2010). Chapter 9 Tables. Available at www.hm-treasury.gov.uk/pesa2010_section4.htm

HPA (2009). Influenza specimens detected in England and Wales, 1991–2009; positive influenza samples detected by regional laboratories' available at
www.hpa.org.uk/web/HPAwebFile/HPAweb_C/1194947397287

HSE (2010). Table STRAGE1W12 - 2008/09. Available at www.hse.gov.uk/statistics/lfs/0809/strage1w12.htm

IC (2008). Health Survey for England, 2006: CVD and risk factors adults, obesity and risk factors children. Available at
www.ic.nhs.uk/statistics-and-data-collections/health-and-lifestyles-related-surveys/health-survey-for-england/health-survey-for-england-2006:-cvd-and-risk-factors-adults-obesity-and-risk-factors-children

IC (2009a) Smoking, drinking and drug use among young people in England in 2009. Available at
www.ic.nhs.uk/statistics-and-data-collections/health-and-lifestyles-related-surveys/smoking-drinking-and-drug-use-among-young-people-in-england/smoking-drinking-and-drug-use-among-young-people-in-england-in-2009

IC (2009b). Adult Psychiatric Morbidity Survey 2007, results of a household survey. Available at
www.ic.nhs.uk/statistics-and-data-collections/mental-health/mental-health-surveys/adult-psychiatric-morbidity-in-england-2007-results-of-a-household-survey

IC (2010). Health Survey for England, 2009. Available at www.ic.nhs.uk/statistics-and-data-collections/health-and-lifestyles-related-surveys/health-survey-for-england/health-survey-for-england--2009-health-and-lifestyles

International Agency for Research on Cancer (2010). Global Cancer (Globocan) data tool. Available at www.iarc.fr/en/research-groups/index.php

MET, UK Mean Temperature. Available at www.metoffice.gov.uk/climate/uk/datasets/Tmean/ranked/UK.txt

NHS (2009), www.nhsconfed.org/Publications/Documents/Briefing_193_Alcohol_costs_the_NHS.pdf

NHS online (2008), 2007/08 Annual Report, available at www.nhsdirect.nhs.uk/en/About/OperatingStatistics/Annual Report2007-2008

NHS online (2010), 2009/10 Annual Report, available at www.nhsdirect.nhs.uk/en/About/OperatingStatistics/AnnualReport2009-2010

NRS (2010)a, National Records of Scotland, Table 4.5: Infant deaths by sex and cause, Scotland, 1999 to 2009. Available at www.gro-scotland.gov.uk/statistics/theme/vital-events/general/ref-tables/2009/stillbirths-infant-deaths.html

NRS (2010)b National Records of Scotland, Increased winter mortality, mean winter temperature and indicators of level of influenza activity, Scotland, 1951/52 – 2009/10. Available at www.gro-scotland.gov.uk/statistics/theme/vital-events/deaths/increased-winter-mortality/2009-10/tables-and-charts.html

OECD (2010). OECD Health Data 2010 – Frequently Requested Data. Available at www.oecd.org/document/16/0,3343,en_2649_34631_2085200_1_1_1_1,00.html

ONS (1995), Cancer survival: Five-year relative survival rate in most affluent group, and difference (gap) between most affluent and most deprived groups, for cancers with more than 1,000 patients, 1986–1990. Available at www.statistics.gov.uk/statbase/xsdataset.asp?vlnk=979&More=Y

ONS (2009). Smoking-related behaviour and attitudes 2008–09. Available at www.statistics.gov.uk/StatBase/Product.asp?vlnk=1638&Pos=2&ColRank=2&Rank=224

ONS (2010a), Cancer survival in England: one-year and five-year survival for 21 common cancers, by sex and age. Patients diagnosed 2004–2008 and followed up to 2009. Available at www.statistics.gov.uk/StatBase/Product.asp?vlnk=14007

ONS (2010b). United Kingdom Health Statistics no.4, 2010. Available at www.statistics.gov.uk/statbase/Product.asp?vlnk=6637

ONS (2010c). Mortality Statistics: Deaths registered in 2009. Available at www.statistics.gov.uk/statbase/product.asp?vlnk=15096

ONS (2010d). Health expectancies at birth and at age 65 in the United Kingdom 2000–02 to 2006–08. Available at www.statistics.gov.uk/StatBase/Product.asp?vlnk=12964&Pos=1&ColRank=2&Rank=272

ONS (2010e). June 2011 - Cancer incidence and mortality 2006–08 Statistical Bulletin. Available at www.statistics.gov.uk/StatBase/Product.asp?vlnk=14209&Pos=&ColRank=2&Rank=272

ONS (2010f) Alcohol-related death rates in the UK, 1991–2009. Available at www.statistics.gov.uk/statbase/product.asp?vlnk=14496

ONS (2010g). Deaths related to drug poisoning. Available at www.statistics.gov.uk/statbase/ssdataset.asp?vlnk=7892

ONS (2010h). Excess Winter Mortality Statistical Bulletin – November 2010. Available at
    www.statistics.gov.uk/StatBase/Product.asp?vlnk=10805&Pos=1&ColRank=1&Rank=272

ONS (2010i). Suicide rates in the UK 1991–2009. Available at www.statistics.gov.uk/statbase/Product.asp?vlnk=13618

ONS (2011). General Lifestyle Survey 2009 Data. Available at
    www.statistics.gov.uk/StatBase/Product.asp?vlnk=5756&Pos=&ColRank=1&Rank=256

Scot (2010). Scottish Health Survey. Available at www.scotland.gov.uk/Topics/Statistics/Browse/Health/scottish-health-
    survey

UK Focal Point (2009). UK Focal Point on Drugs, Annual Report to the European Monitoring Centre for Drugs and Drug
    Addiction (EMCDDA), 2009. Available at www.nwph.net/ukfocalpoint/

Wales (2010). Welsh Health Survey. Available at http://wales.gov.uk/topics/statistics/theme/health/health-
    survey/results/?lang=en

Notes

i The OECD is a unique forum where the governments of 30 democracies work together to address the economic, social and environmental challenges of globalisation. The Organisation provides a setting where governments can compare policy experiences, seek answers to common problems, identify good practice and work to co-ordinate domestic and international policies.

The OECD member countries are Australia, Austria, Belgium, Canada, the Czech Republic, Denmark, Finland, France, Germany, Greece, Hungary, Iceland, Ireland, Italy, Japan, Korea, Luxembourg, Mexico, the Netherlands, Norway, Poland, Portugal, the Slovak Republic, Spain, Sweden, Switzerland, Turkey, the UK and the United States. The Commission of the European Communities takes part in the work of the OECD.

ii Analyses of the effects of premature death assume that everyone may live to some arbitrarily chosen age and that death at a younger age means that some future years of life have been lost. Calculations of years of life lost are made for deaths from selected causes with the aim of illustrating the relative effects from different diseases.

iii Total Expenditure on Services (TES) is the spending aggregate that is allocated to function and covers most expenditure by the public sector that is included in Total Managed Expenditure (TME).

iv P00–P96 Certain conditions originating in the perinatal (deaths within 7 days of birth) period include;

P00–P04   Foetus and newborn affected by maternal factors and by complications of pregnancy, labour and delivery

P05–P08   Disorders related to length of gestation and foetal growth

P20–P29   Respiratory and cardiovascular disorders specific to the perinatal period

P35–P39   Infection specific to the perinatal period

P50–P61   Haemorrhagic and haematological disorders of the foetus and newborn

P75–P78   Digestive system disorders of foetus and newborn

P90–P96   Other disorders originating in the perinatal period

v Healthy life expectancy (HLE) and disability-free life expectancy are summary measures of population health that combine mortality and ill health. In contrast to life expectancy, these two indicators measure both the quality and quantity of life. Essentially they partition life expectancy into the following two components:

years lived free from ill health or disability

years lived in ill health or with a disability

Life expectancy indicators are independent of the age structure of the population and represent the average health expectation of a synthetic birth cohort experiencing current rates of mortality and ill health over their lifetime.

HLE at birth is defined as the number of years that a newly born baby can expect to live in good or fairly good health if he or she experienced current mortality rates and 'good' or 'fairly good' health rates, based on self-assessed general health for different age-groups during their lifespan.

Disability-free life expectancy, defined as expected years lived without a limiting long-standing illness, is calculated in the same way as HLE, except that is uses the GLF/CHS age-sex rates of 'without limiting long-standing illness' instead of rates of 'good/fairly good' health.

vi In the General Lifestyle Survey, information on chronic sickness was obtained from the following two-part question:

'Do you have any longstanding illness, disability or infirmity? By longstanding, I mean anything that has troubled you over a period of time or that is likely to affect you over a period of time.

IF YES

Does this illness or disability limit your activities in any way?'

'Longstanding illness' is defined as a positive answer to the first part of the question and 'limiting longstanding illness' as a positive answer to both parts of the question.

vii Directly age-standardised incidence rates enable comparisons to be made between geographical areas over time, and between the sexes, which are independent of changes in the age structure of the population. In each year the crude rates in each five-year age group are multiplied by the European standard population for that age group. These are then summed and divided by the total standard population for these age groups to give an overall standardised rate.

ix The NHS Breast Screening Programme provides free breast screening every three years for all women in the UK aged 50 and over. Around one-and-a-half million women are screened in the UK each year.

x There is no organised screening programme for prostate cancer in the UK but an informed choice programme, Prostate Cancer Risk Management, has been introduced. The aim of Prostate Cancer Risk Management is to ensure that men who are concerned about the risk of prostate cancer receive clear and balanced information about the advantages and disadvantages of the PSA test and treatment for prostate cancer.

xi Current guidelines from the Chief Medical Officer for England suggest that consuming 3 to 4 units of alcohol per day for men and 2 to 3 units for women should not lead to significant health risks. Individuals identified at highest risk of alcohol-related harm are those who regularly drink at least twice the recommended daily limit.

xii The Office for National Statistics (ONS) definition of alcohol-related deaths includes only those causes regarded as being most directly a result of alcohol consumption. It does not include other disease where alcohol has been shown to have some causal relationship, such as cancers of the mouth, oesophagus and liver.

The definition includes all deaths from chronic liver disease and cirrhosis (excluding biliary cirrhosis), even when alcohol is not specifically mentioned on the death certificate. Apart from deaths due to poisoning with alcohol (accidental, intentional or undetermined), this definition excludes any other external causes of death, such as road traffic accidents and other accidents.

International Classification of Diseases for alcohol-related illness, Tenth Revision.

F10   Mental and behavioural disorders due to use of alcohol

G31.2   Degeneration of nervous system due to alcohol

G62.1   Alcoholic polyneuropathy

I42.6   Alcoholic cardiomyopathy

K29.2   Alcoholic gastritis

K70   Alcoholic liver disease

K73   Chronic hepatitis, not elsewhere classified

K74   Fibrosis and cirrhosis of liver (excluding K74.3–K74.5 – Biliary cirrhosis)

K86.0   Alcohol induced chronic pancreatitis

X45   Accidental poisoning by and exposure to alcohol

X65   Intentional self-poisoning by and exposure to alcohol

Y15   Poisoning by and exposure to alcohol, undetermined intent

xiii These figures represent the number of deaths where the underlying cause of death is regarded as poisoning, drug abuse or drug dependence and where any substances controlled under the Misuse of Drug Act (1971) was mentioned on the death certificate. The data on drug misuse deaths do not include deaths from other causes that may have been related to drug taking (for example, road traffic accidents or HIV/AIDS).

xiv The UK focal point on drugs is based in the Department of Health, England, with support from the North West Public Health Observatory based at the Centre for Public Health, Liverpool John Moores University. It works closely with the Home Office, other government departments and the devolved administrations (Northern Ireland, Scotland and Wales) in providing information to the EMCDDA.

xv The Health Survey for England, Welsh Health Survey and Scottish Health Survey. It is important to note that comparisons based on survey data should be treated with caution due to differences in survey sampling, methodology and sample size. Differences highlighted in the text are for the purpose of drawing a general picture of the health and health trends of Great Britain, and do not necessarily imply statistical significance. Further information on issues of comparability relating specifically to comparisons of health surveys is available at www.scotland.gov.uk/publications/2010/08/31093025/0

xvi For England, Wales and Scotland, those meeting the recommended levels of physical activity fall in the category 'High' = 30 minutes on at least five days a week for adults while for children aged 2–15 years it is those achieving an hour of moderate activity every day.

xvii The current ONS standard method defines the winter period as December to March, and compares the number of deaths that occurred in this winter period with the average number of deaths occurring in the preceding August to November and the following April to July.

xviii The Adult Psychiatric Morbidity Survey (APMS) series provides data on the prevalence of both treated and untreated psychiatric disorder in the English adult population (aged 16 and over). This survey was conducted by the National Centre for Social Research in collaboration with the University of Leicester for the NHS Information Centre for Health and Social Care. Previous surveys were conducted in 1993 (16–64-year-olds) and 2000 (16–74-year-olds) by the Office for National Statistics, and covered England, Scotland and Wales.

Topics covered include Common mental disorders; Post-traumatic stress disorder; Suicidal thoughts, attempts and self-harm; Psychosis; Antisocial and borderline personality disorders; Attention deficit hyperactivity disorder; Eating disorder; Alcohol misuse and dependency; Drug use and dependency; Problem gambling; Psychiatric co-morbidity.

Social protection

Social protection encompasses the financial assistance and services provided to those in need or at risk of hardship. It is provided by central government, local authorities, private bodies such as voluntary organisations (the 'third sector') and individuals. It provides a safety net to protect the vulnerable in society: those who are unable to make provision for a minimum decent standard of living. Social protection policies aim to reduce poverty and wealth gaps through the national minimum wage, means-tested benefits, payments such as working tax credits to low earners and assistance with child care. Assistance is provided through direct measures such as benefits payments, tax credits or pensions, payments in kind such as free prescriptions, and the provision of services such as local authority (LA) home-care help. Unpaid care, often provided by family and neighbours, also plays an important part.

Key points

Expenditure

- Social security benefit expenditure in the UK increased by 128 per cent from £72 billion in 1979/80 to £165 billion in 2009/10, after allowing for inflation
- In 2009/10 local authorities in the UK spent more than £30 billion on personal social services

Social care

- In 2009/10, more than 183 million hours of home care was provided by local authorities in England compared with just over 151 million hours in 2003/04, an increase of 21 per cent
- In England during 2009/10 nearly 1.7 million adults received caring services, of which almost 1.5 million were community-based services

Older people

- In 2008/09, 29 per cent of all pensioners in the UK had no pension provision other than state retirement pension
- In 1983, 70 per cent of people in Great Britain either agreed or agreed strongly that older people should be encouraged to retire earlier to reduce unemployment; by 2009 this had fallen to 15 per cent

Families and children

- In 2008/09, 71 per cent of lone parents with dependent children in the UK were in receipt of working tax credit, income support or pension credit, compared with 17 per cent of couples with dependent children
- Grandparents remain the most common source of informal child care in Great Britain. In 2008, where the mother was in work, 36 per cent of couples and 33 per cent of lone mothers relied on grandparents to provide informal childcare

Working age and state pension age

Where the term working age is used it refers to those aged 16–59 for women and 16–64 for men. Similarly where the term state pension age is used it refers to those aged 60 and over for women and 65 and over for men. This is because much of the data were collected before the current changes to the age at which women can collect their State Pension. This age is in the process of rising for women from 60 to 65 to equalise with men (this affects women born after 5 April 1950); and then state pension age for both men and women is due to increase from 65 to 66 between 2024 and 2026. Current proposals in the Pension Bill may change this.

Expenditure

The Department for Work and Pensions (DWP) in Great Britain and the Department for Social Development in Northern Ireland are responsible for the administration and payment of all social security benefits, with the exception of child benefit and tax credits which are the responsibility of HM Revenue & Customs (HMRC). Social security benefits include payments relating to unemployment, disability allowances, and retirement pensions and benefits. Allowing for inflation, social security benefit expenditure in the UK increased by 128 per cent from £72 billion in 1979/80 to £165 billion in 2009/10 (**Figure 1**).

Figure 1   **Social security benefit expenditure[1] in real terms[2]**

United Kingdom
Expenditure £ billion at 2009/10 prices

Expenditure per head (£ at 2009/10 prices)

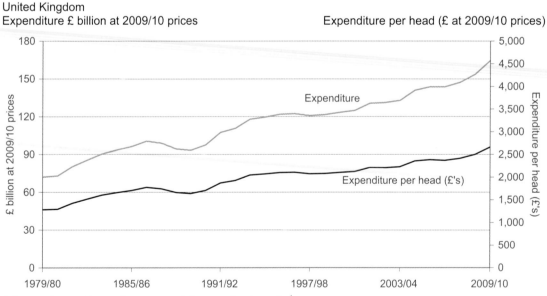

1 See endnote: Expenditure on social protection benefits[i].
2 Adjusted to 2009/10 prices using the GDP market prices deflator (Q2 2010).
Source: Department for Work and Pensions; HM Revenue & Customs; Veterans Agency; Department for Social Development, Northern Ireland

Spending on specific benefits is influenced by a range of factors. Expenditure on various elements of unemployment is affected by the economic cycle, while expenditure on the elderly, primarily pensions, is affected by demographic change. Government priorities also have an impact as its policies attempt to address other issues affecting society. Expenditure on social security benefits has risen each year between 1979/80 and 2009/10 apart from a decrease between 1987/88 and 1989/90, a small fall between 1996/97 and 1997/98 and a very small fall in 2006/07. In 1981/82 and 1991/92 the annual increase in expenditure was 10 per cent, reflecting increases in the number of people who were unemployed or economically inactive during the economic recessions in the early 1980s and 1990s (Social Trends 41: Labour Market chapter), and more than 7 per cent between 2008/09 and 2009/10 at the time of the most recent recession.

Of the £165 billion UK benefit expenditure in 2009/10, £147 billion was managed by the DWP in Great Britain. Most of this, £97 billion (65 per cent of the Great Britain total), was paid to people of state pension age (age 65 and over for men and 60 and over for women) though this total excludes £1 billion of war pensions payments made by the Veterans Agency to ex-services personnel and their dependents throughout the UK. In Northern Ireland, the Department for Social Development administers benefits and in 2009/10 spent nearly £5 billion on welfare benefits and payments.

Expenditure directed at people of working age accounted for £47 billion (32 per cent). A further £3.7 billion was payable to adults for the benefit of children. These payments include elements of income support, disability allowances, housing benefit and council tax benefit paid because of the presence of children in the family, but exclude child benefit payments which are the responsibility of HMRC. Expenditure on those with disabilities is not related to age and is therefore spread across people of state pension age, of working age and children, and totalled £25.8 billion (17.5 per cent).

Child benefits payments, administered by HMRC, totalled nearly £12 billion in the UK in 2009/10. HMRC has also provided financial assistance since 1999/2000 in the form of tax credits which are not included in the expenditure in Figure 1. Child tax credit is available to families on low or moderate incomes, whereas working tax credit is available to adults who are in work but on low or moderate incomes and can be claimed in addition to child tax credit. In the 11 years since their introduction, expenditure on tax credits has risen from £1.1 billion in 1999/2000 to £27.6 billion in 2009/10 when they were being paid to around 6.1 million families in the UK.

The British Social Attitudes Survey asks adults aged 18 and over in Great Britain to give their opinion on the effects of government spending on social security benefits (**Table 1**). Between 1999 and 2009 attitudes towards those receiving benefits have become more negative.

Table 1   **Attitudes to government spending on social security benefits**[1]

Great Britain   Percentages

	Agree/agree strongly			Neither agree or disagree			Disagree/disagree strongly		
	1999	2007	2009	1999	2007	2009	1999	2007	2009
The welfare state encourages people to stop helping each other	32	30	34	34	36	38	32	31	25
The government should spend more money on welfare benefits for the poor even if it leads to higher taxes	40	32	27	30	33	28	28	33	43
Many people who get social security don't really deserve any help	27	36	34	31	35	33	40	27	32
If welfare benefits weren't so generous people would learn to stand on their own two feet	38	53	53	27	23	24	34	22	22

1 Respondents aged 18 and over were asked 'please tick a box to show how much you agree or disagree with the following statements.'
Source: British Social Attitudes Survey, National Centre for Social Research

In 2009 more than half of adults questioned (53 per cent) either agreed strongly or agreed that if welfare benefits weren't so generous people would learn to stand on their own two feet, an increase of 15 percentage points since 1999. Over the same period the number of adults supporting increases in welfare benefits has fallen. In 2009 just over one in four adults (27 per cent) agreed or strongly agreed the Government should spend more money on welfare benefits for the poor, even if it leads to higher taxes, this is a considerable decrease from 4 in 10 adults agreeing with this statement in 1999. Alongside this change in attitude, 2009 expenditure on benefits was £165 billion compared with around £123 billion in 1999, after allowing for inflation, and expenditure per head rose from just over £2,100 to more than £2,600 per head between 1999 and 2009 (refer to **Figure 1**).

Over the same period, not only had people's attitudes towards the amount of money spent on benefits become more negative but their attitudes on the use of the benefit system had also changed. In 2009 over a half (53 per cent) of adults in Great Britain agreed with the statement that if welfare benefits weren't so generous people would learn to stand on their own two feet, compared with 38 per cent in 1999. There was also a slight change in the proportion of people agreeing with the statement that the welfare state encourages people to stop helping each other (34 per cent in 2009 compared with 32 per cent in 1999).As well as provision of additional income through benefits the government also provides services to those in need, many of these through local authorities.

Table 2   Personal social services expenditure

United Kingdom   £ million

	2005/06	2006/07	2007/08	2008/09	2009/10
United Kingdom	24,566	26,044	27,553	29,187	30,385
Sickness & disability	7,019	7,305	7,956	8,469	8,952
Old age	8,617	8,892	9,368	9,929	10,290
Family and children	6,309	6,654	7,024	7,481	8,082
Unemployment	837	1,424	1,391	1,384	1,105
Social exclusion nec	1,784	1,769	1,814	1,924	1,956

Source: HM Treasury, PESA 2010 National Statistics

In 2009/10 local authorities in the UK spent more than £30 billion on personal social services, an increase of more than £5.8 billion since 2005/06, although these figures have not been adjusted to remove the effects of inflation over this period. This was an increase of around 24 per cent in expenditure on personal social services while expenditure on total public sector expenditure on social protection services, also unadjusted for inflation, increased by almost 31 per cent. Over the same period prices, based on the retail prices index (RPI), increased by around 16 per cent. Personal social services include provision of home help and home care; services for looked after children and children on child protection registers; foster care provided by local authorities; and services for the unemployed. More than £10 billion was spent on older people aged 65 and over (**Table 2**). This was the largest category of expenditure in 2009/10 (34 per cent of expenditure) a small decrease from 35 per cent of expenditure in 2005/06. Spending on sickness and disability was the next largest category at nearly £9 billion, 29 per cent of expenditure. Expenditure on family and children is not restricted to any category of person and will include provision of goods, services and benefits and was the third largest category of expenditure at more than £8 billion, more than a quarter (27 per cent) of expenditure.

Eurostat collects social protection expenditure information across the 27 member states of the European Union (EU-27) as part of the European System of Integrated Social Protection Statistics (ESSPROS). ESSPROS defines social protection as encompassing all interventions from public or private bodies intended to relieve households and individuals of the burden of a defined set of risks or needs. It should be noted that the UK makes much more use of tax credits as a means of social protection than most other EU nations and these, totalling £24 billion in 2008/09, are not included in the estimates of expenditure.

Figure 2 **Expenditure[1] on social protection as a percentage of GDP: EU-27 comparison, 2008**

Percentages

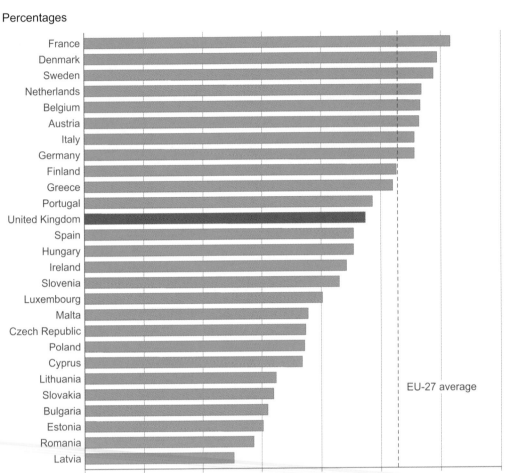

1 Social protection expenditure and receipts are calculated in line with the methodology of the latest 'European system of social protection statistics' (Esspros) manual. Expenditure includes social benefits, administrative costs and other expenditure linked to social protection schemes.
Source: Eurostat

In 2008 UK spending on social protection, excluding tax credits, was equivalent to 23.7 per cent of gross domestic product (GDP), below the EU-27 average of 26.4 per cent (**Figure 2**). However, when expressed in terms of expenditure per head and in purchasing power standard (PPS[ii]), UK expenditure was 6,900 PPS, higher than the EU-27 average of 6,600 PPS per head.

As a percentage of GDP, expenditure on social protection was highest in France, at 30.8 per cent, followed by Denmark (29.7 per cent) and Sweden (29.4 per cent). Of all the EU-27 countries, Latvia recorded the lowest expenditure on social protection as a percentage of GDP, at 12.6 per cent, followed by Romania and Estonia (14.3 per cent and 15.1 per cent respectively). Of the EU-15 countries Luxembourg spent the least at 20.1 per cent, less than Slovenia (21.5 per cent) and Hungary (22.7 per cent) two of the recent accession countries.

Social care

Since the early 1990s, government policy has been to provide help and assistance through local authorities to people who need care to continue to live in their own homes as independently as possible. This can include financial help or the provision of services to those who qualify. Such services may involve routine household tasks within or outside the home, personal care of the client, or respite care to support the clients' regular carers.

Figure 3   **Actual number of contact hours of home care provided during the year: by sector[1,2]**

England
Hours (millions)

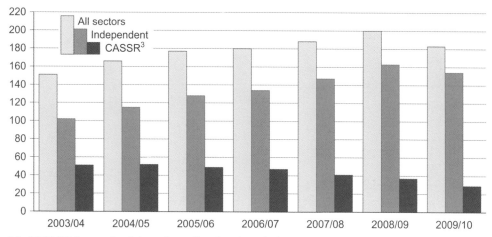

1 In 2008/09 the methodology for estimating for missing data was changed.
2 Components may not add to totals due to the estimation methodology for years prior to 2008/09.
3 Councils with social services responsibility.
Source: The NHS Information Centre for health and social care, Community Care Statistics 2009-10: Social Services Activity Report, England

As well as council-run care homes, local authorities provide home care services to those with physical disabilities (including frailty associated with ageing), dementia, mental health problems and learning difficulties. In 2009/10, 183 million hours of home care was provided by councils in England to households compared with just over 151 million hours in 2003/04, an increase of 21 per cent (**Figure 3**). However, this has fallen by 9 per cent since 2008/09 when around 200 million hours of home care was provided. All the increase in care provision between 2003/04 and 2009/10 was in care provided by the independent sector, which increased by 51 per cent, while at the same time care provided by councils with social services responsibilities decreased by 43 per cent. In 2003/04 the independent sector provided 68 per cent of home care, by 2009/10 this had increased to 84 per cent.

Table 3   Estimated number of clients receiving services: by service type and age group, 2009/10

England   Thousands

	All aged 18 and over	18–64	65 and over
Total number of clients receiving services[1]	**1,698**	**550**	**1,148**
Community-based services[2]	**1,464**	**507**	**958**
Home care	557	104	453
Equipment and adaptations	512	118	394
Professional support	445	240	204
Day care	195	89	106
Meals	100	7	93
Direct payments and personal budgets	166	74	92
Short-term residential – not respite	76	14	62
Other	119	50	69
Residential care			
Independent sector residential care/LA-staffed residential care	215	48	167
Nursing care	90	9	82

1 The 'Total of clients receiving services' is the number of clients receiving one or more services at some point during the year excluding double counting.
2 A client may have received more than one type of community-based service during the year and thus there may be some double counting across service categories, but each client is counted only once in the total of community-based services.
Source: The NHS Information Centre for health and social care, Community Care Statistics 2009-10: Social Services Activity Report, England

In England during 2009/10 nearly 1.7 million adults received caring services: of these almost 1.5 million received community-based services, such as meals on wheels, house cleaners, housing modifications for those with disabilities or the elderly or even day-care centres (**Table 3**). The largest users of services, around two-thirds of the total, were the 1.1 million clients aged 65 and over. Within the 65 and over age group the most commonly received services were 'home care' and 'equipment and adaptations', 453,000 and 394,000 clients respectively.

There were also more than 550,000 clients aged 18 to 64. In this age group the most common service was 'professional support', received by 240,000 clients. This category includes education of individuals regarding health matters and advice on health and mitigation of health risks. Those over 65 dominated every service group except 'professional support' where those aged 18 to 64 made up 54 per cent of the clients. This was particularly so for 'meals', 'nursing care', 'short-term residential – not respite' and 'home care', where those aged over 65 made up 80 to 90 per cent of the clients.

Sick and disabled people, depending upon the nature and severity of their condition, are entitled to a number of financial benefits. Incapacity benefit (IB) and severe disablement allowance (SDA) are benefits principally for people of usual working age who are unable to work because of illness and/or disability, although a small number of beneficiaries are older. These benefits can be claimed in addition to other benefits. It should be noted that from 27 October 2008 Employment and Support Allowance replaced Incapacity Benefit and Income Support paid on incapacity grounds for new customers.

In 2009/10 there were nearly 2.7 million working age recipients of IB and other benefits in the UK (**Table 4,** overleaf). This was around 0.3 million more than in 2008/09, but still lower than in recent years. There has been a largely downward trend from 2004/05 when the number of recipients was more than 2.8 million. The decrease in IB recipients in 2008/09 and 2009/10 is, in part, offset by the recipients of Employment and Support Allowance (ESA), so that the net reduction between 2008/09 and 2009/10 in recipients of IB and ESA was around 150,000.

Disability living allowance (DLA) is a benefit for people who are disabled, have either personal care needs or mobility needs, or both, and who are aged under 65. Attendance allowance (AA) is paid to people who are ill or disabled after their 65th birthday and who need someone to help with their personal care. In 2009/10 there were almost 5 million people in receipt of DLA and/or AA in the UK, compared with around 4.4 million in 2004/05. Around two-thirds of these were claiming DLA over the same period and while the number of those in receipt of DLA or AA has increased, the ratio between them has remained steady.

Table 4   **Recipients of selected benefits for sick and disabled people[1,2]**

United Kingdom   Thousands

	2004/05	2005/06	2006/07	2007/08	2008/09	2009/10
Working-age recipients of Incapacity and other benefits[3,4]	**2,819**	**2,765**	**2,720**	**2,679**	**2,661**	**2,664**
Incapacity Benefit only	836	794	753	718	597	463
Incapacity Benefit and Income Support/Pension Credit	646	626	615	601	527	429
Incapacity Benefit and Disability Living Allowance	544	550	553	558	552	514
Incapacity Benefit, Income Support/Pension Credit and Disability Living Allowance	471	484	499	517	536	520
Employment and Support Allowance only[3]	..	..	..	..	151	371
Employment and Support Allowance and Disability Living Allowance[3]	..	..	..	..	22	98
Severe Disablement Allowance only	9	8	7	6	6	5
Severe Disablement Allowance and Income Support/Pension Credit	15	13	12	10	9	8
Severe Disablement Allowance and Disability Living Allowance	56	53	48	44	40	37
Severe Disablement Allowance and, Income Support/Pension Credit and Disability Living Allowance	180	172	167	161	155	149
Other combinations	61	64	66	63	67	69
Attendance Allowance/Disability Living Allowance[5]	**4,355**	**4,479**	**4,601**	**4,723**	**4,860**	**4,993**
Attendance Allowance[6]	1,477	1,524	1,567	1,603	1,638	1,673
Disability Living Allowance (All ages)[6]	2,879	2,955	3,033	3,120	3,222	3,320

1 See endnote: Benefit units[iii].
2 Figures are taken from the February of each year.
3 From 27 October 2008 Employment and Support Allowance (ESA) replaced Incapacity Benefit and Income Support paid on the grounds of incapacity for new claims. Figures for Northern Ireland not available.
4 The age at which women reach State Pension age will gradually increase from 60 to 65 between April 2010 and April 2020. This will introduce a small increase in the number of working-age benefit recipients and a small reduction in the number of pension-age recipients. Figures from May 2010 onwards reflect this change.
5 Individuals receiving both Attendance Allowance and Disability Allowance are counted twice.
6 Includes those in receipt of an allowance but excludes those where payment is currently suspended, (for example, because of a stay in hospital).

Source: Department for Work and Pensions; Department for Social Development, Northern Ireland

Older people

In the UK much of central government expenditure on social protection for older people is through payment of the State Pension. Nearly everyone of state pension age (currently age 65 [iv] for men and 60 for women) receives this pension, whatever the level of their other income. Some also receive income-related state benefits, such as council tax benefit or pension credit.

Table 5   **Pension receipt: by type of pensioner benefit unit[1], 2008/09**

United Kingdom   Percentages

	Pensioner couples	Single male pensioners	Single female pensioners	All pensioners
State Pension only[2]	20	29	40	29
State Pension Plus				
Occupational, but not personal pension[3]	52	52	50	51
Personal, but not occupational pension[4]	12	11	4	8
Both occupational and personal pension	10	5	2	6
No state pension, but some occupational or personal pension[5]	3	1	1	2
No state pension, occupational pension or personal pension	4	2	3	3

1 See endnote: Benefit units[iii].
2 State pension includes basic and additional state pension, Widow's pension and Widowed parent's allowance.
3 Occupational pension includes annuities bought with lump sums from occupational pensions.
4 Personal pension includes annuities bought with lump sums from personal pensions, trades union and friendly society pensions.
5 Combinations can include: No state pension and some occupational pension only; no state pension and some personal pension only; no state pension and some occupational and personal pension.
Source: The Pensioners' Incomes Series, Department for Work and Pensions

People can also make their own provision for retirement to supplement the state pension through occupational, personal or stakeholder pensions[iv]. In 2008/09, 29 per cent of all pensioners in the UK had no pension provision other than state pension (**Table 5**). Single women were more likely to have a state pension only (40 per cent) compared with single men or pensioner couples (29 per cent and 20 per cent respectively). Over half (52 per cent) of single male pensioners in the UK had an occupational pension in addition to the state pension, compared with 50 per cent of single female pensioners and 52 per cent of pensioner couples. The proportions of pensioner benefit units[iii] who received a personal pension as well as the state pension were much lower than those who received an occupational pension; 11 per cent of single male pensioners, 4 per cent of single female pensioners and 12 per cent of pensioner couples. The lower proportions for women may be in part because women traditionally had lower employment rates than men (see Chapter 4: Labour market, Figure 4.4). Women were also less likely to have been self-employed, an employment status where a personal pension is the main source of private pension provision.

Table 6   **Receipt of selected social security benefits among pensioners: by type of benefit unit[1], 2008/09**

United Kingdom   Percentages

	Single male pensioners	Single female pensioners	Pensioner couples
Any income-related benefit[2]	38	43	19
Specific income-related benefits:			
Council tax benefit	33	38	17
Pension credit	20	29	11
Housing benefit	24	22	7
Non-income-related: disablement benefits[3]	23	23	26

1 Pensioner benefit units. See endnote: Benefit units[iii].
2 Includes benefits not listed here. Components do not sum to the total as each benefit unit may receive more than one benefit.
3 Disability living allowance (care and mobility components); severe disablement allowance; industrial injuries disability benefit; armed forces compensation scheme; and attendance allowance.
Source: Family Resources Survey, Department for Work and Pensions

In 2008/09, 38 per cent of single male pensioners and 43 per cent of single female pensioners in the UK received income-related benefits, compared with 19 per cent of pensioner couples (**Table 6**). Council tax benefit was the most commonly received benefit by all groups, followed by pension credit and housing benefit. With the exception of housing benefit, single female pensioners are more likely than single male pensioners or pensioner couples to receive income related benefits. The largest difference between single male and single female pensioners was receiving pension credit with 29 per cent of women receiving this compared with 22 per cent of men. This is most likely because fewer women receive the full rate of state retirement pension. For pensioner couples the proportion was again lower, at 11 per cent. Single women were also more likely to receive council tax benefit (38 per cent) than either single men (33 per cent) or couples (17 per cent). However, slightly more single men than women received housing benefit (24 per cent compared with 22 per cent), again for couples the figure was much lower at 7 per cent. Receipt of non-income-related benefits was more even with 23 per cent of single male and female pensioners being in receipt of disablement benefits compared with 26 per cent of couples, the only area where couples were more likely to be in receipt of benefits than single pensioners.

Pension credit is a means-tested benefit comprising guarantee credit and savings credit. Guarantee credit is for people aged 60 and over living in the UK. It ensured a minimum income of £132.60 per week for single pensioners and £202.40 for pensioner couples in 2010/11. The savings credit element is for those with some savings, whether single or living with a partner, where either partner is aged 65 and over. The maximum savings credit payable in 2010/11 was £20.52 per week for single people or £27.09 for people with a partner. Savings credit is generally available to single people with an income of up to £184 per week and couples with an income of up to £270 per week, although these thresholds may be higher depending on a range of factors such as disability, caring duties or certain housing costs such as mortgage interest payments.

Table 7   **Attitudes towards older people in the labour force**[1]

Great Britain   Percentages

	Agree		Neither agree nor disagree		Disagree	
	1983	**2009**	**1983**	**2009**	**1983**	**2009**
Men	73	17	12	21	14	59
18–24	70	25	18	27	13	46
25–40	70	12	12	27	17	58
41–64	79	17	10	17	10	64
65 and over	72	21	11	19	16	57
Women	67	13	15	21	18	64
18–24	67	16	17	24	16	56
25–40	62	7	17	22	21	69
41–59	66	12	12	22	20	64
60 and over	71	18	14	17	12	61
All aged 18 and over	**70**	**15**	**13**	**21**	**16**	**61**

1 Respondents aged 18 and over were asked to tick a box to show how much they agreed or disagreed with the statement, 'older people should be encouraged to retire earlier to reduce unemployment'.
Source: British Social Attitudes Survey, National Centre for Social Research

Views about older people and retirement have changed over the last 25 years (**Table 7**). In 1983, 70 per cent of people aged 18 and over in Great Britain either agreed or agreed strongly that older people should be encouraged to retire earlier to reduce unemployment, in 2009 this had fallen to 15 per cent. There were differences between men and women, with more men being in agreement than women (17 per cent and 13 per cent respectively in 2009). There was also a noticeable difference was between age groups with a higher proportion of those entering the job market (18–24-year-olds) and those of retirement age agreeing that older people should retire early in 2009. However, these proportions were still substantially lower than in 1983.

Families and children

The Government provides a number of social security benefits targeted at families with children in the UK. They include tax credits, income-related benefits paid to low-income families, such as housing benefit, council tax benefit and income support and non-income-related benefits, such as child benefit and incapacity or disablement benefits.

Table 8   Receipt of selected social security benefits among families: by type of benefit unit[1], 2008/09

United Kingdom   Percentages

	Lone parent with dependent children[2]	Couple with dependent children[2]
Any benefit or tax credit[3]	97	97
Income-related		
Council tax benefit	44	7
Housing benefit	42	6
Jobseeker's allowance	2	3
Tax credits		
Working tax credit/income support/pension credit	71	17
Child tax credit	75	53
Non-income-related		
Child benefit	94	95
Disablement benefits[4]	7	6

1 Families where household reference person is under state pension age. See endnote: Benefit units[iii].

2 Children aged under 16, or aged 16 to 19 and not married or in a civil partnership and living with their parents and in full-time non-advanced education or in unwaged government training.

3 Includes all benefits not listed here. Components do not sum to the total as each benefit unit may receive more than one benefit.

4 Disability living allowance (care and mobility components), severe disablement allowance, industrial injuries disability benefit, armed forces compensation scheme and attendance allowance.

Source: Family Resources Survey, Department for Work and Pensions

In 2008/09 child tax credit was the most common source of assistance among families in the UK, with three-quarters (75 per cent) of lone parents with dependent children in the UK and more than half (53 per cent) of couples with dependent children in receipt (**Table 8**). As with working tax credit the amount that can be received differs depending on circumstances: lone parents are likely to receive larger amounts because their income is less than couples and they are just as likely to use paid childcare. This may reflect the employment status of lone-parent mothers, who head the majority of lone-parent families and are less likely to be employed than mothers with a partner, and consequently less likely to have a partner who can provide informal childcare (see also Chapter 2: Households and families). While the numbers in receipt of tax credits is high among all families, the receipt of income-related benefits is much higher among lone-parent families than couples. More than half of all lone-parent families receive some combination compared with less than 1 in 10 couples (51 per cent and 9 per cent respectively). The most common income-related benefit is council tax benefit (44 per cent and 7 per cent respectively) closely followed by housing benefit (42 per cent and 6 per cent respectively). The receipt of non-income related benefits among families is much more even with around 9 out of 10 receiving a non-income-related benefit; this is primarily child benefit which is received by 94 per cent of lone parents and 95 per cent of couples.

According to the Department for Work and Pensions 2008 Families and Children Study (FACS 2008) lone parents with dependent children in Great Britain were more likely than couples with dependent children to have loans other than a mortgage, 52 per cent compared with 44 per cent. Lone parents were also more reliant on loans from friends or relatives, 16 per cent compared with 8 per cent of couple families and less likely to have bank overdrafts or loans. Lone parents were also more likely to apply for a Social Fund[v] loan, 12 per cent of lone parents compared with 1 per cent of couples. Lone parents working up to 15 hours per week were more likely than those working 16 hours or more to borrow money using these methods. Just over a fifth (21 per cent), of lone parents working up to 15 hours borrowed from friends or relatives compared with 11 per cent of those working 16 hours or more. The difference was greater for those with Social Fund loans, where a quarter (24 per cent) of lone parents working up to 15 hours received such a loan compared with 1 per cent of those working 16 hours or more. They were also more reliant on loans from finance companies than banks or building societies, when compared with lone parents working 16 or more hours or couples.

Table 9   **Childcare arrangements for children with working mothers: by family characteristics, 2008**

Great Britain   Percentages[1]

	Child care not required	Formal child care[2]	Informal child care[3]				
			Ex partner/ non- resident parent	Grand- parent	Older sibling/ other relative informal[4]	Other informal	Total informal
Family type							
Lone parent	40	30	16	33	5	10	46
Couple	42	31	2	36	3	9	44
Family type working status							
Lone parent: 1 to 15 hours	53	21	6	19	8	4	32
Lone parent: 16 hours and above	39	31	17	34	5	10	47
Couple – both: 16 hours and above	39	33	2	38	4	9	45
Couple – one only: 16 hours and above	52	22	1	31	3	9	38
Age of child							
0–4	21	56	4	46	9	7	52
5–10	31	34	6	46	14	15	56
11–16	70	6	5	18	9	5	27

1 Percentages do not sum to 100 per cent as respondents could give more than one answer.
2 Respondents could give more than one source of informal child care.
3 Includes nurseries/crèches, nursery schools, playgroups, registered childminders, after school clubs/breakfast clubs, and holiday play schemes.
4 A friend, neighbour or babysitter, who came to the home.
Source: Families and Children Study, Department for Work and Pensions

The Family and Children Study (FACS) also showed that in 2008 in Great Britain, 60 per cent of working lone-parent families and 58 per cent of couple families, where the mother worked, made use of some form of childcare. While the proportions of couple families and lone-parent families using formal and informal childcare were similar, lone parents were more likely than couples to make use of most types of informal childcare (which can be provided by family members, partners, ex-partners or friends) except for grandparents. As children get older, the use of formal childcare decreases. In 2008, 56 per cent of children aged under five whose mothers worked were looked after under formal childcare arrangements (**Table 9**). The proportion of children of primary school age (aged 5 to 10) was much less (34 per cent), and decreased further to around 6 per cent when they reached secondary education age (aged 11 to 16). Use of informal childcare changes much less and is greater among children of primary school age than those of pre-school age. The decrease in use of informal childcare between primary school age and secondary education age (aged 11 to 16) is also less than that of formal child care, with more than half of children under 10 (52 per cent of those aged 0 to 4 and 56 per cent of those aged 5 to 10) and around a quarter (27 per cent) of children aged 11 to 16 receiving this form of childcare.

The use of child care by households with non-working mothers was much lower than in those with working mothers. In households with a working mother 44 per cent used informal childcare, this dropped to 24 per cent of households with non-working mothers. Formal childcare was used by 31 per cent of families with a working mother and by half this number for families where the mother did not work (15 per cent).

When a child is assessed as being subject to a continuing risk of significant harm they may be placed on a local authority's 'at risk' register. These registers are maintained and managed by social services departments.

Table 10   Children and young persons on the at risk register[1]

United Kingdom   Number of children

	2003	2004	2005	2006	2007	2008 [2]	2009
Neglect	13,100	13,400	13,900	14,500	15,500	16,600	19,200
Emotional abuse	6,000	6,100	6,300	7,000	8,300	9,900	11,100
Physical abuse	5,800	5,500	5,200	4,900	4,800	5,400	5,400
Sexual abuse	3,300	3,100	3,000	2,900	2,600	2,000	2,000
Multiple/not specified	4,500	4,000	3,500	3,200	3,400	2,500	2,900
Total number of children	32,700	32,100	31,900	32,500	34,600	36,400	40,600

1 At 31 March each year. Children and young persons aged under 18.
2 Data revised.
Source: Department for Children, Schools and Families; Welsh Government; Scottish Government; Department of Health, Social Services and Public Safety, Northern Ireland

While the number of children on 'at risk' registers throughout the UK remained roughly the same between 2003 and 2006 there has been an increase since 2006. As at March 2009 there were more than 40,000 children listed (Table 10). The number of children on the 'at risk' register increased by 11.5 per cent between 2008 and 2009 which was the largest year-on-year increase over the period and represents a 24.2 per cent increase since 2003. However, the overall increase was not consistent across each of the reasons for being on the register. Neglect was the most common reason given for a child being placed on the register in 2009 (47 per cent) followed by emotional abuse (27 per cent). Although these percentages have increased, they have been the two most common reasons for a child being on the register each year since 2003. The number of children on the register because of neglect or emotional abuse increased 46.6 per cent and 85.0 per cent respectively between 2003 and 2009 while those in all other categories fell. The number of children on the register because of physical abuse fell by 6.9 per cent and as a result of sexual abuse by around 39.4 per cent. The number of children classified to multiple reasons or unspecified reasons also fell by 35.6 per cent although this may be due in part to more children being classified to specific categories.

References

HMRC, 2009/10, Social security benefits expenditure. Available at:

www.hmrc.gov.uk/stats/tax_receipts/tax-receipts-and-taxpayers.xls

DWP, 2009/10a, Social security benefits expenditure. Available at:

http://research.dwp.gov.uk/asd/asd4/index.php?page=expenditure

DSDNI, 2009/10a, Social security benefits expenditure. Available at:

www.dsdni.gov.uk/index/ssa.htm

HMT, 2009/10, Personal social services expenditure, HM Treasury. Available at:

www.hm-treasury.gov.uk/pesa2011_section2.htm

Eurostat, 2008, Expenditure on social protection as a percentage of GDP. Available at:

www./epp.eurostat.ec.europa.eu/portal/page/portal/social_protection/data/main_tables

NHSIC, 2009/10a, Adult home care. Available at:

www.ic.nhs.uk/statistics-and-data-collections/social-care/adult-social-care-information

NHSIC, 2009/10b, Provision of social care services. Available at:

www.ic.nhs.uk/statistics-and-data-collections/social-care/adult-social-care-information

DWP, 2009/10b, Benefits for sick and disabled people. Available at:

http://statistics.dwp.gov.uk/asd/index.php?page=statistics_a_to_z

DSDNI, 2009/10b, Benefits for sick and disabled people. Available at:

www.dsdni.gov.uk/index/ssa.htm

DWP, 2008/9a, Family Resources Survey (FRS), 2008/09. Pension receipt by pension unit. Available at:

www.statistics.dwp.gov.uk/asd/frs/

DWP, 2008/9b, Family Resources Survey (FRS), 2008/09. Receipt of selected benefits among pensioners, by type of benefit unit. Available at:

www.statistics.dwp.gov.uk/asd/frs/

DWP, 2008/9c, Family Resources Survey (FRS), 2008/09. Receipt of selected benefits among families, by benefit unit Available at:

www.statistics.dwp.gov.uk/asd/frs/

BSA, 2009a, Attitudes toward government spending on benefits, National Centre for Social Research: Available at:

www.natcen.ac.uk

BSA, 2009b, Attitudes toward older people in the labour market, National Centre for Social Research: Available at:

www.natcen.ac.uk

DWP, 2008, Families and children study (FACS) 2008. Childcare arrangements for working mothers. Available at: www.statistics.dwp.gov.uk/asd/asd5/facs/

DfES, 2009, Children and young people on the at risk register. Available at:

www.education.gov.uk/cgi-bin/rsgateway/search.pl?cat=3&subcat=3_1&q1=Search

WG, 2009, Children and young people on the at risk register. Available at:

www.statswales.wales.gov.uk

SG, 2009, Children and young people on the at risk register. Available at:

www.scotland.gov.uk/Publications

DHSSPSNI, 2009, Children and young people on the at risk register. Available at:

www.dhsspsni.gov.uk/index/hss/child_care/child_protection.htm

Notes

[i] Cash benefits

Income support: Periodic payments to people with insufficient resources. Conditions for entitlement may be related to personal resources and to nationality, residence, age, availability for work and family status. The benefit may be paid for a limited or an unlimited period. It may be paid to the individual or to the family, and be provided by central or local government.

Other cash benefits: Support for destitute or vulnerable people to help alleviate poverty or assist in difficult situations. These benefits may be paid by private non-profit organisations.

Benefits in kind

Accommodation: Shelter and board provided to destitute or vulnerable people, where these services cannot be classified under another function. This may be short term in reception centres, shelters and others, or on a more regular basis in special institutions, boarding houses, reception families, and others.

Rehabilitation of alcohol and drug abusers:

Treatment of alcohol and drug dependency aimed at reconstructing the social life of the abusers, making them able to live an independent life. The treatment is usually provided in reception centres or special institutions.

Other benefits in kind: Basic services and goods to help vulnerable people, such as counselling, day shelter, help with carrying out daily tasks, food, clothing and fuel. Means-tested legal aid is also included.

Employment and support allowance

Employment and support allowance (ESA) was introduced in October 2008 to replace incapacity benefit (IB) and incapacity-related income support (IS). The figures relating to ESA in Table 8.9 (Recipients of selected benefits for sick and disabled people) have been thoroughly quality assured to National Statistics standards. However it should be noted that this is a new benefit using a new data source which may not have reached steady state in terms of operational processing and retrospection.

[ii] Purchasing power parities

The international spending power of sterling depends both on market exchange rates and on the ratios of prices between the UK and other countries. Purchasing power parities (PPPs) are indicators of price level differences across countries. PPPs tell us how many currency units a given quantity of goods and services costs in different countries. PPPs can thus be used as currency conversion rates to convert expenditures expressed in national currencies into an artificial common currency (the Purchasing Power Standard, PPS), eliminating the effect of price level differences across countries.

The main use of PPPs is to convert national accounts aggregates, like the gross domestic product (GDP) of different countries, into comparable volume aggregates. Applying nominal exchange rates in this process would overestimate the GDP of countries with high price levels relative to countries with low price levels. The use of PPPs ensures that the GDP of all countries is valued at a uniform price level and thus reflects only differences in the actual volume of the economy.

PPPs are also applied in analyses of relative price levels across countries. For this purpose, the PPPs are divided by the current nominal exchange rate to obtain a price level index (PLI) which expresses the price level of a given country relative to another, or relative to a group of countries like the EU-27; more information is available at:
epp.eurostat.ec.europa.eu/portal/page/portal/purchasing_power_parities/introduction

[iii] Benefit units

A benefit unit is a single adult or couple living as married and any dependent children living with them in the same household, where the head is below state pension age (60 for women and 65 for men) and where one or both are in receipt of a benefit. A pensioner benefit unit is a single person over state pension age or a couple where one or both adults are over state pension age.

[iv] Pension schemes

A pension scheme is a plan offering benefits to members upon retirement. Schemes are provided by the state, employers and insurance firms, and are differentiated by a wide range of rules governing membership eligibility, contributions, benefits and taxation.

Occupational pension scheme: An arrangement (other than accident or permanent health insurance) organised by an employer (or on behalf of a group of employers) to provide benefits for employees on their retirement and for their dependants on their death.

Personal pension scheme: A scheme where the contract to provide contributions in return for retirement benefits is between an individual and an insurance firm, rather than between an individual and an employer or the state. Individuals may choose to join such schemes, for example, to provide a primary source of retirement income for the self-employed, or to provide a secondary income to employees who are members of occupational schemes. These schemes may be facilitated (but not provided) by an employer.

Stakeholder pension scheme: Available since 2001, a flexible, portable, defined-contribution personal pension arrangement (provided by insurance companies with capped management charges) that must meet the conditions set out in the *Welfare Reform and Pensions Act 1999* and be registered with the Pensions Regulator. They can be taken out by an individual or facilitated by an employer. Where an employer of five or more staff offers no occupational pension and an employee earns more than the lower earnings limit (the entrance level for paying tax), the provision of access to a stakeholder scheme with contributions deducted from payroll is compulsory.

[v] Social fund

The social fund is available to people on low incomes faced with expenses they find difficult meeting from their normal income. Payments come in the form of payments, grants or loans and can cover maternity costs, funeral costs, fuel costs, items of clothing and footwear, furniture items and items relating to the safety and well-being of individuals and families.

Maternity grant: also known as Sure Start maternity grant is a fixed amount of £500 to help people on low income buy clothes and equipment for a new born baby, it does not have to be repaid.

Funeral payment: is a payment to people on low income to help with the essential costs of a funeral. Proof has to be provided of expense and the payment does not have to be repaid but it can be recovered from the estate of the person who has died.

Budgeting loan: is a loan to people on low income to help pay essential lump sum payments which are difficult to budget for. It is an interest free loan which must be paid back to the social fund.

Crisis loan: is a loan to people on low income who need money quickly because of expenses in an emergency or disaster. It is an interest free loan which must be paid back to the social fund.

Household and families

People live in different types of households and families during their lifetime. Most begin life in the parental home and later they may set up home alone, with other non-related adults or by starting a family. Families are started when people form partnerships or marry, or when they have children. Understanding the distribution of the population by household and family type is important for many different organisations in the public and private sectors, including policy makers dealing with issues such as health, housing and benefits. Issues such as unemployment and poverty can often be better understood by looking at the characteristics of households and families. Information about households and families also shows how society is changing. This chapter provides the latest data on the number and composition of households and families in the UK and looks at trends over time.

Key Points

Household composition

- There were 25.3 million households in Great Britain in 2010, an increase of 9.0 million since 1961 and 1.4 million since 2001

- Average household size has decreased from 3.1 persons in 1961 to 2.4 persons in 2010

- A smaller proportion of households in Great Britain have children living in them in 2010 than in 1961, and those households with children have fewer children living in them

People living in households

- The number of people living in households in the UK has increased by 3.1 million from 58.3 million in 2001 to 61.4 million in 2010

- The number of people living alone increased from 7.0 million to 7.5 million between 2001 and 2010

- The proportions of all people living alone in specific age groups increases with age; in 2010 about three per cent of those age 16 to 24 lived alone compared to over 45 per cent of those aged 75 and over

Families

- In 2010 there were an estimated 17.9 million families, an increase from 17.0 million in 2001 with an increase of 0.6 million cohabiting couple families and 0.4 million lone parent families offset by a decrease of 0.1 million in the number of married couple families

- There were an estimated 50.8 million people living in families in 2010, an increase from 48.8 million in 2001

- The most common type of family in the UK in 2010 consisted of a married couple with or without children, although there had been a decrease from an estimated 72.4 per cent of all families in 2001 to 68.0 per cent in 2010

- Families consisting of a cohabiting couple with or without children increased from 12.5 per cent of all families in 2001 to 15.3 per cent 2010, and lone parent families increased from 14.8 per cent in 2001 to 16.2 per cent in 2010
- In 2010 there were an estimated 7.7 million families with dependent children and 13.3 million dependent children living in those families
- The most common type of family in the UK at the time of the survey in 2010 contained one child (46.3 per cent of all families in 2010)

Family formation

- Around two thirds of marriages (67 per cent) in 2009 in England and Wales were by civil ceremony, a similar proportion to 2008 but a considerable increase compared with 1981 when only 49 per cent of marriages were by civil ceremony
- In 2009 in the UK nearly 6,300 civil partnerships were registered, a decrease of nearly 900 compared to 2008

Divorces and dissolution

- There has been a consistent downward trend in divorces in England and Wales between 2003 and 2009: the decrease between 2008 and 2009 was about 6.4 per cent (from 121,700 to 113,900)
- Between 1989 and 2009 the total number of children of divorcing couples of all ages decreased from just over 216,000 to nearly 154,000; this is partly because of the overall decrease in the number of divorces and partly because the average number of children involved in each divorce had reduced

Births

- In 2009 there were 706,200 live births registered in England and Wales, compared with 783,200 in 1971 and 708,700 in 2008
- The age distribution of women giving birth in England and Wales has changed considerably: in 1971 nearly four out of five births were to women aged less than 30, by 2009 only just over half were to women of this age
- In 1971 45.5 per cent of births outside marriage in England and Wales were joint registrations, by 2009 this had increased to 86.6 per cent and nearly two thirds (65.7 per cent) of all registrations outside marriage were from parents living at the same address

Conceptions and abortions

- Provisional estimates for 2009 suggest that the number of conceptions in England and Wales had increased by 0.9 per cent since 2008
- Between 1991 and 2009 the number of conceptions to women younger than 30 decreased markedly while the number to women aged 30 and over increased
- The proportion of conceptions resulting in legal abortion decreased from 21.8 per cent in 2008 to 21.0 per cent in 2009, with a decrease in all age groups

Household[i] composition

Households are defined as people who live and eat together or people who live alone. Families are defined by marriage, civil partnership or cohabitation or, where there are children in the household, child/parent relationships exist. Most households consist of a single family or someone living alone (as shown in Table 2). This first section looks at people living in private households and excludes those living in institutions such as care homes, prisons, hospitals and other communal establishments.

There were an estimated 25.3 million households in Great Britain in 2010, an increase of 1.4 million from 2001 and 9.0 million since 1961. The proportion of households with three or more people has fallen from 57 per cent in 1961 to 36 per cent in 2010. Consequently the average household size fell from 3.1 people in 1961 to 2.4 people in 2010, as seen in **Table 1**.

Table 1   **Households:[1] by size**

Great Britain   Percentages

	1961	1971	1981	1991	2001	2010
One person	12	18	22	27	29	29
Two people	30	32	32	34	35	35
Three people	23	19	17	16	16	16
Four people	19	17	18	16	14	14
Five people	9	8	7	5	5	4
Six or more people	7	6	4	2	2	2
All households (millions = 100%)	16.3	18.6	20.2	22.4	23.9	25.3
Average household size (number of people)	3.1	2.9	2.7	2.5	2.4	2.4

1 Data are at Q2 (April–June) each year and are not seasonally adjusted. A household is a set of people who live and eat together or a person living alone.
Source: Census, Labour Force Survey, Office for National Statistics

Part of the decrease in average household size in Great Britain can be attributed to a reduction in the proportion of families with children and the decrease in the number of children within those families, as shown in **Table 2**.

Table 2   **Households:[1] by type of household and family**

Great Britain   Percentages

	1961	1971	1981	1991	2001	2010
One person households	12	18	22	27	29	29
One family households						
Couple[2]						
No children	26	27	26	28	29	28
1–2 dependent children[3]	30	26	25	20	19	18
3 or more dependent children[3]	8	9	6	5	4	3
Non-dependent children only	10	8	8	8	6	6
Lone parent[2]						
Dependent children[3]	2	3	5	6	7	7
Non-dependent children only	4	4	4	4	3	3
Two or more unrelated adults	5	4	5	3	3	3
Multi-family households	3	1	1	1	1	1
All households						
(=100%) (millions)	16.3	18.6	20.2	22.4	23.9	25.3

1 Data are at Q2 (April–June) each year and are not seasonally adjusted.

2 These households may contain individuals who are not family members. Couples include a small number of same-sex couples and civil partners.

3 Dependent children are children living with their parent(s) aged under 16, or aged 16 to 18 in full-time education, excluding all children who have a spouse, partner or child living in the household. These families may also contain non-dependent children.

Source: Census, Labour Force Survey, Office for National Statistics

There was little change in the proportions of different types of families within households between 2001 and 2010. Over the longer term the proportion of households which consisted of one family with children decreased from 54 per cent to 37 per cent between 1961 and 2010. Over the same time period the proportion of households containing couples with one or two dependent children went down from 30 per cent to 18 per cent (from about 4.9 million to 4.6 million households) and those with 3 or more dependent children from 8 per cent to 3 per cent of all households (from about 1.3 million to 0.8 million households).

Another contributor to the reduction in average household size, as reported in **Table 1**, is the increase in the proportion of people living alone. In 2010, 29 per cent of all households in Great

Britain contained just one person, the same proportion as in 2001, but a considerable increase since 1961 when only 12 per cent of households were one person living alone.

People living in households

This section examines in more detail the people living in households in the UK and compares changes between 2001 and 2010. In 2010 there were an estimated 61.4 million people living in households in the UK an increase of 3.1 million since 2001.

Table 3   People living in households: by type of household[1]

United Kingdom   Millions and percentages

	2001	2010	2001	2010
	(Millions)		(Percentages)	
One person household	7.0	7.5	12.0	12.3
Under 65	3.7	4.2	6.4	6.8
65 or over	3.3	3.4	5.7	5.5
One family households	48.4	50.4	83.0	82.1
Couple[2]	42.0	43.0	72.0	70.1
No children	14.3	15.2	24.6	24.7
1-2 dependent children[3]	17.1	17.5	29.3	28.6
3 or more dependent children[3]	5.3	4.8	9.1	7.8
Non-dependent children only	5.3	5.5	9.0	9.0
Lone parent[2]	6.4	7.4	11.0	12.0
Dependent children[3]	4.7	5.3	8.1	8.6
Non-dependent children only	1.7	2.1	2.9	3.4
Two or more unrelated adults	1.9	2.2	3.3	3.6
Multi-family households	1.0	1.3	1.7	2.1
All people in households	58.3	61.4	100.0	100.0

1 Data are at Q2 (April–June) each year and are not seasonally adjusted.

2 These households may contain individuals who are not family members. Couples data for 2010 include a small number of same-sex couples and civil partners.

3 Dependent children are children living with their parent(s) aged under 16, or aged 16 to 18 in full-time education, excluding all children who have a spouse, partner or child living in the household. These families may also contain non-dependent children.

Source: Census, Labour Force Survey, Office for National Statistics

Between 2001 and 2010 there were increases in the numbers of people living in all types of household in the UK apart from that consisting of a couple with three or more dependent children where there was a decrease of nearly half a million.

There were some changes in the proportions of households of different type: there were smaller proportions of people living in couple households with dependent and non-dependent children in 2010 as compared to 2001, and larger proportions living in lone parent, multi-family and one person, households. This reflects the trend towards fewer families with children and families with fewer children as discussed earlier for Great Britain.

In the UK between 2001 and 2010 there was an increase in the both the estimated number of people living alone from 7.0 million to 7.5 million and the proportion that these formed of all households from 12.0 per cent to 12.3 per cent (**Table 3**).

Not only have there been changes in the number and proportion of single person households but there are differences between age groups. In 2010 in the UK 55 per cent of all people living alone were under 65, an increase from 53 per cent in 2001.

Figure 1   Proportion of people living alone: by age group

United Kingdom

Percentages

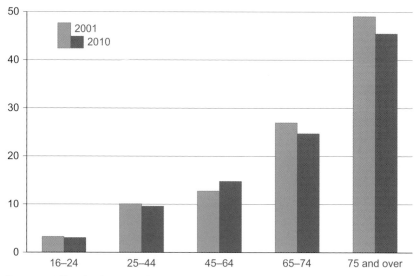

Source: Office for National Statistics

As age increases so the proportion of the age group living alone also increases. In 2010 in the UK, around three per cent of those aged 16 to 24 lived alone compared to around 25 per cent of those aged 65 to 74 and over 45 per cent of those aged 75 and over. There had been slight changes in the proportions of the age groups who were living alone between 2001 and 2010 with decreases for all age groups apart from those aged 45 to 64. The largest changes were in those aged 75 and over which had decreased from 49 per cent of the age group in 2001 to 45 per cent in 2010 and those aged 65 to 74 which had decreased from 27 per cent to 25 per cent of the age group (**Figure 1**).

The decrease in the proportion of the older age groups living alone is linked to the fall in the proportions who are widowed. In England and Wales between 2001 and 2009 the estimated percentage of widowed persons changed from 20 per cent to 15 per cent of those aged 65-74 and from 51 per cent to 46 per cent of those aged 75 and over (ONS 2011a).

Families

The previous sections examined the composition of households in Great Britain and the UK. This section describes the different types of family[ii] in the UK and the people who live in them. In 2010 there were about 17.9 million families in the UK, an estimated increase of 0.9 million (5.6 per cent) since 2001. The growth in the number of families between 2001 and 2010 is made up of increases in the numbers of cohabiting couple by 0.6 million and lone parent families by 0.4 million offset by a reduction in the number of married couple families by 0.1 million. Between 2001 and 2010 the number of people living in families increased by 4.1 per cent from 48.8 million to 50.8 million **(Table 4)**.

Table 4   **Families and number of people living in families: by family type**

United Kingdom   Percentages

	Families		People in families	
	2001	**2010**	**2001**	**2010**
Married couple family	72.4	68.0	74.7	70.2
Civil partner family	-	0.2	-	0.2
Cohabiting couple family	12.5	15.3	11.7	14.7
Same sex cohabiting couple family	0.3	0.3	0.2	0.2
Lone parent family	14.8	16.2	13.4	14.7
Lone mother family	12.7	14.1	11.7	12.9
Lone father family	2.1	2.1	1.7	1.8
All families and people in families (millions = 100%)	17.0	17.9	48.8	50.8

Source: Labour Force Survey, Office for National Statistics

Married couple families were the most common in the UK each of these two years although there had been a decrease from 72.4 to 68.0 per cent in this type of family between 2001 and 2010. There had been an increase between 2001 and 2010 in the proportion of families which were cohabiting couples from 12.5 per cent to 15.3 per cent, and in lone parent families from 14.8 per cent to 16.2 per cent. Almost all the growth in lone parent families was in those headed by a lone mother.

Of all those living in families just over 70 per cent (35.7 million) lived in a married couple family in 2010, while the proportions living in cohabiting families and lone parent families were each nearly 15 per cent or 7.5 million people.

The introduction of Civil Partnerships in 2004 has resulted in approximately 45,000 civil partner families by 2010. In addition in 2010 there were approximately 51,000 same sex cohabiting families.

In 2010 there were 7.7 million families with dependent children[iii], an increase of 0.3 million (3.7 per cent) since 2001. The number of dependent children living in families in 2010 was 13.3 million a slight decrease of 0.1 per cent since 2001.

Table 5   Families[1] with dependent children[2]

United Kingdom   Percentages

	Families		Dependent children	
	2001	2010	2001	2010
Married couple family	65.4	60.4	68.0	63.0
One child	24.1	24.4	13.4	14.1
Two children	29.5	26.3	32.8	30.3
Three or more children	11.8	9.8	21.7	18.6
Cohabiting couple family	10.9	14.0	10.1	13.4
One child	5.8	7.3	3.2	4.2
Two children	3.6	4.8	4.0	5.5
Three or more children	1.6	1.9	2.9	3.7
Lone parent family	23.6	25.5	21.9	23.6
One child	12.6	14.6	7.0	8.4
Two children	7.6	7.8	8.5	9.1
Three or more children	3.3	3.1	6.3	6.1
All families	100.0	100.0	100.0	100.0
One child	42.5	46.3	23.7	26.8
Two children	40.8	38.9	45.4	44.9
Three or more children	16.7	14.8	30.9	28.3

1 Excludes a small number of Civil Partnership and same sex cohabiting couple families.
2 Excludes dependent children who do not live in families.
Source: Labour Force Survey, Office for National Statistics

The majority of dependent children in the UK live in families of which there are three main types: a married couple, a cohabiting couple or a lone parent family. The proportions of these types of family with dependent children have changed between 2001 and 2010. Married couple families decreased from 65.4 per cent of all families with dependent children in 2001 to 60.4 per cent in 2010 **(Table 5)**. The numbers of these families had also gone down from 4.8 million in 2001 to 4.6 million 2010. The proportion of cohabiting couple families with dependent children increased between 2001 and 2010 from 10.9 per cent to 14.0 per cent, and lone parent families from 23.6 per cent to 25.5 per cent of all families with dependent children.

Of all dependent children living in families, 63.0 per cent (8.4 million) lived in a married couple family in 2010 a decrease from 68.0 per cent (9.0 million) in 2001. The proportion living in cohabiting couple families increased from 10.1 per cent (1.3 million) in 2001 to 13.4 per cent (1.8 million) in 2010. Over the same time period the proportion of dependent children living in lone parent families increased from 21.9 per cent to 23.6 per cent (2.9 million to 3.1 million).

At the time of the survey in 2010 families with one dependent child were the most common, comprising 46.3 per cent of all families with dependent children, an increase from 42.5 per cent in 2001. Over half of all cohabiting couple and lone parent families had a single dependent child. However, for married couple families the most frequent number of dependent children was two. The proportion of all families with three or more dependent children decreased from 16.7 per cent in 2001 to 14.8 per cent in 2010, an indicator of the decrease in family size for families with dependent children. Note that all these types of family could also have non-dependent children.

Family formation

The previous sections showed estimates of households and families at specific points in time. The next sections discuss the events which can cause changes to household and family types, such as marriage, civil partnership, divorce and dissolution and births.

The Marriage Act 1836 and the Registration Act 1836 came into force in 1837 in England and Wales and provided the statutory basis for regulating and recording marriages. There were 118,000 marriages registered in 1838, the first full year of civil registration in England and Wales. Annual numbers of marriages rose steadily from the 1840s to the 1940s, apart from peaks and troughs around the two world wars.

The provisional number of marriages registered in England and Wales in 2009 was 231,490 **(Figure 2).** This currently represents the lowest numbers of marriages in England and Wales since 1895 (228,204). However, it is estimated that a further one per cent of 2009 marriage returns will be received from register offices and the clergy over the next year allowing final figures to be published (ONS, 2011b). It is therefore expected that final 2009 marriage figures will be similar in total to 2008 (235,794).

Figure 2   **Marriages: by previous marital status**

England and Wales
Thousands

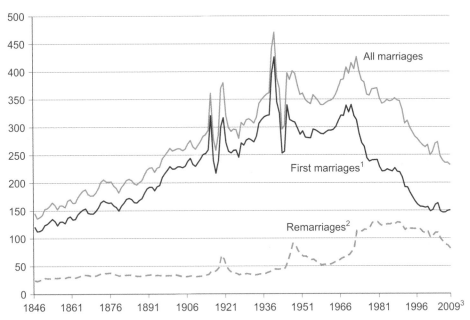

1 For both parties

2. For one or both parties.

3. Figures for 2009 are provisional.

Source: Office for National Statistics (ONS 2009; 2011c)

The number of marriages in England and Wales that were the first for both partners peaked in 1940 at 426,100 when 91 per cent of all marriages were the first for both partners. First marriages fell below three-quarters (73 per cent) of all marriages in 1972 and continued to decrease, reaching a low of 58 per cent in 1997. Provisional figures for 2009 show that there were around 150,600 marriages which were first for both partners, almost two-thirds (65 per cent) of all marriages. The last time the proportion of marriages that were first marriages was this high was in 1980. Remarriages rose by about a third between 1971 and 1972, following the introduction of the Divorce Reform Act 1969 in England and Wales, and then levelled off. Provisional estimates for 2009 show that 35 per cent of all marriages (80,900) were remarriages for one or both parties. This is a decrease since 2008 and a continuation of the slight downward trend since 2004.

In England and Wales, the number of unmarried adults rose between 2008 and 2009 (ONS 2011a; 2011d), but the provisional number choosing to marry remained stable, producing the lowest marriage rates since they were first calculated in 1862. In 2009, the provisional marriage rate for men was 21.3 men marrying per 1,000 unmarried men aged 16 and over, down from 22.0 in 2008. The provisional marriage rate for women in 2009 was 19.2 women marrying per 1,000 unmarried women aged 16 and over, down from 19.9 in 2008 (ONS, 2011b).

In Scotland, the number of marriages decreased from 28,903 in 2008 to 27,524 in 2009, a fall of 4.8 per cent, while in Northern Ireland the number of marriages decreased by 6.8 per cent to 7,931 (ONS 2011e).

Since 1999, there have been more civil ceremonies in England and Wales than religious ceremonies. Of the 231,490 marriages that were registered in England and Wales in 2009, two thirds (67 per cent) were solemnised in civil as opposed to religious ceremonies and 48 per cent of all marriages were in Approved Premises. This is a considerable increase since 1981 when only 49 per cent of all marriages were civil ceremonies (ONS 2011c). As well as the changes in the type and place of ceremony there has also been a change in the seasonal distribution of marriages: in 1981 62 per cent of marriages took place between April and September but this had risen to 70 per cent in 2009 (ONS, 2011c).

The Civil Partnership Act 2004 came into force on 5 December 2005 in the UK; when couples could give notice of their intention to form a civil partnership[iv]. The Act enables same-sex couples aged 16 and over to obtain legal recognition of their relationship. The first day that couples could formally form a partnership was 19 December 2005 in Northern Ireland, 20 December 2005 in Scotland and 21 December 2005 in England and Wales. The total number of partnerships formed since the Civil Partnership Act came into force in December 2005 up to the end of 2009 is 40,237. The highest number of civil partnerships registered in the UK in a month was in December 2005 (1,953) (ONS, 2010a). The high number of partnerships formed in this month, and throughout the following 12 months, reflected the number of same-sex couples in long-term relationships who took advantage of the opportunity to formalise their relationship as soon as possible after the legislation was implemented.

Figure 3   Civil partnerships: by sex

United Kingdom
Thousands

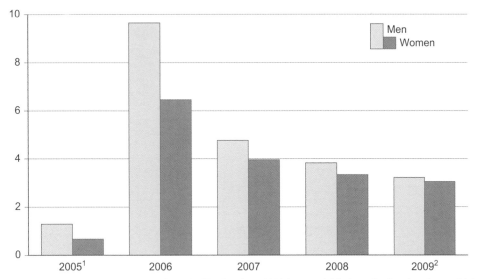

1 In 2005 there were only 11 days in England and Wales and 12 days in Scotland on which couples could normally register a partnership.

2 Figures for the UK for 2009 are provisional.

Sources: Office for National Statistics, General Register Office for Scotland, Northern Ireland Statistics and Research Agency (ONS, 2010a)

Provisionally, there were a total of 6,281 civil partnerships registered in the UK in 2009, a fall of 12.4 per cent on the previous year continuing the trend seen in 2007. In 2009 3,227 (51 per cent) were male and 3,054 were female partnerships **(Figure 3)**.

There were decreases in the number of civil partnerships in England (from 6,276 to 5,443), Wales (from 282 to 244) and Scotland (from 525 to 498) between 2008 and 2009. However, the number of civil partnerships in Northern Ireland increased from 86 to 96 (ONS, 2010a).

Divorces and dissolution

Another way in which family structures change is following divorce or, for civil partnerships, dissolution. Between 1918 and 1938 the number of divorces each year in England and Wales gradually increased from 1,100 to 6,300 **(Figure 4)**. Following the Act of Parliament in 1938 that extended the grounds on which divorce was allowed, numbers increased considerably throughout the 1940s, to a peak of around 60,300 in 1947. Although the number of divorces then fell to 22,700 in 1958, there was a further increase during the 1960s.

Figure 4   **Number of couples divorcing**

England and Wales
Thousands

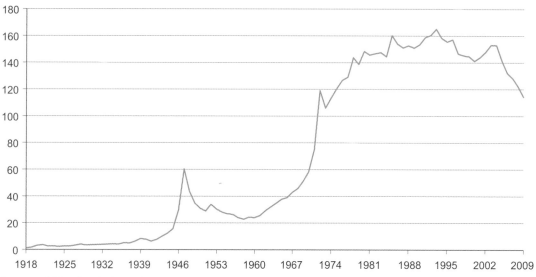

Source: Office for National Statistics (ONS, 2011f)

The Divorce Reform Act of 1969, which was subsequently consolidated into the Matrimonial Causes Act 1973, had a considerable impact on divorce numbers in England and Wales. In 1972 there were 119,000 divorces, an increase of almost 60 per cent on the previous year. From 1972 onwards, there was a generally upward trend in divorces in England and Wales, reaching the highest recorded number of 165,000 in 1993.

The numbers of divorces were variable between 1993 and 2002, but there has been a consistent downward trend from 2003 to 2009. In 2009 there were about 113,900 divorces in England and Wales compared with 121,700 in 2008, a decrease of 6.4 per cent.

In Scotland, there were less than 10,200 divorces registered in 2009/10, a fall of 9.8 per cent on the previous year. In Northern Ireland in 2009, less than 2,200 divorces were recorded, a decrease of 21.5 per cent compared with the previous year (Scottish Government, 2010a; NISRA, 2010a).

In order to obtain the dissolution of a civil partnership, a couple must have been in a registered partnership, or a recognised foreign relationship, for at least 12 months. In 2009 there were 351 civil partnership dissolutions granted in the UK, 127 to male couples and 224 to female couples, an increase from 180 in 2008 and 41 in 2007 (ONS, 2010b).

As already discussed family type is changed when divorce occurs, and when a divorcing couple have children, this affects the family type in which those children live. There has been a considerable change not only in the number of children living in families affected by divorce but also in the distribution of their ages. Between 1989 and 2009 the total number of children of divorcing couples of all ages decreased from just over 216,000 to less than 154,000; this decrease is partly because of the overall decrease in the number of divorces and partly because the average number of children involved in each divorce had reduced (ONS 2011g).

Figure 5   Number of children[1] of divorced couples: by age[2] group

England and Wales

Thousands

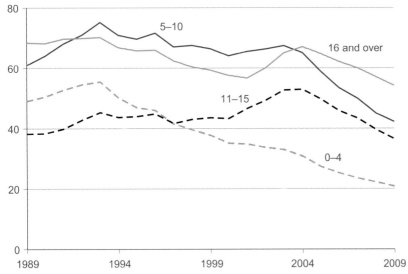

1 Children are those treated as children of the family, and can include children born outside marriage, children of previous marriages, adopted and step children.

2 Ages are those at petition to divorce.

Source: Office for National Statistics (ONS, 2011g)

Not only was there a decrease in the total number of children affected by divorce, but there was a change in the ages at which children were affected by divorce. This is particularly noticeable for children aged 0 to 4, where, after an increase to about 55,500 in 1993, numbers fell in each year to reach 20,800 in 2009. By 2004, the highest number of children who were affected by divorce were those aged 16 and over. From 2004 onwards numbers in each of the age groups decreased in line with the decrease in the overall number of divorces **(Figure 5)**.

Births

One of the largest changes over time, as noted above, is in the types of family which have dependent children; there has been a decrease in the proportion living in married couple families and an increase in the proportion that are living in cohabiting couple and lone parent families. This section examines changes in the numbers of children born within and outside marriage together with the changes in the ages of their mothers. There is also a discussion of the differences over time in the registration of their births and how this relates to the change in the types of family with dependent children.

The number of births in England and Wales increased for seven successive years between 2001 and 2008, rising from 594,600 in 2001 to 708,700 in 2008. However, the number of live births decreased by about 2,500 to 706,200 in 2009.

Table 6   Live births: by age of mother and registration type[1]

England and Wales

Numbers of births

| | Age of mother at birth | | | | | | All ages |
	Under 20	20–24	25–29	30–34	35–39	40 and over	
All							
1971	82,600	285,700	247,200	109,600	45,200	12,700	783,200
1981 [2]	56,600	194,500	215,800	126,600	34,200	6,900	634,500
1991	52,400	173,400	248,700	161,300	53,600	9,800	699,200
2001	44,200	108,800	159,900	178,900	86,500	16,300	594,600
2008	44,700	136,000	193,000	192,500	116,200	26,400	708,700
2009	43,200	136,000	194,100	191,600	114,300	27,000	706,200
Outside marriage							
1971	21,600	22,000	11,500	6,300	3,200	1,100	65,700
1981 [2]	26,400	28,800	14,300	7,900	27,300	900	81,000
1991	43,400	77,800	52,400	25,700	9,800	2,100	211,300
2001	39,500	68,100	56,800	45,200	23,300	5,100	238,100
2008	42,000	97,700	82,600	54,400	34,600	9,500	320,800
2009	40,900	100,100	85,600	55,800	34,100	9,600	326,200
Within marriage							
1971	61,100	263,700	235,700	103,400	42,100	11,600	717,500
1981 [2]	30,100	165,700	201,500	118,700	31,500	6,000	553,500
1991	8,900	95,600	196,300	135,500	43,800	7,700	487,900
2001	4,600	40,700	103,100	133,700	63,200	11,100	356,500
2008	2,700	38,200	110,400	138,100	81,600	16,900	387,900
2009	2,300	35,900	108,500	135,800	80,200	17,400	380,100

1. The Human Fertilisation and Embryology Act 2008 contained provisions enabling two females in a same-sex couple to register a birth from 1st September 2009 onwards. Due to the small numbers in 2009, births registered to a same-sex couple in a civil partnership (22 in 2009) are included with marital births while births registered to a same-sex couple outside a civil partnership (2 in 2009) are included with births outside marriage.

2. For 1981 data the processing was delayed due to the late submission of registrations. As a result the data for 1981 is estimated and figures for age of mother are based on a ten per cent sample.

Source: Office for National Statistics (ONS, 2010c)

The average age for women giving birth in England and Wales has increased from just over 26 and a half years in 1971 to just under 29 and a half years in 2009 (ONS, 2010c) and this is reflected in the age distribution in **Table 6**. In 1971, nearly four out of five of all live births (79 per cent) were to women aged less than 30: by 2009 just over half of all live births (53 per cent) were to women of this age. The number of live births decreased for women in each of the three age groups under 20,

20 to 24 and 25 to 29 and increased in women aged 30 to 34, 35 to 39 and 40 and over between 1971 and 2009.

In 1971 there were 65,700 live births outside marriage in England and Wales, 8.4 per cent of all live births in that year. By 1991 the number of live births outside marriage had risen to 211,300, more than 30.2 per cent of all live births in that year. Live births outside marriage have continued to increase both numerically and as a proportion of all births reaching 326,200 (46.2 per cent) in 2009, an increase of about 5,400 (1.7 per cent) compared to 2008 and nearly five times as many as were born outside marriage in 1971. Over the same time period the number of live births within marriage had decreased by 47 per cent from 717,500 to 380,100 **(Table 6)**.

However, the increases and decreases in overall births, and those within and outside marriage were not the same for all age groups. The age distribution of women for births within marriage reflects the increase already mentioned in the average age at birth and also in average age for women at marriage. There have been considerable decreases in the number of births within marriage for each of the three age groups under 20, 20 to 24 and 25 to 29. For example, the number of births within marriage in the under 20 age group decreased from 61,100 in 1971 to 2,300 in 2009 (a decrease of 58,800 or 96 per cent). In the older age groups there have been increases in births within marriage: for example in the 35 to 39 age group the increase between 1971 and 2009 was 38,000 live births (from 42,100 to 80,200 or 91 per cent).

By contrast, for births outside marriage there have been increases in the number of live births in all age groups, particularly since 2001.

Table 7   **Live births outside marriage: by registration type[1]**

England and Wales   Percentages

	Joint registration same address[2]	Joint registration different addresses[2]	Sole Registration
1971		45.5	54.5
1981 [3]		58.2	41.8
1991	54.6	19.8	25.6
2001	63.2	18.4	18.4
2008	65.5	20.3	14.2
2009 [4]	65.7	20.9	13.4

1 Births outside marriage can be registered by both parents (joint) or by the mother alone (sole).

2 Usual address(es) of parents.

3 For 1981 data the processing was delayed due to the late submission of registrations. As a result the data for 1981 is estimated and figures for age of mother are based on a ten per cent sample. Figures have been rounded to the nearest ten.

4. The Human Fertilisation and Embryology Act 2008 contained provisions enabling two females in a same-sex couple to register a birth from 1st September 2009 onwards. Due to the small numbers in 2009, births registered to a same-sex couple outside a civil partnership (2 in 2009) are included with births outside marriage.

Source: Office for National Statistics (ONS, 2010c; 2010d)

There have also been changes over time in the registration status of children born outside marriage. In 1971 45.5 per cent of children born outside marriage were registered jointly (**Table 7**). When data began to be reported about the address status of those who had jointly registered births outside marriage in 1991, nearly three quarter (74.4 per cent) were jointly registered and more than half of these (54.6 per cent of all registrations outside of marriage) were from couples living at the same address (for more information about children in cohabiting couple families see Figure 5). By 2009, 65.7 per cent of births outside of marriage were registered by parents living at the same address, 20.9 per cent were registered by parents living at different addresses and 13.4 per cent were solely registered. The number of sole registrations of births has remained fairly stable between 2001 and 2009, varying from 43,000 to 46,000 (ONS, 2010d).

In Scotland, the proportion of births outside marriage rose to 50 per cent for the first time in 2008 and increased slightly in 2009 (General Register Office for Scotland, 2010). In Northern Ireland in 2009, there were almost 10,000 births outside marriage, around 40 per cent of all births (NISRA, 2010b).

Conceptions and Abortions

Information about conceptions[v] also shows a change in age structure. Provisional estimates in 2009 are that there were 896,300 conceptions in England and Wales, an increase of nearly 8,000 (0.9 per cent) from 888,600 in 2008. The number of conceptions in 2009 was also higher than in 1991 and 2001. There was an increase in the overall rate of conception between 2008 and 2009 of one additional conception per 1,000 women (from 80 to 81 conceptions per 1,000 women aged 15 to 44, see footnote 4 to **table 8**).

Table 8   **Conceptions:[1] by age of woman at conception**

England and Wales[2]

	Under 16	Under 18	Under 20	20–24	25–29	30–34	35–39	40 and over	All ages
Age of woman at conception									
Numbers (thousands)									
1991	7.5	40.1	101.6	233.3	281.5	167.5	57.6	12.1	853.7
2001	7.9	41.0	96.0	161.6	199.3	196.7	92.2	17.8	763.7
2008	7.6	41.4	103.3	198.5	237.8	207.1	115.6	26.5	888.6
2009[3]	7.2	38.3	97.9	199.5	242.2	213.3	116.5	26.8	896.3
Rates (conceptions[4] per thousand women in age-group)									
1991	8.9	44.6	64.1	120.2	135.1	90.1	34.4	6.6	77.7
2001	8.0	42.7	60.8	102.5	114.2	96.7	44.3	9.6	70.3
2008	7.8	40.7	60.1	108.7	133.2	121.7	58.1	12.6	79.9
2009[3]	7.5	38.3	57.3	108.5	133.8	125.9	60.1	12.8	80.9
Percentage terminated by abortion									
1991	51.1	39.9	34.5	22.2	13.4	13.7	22.0	41.6	19.4
2001	55.8	45.7	40.4	29.7	18.4	14.6	20.4	34.6	23.2
2008	61.5	49.4	42.4	28.0	17.4	12.8	16.3	30.0	21.8
2009[3]	59.8	48.8	41.9	27.1	16.5	12.4	15.8	29.1	21.0

1 Conception figures are estimates derived from birth registrations and abortion notifications.

2 Data are for residents of England and Wales.

3 Figures for 2009 are provisional.

4 Revised mid–2002 to mid–2008 population estimates published on 13 May 2010 have been used in the calculation of conception rates. Figures may therefore differ from those published previously. Rates for women of all ages, under 16, under 18, under 20 and 40 and over are based on the population of women aged 15-44, 13-15, 15-17, 15-19 and 40-44 respectively.

Source: Office for National Statistics (ONS, 2011h)

However, these increases were not uniform across age groups. For all age groups from 25 to 29 to those aged 40 and over there were increases between 2008 and 2009 in the number of conceptions and in the rates of conception per 1,000 women. For women in the under 20 age group (and the constituent parts of women aged under 18 and under 16) there were decreases in both the numbers and rates of conception between 2008 and 2009. For the age group 20-24 there was a slight increase in the number of conceptions over this time period, but a slight decrease in the rate of conception, which can be explained by an increase in the number of women in this age group.

Over the longer time period of 1991 to 2009 there were also increases in the overall number and rates of conception, but the difference in the age groups is more marked. While there was an overall increase of an estimated 42,600 in the number of conceptions between 1991 and 2009, this was the result of a decrease of approximately 76,800 conceptions in women under 30 and an increase of 119,400 in conceptions in women over 30 and over.

Proportions of conceptions resulting in legal abortion were highest in the lower age groups: 48.8 per cent of conceptions in women under 18 and 59.8 per cent in girls aged less than 16 led to a legal abortion according to provisional estimates for 2009. The percentage of all conceptions which were terminated by legal abortion decreased from 21.8 per cent in 2008 to 21.0 per cent in 2009 with a decrease in the percentages in all age groups.

The overall percentage of conceptions leading to a legal abortion increased from 19.4 per cent to 21.0 per cent between 1991 and 2009. However, the largest increases over this time period were in the younger age groups which include girls and women up to the age of 30. For those aged 30 and over, there were decreases in all age groups, with a particularly marked fall in the 40 and over age group from 41.6 per cent in 1991 to 29.1 per cent in 2009.

In Scotland, provisional figures for 2009 show that there were a total of 12,950 abortions performed in Scotland for Scottish residents, a decrease of 6.0 per cent since 2008. The rate per thousand women aged 15 to 44 had decreased from 13.2 to 12.4 (Scottish Government, 2010b).

In Northern Ireland, abortion is illegal and is only considered lawful in exceptional circumstances. As there are such a small number of abortions, and in order to protect patient confidentiality, there are no comparable conception figures for Northern Ireland.

References

General Register Office for Scotland (2010). Live births, numbers and percentages, by marital status of parents and type of registration, Scotland, 1974 to 2009 . Available at www.gro-scotland.gov.uk/statistics/theme/vital-events/general/ref-tables/2009/births.html

NISRA (2010a). Additional Tables for Marriages, Divorces and Civil Partnerships in Northern Ireland, 2009. Available at www.nisra.gov.uk/demography/default.asp25.htm

NISRA (2010b). Live births by number of previous children and marital status of parents, 1976 to 2009. Available at www.nisra.gov.uk/demography/default.asp98.htm

ONS (2009). Historic marriage tables: Previous marital status. Available at www.statistics.gov.uk/statbase/Product.asp?vlnk=581

ONS (2010a). Civil partnerships formations data. Available at www.statistics.gov.uk/StatBase/Product.asp?vlnk=14675&Pos=4&ColRank=1&Rank=272

ONS (2010b). Civil partnerships dissolutions data. Available at www.statistics.gov.uk/StatBase/Product.asp?vlnk=14675&Pos=4&ColRank=1&Rank=272

ONS (2010c). Characteristics of Mother 1 2009: 21/10/10. Available at www.statistics.gov.uk/statbase/Product.asp?vlnk=14408

ONS (2010d). Live births outside marriage: age of mother and type of registration, 1971 onwards (England and Wales): Population Trends. Available at www.statistics.gov.uk/StatBase/ssdataset.asp?vlnk=9557&Pos=&ColRank=1&Rank=272

ONS (2011a). Mid-2009 Marital Status Estimates. Available at www.statistics.gov.uk/statbase/product.asp?vlnk=15107

ONS (2011b). Marriages in England and Wales 2009: Statistical bulletin. Available at www.statistics.gov.uk/statbase/Product.asp?vlnk=14275

ONS (2011c). Marriage summary statistics 2009 (provisional). Available at www.statistics.gov.uk/statbase/Product.asp?vlnk=14275

ONS (2011d). Mid-2002 to Mid-2008 revised Marital Status Estimates (revised). Available at www.statistics.gov.uk/statbase/product.asp?vlnk=15107

ONS (2011e). Marriages. Available at www.statistics.gov.uk/cci/nugget.asp?id=322

ONS (2011f). Number of divorces, age at divorce and marital status before marriage. Available at www.statistics.gov.uk/statbase/Product.asp?vlnk=14124

ONS (2011g). Children of divorced couples. Available at www.statistics.gov.uk/StatBase/Product.asp?vlnk=14124&Pos=3&ColRank=1&Rank=160

ONS (2011h). Conceptions to women by age, year and quarter. Available at
www.statistics.gov.uk/statbase/product.asp?vlnk=15055

Scottish Government (2010a). Table 1: Divorces and dissolutions granted, 2000-01 - 2009-10. Available at
www.scotland.gov.uk/Publications/2010/12/17151409/3

Scottish Government (2010b). Abortions by place, age, deprivation, gestation, parity, repeat abortions and grounds for
termination. Available at www.isdscotland.org/isd/1918.html

Notes

[i] A household is a person living alone or a group of people who have the address as their only or main residence and who either share one meal a day or share the living accommodation.

[ii] A family is a married or cohabiting couple living together with or without children or a lone parent lining with his or her children. A family could also consist of grandparent(s) with their grandchild or grandchildren if the parent(s) are absent.

[iii] In general, a dependent child is a child aged under 16 (under 15 in earlier Census data) or one aged 16 to 18 in full-time education who has never married and is living a family with their parent(s)

[iv] Civil partners have equal treatment to married couples in a number of legal matters such as tax, employment benefits, pension benefits, maintenance and recognition for immigration and nationality purposes.

[v] Conception estimates include pregnancies that result in one or more live births or stillbirths or which are terminated by a legal abortion. They do not include miscarriages or illegal abortions.

e-Society

This is the first Social Trends chapter to focus on e-Society. For most people, new technology plays a crucial part in their daily lives, from use of a computer and having Internet access at home or work, to texting or making calls on a mobile phone. Even if people do not make direct use of this technology, they are surrounded by networks through which information constantly flows. It allows anyone to create new information, provides convenient access to information and enables people to interact with information produced by others, especially on the Internet. Digital television and radio services allow a greater number of channels to be broadcast and allow viewers to interact with what they see and hear. People can take new technology with them virtually anywhere they go; computers can be portable and phones can be mobile.

Key points:

Household access to the Internet

- In 2010, 19.2 million households in the UK had Internet access, 73 per cent of households. This compares with 57 per cent in 2006, equivalent to 14.3 million households
- In the UK in 2008, over 8 in 10 (83 per cent) households with dependent children had Internet access
- In 2008, households in the highest 10 per cent of the income distribution in the UK were over three-and-a-half times as likely as those in the lowest 10 per cent to have an Internet connection, 96 per cent of households compared with 26 per cent

Use of the Internet and other technologies

- Just over a third (34 per cent) of adults aged 15 and over in the UK stated that they or someone else in their household had watched online television or videos in 2009
- Over three-quarters (78 per cent) of all those who had accessed the Internet in the three months prior to interview had done so every day or almost every day, while a fifth (17 per cent) had accessed it at least once a week but not every day

Online communication and social networking

- The proportion of Internet users in the UK aged 16 and over who had their own social networking site profile doubled between 2007 and 2009, from 22 per cent to 44 per cent

Children's use of new technology

- Just over a quarter (27 per cent) of children aged 5 to 15 owning a mobile phone in 2009 in the UK had first acquired one by the time they were eight years old and just under two-thirds (65 per cent) by the time they were 10 years old
- Nearly 3 in 10 (59 per cent) parents and guardians of those aged 6 to 17 in the UK were very or rather worried that their child might see sexually or violently explicit images on the Internet, while 46 per cent were very or rather worried that their child could become a victim of online grooming

New technology in education and work

- The number of users of computers with Internet access in the workplace in the UK increased by 27 per cent between 2004 and 2008, from the equivalent to 5.9 million employees in 2004 to 7.5 million in 2008

e-commerce and online banking

- Among EU-27 member states, the use of the Internet to order goods and services was most common in the UK: in 2009, 66 per cent of adults aged 16 to 74 in the UK had done so in the 12 months prior to interview

- Losses through online banking fraud largely due to malware which targets vulnerabilities in customers' PCs, rather than the banks' own systems totalled £59.7 million in the UK in 2009

e-government

- 46 per cent of adults aged 16 and over in the UK who had accessed the Internet in the 12 months prior to interview had obtained information from a public authority website in 2010

Household access to the Internet

Figure 1   **Household Internet access**

United Kingdom
Percentages

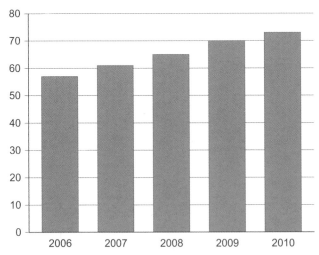

Source: Opinions Survey, (ONS, 2010)

The proportion of households with Internet access at home has been increasing year on year (**Figure 1**). In 2010, 19.2 million households in the UK had Internet access, 73 per cent of households. This compares with 57 per cent in 2006, equivalent to 14.3 million households. Internet access varied between the UK regions in 2010, with the highest levels of access in London at 83 per cent and the South East at 79 per cent. The lowest levels of Internet access were in the North East at 59 per cent and Scotland at 64 per cent (ONS, 2010).

Access to new technology and particularly the Internet is not universal. The gap between those who can access the Internet and other information communication technologies (ICTs) and those who cannot is often referred to as the 'digital divide'. Adults without an Internet connection at home are more likely to be older (particularly those over retirement age), have no formal educational qualifications or have lower annual household incomes (ONS, 2010).

According to the ONS Living Costs and Food Survey, in the UK in 2008 more than 8 in 10 (83 per cent) of households with dependent children[i] had Internet access. Households consisting of a couple with children were the most likely of all types of household to have access in 2008 (88 per cent), while lone parent households were the least likely of all households with children to have Internet access (63 per cent). Older households were the least likely to have Internet access. Fewer than 4 in 10 (37 per cent) of one person households over state pension age had Internet access in 2008 compared with just under 8 in 10 (79 per cent) of one person households under state pension age.

According to the same survey, rates of Internet access rose for all types of households in the UK between 2000–01 and 2008. For most types of households, the proportion with Internet access rose by about 40 percentage points over the period. However, the increase was only 26 percentage points for one person households over state pension age.

According to the ONS Opinion Survey, in 2009, just under two-thirds (63 per cent) of households, equivalent to 16.5 million households, had broadband Internet access[ii]. This was an increase of 6.6 million households since 2006. The proportion of UK households with a dial up connection fell by 10 percentage points between 2006 and 2009 to reach 7 per cent, equivalent to 1.8 million households. Nine in 10 households (90 per cent) with Internet access had a broadband connection in 2009, an increase from 69 per cent in 2006 (ONS, 2009a)

Table 1   **Households with broadband connection:[1] EU comparison, 2009**

Percentages

Top 6 countries		Bottom 6 countries	
Sweden	79	Portugal	46
Netherlands	77	Slovakia	42
Denmark	76	Italy	39
Finland	74	Greece	33
Luxembourg	71	Bulgaria	26
United Kingdom	69	Romania	24
		EU-27 average	56

1 Proportion of households with broadband access with at least one member aged 16 to 74.
Source: Eurostat (table isoc_pibi_hba)

Broadband access also varies across the EU. In 2009 Sweden ranked highest, with 79 per cent of households having broadband access, while the UK ranked sixth, at 69 per cent which was 13 percentage points above the EU-27 average **(Table 1)**. Romania ranked the lowest with less than a quarter of households having a broadband connection (24 per cent), 32 percentage points lower than the EU-27 average.

In all EU-27 countries broadband access increased substantially between 2006 and 2009. The percentage of households in Romania with a broadband connection increased by 19 percentage points, from 5 per cent to 24 per cent but the largest increase among countries ranked in the bottom six was recorded by Slovakia, increasing 31 percentage points from 11 per cent in 2006. Within the top six countries, the largest increase was seen in Sweden, 28 percentage points since 2006 (Eurostat table isoc_pibi_hba).

Table 2   **Household ownership of selected new technology: by income group,[1] 2008**

United Kingdom   Percentages

	Internet connection	Mobile phone	Satellite receiver[2]	Home computer
Lowest decile group	26	61	63	33
2nd	33	62	73	42
3rd	40	66	74	47
4th	54	77	82	65
5th	68	83	86	75
6th	76	86	86	83
7th	85	87	88	91
8th	88	87	91	93
9th	94	89	92	95
Highest	96	89	91	98

1 Households are ranked according to their income and then divided into 10 groups of equal size. The lowest decile group is the 10 per cent of households with the lowest incomes.

2 Digital television service. Includes digital and cable receivers.

Source: Living Costs and Food Survey (ONS, 2009b)

There is a relationship between ownership of new technology and household income. Household ownership of home computers and Internet access increase considerably as household income increases. In 2008 households in the highest 10th of the income distribution (the highest decile group were over three-and-a-half times as likely as those in the lowest 10 per cent to have an Internet connection, 96 per cent of households compared with 26 per cent **(Table 2)**. They were also nearly three times likely to own a home computer, 98 per cent compared with 33 per cent. Household ownership of mobile phones and a digital television service in the UK are also linked to income, although to a lesser extent. Households in the highest income group were nearly one-and-a-half times more likely to have a satellite receiver or a mobile phone than those in the lowest income group.

Figure 2

Reasons why households do not have Internet access[1]

United Kingdom
Percentages

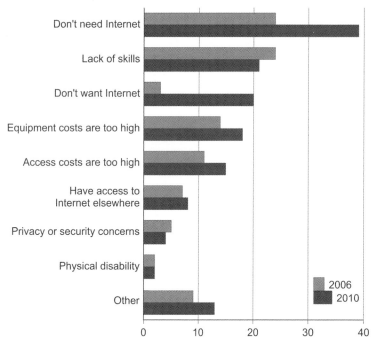

1. Respondents were asked 'What are the reasons for not having access to the Internet at home?'
Source: Opinions Survey, (ONS, 2006, 2010)

There are many possible reasons why households in the UK do not have access to the Internet. Not having a need for access was the most common reason reported in 2010 at 39 per cent, an increase of 15 percentage points since 2006 **(Figure 2)**. Just over a fifth (21 per cent) of households did not have access because of a lack of skills in the household, a fall of 3 percentage points since 2006. A fifth (20 per cent) of households with no access simply did not want the Internet, a rise of 17 percentage points since 2006.

Use of the Internet and other technologies

According to Ofcom, people who used new technology in 2010 in the UK spent almost half (45 per cent) of their waking hours watching television, using their mobiles and other communication devices such as the Internet (Ofcom, 2010a). Given this intensity of use, in 2009 Ofcom asked adults aged 16 and over which media activity they would miss doing the most.

Table 3   **Media activities that would be missed most: by age group,[1] 2009**

United Kingdom   Percentages

	16–24	25–34	35–44	45–54	55–64	65 and over	All aged 16 and over
Television	36	47	52	49	57	60	50
Internet	18	20	19	17	12	3	15
Mobile phone	32	14	9	7	4	1	11
Radio	2	3	7	10	16	18	9
Newspapers or magazines	1	2	3	3	4	11	4
Other[2]	11	14	10	14	7	7	11

1 Respondents were asked 'Which one of these would you miss doing the most?'

2 Other includes listening to music on a hi-fi, CD or tape player, playing console or computer games, listening to portable music devices or an MP3 player, watching videos DVDs or using a portable media player.

Source: UK Adults' Media Literacy (Ofcom, 2010b)

In each age group, watching television would be the most missed media activity **(Table 3)**. However, there are differences according to age. Adults aged 16 to 24 were less likely than older age groups to miss watching the television (36 per cent compared with 57 per cent and 60 per cent of the two oldest age groups shown). Nearly a third (32 per cent) of those aged 16 to 24 stated that they would miss using a mobile phone the most, compared with 14 per cent of those aged 25 to 34 and only 1 per cent of those aged 65 and over. The Internet would be missed by around a fifth of each age group among those aged 16 to 54. People aged 65 and over were more likely to miss more traditional media activities such as listening to the radio or reading newspapers and magazines.

The mobile phone is an increasingly powerful portable media device that allows people to undertake a wide range of activities. Beyond making voice calls, over 8 in 10 of adults (83 per cent) aged 15 and over in the UK used their mobile phone to send text messages and 56 per cent used it for voice mail in 2009 (Ofcom 2009c) . The only other function used by more than half (52 per cent) of mobile phone users is taking and storing photos. The next most common use was picture messaging, performed by just over a quarter (27 per cent) of mobile phone users, while 19 per cent used their mobile phone to either listen to radio, MP3s or podcasts or used it as a personal organiser.

Digital convergence is a term used to describe the growing tendency for different content formats such as audio, video, text or pictures to reach consumers via a range of digital networks such as a computer, television or mobile phone[iii]. In 2009, just over a third (34 per cent) of adults aged 15 and over in the UK stated that they or someone else in their household had watched online television or videos (Ofcom, 2009b). Three in 10 (30 per cent) stated that they or someone else in their household had used the Internet to access a social networking site. Two in 10 (20 per cent) stated that they had used a mobile phone to access the Internet, a similar proportion (17 per cent) listened to audio content on their mobile phone, and 12 per cent stated that they or someone else in their household made voice calls or listened to the radio over the Internet.

In 2010, just under a fifth of adults (18 per cent) had never used the Internet; however, this differed by educational qualifications. Over half (55 per cent) of adults aged 16 and over in the UK with no qualifications had never used the Internet. In comparison only 2 per cent of adults with a degree or equivalent qualification had never used the Internet (ONS, 2010). When interviewed in 2010, just over three-quarters (77 per cent) of the UK population aged 16 and over had accessed the Internet in the three months prior to interview. Level of Internet use varies by the age of the user. Those aged 16 to 24 had the highest level of use, with 97 per cent using it within the three months prior to interview, compared with just under a third (32 per cent) of those aged 65 and over (ONS, 2010).

Figure 3   **Frequency of Internet use:[1] by age group, 2010**

United Kingdom

Percentages

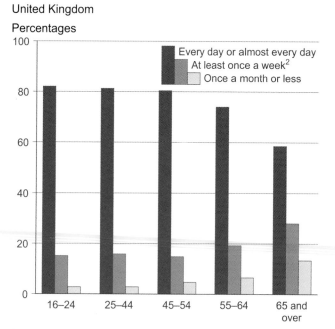

1 UK adults who have used the Internet in the three months prior to interview.

2 Not every day

Source: Opinions Survey (ONS, 2010)

Over three-quarters (78 per cent) of all those who had accessed the Internet in the three months prior to interview had done so every day or almost every day, while a fifth (17 per cent) had accessed it at least once a week but not every day. The proportion of those using the Internet every day or almost every day decreases with age. Those aged 16 to 24 accessed the Internet the most, with 82 per cent using it every day or almost every day **(Figure 3)**. Internet users aged 65 and over used it the least, with just under 6 in 10 (59 per cent) using it every day or almost every day.

There are also geographical differences in Internet use across the UK. In 2010 just under 3 in 10 adults (29 per cent) aged 16 and over in the North East had never used the Internet, followed by around a fifth of adults in Scotland (22 per cent), Yorkshire and the Humber (21 per cent) and West Midlands (20 per cent). Only 13 per cent of adults in London had never used the Internet (ONS, 2010).

Table 4   **Selected activities performed on the Internet:[1] by sex, 2010**

United Kingdom   Percentages

	Men	Women	All
Sending/receiving emails	90	89	90
Finding information about goods and services	77	73	75
Using services related to travel and accommodation	64	63	63
Internet banking	57	51	54
Reading or downloading online news, newspapers, magazines	56	46	51
Listening to web radio or watching web television	52	39	45
Posting messages to chat sites, blogs, newsgroups etc.	44	42	43
Playing or downloading games, images, films or music	45	34	40
Seeking health related information	34	44	39
Uploading self created content	36	40	38
Consulting the Internet with the purpose of learning	39	31	35
Looking for information about education, training or courses	30	33	32
Downloading software	41	19	30
Looking for a job or sending a job application	28	24	26
Telephoning over the Internet/video calls (via webcam)	27	20	23
Selling goods or services over the Internet	25	17	21

1 Adults aged 16 and over who had accessed the Internet in the three months prior to interview.
Source: Opinions Survey (ONS, 2010)

The Internet is used for a range of activities. The most common activity in 2010 was sending or receiving emails by 9 in 10 adults (90 per cent) aged 16 and over in the UK in 2010 who had used the Internet in the three months prior to interview **(Table 4)**. This was also the most common activity for both men and women (90 per cent of men and 89 per cent of women) who had used the Internet in the three months prior to interview.

Three-quarters of adults (75 per cent) used the Internet to find information about goods and services and 63 per cent used services related to travel and accommodation. Men were more likely than women to download software (41 per cent of men compared with 19 per cent of women) or to listen to web radio or watch web television (52 per cent compared with 39 per cent). Women were more likely than men to seek health related information (44 per cent of women compared with 34 per cent of men).

Online communication and social networking

The increase in popularity of modern technologies such as mobile phones and the Internet has changed the way that people communicate with each other. Online communication tools such as telephone calls over the Internet, video calls via webcams, social networking sites, email and instant messaging play an increasing role in how people keep in touch with existing friends and family and make new acquaintances.

Social networking sites offer new and varied ways to communicate via the Internet, whether through computers or mobile phones. Users can communicate via their 'profile' both with a list of contacts over which they have control – their 'friends' – and with others, either on a one-to-one basis through messages similar to emails, or in a more public way such as a comment posted for all to see.

Figure 4   **People who have set up own social networking site profile:[1] by age**

United Kingdom
Percentages

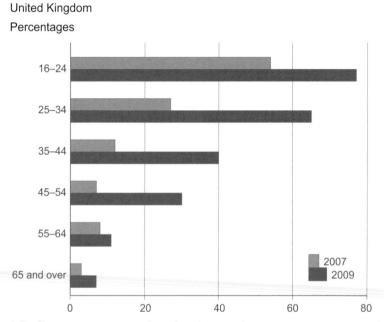

1 Profiles are a representation of each user often containing personal information such as their name, email address, phone number and photographs.
Source: UK Adults' Media Literacy (Ofcom, 2010b)

According to Ofcom, the proportion of Internet users in the UK aged 16 and over who had their own social networking site profile doubled between 2007 and 2009, from 22 per cent to 44 per cent. The proportion rose for all age groups but the largest rises were among those aged 25 to 34 (38 percentage points) and those aged 35 to 44 (28 percentage points) **(Figure 4)**. Women were more likely than men to have set up a social networking site profile (48 per cent compared with 40 per cent in 2009).

Users of social networking sites reported that they used them to talk to friends and family they see a lot (78 per cent), those they rarely see (75 per cent), and to look for old friends and people they have lost contact with (47 per cent) (Ofcom, 2010b). In 2009, just under half of all Internet users in the UK said that using the Internet had increased the contact they have with friends (49 per cent) or family (47 per cent) who live further away. Lower proportions stated that their contact with friends (24 per cent) or family (18 per cent) who live nearby had increased. Just over one in five Internet users said that they had increased contact with people with whom they share personal interests and hobbies (22 per cent), and around 1in 10 had increased contact with people with different interests and hobbies (11 per cent).

Social networking site users can manage the security settings of their profiles to control who can see their pages and the information contained on them. Many profiles can be limited so that only a user's 'friends' are allowed to see their profile pages. The use of such controls has grown: in 2009, 80 per cent of social networking site users in the UK had a profile that could be seen only by their friends, compared with 48 per cent in 2007. The proportion of users with open profiles, that could be seen by anyone, fell from 44 per cent in 2007 to 17 per cent in 2009 (Ofcom, 2010b). This seems to indicate that social networking users are becoming more security conscious. See also Internet security.

Although many Internet users use online communication to keep in touch with existing friends and family, they may also use the Internet as a means to meet new people.

Figure 5   **Internet users[1] who met people online: by place met, 2009**

Great Britain
Percentages

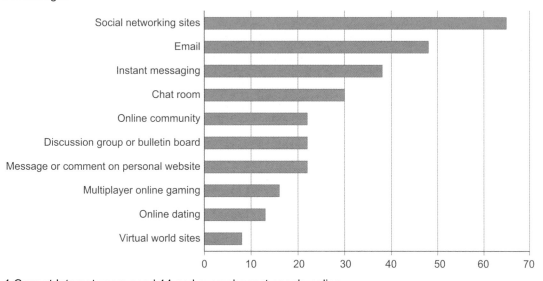

1 Current Internet users aged 14 and over who met people online.
Source: Oxford Internet Survey, (Dutton, Helsper and Gerber, 2009)

According to the 2009 Oxford Internet Survey the most common place for Internet users aged 14 and over in Great Britain to meet others online was social networking sites (with 65 per cent of people who met people online meeting them through social networking sites) **(Figure 5)**. This was followed by email (48 per cent), instant messaging (38 per cent) and chat rooms (30 per cent). Just over a fifth of those who met someone online met them through comments on personal websites or online communities or discussion groups or bulletin boards all at 22 per cent.

Internet security

Some Internet users may have unfavourable experiences online. For example, Internet security can be compromised in a variety of ways. According to the ONS Opinions Survey, in 2010 over half (54 per cent) of those aged 16 and over in the UK who had accessed the Internet in the 12 months prior to interview, had received unsolicited emails (also known as spam or junk mail) (ONS, 2010). These are often of a commercial nature, sent indiscriminately to multiple mailing lists, individuals, or newsgroups. Just over 3 in 10 Internet users (31 per cent) had caught a virus or other infection on their computer resulting in loss of information or time, and 5 per cent had experienced financial losses due to fraud when using a payment card. Abuse of personal information sent on the Internet and/or other privacy violations was relatively rare, having been experienced by 4 per cent. Financial losses as a result of responding to fraudulent messages (phishing)[iv] or being redirected to a fake site and providing personal information was experienced by 3 per cent. Two per cent of users reported that children had accessed inappropriate websites or had been connecting with potentially dangerous people from a computer in the household.

To overcome some of these security problems many people use some kind of security software or tool. In 2010, 85 per cent of UK adults who had used some sort of security software in the 12 months prior to interview had used a virus checking program or anti-spy ware program. Other common forms of security were hardware or software firewalls, used by 63 per cent, and email filtering to prevent spam used by 45 per cent (ONS, 2010).

Entering personal details online can be problematic since it may lead to unauthorised access to sensitive information such as usernames, passwords, Internet banking logons and credit card details which may then be used fraudulently. As knowledge about the potential risks of the Internet grows, there are an increasing number of users taking more care over Internet security.

Figure 6   **Internet users who would be happy to enter personal details online: by type of details[1]**

United Kingdom

Percentages

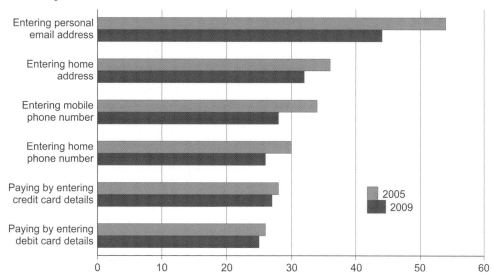

1 Internet users aged 16 and over and stated that they would be happy to do this when asked 'I'm going to read out some types of information you could be asked to enter when you're on the internet, and for each one I'd like you to say how you would feel about doing this in terms of any security concerns'.

Source: UK Adults' 'Media Literacy (Ofcom 2010b)

People are becoming more concerned about providing personal information online. Between 2005 and 2009 the proportion of UK Internet users aged 16 and over who were happy to provide six main types of personal information fell **(Figure 6)**. Less than half (44 per cent) of respondents in 2009 said they would be happy to provide their personal email address compared with 54 per cent in 2005. Those willing to provide their home address decreased from 36 per cent to 32 per cent over the same period. Those happy to enter credit card or debit card details remained at around the same level in both years at around 27 per cent and 25 per cent respectively.

Children's use of new technology

Adults in older age groups are known as 'digital immigrants' as they grew up without digital technology and adopted it later. However, children under 16 are 'digital natives', since digital technology already existed when they were born, and hence they have grown up with it around them. According to Ofcom, around 9 in 10 (92 per cent) children aged 5 to 15 live in a household with a digital television service. Four in five (82 per cent) children aged 5 to 15 live in a household with access to the Internet through a home computer and 9 in 10 children aged 5 to15 (89 per cent) live in a household with a games console (Ofcom, 2010c).

Figure 7   **Age at which child first acquired a mobile phone,[1] 2009**

United Kingdom
Percentages

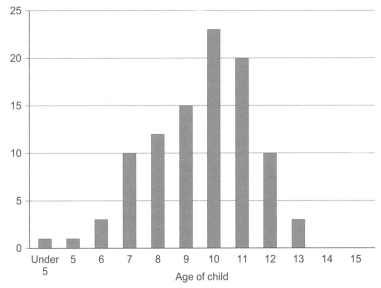

1 Parents of children aged 5 to 15 with a mobile phone were asked the question ' How old was your child when they first got a mobile phone that makes and receives calls?'

Source: UK Children's Media Literacy (Ofcom, 2010c)

Personal ownership of a mobile phone increases with age. In 2009 just under 1 in 10 (9 per cent) children aged 5 to 7 owned a mobile phone compared with 50 per cent of those aged 8 to 11 and 88 per cent of those aged 12 to 15 (Ofcom,2010c). Just over a quarter (27 per cent) of children aged 5 to 15 owning a mobile phone in 2009 had first acquired one by the time they were eight years old and just under two-thirds (65 per cent) by the time they were 10 years old **(Figure 7)**. Girls were more likely than boys to have a mobile phone by the time they are 10 years old (68 per cent of girls compared with 61 per cent of boys).

Table 5

Main reasons for children's dislikes of selected ICTs:[1] by age group, 2009

United Kingdom   Percentages

	8–11	12–15
Internet		
Websites that take too long to load	36	42
Too many adverts	16	23
Mobile phone		
It costs too much money	36	49
People can send hurtful messages to other people	12	15
Sometimes people get bullied on them	13	14
Online gaming		
Sometimes spend too much time on them	19	34
Someone might pretend to be my age and get to know me	15	16
Strangers might find out information about me	14	16

1 Children aged 8 to 15 were shown a list of dislikes and asked if any of them related to their use of the media shown in the table.
Source: UK Children's Media Literacy (Ofcom, 2010c)

New technologies are perceived to have drawbacks as well as advantages. Children aged 8 to 15 who used the Internet, watched television, used a mobile phone or played games over the Internet were prompted with a list of dislikes and were asked if any of them applied to them. Children aged 8 to 11 and 12 to 15 were most likely to state that 'websites take too long to load' (36 per cent and 42 per cent respectively) and that there were 'too many adverts' on the Internet (16 per cent and 23 per cent respectively) **(Table 5)**.

Cost issues were the main drawback associated with mobile phones, with over a third (36 per cent) of those aged 8 to 11 and just under a half (49 per cent) of those aged 12 to 15 agreeing that mobile phones 'cost too much money'. 'Spending too much time' was the most common drawback identified by just under a fifth (19 per cent) of those aged 8 to 11 and just over a third (34 per cent) of those aged 12 to 15 who played games over the Internet. Around 14 to 16 per cent of users of the Internet among both age groups of felt that 'someone might pretend to be my age and get to know me' or 'strangers might find out information about me' as things they did not like about online gaming (Ofcom, 2010c). For more information on children's use of new technology see also Social Networking and New technology in education and work.

Table 6   **Parents' concerns[1] about online risks, 2008**

United Kingdom   Percentages

	Very much worried	Rather worried	Rather not worried	Not at all worried	Don't know/Not applicable
Might see sexually/violently explicit images on the Internet	37.4	21.4	13.4	27.4	0.4
Might be a victim of online grooming[2]	32.2	14.2	11.2	41.2	1.2
Might get information about self-harm, suicide, anorexia	25.8	16.2	10.4	46.2	1.4
Might see sexually/violently explicit images via the mobile phone	25.8	10.4	9.4	42.2	12.2
Could be bullied online by other children	24.2	15.2	16.6	42.6	1.4
Could be bullied by other children via the mobile phone	23.8	13.4	9.4	39.8	13.6
Might become isolated from other people if spending too much time online	21.2	19.6	10.2	48.4	0.6
May give out personal/private information online	16.4	17.0	24.0	42.2	0.4

1 Parents or guardians of children aged 6 to 17 were asked the question 'How worried are you that when your child is using the Internet or mobile phone, he/she might...'

2 Child grooming is the deliberate actions taken by an adult to form a trusting relationship with a child, with the intent of later having sexual contact.

Source: Flash Eurobarometer 248 (European Commission, 2008)

Parents are particularly concerned about their children using the Internet or a mobile phone. According to a Flash Eurobarometer[v] report in 2008, 59 per cent of parents and guardians of those aged 6 to 17 in the UK were very or rather worried that their child might see sexually or violently explicit images on the Internet, while 46 per cent were very or rather worried that their child could become a victim of online grooming **(Table 6)**. Child grooming is the term used to describe deliberate actions taken by an adult to form a trusting relationship with a child, with the intent of later having sexual contact. Parents or guardians were also very or rather worried that their child might get information about self-harm, suicide, anorexia (42 per cent) or might become isolated from other people if spending too much time online (41 per cent).

Children also use social networking sites. According to Ofcom, in 2009 31 per cent of children aged 8 to 11 in the UK and 69 per cent of those aged 12 to 15, used the Internet at home for social networking at least once a week. One in four (25 per cent), Internet users aged 8 to 12 had a page or profile on Facebook, Bebo or MySpace, despite the fact that the minimum age for setting up a profile on these social networking sites is 13 years (Ofcom, 2010c).

According to the *National Letter Writing Day* report produced by World Vision, more children aged 7 to 14 in the UK are communicating via the social networking site, Facebook, or by e-mail than using more traditional methods such as handwritten letters. In 2010, 49 per cent of children had written an email or a message on Facebook in the week prior to being interviewed, compared with only 14 per cent who had written a handwritten letter in the same period. Likewise, 52 per cent received a message on Facebook or email compared with 9 per cent who had received a handwritten letter (World Vision, 2010).

New technology in education and work

New technology has had an impact on education, training and the labour market. Children use computers and the Internet at school and at home for educational purposes as do adults for training, while computers and the Internet are becoming commonplace in the workplace. The use of new technology also allows people to find jobs online and to be able to work from their home.

Figure 8   **Use of Internet for schoolwork or homework,[1] 2009**

United Kingdom

Percentages

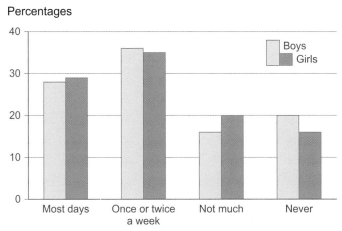

1 Children aged between 5 and 15 who use the Internet at home were asked how often they used the internet for schoolwork and homework and were given the above responses to choose from.

Source: Media Literacy Tracker 2009 (Ofcom, 2010d)

In 2009, similar proportions of boys and girls in the UK aged between 5 and 15 used the Internet on 'most days' (28 and 29 per cent respectively), or once or twice a week (36 and 35 per cent) for schoolwork or homework **(Figure 8)**. More boys than girls never used the Internet for this purpose – 20 per cent of boys compared with 16 per cent of girls.

Using the Internet for school or homework increases with age. Among 12 to 15-year-olds, 45 per cent used the Internet for school or homework most days. This proportion dropped to 23 per cent for 8 to 11-year-olds, and to just 10 per cent for 5 to 7-year-olds (Ofcom, 2010d).

Table 7   **Children's trust in internet content for schoolwork or homework, 2009[1]**

United Kingdom   Percentages

	Boys		Girls	
	Aged 8–11	Aged 12–15	Aged 8–11	Aged 12–15
All is true	42	37	37	36
Most is true	41	52	46	49
Some is true	11	8	9	12
Don't know	6	3	8	4

1 Children aged between 8 and 15 who use the internet to visit sites for schoolwork or homework were asked 'Do you believe that all of the information you see is true, most of it is true or just some of it is true?'

Source: Media Literacy Tracker 2009 (Ofcom, 2010d)

Trust in Internet content varies by age and gender. In 2009 39 per cent of pupils aged 8 to 11 and 36 per cent of those aged 12 to 15 in the UK believed that all of the information they see on the Internet for schoolwork or homework is true (Ofcom, 2010d). Forty-four per cent of 8 to 11-year-olds believed that 'most is true' compared with 51 per cent of children aged 12 to 15.

Just over 4 in 10 (42 per cent) of boys and under 4 in 10 (37 per cent) girls aged 8 to 11 believed that all of the information they see on the Internet for homework or schoolwork is true **(Table 7)**. The percentage of boys believing this dropped to 37 per cent at age 12 to 15 while the percentage of girls aged 12 to 15 remained fairly stable at 36 per cent. Just over 4 in 10 (41 per cent) of boys and 46 per cent of girls aged between 8 and 11 believed that of the information seen on the Internet, 'most is true'. Around half of both boys and girls aged 12 to 15 stated that most of the Internet content used for schoolwork and homework was mostly true (52 per cent and 49 per cent respectively).

The number of users of computers with Internet access in the workplace in the UK increased by 27 per cent between 2004 and 2008, from the equivalent to 5.9 million employees in 2004 to 7.5 million in 2008. The largest increase over the period was for businesses employing over 1,000 staff at 36 per cent, from 2.2 million in 2004 to 3.0 million in 2008. This was followed by businesses employing between 10 and 49 employees, from 1.3 million to 1.7 million, a 31 per cent increase. Those employing between 50 and 249, and 250 and 999, employees increased by 23 per cent (1.3 to 1.6 million), and 18 per cent (1.1 to 1.3 million) respectively (ONS, 2008).

Between 2004 and 2008 there was also an increase in the proportion of workers using computers with Internet access as a proportion of all workers using computers. Firms employing between 10 and 49 staff saw an increase of around 8 percentage points (81.3 per cent to 89.5 per cent) over the period. However, companies employing larger numbers of staff increased only slightly, by 0.5 percentage points (71.0 per cent to 71.4 per cent) for those with over 1,000 staff and around 3 percentage points (78.6 per cent to 81.3 per cent) for those employing between 250 and 999 staff (ONS, 2008).

Figure 9   Teleworkers[1] by region, 2009[2]

United Kingdom

Percentages

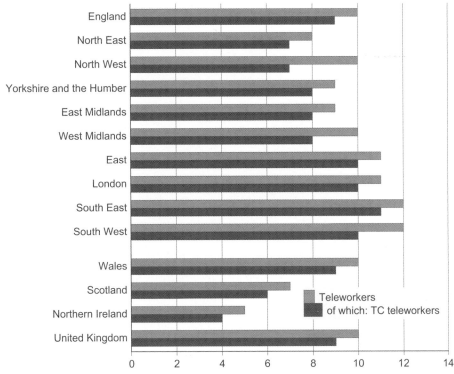

1 Teleworkers are defined in the Labour Force Survey as those people who work mainly at home or mainly in different places using home as a base, who use both a telephone and a computer to carry out their work at home. TC Teleworkers are a subgroup of Teleworkers who could not work at home (or use home as a base) without using both a telephone and computer. Proportion of all in employment.

2 Data are at Q2 (April–June), are not seasonally adjusted.

Source: Labour Force Survey, Office for National Statistics

In England, the Government Office Regions with the highest proportion of teleworkers in 2009 were the South East and South West, both at 12 per cent of all those in employment **(Figure 9)**. These regions were closely followed by London and the East at 11 per cent. The region with the lowest proportion of teleworkers was the North East at 8 per cent. This compares with the UK, England and Wales averages each at 10 per cent. Northern Ireland had the lowest rate of the countries of the UK at 5 per cent.

The English region with the highest percentage who couldn't work at home without both a telephone and a computer (TC teleworkers) was the South East at 11 per cent of all in employment. The North East and North West had the lowest rates at 7 per cent each. The UK, Wales and England averages for TC teleworkers were each 9 per cent, with Scotland at 6 per cent. Northern Ireland also had the lowest rate for TC teleworkers at 4 per cent.

e-Commerce and online banking

e-Commerce is the buying and selling of products or services over electronic systems such as the Internet and other computer networks. According to the ONS experimental Internet sales series, the value of Internet retail sales in Great Britain increased from an average weekly value of £169.3

million in November 2006 to £446.1 million in July 2010. In July 2010 the value of Internet retail sales was 8.0 per cent of total retail sales.

Table 8   **Buying or ordering goods or services over the Internet:[1] EU-27 comparison**

Percentages

	2006	2007	2008	2009		2006	2007	2008	2009
United Kingdom	**45**	**53**	**57**	**66**	Spain	15	18	20	23
Denmark	55	56	59	64	Poland	12	16	18	23
Netherlands	48	55	56	63	Latvia	8	11	16	19
Sweden	55	53	53	63	Estonia	7	9	10	17
Luxembourg	44	47	49	58	Cyprus	7	10	9	16
Germany	49	52	53	56	Hungary	7	11	14	16
Finland	44	48	51	54	Portugal	7	9	10	13
France	22	35	40	45	Italy	9	10	11	12
Austria	32	36	37	41	Greece	5	8	9	10
Ireland	28	33	:	37	Lithuania	4	6	6	8
Belgium	19	21	21	36	Bulgaria	2	3	3	5
Malta	14	20	22	34	Romania	1	3	4	2
Slovakia	11	16	23	28					
Czech Republic	13	17	23	24	**EU-27 average**	**26**	**30**	**32**	**37**
Slovenia	13	16	18	24					

1 People aged 16 to 74, buying or ordering goods or services for private use over the Internet in the 12 months prior to interview.

Source: Eurostat (table isoc_ec_ibuy)

Among EU-27 member states the use of the Internet to order goods and services was most common in the UK: in 2009, 66 per cent of adults aged 16 to 74 in the UK had done so in the 12 months prior to interview **(Table 8)**. Denmark had the second highest proportion at 64 per cent followed by the Netherlands with 63 per cent. Seventeen countries fell below the EU-27 average of 37 per cent in 2009 with Lithuania, Bulgaria and Romania having the lowest proportions with 8 per cent, 5 per cent and 2 per cent respectively (see Table 1 for proportion of households with Internet access in these countries). All member states recorded increases in the use of the Internet for these purposes between 2006 and 2009, but the increase for France was the greatest at 23 percentage points.

While the majority of Internet users in the EU-27 are confident that transactions over the Internet are completely or rather safe (58 per cent), there is a minority of users who do not have confidence in online transactions. According to a 2008 Flash Eurobarometer report, just over 1 in 10 (11 per cent)

Internet users in the EU held the opinion that such transactions are not safe at all and just under 2 in 10 (19 per cent) believed that they were not really safe. These proportion were slightly lower in the UK with 5 per cent of Internet users stating that such transaction are not safe at all and 11 per cent stating they were not really safe (Eurobarometer, 2009).

Table 9   **Adults who used Internet banking:[1] EU-27 comparison**

Percentages

	2006	2007	2008	2009		2006	2007	2008	2009
Estonia	79	83	84	87	Spain	32	31	35	39
Finland	81	84	87	87	Slovenia	32	36	38	39
Netherlands	73	77	79	82	Poland	23	29	35	38
Sweden	66	71	73	79	Slovakia	25	27	37	38
Denmark	69	70	73	77	Portugal	27	29	32	37
Latvia	44	50	64	66	Italy	25	31	32	34
Belgium	46	52	57	62	Cyprus	18	31	30	32
Luxembourg	58	58	60	62	Czech Republic	22	24	25	31
France	39	51	59	60	Hungary	18	23	23	27
Lithuania	35	43	51	56	Greece	9	12	13	13
Malta	42	48	52	56	Romania	3	7	7	7
United Kingdom	**42**	**45**	**49**	**55**	Bulgaria	6	5	4	4
Germany	46	49	51	53					
Austria	44	44	47	48	**EU-27 average**	**40**	**44**	**47**	**50**
Ireland	40	42	:	46					

1 Individuals aged 16 to 74 who had used the Internet in the last three months who had used the Internet for given activity within the three months prior to survey.
Source: Eurostat (table isoc ci i)

Apart from ordering goods and services online, the Internet can be used for other financial transactions such as Internet banking. Among EU-27 member states in 2009 Estonia and Finland had the highest proportions of adults aged 16 to 74 who had used the Internet in the three months prior to interview for Internet Banking both at 87 per cent **(Table 9)**. Over half of adults (55 per cent) in the UK have used Internet banking, a rise of 6 percentage points compared with 2008 and 5 percentage points higher than the EU-27 average of 50 per cent. Bulgaria and Romania had the lowest proportions at 4 per cent and 7 per cent respectively. Since 2006, Latvia has shown the largest growth (22 percentage points) in the proportion of adults using Internet banking, rising from 44 per cent in 2006 to 66 per cent in 2009. In comparison the use of Internet banking in the UK rose by 13 percentage points over the same period.

Losses through online banking fraud largely due to malware[vi] which targets vulnerabilities in customers' PCs, rather than the banks' own systems totalled £59.7 million in the UK in 2009. These losses have risen from £12.2 million in 2004, increasing each year except between 2006 and 2007 when they fell from £33.5 million to £22.6 million. There were also more than 51,000 phishing incidents recorded during 2009, a 16 per cent increase on the amount seen in 2008 (UK Cards, 2010).

e-Government

Information and communication technology (ICT) allows citizens to access public services through media such as the Internet at times and in ways that suit them. An increasing amount of national and local government services are now available on the Internet.

According to the ONS Opinions Survey, 46 per cent of adults aged 16 and over in the UK who had accessed the Internet in the 12 months prior to interview had obtained information from a public authority website in 2010. Just over 3 in 10 (31 per cent) had downloaded official forms while under 3 in 10 (27 per cent) had sent filled in forms over the Internet electronically. Men tended to use online public services more than women. Just under half (49 per cent) of men UK who had accessed the Internet in the 12 months prior to interview had obtained information from government websites compared with 43 per cent of women, while a third (33 per cent) had downloaded official forms compared with 28 per cent of women.

Table 10   **Online availability of public services: EU-27 comparison[1]**

Percentages

	2006	2007	2009		2006	2007	2009
Austria	83	100	100	Italy	58	70	70
Malta	75	95	100	Luxembourg	25	40	68
Portugal	60	90	100	Latvia	10	30	65
United Kingdom	**71**	**89**	**100**	Hungary	50	50	63
Slovenia	65	90	95	Czech Republic	30	55	60
Sweden	74	75	95	Lithuania	40	35	60
Estonia	79	70	90	Slovakia	20	35	55
Finland	61	67	89	Poland	20	25	53
Denmark	63	63	84	Cyprus	35	45	50
Ireland	50	50	83	Greece	30	45	45
Spain	55	70	80	Romania	.	35	45
France	65	70	80	Bulgaria	.	15	40
Netherlands	53	63	79				
Germany	47	74	74	**EU27**	.	**59**	**74**
Belgium	47	60	70				

1 Percentage of online availability of 20 basic public services. The indicator shows the percentage of the 20 basic services which are fully available online that is for which it is possible to carry out full electronic case handling. For example if in a country 13 of the 20 services were measured as being 100 per cent available on-line and one service was not relevant (for example does not exist), the indicator is 13/19 which is 68.4 per cent. Measurement is based on a sample of URLs of public web sites agreed with Member States as relevant for each service.

Source: EuroStat (table tsiir120)

In 2009 out of 20 basic public services (12 for citizen and 8 business services) 74 per cent were available online on average across the EU-27 member states, an increase from 59 per cent in 2007 **(Table 10)**. Citizen services included car registration and library services, while business services included environment-related permits and public procurement. In 2009 this online availability measure varied from 100 per cent in Austria, Malta, Portugal and the UK, while Bulgaria had the lowest online availability at 40 per cent. The growth of online public service provision also varied from country to country with some countries recording large increases between 2006 and 2009, such as Latvia (55 percentage points), Luxembourg (43 percentage points) and Portugal (40 percentage points). Public service online availability in the UK increased by 29 percentage points between 2006 and 2009.

Directgov is the UK government's website for citizens of England and Wales, providing a single point of access to public sector information and services. The site enables people to complete tasks online such as booking a driving test, finding a job, paying road tax and finding local services such as NHS clinics and nurseries. There is a similar site for Northern Ireland (nidirect).

Figure 10   **Number of visits to Direct.gov[1]**

United Kingdom

Millions

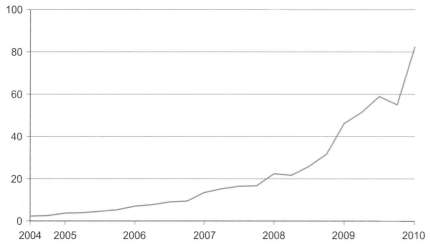

1 Data are at July to December for 2004 and January to March for 2010.

Source: Direct.gov

According to data from Directgov, the number of visits to the Directgov website has increased since it began from 2.3 million in Q3 2004 to 82.5 million in Q1 2010 **(Figure 10)**. In 2009 the site received an average (mean) of almost 52.9 million visits per quarter. Directgov offers information on a number of services in the UK. In 2009 the three most visited were motoring (35.1 million visits), money, tax and benefits (20.8 million visits), and education and learning (17.3 million visits).

Around half of the 70 million motoring transactions carried out each year where users have a choice of channel to use take place using the Department for Transport's electronic and online services. There was a steady increase in the proportion of candidates booking their theory and practical driving tests electronically in the UK between March 2007 and March 2009. In March 2009, just over four-fifths (82 per cent) of theory tests (around 1.4 million) were booked online or electronically, compared with 69 per cent in March 2007. Just under three-quarters (73 per cent) of practical tests (around 1.6 million) were booked online or electronically in March 2009 compared with 59 per cent in March 2007. Candidates can also change the date of their booked practical test online if they need to. More than half (54 per cent) were amended this way in March 2009 (DfT, 2009).

Renewing car tax or making a Statutory Off-Road Notification (SORN) through the Electronic Vehicle Licensing (EVL) system enables customers to complete a transaction either online or over the telephone. According to the Department for Transport, around 17 million of 45 million car tax renewals were carried out this way in 2008/09, a rise of 3 million from 2007/08 (DfT, 2009).

Figure 11   Her Majesty's Revenue and Customs online returns

United Kingdom

Percentages

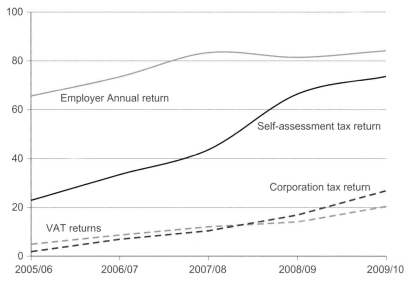

Source: HM Revenue and Customs

Her Majesty's Revenue and Customs (HMRC) is primarily responsible for the collection of taxes and the payment of some forms of state support. In 2006 Lord Carter of Coles report 'Review of HMRC online services', recommended that HMRC should aim for universal electronic delivery of tax returns by 2012 (Carter, 2006). Although it is not compulsory to file Self-Assessment tax returns online, in 2009/10, 74 per cent (6.6 million) were filed online, an increase of 51 percentage points from 2005/06 when 23 per cent (2.0 million) were filed online **(Figure 11)**.

All employers who use Pay as You Earn (PAYE) to deduct their employee's income tax are required to submit the Employer Annual Return (P35) form to HMRC. This form summarises the end of year payroll totals of these deductions for all their employees combined. Since 2006, all employers with 50 or more employees were required to file their returns online and since April 2010 all employers, other than those with a legitimate exemption, are required to file this form online. This has resulted in an increase in online filing of P35s from just under two-thirds (66 per cent) in 2005/06, equivalent to 1.1 million returns, to 84 per cent in 2009/10, a rise of 19 percentage points. From April 2009 all employers with 50 or more employees have been required to send their starter and leaver information online (forms P45, P46 etc.) and from April 2011 all employers will be required to send these forms online too.

There has been an online filing service for VAT returns for several years, but until very recently the extent of customer usage was comparatively low, at less than 20 per cent of all returns received. However, as from 1 April 2010, it was made compulsory for the following customers to file their returns online and pay any VAT due electronically:

- all existing customers whose turnover was £100,000 or more (excluding VAT) – which accounts for about 1.1million customers (out of the 1.9 million customer base)

- all new customers registering for VAT on or after that date

Since the vast majority of VAT customers file on a quarterly basis, that meant that the first set of compulsory online returns were due in by 7 August 2010 (covering the period April – June). Just over 71 per cent of the returns received from 8 July to 7 August were filed online. Additionally, registrations for VAT online services (the first step to being able to file online) reached nearly 1.4 million (an increase of about one million on the same date last year), indicating that in excess of 250,000 customers with a turnover of under £100,000 for whom it is not compulsory to make online returns have also converted to online filing.

The Internet has made health information more easily available and accessible. Many organisations in the UK provide health information on the web including NHS Choices, NHS Direct, BBC Health and the private healthcare provider, BUPA. From October 2008 the Health A to Z section of NHS Direct online services was integrated with NHS Choices, which acts as a digital gateway and public front to the NHS, providing a one-stop shop for health and social care.

Table 11   Using Internet to find health information, 2009[1]

England | | | | | Percentages

	Have already done so	Very or fairly likely	Nether likely nor unlikely	Very or fairly unlikely	Would not look for this information on the Internet
To help better manage an existing health condition for myself or a family member	8	36	9	25	22
To check symptoms to determine if I, or a family member, need to go to the GP or A & E	8	30	8	30	24
To help me choose between different treatment options	5	30	9	32	24
To find out which vaccines I, or a family member, need to get	4	28	9	33	26
To find out if I, or my family, have a high risk of developing a condition and should be tested for it	3	29	9	34	25
To find out about healthier lifestyle changes[2]	5	26	9	34	25
To help me choose a hospital or other health service	3	23	10	39	25

1 Respondents were asked, ' How likely are you to use Internet to find information in each of the following situations'?
2. For example quitting smoking or losing weight.
Source: NHS Choices; TNS CAPI, Public Omnibus Survey

The NHS Choices Public Omnibus Survey 2009 found over half (52 per cent) of people aged 16 or over in England had used the Internet to look up health information generally. This survey also asked people how likely they were to use the Internet to find information for selected health related situations. Fairly small proportions had already used the Internet to find health information, but much higher proportions said that they were very or fairly likely to do so in the future **(Table 11)**. Eight per cent of adults aged 16 and over in England stated they had already used the Internet to check symptoms to determine if they or a family member need to go to a GP or A & E, with 30 per cent stating they were very or fairly likely to use it for this purpose. Choosing a hospital or other health service was the least common health related situation for which people said they would use the Internet, with 3 per cent already having done so and 23 per cent very or fairly likely to do so. A similar proportion of people (22 per cent to 26 per cent) would not look for information on the Internet relating to health related situations that are shown in Table 11.

References

Carter, 2006 - Review of HMRC Online Services. Available at www.hmrc.gov.uk/budget2006/carter-review.htm

DfT, 2009 Annual Report and Resource Accounts 2008-09. Available at www.dft.gov.uk/about/publications/apr/ar2009/arra.pdf

Dutton, W., Helsper, E., and Gerber,M. (2009) The Internet in Britain: 2009. Oxford Internet Institute, University of Oxford.

Eurobarometer 2009, Confidence in Information Society. Available at www.ec.europa.eu/public_opinion/flash/fl_250_en.pdf

European Commission (2008. Towards a safer use of the Internet for children in the EU – a parents' perspective: Summary. Available at www.ec.europa.eu/public_opinion/archives/flash_arch_254_240_en.htm

Ofcom (2009a), Accessing the Internet at home: A quantitative and qualitative study among people without the Internet at home by Ipsos Mori. Available at www.stakeholders.ofcom.org.uk/binaries/research/telecoms-research/bbathome.pdf

Ofcom (2009b), CMR 2009: Nations and Regions - Convergence. Available at www.stakeholders.ofcom.org.uk/binaries/research/cmr/converge1.pdf

Ofcom (2009c) the Communications Market Report: United Kingdom, 2009. Available at www.stakeholders.ofcom.org.uk/market-data-research/market-data/communications-market-reports/cmr09/

Ofcom (2010a), the Communications Market Report: United Kingdom, 2010. Available at www.stakeholders.ofcom.org.uk/market-data-research/market-data/communications-market-reports/cmr10/uk/

Ofcom (2010b). UK adults' media literacy. Available at www.stakeholders.ofcom.org.uk/binaries/research/media-literacy/adults-media-literacy.pdf

Ofcom (2010c). UK children's media literacy. Available at www.stakeholders.ofcom.org.uk/binaries/research/media-literacy/ukchildrensml1.pdf

Ofcom (2010d). Ofcom Media Literacy Tracker 2009 consolidated. Available at www.stakeholders.ofcom.org.uk/binaries/research/statistics/mlt_chlidren.pdf

ONS (2006), Internet access, households and individuals 2006 – First release, available at www.statistics.gov.uk/pdfdir/inta0806.pdf

ONS (2007) Focus on the Digital Age – available at www.statistics.gov.uk/StatBase/Product.asp?vlnk=14797&Pos=4&ColRank=1&Rank=144

ONS (2008) 2008 e-commerce Survey of Business datasets. Available at
www.statistics.gov.uk/downloads/theme_economy/ecommerce-2008/2008-datasets.pdf

ONS (2009a). Internet access households and individuals 2009 - Statistical bulletin. Available at
www.statistics.gov.uk/pdfdir/iahi0809.pdf

ONS (2009b). Family Spending 2009. Available at www.statistics.gov.uk/statbase/product.asp?vlnk=361

ONS (2010). Internet access households and individuals 2010 - Statistical bulletin. Available at
www.statistics.gov.uk/StatBase/Product.asp?vlnk=5672

UK Cards, 2010, Banking Fraud Figures Available at
www.cardwatch.org.uk/images/uploads/Fraud%20Figures%20Release%2010%20Mar%2010.pdf?Title=Pr
essReleases

World Vision 2010, National Letter Writing Day Available at
www.worldvision.org.uk/server.php?show=nav.3585

Notes

ⁱ A dependent child is defined as a person aged 15 and under in a household or aged 16 to 17 in full-time education and who is not married.

ⁱⁱ Narrowband: the computer uses the telephone line to dial up for an Internet connection. Because narrowband access uses normal telephone land lines, the quality of the connection can vary and data rates are limited. A narrowband user cannot be online and use the telephone at the same time.

Broadband provides faster data transferral. High-speed Internet connectivity is provided by Digital Subscriber Line (DSL), cable, satellite and wireless service providers. This means that moving from one web-page to another or downloading large amounts of information, such as software, music or games, takes less time. It is also useful when the user has a particular need for quick communication or is engaged in real-time communication, for example, using web-radio or a chat room connection. A broadband connection allows users to use the telephone while online.

ⁱⁱⁱ Examples of digital convergence include:
- A mobile handset can receive voice calls, data, pictures, audio, video and text, all over a 2G/3G network
- Audio-visual content can be accessed using satellite, cable, digital terrestrial and analogue terrestrial platforms, as well as through a fixed broadband connection or over a mobile network

^{iv} Phishing: the practice of sending emails at random, pretending to come from a genuine company, and attempting to trick users into disclosing information.

^v Flash Eurobarometers are ad hoc thematical telephone interviews conducted at the request of any service of the European Commission. Flash surveys enable the Commission to obtain results relatively quickly and to focus on specific target groups, as and when required.

^{vi} Malware: malicious software, which includes computer viruses that are installed on a computer without the user's knowledge, typically by users clicking on a link in an unsolicited email, or by downloading suspicious software. Malware is capable of logging keystrokes thereby capturing passwords and other financial information.

Lifestyles and social participation

Lifestyle is defined as a way of living: the things that a particular person or group of people usually do. Lifestyles are based on individual choices, characteristics, personal preferences and circumstances. In their free leisure time many choose to engage in the arts and culture, read a book, visit the cinema, go on holiday and participate in sporting activities. Social participation includes looking after the family or home and care giving; interpersonal roles of friend and family member; life roles such as student, worker and volunteer; and community roles such as participant in religious, activity based, or voluntary help organisations.

Key points:

Leisure and entertainment activities

- In 2009/10, almost 9 in 10 (89 per cent) of adults aged 16 and over in England watched television in their spare time

- In 2009/10, adults in the UK aged 16 and over spent an average of 3 and a half hours a day watching television, 2 and a half hours using a computer and 1 hour listening to radio

- In 2009, UK teenagers and young adults aged 15 to 24 were the most frequent cinema goers, with 61 million cinema admissions

- In 2009, almost all (98.0 per cent) of single music tracks were purchased digitally, with digital sales increasing by 91.9 per cent between 2007 and 2009

- Sales of books by UK publishers fell by 5.9 per cent from 492 million books in 2007 to 463 million in 2009

- Between 2005/06 and 2009/10 the proportion of adults aged 16 and over visiting a public library in England fell from 48 per cent to 39 per cent

- In 2009, 22 per cent of children aged 8 to 16 stated they enjoy reading very much compared to 10 per cent who do not enjoy reading at all

- In 2010, less than half of adults in Great Britain aged 15 and over read a national daily newspaper (41 per cent): on average since 1981 the proportion reading national newspapers has fallen by approximately 10 percentage points every 10 years

Holidays and day trips

- Holiday visits abroad decreased by 15 per cent from 45.5 million visits in 2008 to 38.5 million visits in 2009, the lowest levels since 2000

- In 2009 Spain remained the most popular destination for UK residents going abroad on holiday (26 per cent of holiday visits), the Irish Republic was the most common destination for UK residents travelling abroad to visit friends and relatives (14 per cent of visits)

- UK residents aged 45 to 54 took the most holiday visits abroad in 2009, with 7.6 million visits

- In 2008/09 around 563,000 households in England had a second home, amounting to 651,000 properties, 58 per cent of which were located outside the UK

- Domestic holiday tourism grew by 12 per cent from 75 million trips within the UK in 2008 to 84 million in 2009

- The most popular type of heritage site visited by adults aged 16 and over in England in 2009/10 was an historical city or town, with 55 per cent of adults visiting these

Sporting activities

- The proportion of adults aged 16 and over in England who participate in active sport for at least 30 minutes in the last four weeks decreases with age: 75 per cent of those aged 16 to 24 compared with 18 per cent of those aged over 75 (figures for 2009/10)

- In 2009, 40 per cent of UK adults who did not practice sport said that lack of time was the main reason

- Over half (55 per cent) of children in school years 1 to 13 in England participated in at least 3 hours of high quality Physical Education (PE) and out of hours sport in a typical week in 2009/10

Social and political participation

- A total of 29.7 million valid votes were cast in the 2010 UK general election, a turnout rate of 65.1 per cent, higher than in the previous two general elections

- In England in 2009/10, 29 per cent of adults aged 16 and over volunteered informally at least once a month and 54 per cent at least once a year, compared with 35 per cent and 62 per cent in 2008/09

- In 2009/10, 34 per cent of adults aged 16 and over in England had engaged in some sort of civic participation, a decrease from 38 per cent in 2001

- The estimated total amount donated to charity in 2009/10 was £10.6 billion, up 3.9 per cent compared with 2008/09 when £10.2 billion was donated. However donations have not returned to the pre recession record level of £11.3 billion recorded in 2007/08

Religion

- In 2008/09, 32 per cent of adults aged 16 and over in England and Wales who reported being Christian actively practiced their religion, compared with 80 per cent of those who reported being Muslim

- In 2008/09, 30 per cent of adults aged 16 and over in England and Wales who practiced their religion stated that this influenced the school to which they sent or would send their child

Leisure and entertainment activities

Leisure, or free time, is a period of recreational time spent on non-compulsory activities when individuals can choose to spend their time doing the things they enjoy.

People spend this time taking part in a wide range and variety of activities, depending on individual preferences and lifestyles.

Table 1   **Selected activities performed in free time:[1] by age, 2009/10**

England   Percentages

	16–24	25–34	35–44	45–64	65 and over	All aged 16 and over
Watching television	88	85	88	89	92	89
Spending time with friends/family	87	85	85	83	82	84
Listening to music	90	78	76	74	69	76
Shopping	71	73	74	69	69	71
Reading	53	62	65	72	73	67
Eating out at restaurants	66	71	70	72	65	69
Days out	54	65	68	67	59	63
Internet/emailing	79	77	71	57	24	59
Sport/exercise	63	63	60	55	35	54
Gardening	16	36	51	64	62	49
Going to pubs/bars/clubs	59	63	50	44	33	48
Going to the cinema	72	61	55	42	21	48

1 Respondents were shown a list of activities and asked to pick the things they did in their free time in the last year prior to interview. The most popular activities performed by all adults aged 16 and over are shown in the table.

Source: Taking Part: The National Survey of Culture, Leisure and Sport, Department for Culture, Media and Sport (2010)

Watching television has been a common pastime for decades and continues to be so in 2009/10. The latest data from the Taking Part Survey[i] show that watching television in their free time was still the most common activity reported by adults aged 16 and over in England (**Table 1**). Eighty nine per cent of all adults watched television in their free time and it was the most popular activity for age groups from 35 upwards. However, for those aged 16 to 24 spending time listening to music was selected by the highest proportion of respondents (90 per cent). Those aged 25 to 34 reported spending time with friends and family as their joint top activity along with watching television, with 85 per cent of respondents in this age group saying that they did these activities in their free time.

Overall, for adults aged 16 and over, spending time with family and friends was the second most popular activity at 84 per cent, listening to music came next at 76 per cent and shopping was fourth at 71 per cent.

The overall averages also hide differences between the age groups for other activities. Comparing the 16 to 24 age group with those aged 65 and over, the activities which were reported less frequently as age increased were listening to music (90 per cent and 69 per cent respectively); Internet and emailing (79 per cent and 24 per cent); sport and exercise (63 per cent and 35 per cent); going out to pubs, clubs or bars (59 per cent and 33 per cent); and going out to the cinema (72 per cent and 21 per cent). Again comparing the youngest and oldest age groups, the activities which were reported more frequently as age increased were reading (53 per cent and 73 per cent) and gardening (16 per cent and 62 per cent).

Figure 1   Minutes per day spent using each medium: by age, 2009/10

United Kingdom

Hours and minutes per day

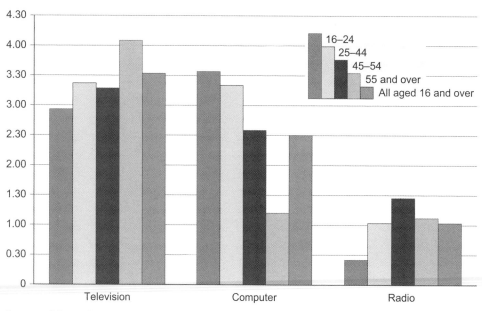

Source: Ofcom (2010)

Estimates from Ofcom show that on average in 2009/10, adults aged 16 and over in the UK spent 3 hours and 32 minutes a day watching television, 2 and a half hours using a computer per day and 1 hour and 2 minutes a day listening to a radio (**Figure 1**). Those aged 55 and over, spent the most time a day watching television at 4 hours and 5 minutes a day, while those aged 16 to 24 spent the least at an average of 2 hours and 56 minutes a day.

Radio listening was highest among those aged 45 to 54 at 1 hour 27 minutes and, as was the case with time spent watching television, people aged 16 to 24 spent the least time listening to the radio at 25 minutes a day.

Conversely, people aged 16 to 24 spent the highest amount of time using a computer, an average of 3 hours and 34 minutes a day. The amount of time spent using a computer decreased with age, with those aged 25 to 44 spending 3 hours and 20 minutes a day doing so, falling to 2 hours and 35 minutes a day for those aged 45 to 54 and to 1 hour and 12 minutes a day for those aged 55 and over.

As shown in Table 3 of the *Social Trends 41* e-society chapter[ii], released in November 2010, Ofcom research also shows that watching television is the media activity adults claim they would miss the most if they were deprived of it. In 2009 half of adults in the UK aged 16 and over (50 per cent) cited television as their most-missed medium, although this varied with age. Among younger adults (16 to 24-year-olds) the figure drops to 36 per cent, compared with 57 per cent among adults aged 55 to 64 (Ofcom, 2010).

Going to the cinema to watch the latest film releases remains a common pastime for many. According to the UK Film Council, cinema-going was not affected by the recession. There were 174 million cinema visits in the UK in 2009, an increase of 5.6 per cent compared with 2008, while box office receipts grew to a record £944 million. The number of admissions in 2009 was the highest since 2002 when admissions reached 176 million. However, cinema admissions were at their highest in 1946 when there were 1.6 billion ticket sales (UK Film Council, 2010).

Figure 2   Annual cinema admissions: by age

United Kingdom

Millions

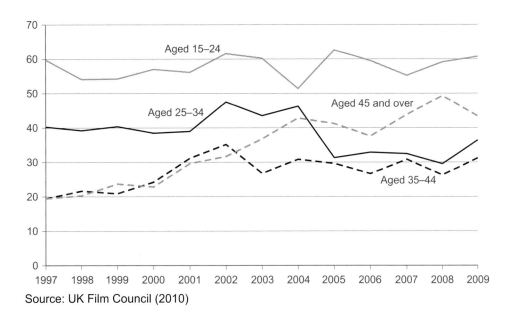

Source: UK Film Council (2010)

As in previous years, teenagers and young adults in the UK aged 15 to 24 were the most frequent cinema-goers in 2009, accounting for 61 million cinema admissions (**Figure 2**). The number of admissions for people aged 45 and over gradually increased from 19 million in 1997 to 49 million in 2008, while those aged 25 to 34 fell from 40 million admissions to 30 million over the same period.

Between 2008 and 2009 changes in cinema admissions differed by age: while there were increases in the 15 to 24, 25 to 34 and 35 to 44 age groups, there was a decrease of 12 per cent for people aged 45 and over. However, the over 45s are still the second largest group of cinema-goers, after overtaking people aged 25 to 34 in 2005. In 2009 people aged 45 and over accounted for 43 million admissions, followed by those aged 25 to 34 at 36 million admissions and those aged 35 to 44 at 31 million admissions.

A survey of cinema-goers' opinions, conducted by YouGov in 2010, found that half of cinema-goers (50 per cent) who had visited the cinema in the previous 6 months thought that the cinema had become too expensive. However, 61 per cent of cinema-goers also agreed that 'you can't beat watching a film on the big screen'. Additionally, 27 per cent agreed that films are a 'great way to escape from the modern world', while 19 per cent agreed that 'the cinema was too noisy when they preferred it to be quiet' and 14 per cent thought that there was 'not enough choice these days at the cinema' (YouGov, 2010a).

According to the Entertainment Retailers Association (ERA), sales in the recorded music sector in the UK in 2009 were only slightly affected by the recession. Unit sales were down just 0.5 per cent and the value of sales was down only 0.8 per cent from 2008 (Entertainment Retailers Association, 2010).

Figure 3   Retail sales of music (singles and albums units sold)

United Kingdom
Millions

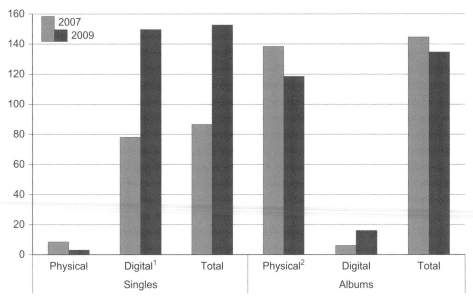

1 Combines single track and album sales.
2 Up-weighted from Official Charts Company data to reflect 100 per cent of the market.
Source Official Charts Company (ERA, 2010)

Estimates from the Official Charts Company (OCC) shows that almost all single music tracks (98.0 per cent) were purchased digitally instead of in physical formats in the UK in 2009 and digital sales increased by 91.9 per cent between 2007 and 2009. Overall volume of sales of singles have grown. In 2007 consumers purchased a combined 87 million physical and digital singles. This increased by 76.3 per cent in 2009 to 153 million (**Figure 3**). In part, this increase could be attributed to the increased availability of tracks to download as singles on music download services such as iTunes, where people can easily purchase individual tracks rather than whole albums. This could also be one of the reasons for the decrease of 7.0 per cent in the number of albums sold, from 145 million units in 2007 to 135 million units in 2009 (Entertainment Retailers Association, 2010).

While sales of albums in digital format increased by 160 per cent between 2007 and 2009, digital sales of albums are still much lower than for digital singles, accounting for 12 per cent of all album sales, with 16 million digital units sold in 2009 compared with 119 million physical units sold. The sales of albums in physical format fell between 2007 and 2009, dropping 14 per cent from 138 million units in 2007 to 119 million in 2009 (Entertainment Retailers Association, 2010).

The value of the UK book market in 2009 at end-purchaser prices was estimated at £3.4 billion according to The Publishers Association. This represented a decrease of 2.9 per cent from 2008, when the value was £3.5 billion, but an increase of 3.8 per cent from £3.3 billion in 2005 (Publishers Association, 2009).

Figure 4   **UK sales by UK publishers (units sold): by category**

United Kingdom

Millions

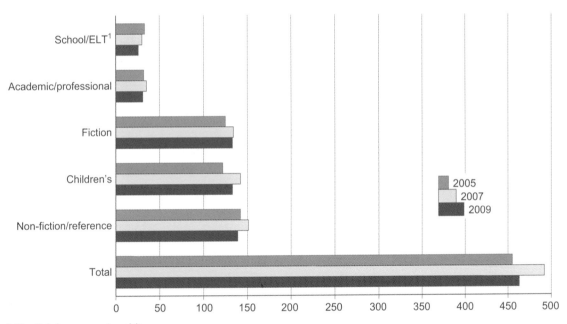

1 English language teaching.

Source: The Publishers Association (2009)

Overall in 2009 there were decreases in UK publishers' net book unit sales to the UK market in each of the five main categories when compared with 2007, while between 2005 and 2007 total unit sales increased (**Figure 4**). However, although there was a 5.9 per cent drop in unit sales to 463 million in 2009 from 492 million in 2007, sales in 2009 remained 1.8 per cent higher than the 455 million units sold in 2005.

Between 2005 and 2009, the overall growth in book sales was driven by increases in children's and fiction books: 9.5 per cent and 6.3 per cent respectively. During the same period, sales in all other categories decreased, with school/English language teaching (ELT) showing the largest decrease at 22.7 per cent.

Other data from the Publishers Association show that the total revenue from UK publishers' sales of digital products is rising, reaching just over £150 million in 2009. This could be split approximately by £5 million digital sales to the general consumer, £8 million sales for consumer reference, £8–9 million sales for school/ELT and £130 million sales for academic/professional. Overall, digital sales represent around 4 to 5 per cent of the combined physical and digital sales of UK publishers in 2009 (Publishers Association, 2009).

Reading is a common pastime, with many choosing to borrow books from libraries as an alterative to purchasing personal copies. According to data from Public Lending Right (PLR) in 2008/09, fiction remained the most common genre of borrowed books from UK libraries, accounting for 44.3 per cent of loans. The next most common genre was children's and educational books at 34.8 per cent, followed by family, home and practical interests at 5.3 per cent (Public Lending Right, 2009).

Overall the number of books issued by public libraries in England has fallen from 279 million in 2004/05 to 264 million in 2008/09. The number of adult fiction books issued decreased from 135 million to 122 million over the same period. Adult non-fiction issues fell from 68 million to 60 million and child non-fiction from 12 million to 11 million. However, child fiction books issued increased in number from 63 million books in 2004/05 to 69 million in 2008/09 (Museums, Libraries & Archives, 2010a).

There were 10 million active borrowers (those that visit the library for the purpose of borrowing books) from public libraries in England in 2008/09, a decline of 10 per cent from 11 million borrowers in 2004/05. However the number of books issued each year per active borrower increased over the same period from 24 books per active borrower in 2004/05 to 26 books in 2008/09 (Museums, Libraries & Archives, 2010a).

Figure 5   Proportion of adults[1] who have visited a public library in the last year

England

Percentages

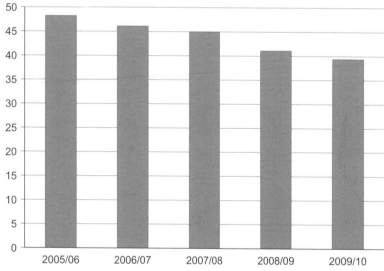

1 Adults aged 16 and over.

Source: Taking Part: The National Survey of Culture, Leisure and Sport, Department for Culture, Media and Sport (2010)

The Taking Part Survey shows that between 2005/06 and 2009/10 there was a steady decrease in the proportion of adults aged 16 and over visiting a public library in England, from 48 per cent to 39 per cent (**Figure 5**). The largest year-on-year decrease was between 2007/08 and 2008/09 with a fall of 3.9 percentage points.

In 2009/10, women were more likely than men to have visited a public library in the last 12 months, 43 per cent having done so compared with 36 per cent of men. Looking at the frequency with which adults visit the library, 5.4 per cent visited a public library at least once a week; 12.8 per cent visited at least once a month; 10.9 per cent visited 3 to 4 times a year and 7.9 per cent visited 1 to 2 times a year (Department for Culture, Media and Sport, 2010).

The Taking Part Survey also reported that in 2009/10, 93.8 per cent of those people who had visited a public library had done so in their own time while 10.3 per cent visited for the purpose of academic study and 3.1 per cent for paid work (Department for Culture, Media and Sport, 2010).

Figure 6   **Children's[1] attitude towards reading, 2009**

United Kingdom

Percentages

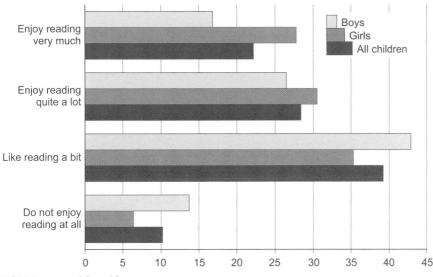

1 Children aged 8 to 16.

Source: The National Literacy Trust (forthcoming publication)

Research from the National Literacy Trust found that the majority of children get some amount of enjoyment out of reading. **Figure 6** shows that among children aged 8 to 16, 22 per cent stated that they enjoy reading very much, while 28 per cent said they enjoy reading quite a lot. However the most frequent response was that they like reading a bit (39 per cent) while 10 per cent stated that they did not enjoy reading at all.

Overall, girls enjoyed reading more than boys, with 28 per cent of girls compared with 17 per cent of boys saying that they enjoy reading very much and 31 per cent of girls and 27 percent of boys stating the enjoy reading quite a lot.

Since the literacy trust first conducted this survey in 2005, levels of enjoyment of reading have remained unchanged. However, the gap in reading enjoyment between boys and girls appears to have widened, increasing from a percentage point difference of 11 per cent in 2005 to a 15 per cent point difference in 2009 (National Literacy Trust, forthcoming publication).

Table 2   Readership of national daily newspapers[1]

Great Britain   Percentages

	1971	1981	1991	2001	2010
The Sun	17	26	22	20	16
Daily Mail	12	12	10	12	10
Daily Mirror	34	25	22	12	7
The Daily Telegraph	9	8	6	5	4
The Times	3	2	2	3	3
Daily Express	24	14	8	4	3
Daily Star	-	9	6	3	3
The Guardian	3	3	3	2	2
The Independent	-	-	2	1	1
Financial Times	2	2	2	1	1
Any national daily newspaper[2]	-	72	62	53	41

1 In the 12 months to June each year. Proportion of adults, aged 15 and over, who have read or looked at the individual newspaper for at least two minutes on the day before interview.

 2 Includes the above newspapers and The Daily Record in 1981, and The Sporting Life and the Racing Post in 2001.

Source: National Readership Survey (2010)

The estimated proportion of adults aged 15 and over in Great Britain who read a national daily newspaper has been decreasing over the past 30 years, from 72 per cent of adults in 1981 to 41 per cent in 2010 according to the National Readership Survey (**Table 2**). On average since 1981 the proportion reading national newspapers has fallen by approximately 10 percentage points every 10 years.

The most commonly read newspaper in 2010 was The Sun, though readership has decreased from 26 per cent of adults who read newspapers in 1981 to 16 per cent in 2010. In fact, most tabloid newspapers experienced substantial falls in readership over this period. The Daily Mirror suffered the largest decrease, falling from being the most commonly read in 1971, when 34 per cent of adults read it, to 7 per cent in 2010. The Daily Express has also suffered a similar fate, falling from 24 per cent in 1971 to 3 per cent in 2010.

The readership of most other newspapers has also remained stable, fluctuating by only one or two percentage points over the period. These are mainly the broadsheets, which have kept their smaller but more targeted audiences.

The decline in the proportion of those reading national newspapers may be affected by the availability of news websites which are free on the Internet. A recent survey by YouGov asked whether respondents would consider paying for access to online news sites. Only 2 per cent stated yes they definitely would, while a further 4 per cent said they would pay but only for special content, for instance content not available elsewhere. A further 6 per cent stated they might possibly pay for online content, while the majority (83 per cent) stated that they would not consider paying for access to newspapers online (YouGov, 2010b).

Holidays and day trips

During extended periods of free time, many people choose to take holidays away from home to get away from their everyday lives. The choice of destination is based not only on the amount of money available to spend on a holiday but also on individual preferences, which may range from gaining new experiences, seeing new cultures, enjoying a different climate or spending time relaxing.

Holidays are such an important part of life for many that they spend all year saving up for their week or two away. However, according to the International Passenger Survey, in 2009 UK residents cut back substantially on the number of holidays taken abroad: holiday visits abroad decreased by 15 per cent from 45.5 million visits in 2008 to 38.5 million in 2009. This was the lowest level since 2000 when 36.7 million holiday visits were taken (Office for National Statistics, 2010).

Table 3   UK residents' holiday visits abroad: by destination[1]

United Kingdom   Percentages[2]

	1981	1991	2001	2008	2009
Spain	22	21	28	27	26
France	27	26	18	17	18
Italy	6	4	4	5	5
United States	5	7	6	5	5
Portugal	3	5	4	5	4
Greece	7	8	8	4	4
Turkey	-	1	2	4	4
Ireland	4	3	4	3	3
Cyprus	1	2	4	2	2
Netherlands	2	4	3	2	2
Other countries	23	20	20	26	25
All destinations (=100%) (millions)	13.1	20.8	38.7	45.5	38.5

1 As a proportion of all holidays taken abroad by residents of the UK. Excludes business trips and other miscellaneous visits.

2 Percentages may not add up to 100 per cent due to rounding.

Source: International Passenger Survey, Office for National Statistics (2010)

In 2009, 26 per cent of UK residents travelling abroad for their holiday went to Spain (**Table 3**). France is also a popular destination, in second place in the top 10 destinations with 18 per cent of holiday visits. However, France has seen a decline in popularity over the years, falling from 27 per cent in 1981.

Both Italy and the United States had 5 per cent of visits in 2009, followed by Portugal, Greece and Turkey with 4 per cent. Turkey has seen a rise in the share of visits for holiday purposes, increasing from 1 per cent in 1991 to 4 per cent in 2009. In contrast, the percentage of those visiting Greece for a holiday has fallen by half, from 8 per cent in 1991 to 4 per cent in 2009.

Those taking trips abroad to visit friends and relatives also decreased in 2009: by 6.4 per cent from 12.4 million visits in 2008 to 11.6 million visits in 2009 (Office for National Statistics, 2010).

Table 4   UK residents' visits to friends and relatives[1] abroad: by destination

United Kingdom				Percentages[2]
	1999	2003	2006	2009
Irish Republic	19	16	15	14
France	12	13	11	11
Poland	1	1	6	9
Spain	6	9	9	8
Germany	7	6	6	5
USA	9	7	6	5
India	3	3	3	4
Italy	3	4	4	4
Netherlands	5	4	3	3
Pakistan	2	3	3	3
Other countries	34	34	35	36
All destinations (=100%) (millions)	6.6	8.5	12.0	11.6

1 As a proportion of all visits to friends and relatives taken abroad by residents of the UK. Excludes business trips and other miscellaneous visits.

2 Percentages may not add up to 100 per cent due to rounding.

Source: International Passenger Survey, Office for National Statistics (2010)

For visits for this purpose the Irish Republic remained the most common destination throughout the period shown in the table, accounting for 14 per cent of such trips in 2009 (**Table 4**). However, although the Irish Republic remained top of the list for visits, there has been a steady decrease in the proportion of visits made there to visit friends and relatives from 19 per cent in 1999. The second most common country visited to see friends and relatives was France with 11 per cent of visits, followed by Poland with 9 per cent. Poland has seen the largest rise of the top 10 destinations, increasing from 1 per cent of all visits in 1999. This reflects the change in international migration patterns following Poland's accession to the European Union in May 2004.

Figure 7   **Holiday visits abroad by UK residents: by age**[1]

United Kingdom

Millions

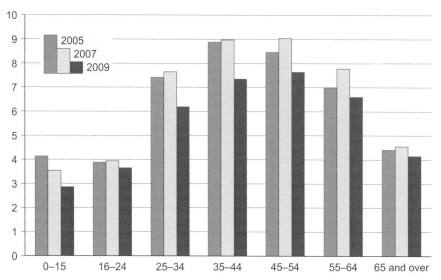

1 Does not include visits for UK residents whose age was unknown.

Source: International Passenger Survey, Office for National Statistics (2010)

In 2009 people aged 45 to 54 took the most holidays abroad (7.6 million visits or 19.9 per cent of all holidays visits abroad), people aged between 35 and 44 made 7.3 million visits (19.1 per cent) and those aged 55 to 64 made 6.6 million visits (17.2 per cent) (**Figure 7**).

In comparison, people aged 65 and over took 4.1 million visits abroad (10.8 per cent), young adults, aged 16 to 24 made 3.6 million visits, accounting for 9.5 per cent of visits, and those aged 0 to 15 years went on 2.9 million holiday visits abroad (7.4 per cent).

The number of holiday visits abroad in all age groups was lower in 2009 than 2005. The largest percentage decreases in visits between 2005 and 2009 were by those aged 0 to 15 (31 per cent) and people aged 35 to 44 (17 per cent).

The English Housing Survey[iii] estimates that around 563,000 households in England in 2008/09 had one or more second homes, either in the UK or abroad, and that these households owned 651,000 properties.

Figure 8   **Households in England with a second home abroad:[1] by location of second home, 2008/09**

England
Thousands

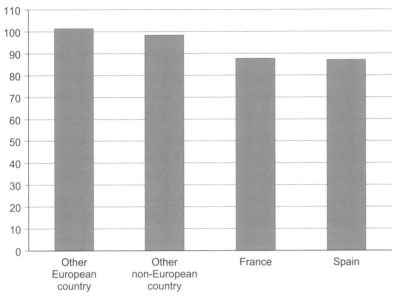

1 The definition of second homes excludes properties owned elsewhere that are let out as someone else's main residence.
Source: English Housing Survey, Department for Communities and Local Government (2009a)

The most often reported reason for a second home was its use as a holiday home or weekend residence (50 per cent of responding households). About 58 per cent or 375,000 properties used as second homes were located outside the UK, with nearly three-quarters located in Europe. The most popular locations were France (88,000 properties) and Spain (87,000) (**Figure 8**). There were 101,000 properties throughout other European countries which were second homes for English households and around 98,000 in non-European countries (Department for Communities and Local Government, 2009a).

In 2008/09, 36.9 per cent of second homes by households resident in England were themselves located in England (240,000 properties). A further 36,000 (5.5 per cent) of second homes were in other parts of the UK (Department for Communities and Local Government, 2009a).

Table 5   **Domestic trips¹ for holidays and visiting friends and relatives: by country**

United Kingdom   Millions

	England	Northern Ireland	Scotland	Wales	United Kingdom
Holidays					
2006	62.2	1.6	8.5	7.4	79.2
2007	60.9	1.4	8.6	6.5	76.8
2008	59.5	1.5	8.3	6.6	75.4
2009	67.4	1.6	8.9	7.0	84.3
Visiting friends and relatives					
2006	20.3	0.4	1.9	1.1	23.7
2007	21.2	0.4	1.9	1.3	24.7
2008	18.0	0.3	1.6	0.8	20.6
2009	18.1	0.4	1.4	1.0	20.8

1 Trips refer to a visit with at least one night's stay.

Source: Visit England, Visit Scotland, Visit Wales, Northern Ireland Tourist Board (2010)

Domestic holidays within the UK, also known as 'staycations', are becoming more popular, according to statistics from the United Kingdom Tourism Survey[iv]. Figures show that between 2008 and 2009 domestic holidays in the UK increased by 12 per cent. However, between 2006 and 2008 domestic holidays were declining (**Table 5**). The increase between 2008 and 2009 could in part be due to the economic crisis which began in April 2008 with financial constraints meaning that holidays in the UK were preferred to those abroad. As with previous years the majority of domestic holiday trips in 2009 (79.9 per cent, 67 million trips) were taken in England, followed by Scotland with 10.5 per cent of holiday trips, then Wales with 8.3 per cent and Northern Ireland with 1.9 per cent.

The number of trips taken to visit friends and relatives in the UK were very similar in 2008 and 2009 at around 21 million. However, between 2007 and 2008 trips taken to visit friends and relatives decreased by 17 per cent (25 million trips in 2007 compared with 21 million trips in 2008).

The proportion of trips to visit friends and relatives in each UK country is very similar to the proportions for holidays in the UK.

According to the Taking Part Survey, 70 per cent of adults aged 16 and over in England visited a heritage site in 2009/10, largely unchanged since 2005/06 (Department for Culture, Media and Sport, 2010).

Figure 9   **Proportion of adults[1] who have visited a heritage site in the last year, 2009/10**

England
Percentages

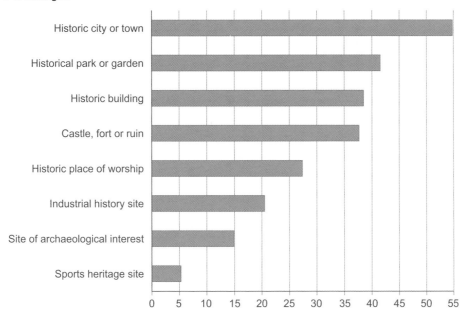

1 Adults aged 16 and over.
Source: Taking Part: The National Survey of Culture, Leisure and Sport, Department for Culture, Media and Sport (2010)

In 2009/10, as in previous years, the most popular type of heritage site visited was an historic city or town, with 55 per cent of adults who had visited a heritage site visiting these, followed by historic parks or gardens at 42 per cent and historic buildings at 39 per cent (**Figure 9**).

In 2009/10, 29.3 per cent of adults had visited an historic site three or four times in the past year and 26.1 per cent had been once or twice, while 12.5 per cent had been at least once a month and 2.5 per cent at least once a week. For people aged 75 and over, 51 per cent had visited one or more heritage sites in the last year. Those aged between 45 and 64 were the most likely to have visited a heritage site, with 77 per cent having done so in 2009/10. Men were marginally more likely to have visited a heritage site than women in 2009/10 (71 per cent compared with 68 per cent) (Department for Culture, Media and Sport, 2010).

According to a 2010 Eurobarometer Survey on attitudes towards tourism when deciding on a holiday destination, 32 per cent of EU citizens named the location's environment as the key consideration. This was followed by cultural heritage (25 per cent) and the options for entertainment (16 per cent). However, UK respondents placed cultural heritage as their top reason for choosing a holiday destination (30 per cent of respondents), followed by entertainment at 24 per cent and the environment at 15 per cent (Eurobarometer, 2010).

Sporting activities

Many people engage in a wide variety of sport or physical activities in their free time. Individuals do this for many different reasons, ranging from improving health to having fun. The 2009/10 Taking Part Survey recorded that over half, 53 per cent, of adults aged 16 and over in England, had taken part in 30 minutes of active sport in the four weeks prior to being interviewed.

Figure 10   **Proportion of adults[1] who have participated in active sport: by age, 2009/10**

England
Percentages

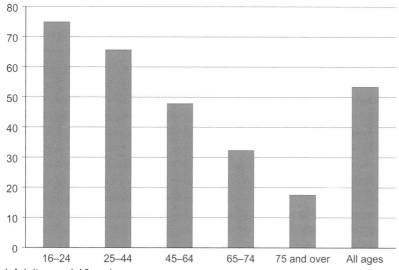

1 Adults aged 16 and over.
Source: Taking Part: The National Survey of Culture, Leisure and Sport, Department for Culture, Media and Sport (2010)

The proportion of those who did participate in active sport in the four weeks prior to interview decreased with age in 2009/10 (**Figure 10).** Of those aged 16 to 24, 75 per cent participated compared to 18 per cent of those aged 75 and over. Additionally, those who take part in active sport every day make up 6.7 per cent of the population, whereas those who take part on 21 to 27 days out of every 28 day period make up 3.3 per cent (Department for Culture, Media and Sport, 2010).

Not only were there differences in participation between the age groups, but there were also differences between men and women: 59 per cent of men had done active sport in the last four weeks prior to interview compared with 48 per cent of women. Among all adults doing sporting activities in the last four weeks, the top activities reported were health, fitness, gym or conditioning activities with 15.1 per cent and indoor swimming or diving with 14.7 per cent reporting having done this, followed by cycling at 10.5 per cent. Outdoor football and jogging, cross-county and road-running came next with around 6.7 per cent stating they did these (Department for Culture, Media and Sport, 2010).

Although exercise and physical activity plays an important role in the lives of many, this is not the case for all and the reasons for not participating in forms of exercise vary from person to person. A Eurobarometer report conducted in October 2009 on sport and physical activity collected reasons preventing participation in sport. The most common reason was given as a lack of time (45 per cent of respondents on average across the EU) (**Figure 11**). A further 13 per cent of respondents on average said that disability or illness prevented them from taking part and 7 per cent did not like competitive activities. Only 3 per cent cited a lack of suitable facilities close to where they live and a further 3 per cent said they do not have friends with whom to do sports (Eurobarometer, 2009).

Figure 11   **Reasons preventing practicing sport more regularly,[1] 2009**

EU–27
Percentages

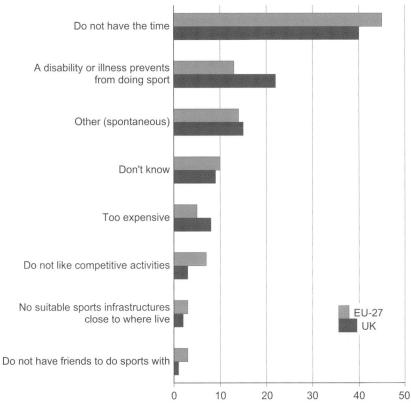

1 Respondents aged 15 and over were asked 'From the following reasons, what is currently preventing you the most from practicing sport more regularly?'.

Source: Eurobarometer (2009)

Not having the time to practice sport was the main reason provided by respondents from the UK, although the UK was below the EU-27 average with 40 per cent of UK respondents citing lack of time as a reason compared with the EU-27 average of 45 per cent.

However, the UK was above the EU-27 average for those citing a disability or illness preventing them from practicing sport. In fact, at 22 per cent, the UK's proportion was the highest across the EU-27. The UK was also above the EU-27 average for those stating that practicing sport was too expensive; with 8 per cent, the UK, along with Greece was the second highest country citing this, behind Portugal where 13 per cent cited cost as a reason.

According to the same Eurobarometer report, 61 per cent of EU citizens who participated in sport or some other form of physical exercise did so to improve their health, while 41 per cent exercise to improve their fitness, 39 per cent to relax and 31 per cent to have fun (Eurobarometer, 2009).

The most common reason given by UK respondents was to improve health (65 per cent). The UK is also above the EU average for improving fitness (53 per cent) and to have fun (37 per cent).Thirty three per cent of UK respondents participated in sport or physical exercise to relax (Eurobarometer, 2009).

The Physical Education and Sport Strategy[v] aims to get more young people in England taking part in high quality physical education (PE) and sport inside and outside of school. Results from the latest survey show that across all school age groups (years 1 to 13), over half (55 per cent) of all pupils participated in at least 3 hours of high quality PE and out of hours school sport in a typical week in 2009/10, (**Figure 12**). This is an increase of 5 percentage points from the 2008/09 survey (Department for Education, 2010).

Figure 12   **Pupils who participate in physical education and out of hour's school sport:[1] by year group**

England

Percentages

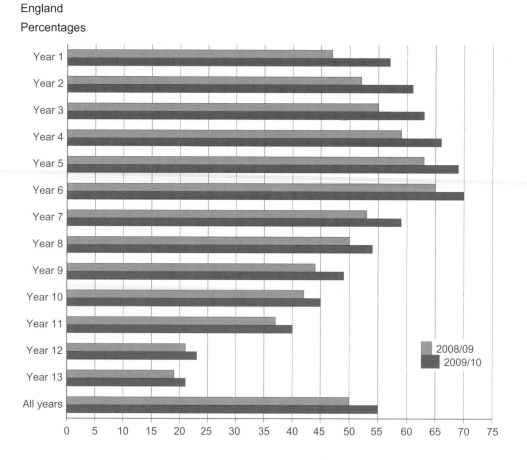

1 Based on pupils who participated in at least three hours of high quality PE and out of hours school sports in a typical week.
Source: Department for Education (2010)

Between 2008/09 and 2009/10 all year groups saw improvements in the percentage of pupils participating in at least 3 hours of high quality PE and out of school sports in a typical week. The largest improvements were for years 1 to 3, while the smallest improvements were for years 12 and 13. Overall, year 1 saw the highest improvement from 47 per cent of pupils in 2008/09 to 57 per cent in 2009/10, followed by year 2 which increased from 52 per cent to 61 per cent and year 3, from 55 per cent to 63 per cent. In comparison, years 12 and 13 both increased by only 2 percentage points from 21 per cent to 23 per cent and 19 per cent to 21 per cent respectively.

Overall, in 2009/10, participation levels were highest in years 5 and 6, with year 5 reaching 69 per cent and year 6 recording the highest participation at 70 per cent. The survey also reported that boys were more likely than girls to participate in at least 3 hours of PE and out of school sport (58 per cent and 52 per cent respectively) (Department for Education, 2010).

Social and political participation

The latest general election in May 2010 saw an increase in those who voted compared with the previous two elections but remained below levels seen in the 1997 election.

Table 6   **General election turnout**[1]

United Kingdom			Percentages
1945	72.8	Oct 1974	72.8
1950	83.9	1979	76.0
1951	82.6	1983	72.7
1955	76.8	1987	75.3
1959	78.7	1992	77.7
1964	77.1	1997	71.4
1966	75.8	2001	59.4
1970	72.0	2005	61.4
Feb 1974	78.8	2010	65.1

1 Percentage of registered electorate who cast a valid vote.
Source: 1945-1997 Rallings and Thrasher (2007); 2001-2010 The Electoral Commission (2010)

Out of the 45.6 million people who were registered to vote in the 2010 general election, a total of 29.7 million valid votes were cast, an overall turnout rate of 65.1 per cent (**Table 6**). This was an increase of approximately 2.5 million voters compared with the 2005 UK general election, when turnout was 61.4 per cent. The 2005 and 2010 elections showed an upward trend in turnout rates since the 2001 general election when turnout fell to 59.4 per cent from 71.4 per cent in 1997. However, turnout figures are still relatively low .The percentage of the electorate who have turned out to vote was highest in 1950 at 83.9 per cent and was above 70.0 per cent between 1945 and 1997 (Electoral Commission, 2010) (Rallings, C. and Thrasher, M, 2007).

For the 2010 general election, turnout in England, Scotland and Wales increased compared with the 2005 general election. Turnout in England rose from 61.3 per cent in 2005 to 65.5 per cent in 2010, Wales increased from 62.6 per cent to 64.8 per cent, while Scotland was up from 60.8 per cent to 63.8 per cent. However, turnout in Northern Ireland decreased by 5.3 percentage points, from 62.9 per cent in 2005 to 57.6 per cent in 2010 (Electoral Commission, 2010).

Among those registered to vote in 2010, turnout among postal voters was higher than for those who voted at polling stations, with 83 per cent of people who were sent a postal ballot pack voting, compared with 63 per cent of those who were required to vote at a polling station. While 15 per cent of eligible voters were issued with a postal vote in 2010 (an increase from 4 per cent in 2001), the majority of votes were cast in polling stations. In total more than 22 million votes, representing just over 82 per cent of all votes, were cast in around 40,000 polling stations across the UK (Electoral Commission, 2010).

Research conducted by Ipsos MORI on behalf of the Electoral Commission for the 2010 UK general election found that the majority of the people in the UK were satisfied with the procedure for voting. In this survey, three-quarters (75 per cent) of respondents (including those who said they did not vote), were very or fairly satisfied with the procedure for voting, with only 13 per cent saying they were dissatisfied (Electoral Commission, 2010).

Among those who said they had voted, 80 per cent said they were satisfied with the voting process. Overall the satisfaction levels were highest among those aged 55 and over, of whom 83 per cent were satisfied compared with 67 per cent of 18 to 34-year-olds (Electoral Commission, 2010).

The 2009 British Social Attitudes survey[vi] found that 57.6 per cent of people thought it was a person's duty to vote. A further 23.3 per cent stated that they only voted if they cared who won and 17.5 per cent thought it was not worth voting. There has been a steady increase in the proportion of people who believe that it is not worth voting, from 8.1 per cent in 1991 to 11.2 per cent in 2000 and 17.5 per cent in 2009 (British Social Attitudes, 2009).

The government's 'Big Society' aims to create a climate that empowers local people and communities, building a big society that will 'take power away from politicians and give it to people' (Num10, 2010). Volunteering, civil participation and charity work play a large role in this vision.

Table 7   Participation[1] in voluntary activities

England   Percentages

	Formal volunteering[2]		Informal volunteering[3]	
	At least once a month	At least once a year	At least once a month	At least once a year
2001	27	39	34	67
2003	28	42	37	63
2005	29	44	37	68
2007/08	27	43	35	64
2008/09	26	41	35	62
2009/10	25	40	29	54

1 Participation by adults aged 16 and over.

2 Formal volunteering: giving unpaid help through groups, clubs or organisations to benefit other people or the environment.

3 Informal volunteering: giving unpaid help as an individual to people who are not relatives.

Source: Citizenship Survey, Department for Communities and Local Government (2010)

The Citizenship Survey[vii] collects information on both formal and informal volunteering. In England in 2009/10, 40 per cent of adults aged 16 and over volunteered formally at least once in the 12 months prior to interview, with 25 per cent having volunteered formally at least once a month (**Table 7**).

Levels of informal volunteering were higher than levels of formal volunteering, for both those who volunteered once a month and at least once a year, however both have shown decreases. In

2009/10, 54 per cent of adults volunteered informally at least once in the 12 months prior to interview, a decrease from 62 per cent in the previous year, the largest decrease observed. An estimated 29 per cent volunteered informally at least once a month, a decrease from 35 per cent in the previous year.

There were some variations by age in the levels of volunteering. In 2009/10, those aged 75 years and over were less likely to participate in formal volunteering at least once a year (29 per cent) than any other age group. Those aged 75 years and over were also less likely to participate in informal volunteering at least once a year (40 per cent) than any other age group (Department for Communities and Local Government, 2010).

Although overall volunteering appears to be decreasing, according to data from Museums, Libraries and Archives (MLA) volunteering in public libraries in England, increased by 22 per cent between 2006/07 and 2008/09. In the museums, libraries and archives sector, 38,570 people volunteered in 2008/09, with over half of these, 20,805 volunteers, being in museums and galleries, a further 15,001 volunteering in libraries and 2,764 volunteers working in archives (Museums, Libraries & Archives, 2010b).

Museums and galleries also received the highest number of volunteer hours per volunteer with an average of 265 volunteered hours of support per volunteer in 2008/09. Despite the lower numbers of volunteers within archives, this area had a higher number of average hours per volunteer at 74 hours, compared with libraries at 33 hours (Museums, Libraries & Archives, 2010b).

A survey conducted by YouGov questioned adults in Wales about their motivation to take part in voluntary activities. It found that 64 per cent of those who volunteered stated they did so to help others. The next most common reason, given by 48 per cent of respondents, was that 'it gives me a sense of personal achievement/satisfaction'. This was followed by 'to promote a cause/campaign' at 34 per cent, to 'meet new people/make friends' at 27 per cent and 26 per cent stated that they volunteered to 'learn/develop new skills' and 'to have fun'. Only 14 per cent said that they volunteered to 'further my career' (YouGov, 2010c).

Figure 13   Participation[1] in civic engagement

England

Percentages

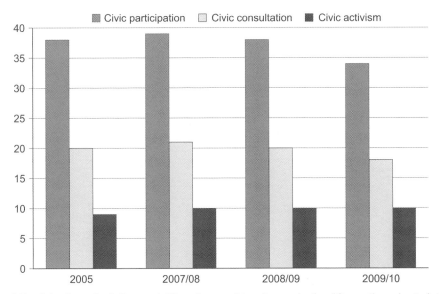

1 Participation of adults aged 16 and over at least once in the 12 months prior to interview.

Source: Citizenship Survey, Department for Communities and Local Government (2010)

Civil engagement is also reported on through the Citizenship Survey, which measures levels of participation in three broad strands: civic participation[viii], civic consultation[ix] and civic activism[x] (Department for Communities and Local Government, 2010).

In 2009/10 in England, 10 per cent of adults aged 16 and over had participated in civic activism in the 12 months prior to interview, slightly higher than in 2005 (9 per cent) but the same level as in 2007/08 (**Figure 13**). The proportion of people engaged in some form of civic participation has been falling gradually, from 38 per cent in 2001 to 34 per cent in 2009/10. Participation in civil consultation has also fallen, with 18 per cent of people actively engaged in 2009/10 compared with 21 per cent in 2007/08 (Department for Communities and Local Government, 2010).

According to a report from Charities Aid Foundation and National Council for Voluntary Organisations, over half of all adults aged 16 and over in the UK donated to charitable causes in 2009/10. In a typical month, 56 per cent donated (equivalent to 28.4 million adults), 2 percentage points higher than in 2008/09. The estimated total amount donated in 2009/10 was £10.6 billion, an increase of 3.9 per cent or around £400 million, after adjusting for inflation, compared with 2008/09 when £10.2 billion was donated. However donations have not returned to the pre recession record level of £11.3 billion recorded in 2007/08 (Charities Aid Foundation/National Council for Voluntary Organisations, 2010).

Table 8   Giving to charity: by age

United Kingdom   Percentages[1]

	2006/07	2007/08	2008/09	2009/10
16–24	42	42	38	39
25–44	57	55	55	58
45–64	60	63	57	63
65 and over	54	57	58	56
All adults	56	56	54	56

1 For some years the percentages differ slightly from those shown in some previous reports, this is because the percentages for all years have been recalculated to be consistent with improvements in methods of weighting and syntax.

Source: Charities Aid Foundation and National Council for Voluntary Organisations (2010)

In 2009/10, as in previous years the likelihood of giving to charitable organisations was lower in the 16 to 24 age group than in the older age groups, the percentage of those in this age group, giving fell from 42 per cent in 2006/07 to 39 per cent in 2009/10. The largest increase in the proportion of people giving between 2008/09 and 2009/10 was by people aged 45 to 64, up by 6 percentage points (**Table 8**). This age group had the highest proportion of people giving to charity in 2009/10, as in all previous years back to 2006/07, except 2008/09 when those aged 65 and over had the highest proportion of people giving to charity.

In 2009/10, as in previous years, women were more likely to donate than men; 61 per cent of women gave to charity compared with 52 per cent of men. In previous years, men who donated gave slightly more on average than women but in 2009/10 women and men gave similar amounts on average (£31). Donors were most likely to support medical research (32 per cent), children and young people (25 per cent) and hospitals (24 per cent). In 2009/10 overseas causes were also supported by 24 per cent of donors, higher than in previous years (Charities Aid Foundation/National Council for Voluntary Organisations, 2010).

In 2009/10 cash was still the most popular method of giving, with half of all donors (50 per cent) using this method compared with 29 per cent who gave by direct debit. Other methods included buying goods (25 per cent) and buying raffle tickets (20 per cent). Although cash was the most common method of giving, it did not account for the largest share of the value of donations. The total amount given by cheque or card was particularly high in 2009/10 and accounted for the largest share of the total amount donated, 29 per cent compared with 23 per cent in 2008/09. The total amount given using this method does fluctuate from year to year, while the total amount given by direct debit is more consistent, although the share of total donations accounted for by direct debits decreased slightly from 24 per cent in 2008/09 to 22 per cent in 2009/10. In 2009/10, 7 per cent of donors had made donations online, an increase of 3 percentage points from 4 per cent in 2008/09 (Charities Aid Foundation/National Council for Voluntary Organisations, 2010).

Religion

The 2008/09 Race, Religion and Equalities Topic Report based on data from the Citizenship Survey, shows that 82 per cent of adults aged 16 and over in England and Wales reported having a religion in 2008/09, while 18 per cent reported having no religion. The largest proportion of those with a religious affiliation reported being Christian, with 72 per cent stating that this was their religion. The next most common religious groups reported were Muslims (4 per cent) and Hindus (2 per cent), while 1 per cent reported being Sikh and 1 per cent reported being Buddhist. A further 3 per cent of people responded 'other religion' (Department for Communities and Local Government, 2009b).

Figure 14   **Adults[1] practicing a religion as a proportion of those having that religion,[2] 2008/09**

England & Wales
Percentages

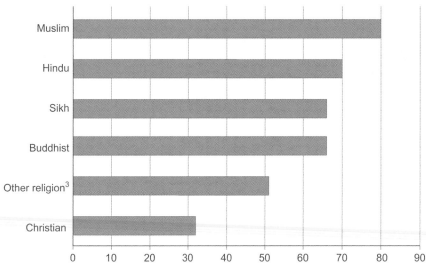

1 Figures based on adults aged 16 and over who reported having a religion.
2 Figures based on combined sample comprised of a core sample and an ethnic minority boost.
3 Jewish respondents included in 'other religion' due to small numbers.
Source: Citizenship Survey, Department for Communities and Local Government (2009b)

The proportion of those who had identified a religion and also said that they actively practised it varied according to the religion. Only 32 per cent of those who reported themselves as Christians actively practised their religion (**Figure 14**). In contrast, 80 per cent of Muslims actively practised their religion, the highest proportion of those with a religion who actively practiced. Two-thirds or more of Hindus, Sikhs and Buddhists actively practised their religion (70 per cent, 66 per cent and 66 per cent respectively). Among people in the 'other religion' category, 51 per cent said that they were actively practising.

Overall, women were more likely than men to say that they actively practised their religion, 42 per cent of women who reported a religion were actively practising compared with 31 per cent of men. People aged 50 and over were also more likely to actively practise their religion than those aged 16 to 29: 41 per cent and 29 per cent respectively (Department for Communities and Local Government, 2009b).

The same report also stated that 94 per cent of people who said that they actively practised their religion felt that they could practise their religion freely in Britain. Additionally, in 2008/09, 52 per cent of people thought that there was more religious prejudice 'today' than there was five years ago, a decrease from 62 per cent in 2007/08 (Department for Communities and Local Government, 2009b).

Figure 15   Influence of religion on day-to-day life,[1] 2008/09

England & Wales
Percentages

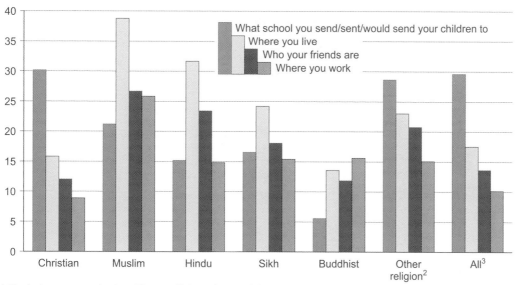

1 Excludes respondents with no religion, those with missing answers or religion data, and those that answered 'don't know' and 'not applicable'.
2 Jewish respondents included in 'other religion' due to a small numbers.
3 'All' category based on core sample. Other categories based on combined sample comprised of a core sample and an ethnic minority boost.
Source: Citizenship Survey, Department for Communities and Local Government (2009b)

In response to the same Survey, the majority of people said that their religion did not affect what school they send (or sent or would send) their children to, where they live, who their friends are or where they work. Thirty per cent of those with a stated religion said that religion influenced their choice of school, while 18 per cent of people who had a religion said that it did influence where they lived, 14 per cent said it influenced who their friends were and 10 per cent said it influenced where they worked (**Figure 15**).

Christian people were more likely than those of other religions (Muslim, Hindu, Sikh and Buddhist) to say that their religion influenced their choice of school: 30 per cent of Christians said this compared with 21 per cent of Muslims, 17 per cent of Sikhs, 15 per cent of Hindus, and 6 per cent of Buddhist respondents. However Christians were less likely than Muslims, Hindus, Sikhs or people in the 'other religion' category to say that their religion influenced where they live, where they work, and who their friends are. For example, only 16 per cent of Christians stated that their religion affected where they lived, compared with 39 per cent of Muslims, 32 per cent of Hindus, 24 per cent of Sikhs, and 23 per cent of people in the 'other religion' category (Department for Communities and Local Government, 2009b).

A higher percentage of Muslims reported religion influencing where they worked (26 per cent) compared with 16 per cent of Buddhists; 15 per cent of Hindu, Sikh and people in the 'other religion' category; and 9 per cent of Christians (Department for Communities and Local Government , 2009b).

Men were more likely than women to say that their religion affected where they live (19 per cent of men compared with 16 per cent of women) and who their friends are (15 per cent compared with 12 per cent) (Department for Communities and Local Government, 2009b).

References

British Social Attitudes (2009). Voting opinions. Available at:
www.britsocat.com/Body.aspx?control=Registration&ReturnUrl=%2fBodySecure.aspx%3fcontrol%3dBritSocAtContentsList&control=BritSocAtContentsList

Charities Aid Foundation/National Council for Voluntary Organisations (2010). UK Giving 2010.
Available at: www.ncvo-vol.org.uk/research/giving

Department for Communities and Local Government (2009a). English Housing Survey 2008-09
Household Report. Available at:
www.communities.gov.uk/publications/corporate/statistics/ehs200809householdreport

Department for Communities and Local Government (2009b). 2008-09 Citizenship Survey: Race,
Religion and Equalities Topic Report. Available at:
www.communities.gov.uk/publications/corporate/statistics/citizenshipsurvey200809equality

Department for Communities and Local Government (2010). Citizenship Survey: 2009-10 (April
2009 – June 2010), England. Available at:
www.communities.gov.uk/communities/research/citizenshipsurvey/quaterlystatisticalreleases/

Department for Culture, Media and Sport (2010). Taking Part: The National Survey of Culture,
Leisure and Sport Adult and Child Report 2009/10. Available at:
www.culture.gov.uk/publications/7386.aspx

Department for Education (2010). PE and Sport Survey 2009/10. Available at:
http://publications.education.gov.uk/default.aspx?PageFunction=productdetails&PageMode=publications&ProductId=DFE-RR032

Eurobarometer (2010). Survey on the attitudes of Europeans towards tourism. Available at:
http://ec.europa.eu/public_opinion/flash/fl_291_en.pdf

Eurobarometer (2009). Sport and Physical Activity. Available at:
http://ec.europa.eu/public_opinion/archives/ebs/ebs_334_en.pdf

Electoral Commission (2010). Report on the administration of the 2010 UK general election.
Available at:
www.electoralcommission.org.uk/publications-and-research/election-reports?query=&meta_s_phrase=UK+Parliamentary+election&sort=relevancy&daat=on

Entertainment Retailers Association (2010). UK and Ireland's statistics. Available at:
www.eraltd.org/content/stats.asp

Museums, Libraries & Archives (2010a). Research Briefing 9: Trends from the CIPFA Public
Library Service Statistics 2004/05 to 2008/09. Available at:
http://research.mla.gov.uk/evidence/view-publication.php?dm=nrm&pubid=1118

Museums, Libraries & Archives (2010b). Volunteering in the mla sector: a discussion. Available at: http://research.mla.gov.uk/evidence/view-publication.php?dm=nrm&pubid=1122

National Literacy Trust (2010). Available at: http://www.literacytrust.org.uk/

National Readership Survey (2010). National Readership estimates. Available at: www.nrs.co.uk/toplinereadership.html

Number 10 (2010). Government launches 'Big Society' Programme. Available at: http://www.number10.gov.uk/news/topstorynews/2010/05/big-society-50248

Ofcom (2010). Communications Market Report. Available at: http://stakeholders.ofcom.org.uk/market-data-research/market-data/communications-market-reports/cmr10/uk/

Office for National Statistics (2010). Travel Trends 2009. Available at: www.statistics.gov.uk/statbase/Product.asp?vlnk=1391

Public Lending Right (2009), 2008-09 Loans of books by category. Available at: www.plr.uk.com/mediaCentre/loansByCategory/loansByCategory.htm

Publishers Association (2009). PA statistics yearbook 2009. Available at: www.publishers.org.uk/index.php?option=com_content&view=category&layout=blog&id=154&Itemid=1295

Radio Joint Audience Research Limited (2010). RAJAR Data Release – Quarter 3, 2010. Available at: www.rajar.co.uk/content.php?page=news

Rallings, C. and Thrasher, M. (2007). British Electoral Facts 1832-2006. Ashgate Publishing Limited: Great Britain

UK Film Council (2010). Statisitcal Yearbook 2010. Available at: http://sy10.ukfilmcouncil.ry.com/Downloads.asp

Visit England, Visit Scotland, Visit Wales, Northern Ireland Tourist Board (2010). The UK Tourist 2009 Report. Available at: www.visitbritain.org/insightsandstatistics/domesticvisitorstatistics/index.aspx

YouGov (2010a). Cinema going habits. Available at: http://today.yougov.co.uk/pdfarchives/cinema-going-habits

YouGov (2010b). Newspapers and online content. Available at: http://today.yougov.co.uk/pdfarchives/newspapers-online-content

YouGov (2010c) Volunteering in Wales. Available at: http://today.yougov.co.uk/pdfarchives/volunteering-wales

Notes

[i] The Taking Part Survey is commissioned by the Department for Culture, Media and Sport in partnership with four of its Non Departmental Public Bodies (Arts Council England, English Heritage, Sport England and the Museums, Libraries and Archives Council).

[ii] www.statistics.gov.uk/cci/article.asp?ID=2604

[iii] The English Housing Survey is conducted by the Department for Communities and Local Government.

[iv] United Kingdom Tourism Survey is jointly funded and managed by Visit England, Visit Scotland, Visit Wales and the Northern Ireland Tourist Board.

[v] The Physical Education and Sport Strategy is run by the Department for Education.

[vi] The British Social Attitudes survey is conducted by the National Centre for Social Research.

[vii] The Citizenship Survey is conducted by the Department for Communities and Local Government.

[viii] Civic participation covers wider forms of engagement in democratic processes, such as contacting an elected representative, taking part in a public demonstration or protest, or signing a petition.

[ix] Civic consultation refers to active engagement in consultation about local services or issues through activities such as attending a consultation group or completing a questionnaire about these services.

[x] Civic activism refers to involvement either in direct decision-making about local services or issues, or in the actual provision of these services by taking on a role such as a local councillor, school governor or magistrate.

11 November 2010

Correction Notice

ST41: International comparisons

A production error was discovered in Figure 8 on page 14, originally published on 11 November 2010.

The figure title and corresponding text incorrectly read 'foreign born population' when it should have read 'foreign citizens'.

This error has now been corrected.

ONS apologises for any inconvenience caused.

Issued by:
Office for National Statistics
Government Buildings
Cardiff Road
Newport NP10 8XG

Telephone:
Media Office   0845 604 1858
Contact Centre   0845 601 3034

International comparisons

This is the first Social Trends chapter to focus on international comparisons. Its aim is to give an overview of the UK in an international context; drawing on international trends and comparisons. Comparing statistics across countries is increasingly important with the rise of globalisation. It also enables the formulation, implementation, monitoring and evaluation of policies in international communities such as the European Union (EU).

The chapter covers a variety of topics including the economy, health, education and crime. In previous editions of Social Trends a limited number of international comparisons have been included in each topic chapter and further international comparisons may still be found in topic articles where relevant.

Key points:

The economy and concerns over the economic situation

- For both the UK and USA GDP per head peaked in 2007 at 29,200 and 37,800 purchasing power standards (PPS) respectively, (PPS is an artificial currency unit that allows comparison between countries). For the EU-27 the peak was in 2008 at an average of 25,100 PPS per head

- In 2008 the level of income inequality in the UK at 34 per cent was joint fifth highest in the EU (alongside Lithuania), up from eighth highest in 2007. This was as a result of income inequality increasing in the UK and falling in both Greece and Estonia

Education and employment

- Between 2000 and 2007, the UK annual average unemployment rate remained relatively stable at around 5 per cent of the labour force, but between 2007 and 2009 it increased by 2.3 percentage points to 7.6 per cent

- The EU average rate of unemployment showed a slightly different pattern, remaining relatively stable at just under 9 per cent between 2000 and 2005 before falling by 1.9 percentage points between 2005 and 2008, returning to the 2005 level in 2009

- Between 2000 and 2008 the proportion of young people aged 15–24 not in education or employment increased in three of the G7 countries. The second largest increase was in the UK with an increase of 1.4 percentage points to 13.0 per cent

Crime and criminal justice

- In spring 2010, 28 per cent of people in the UK selected crime as one of the two most important issues facing the UK, compared with 16 per cent of people across the EU-27

- In 2008, the size of the prison population relative to the total population in the UK ranked ninth highest in the EU and, at 151.2 prisoners per 100,000 population, was higher than the EU-27 average of 125.4

- In 2008 in the UK and most other EU countries the highest proportion of prisoners were sentenced for robbery and other thefts

- A higher proportion of prisoners in the UK in 2008 were sentenced for assault and battery (17.3 per cent) or rape and other sexual offences (10.8 per cent) than in most other EU countries

Population

- Between 2004 and 2009 net migration and natural population change contributed relatively equally to population change in the UK, averaging 3.4 and 3.0 people per 1,000 inhabitants per year respectively

- The proportion of the UK population in 2008 who were foreign citizens was slightly higher than the EU average at 6.6 per cent compared with 6.2 per cent

- Population structures across the EU vary widely with 0.1 per cent of the population of Romania in 2008 being foreign citizens compared with 42.6 per cent of the population of Luxembourg

- Between 1950 and 2010 the world's population has more than doubled from 2.5 to 6.9 billion people. The UK population also increased over this period, though at a much slower rate, from 50.6 million to 61.9 million

- Population in all areas outside Europe grew at a much faster rate between 1950 and 2010 so that Europe's share of world population halved from 21.6 to 10.6 per cent

- In 2010 Asia accounted for 60.3 per cent of world population and the country with the largest population was China with 1.4 billion people

Health

- Between 1997 and 2007 both life expectancy and healthy life expectancy have increased for men and women in the UK

- In comparison with the EU-27 average, men could expect to live 1.6 years longer and women 0.3 years less in the UK than in the EU

- Healthy life expectancy in the UK was higher for both men and women than the EU-27 average in 2007

- In the UK in 2007 the death rate from all cancers for men was lower than the average for the 25 EU countries for which data are available, at 212.3 deaths per 100,000 inhabitants compared with 228.7. However, the opposite was true for women with the UK recording 153.7 deaths per 100,000 inhabitants for women from all cancers compared with an average of 131.5 deaths for the 25 EU countries for which data are available

- In 2008 health expenditure as a percentage of GDP in the UK was the second lowest among G7 countries at 8.7 per cent. This compares with 16.0 per cent of GDP in the USA, which had the highest expenditure

- In 2008, 82.6 per cent of total healthcare expenditure in the UK came from public sources, the highest proportion of all G7 countries. The lowest public expenditure on healthcare as a proportion of the total was recorded by the USA at 46.5 per cent

- In autumn 2009, 70 per cent of citizens across the EU and 86 per cent of citizens in the UK rated the quality of healthcare in their country as 'good' or 'very good'

Political engagement

- Trust in political parties in the UK fell from 18 per cent in autumn 2008 to 9 per cent in autumn 2009
- However, interest in politics in the UK increased in the years leading up to the 2010 General Election, with 12.6 per cent of people saying they were 'very interested' in politics in 2008 compared with 10.9 per cent in 2006

Environment

- Only 4 per cent of people in the UK and across the EU-27 considered the environment to be one of the two most important issues facing their country in spring 2010
- In both the UK and across the EU-27 minimising waste and recycling was regarded as the action that would have the highest impact on solving environmental problems, with 34 per cent of people in the UK and 30 per cent of people across the EU-27 selecting this option in 2009
- Over the period 1998 to 2008 the quantity of municipal waste generated had increased by 4.1 per cent in the UK and 5.6 per cent across the EU-27. However, the quantity of waste sent to landfill or incinerated had fallen by 26.4 per cent in the UK and 13.2 per cent across the EU-27. This could be an indication that more waste is being sent for recycling
- Between 1998 and 2008 the quantity of greenhouse gas emissions has fallen both in the UK and across the EU-27. The fall in UK greenhouse gas emissions was larger than the fall across the EU-27, 10.7 per cent compared with 4.4 per cent

The economy and concerns over the economic situation

This section gives an overview of the economies of the UK and other countries, starting with Gross Domestic Product (GDP). GDP is a key economic indicator, measuring the total economic activity of a country. Expressing it per head adjusts for the population size. **Figure 1** shows that the patterns of change in GDP per head since 2000 for the UK, the EU-27 average, and the USA have been very similar.

Figure 1   **Gross Domestic Product (GDP) per head in PPS[1]: EU/UK/USA comparison**

Thousands

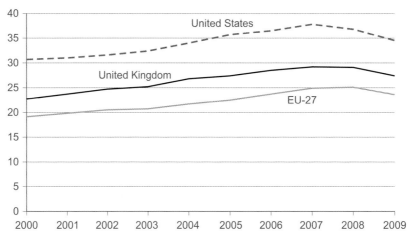

1 Expressing GDP in purchasing power standards (PPS) eliminates differences in price levels between countries, and calculations on a per head basis allows for the comparison of economies significantly different in absolute size.

Source: Eurostat (table tec00001)

Purchasing power standards (PPS) allow the conversion of GDP from national currencies into an artificial common currency which tells us how many currency units a given quantity of foods and services costs in different countries. Looking at GDP per head in PPS:

- For both the UK and USA GDP peaked in 2007 at 29,200 and 37,800 respectively. For the EU-27 the peak was in 2008 at an average of 25,100

- Over the period 2000 to 2009 the UK experienced an average annual change in GDP per head of 2.1 per cent, this compares with 2.4 per cent for the EU-27 and 1.3 per cent for the USA

- Of the EU-27 member states, Luxembourg had the highest per head GDP in 2009 at 63,000, more than twice the UK's GDP of 27,400 (Eurostat table tec00001)

Following the recession inflation has become an increasing concern. **Table 1** shows the 12-month percentage change in consumer prices across the EU-27 in June 2010.

Table 1   **Annual percentage change¹ in consumer prices:² EU comparison, June 2010**

			Percentage change
Hungary	5.2	France	0.8
Romania	4.6	Malta	0.7
Poland	3.5	Belgium	0.6
Greece	2.7	Spain	0.5
United Kingdom	**2.6**	Germany	0.4
Sweden	2.1	Netherlands	0.4
Bulgaria	1.6	Czech Republic	0.3
Luxembourg	1.6	Slovakia	0.3
Denmark	1.4	Estonia	0.0
Slovenia	1.3	Portugal	-0.3
Finland	1.3	Latvia	-1.6
Cyprus	1.0	Ireland	-2.5
Italy	0.9		
Lithuania	0.9		
Austria	0.9	**EU-27**	**1.3**

1 Twelve-month average rate of change.

2 All item Harmonised Indices of Consumer Prices (HICP), a set of EU consumer price indices (CPIs) calculated according to a harmonized approach and a single set of definitions to allow comparisons across countries.

Source: Eurostat (table prc_hicp_mv12r)

The Harmonised Indices of Consumer Prices (HICP)[i] allow inflation levels to be compared across EU member states. In June 2010 Hungary had the highest level of inflation at 5.2 per cent while inflation was fifth highest in the UK at 2.6 per cent, twice the average for the EU-27 (1.3 per cent).

Prices, as measured by the HICP, fell between June 2009 and June 2010 in Portugal, Latvia and Ireland, with Ireland recording the largest fall at -2.5 per cent.

While indicators such as GDP per head give an indication of the overall state of an economy they do not give a complete picture of economic wellbeing as, for example, they do not take into consideration the distribution of income and wealth across the economy. The extent of household income inequality is commonly measured using the Gini coefficient[ii] for which higher values represent higher levels of inequality, as shown in **Figure 2**.

Figure 2   Household income inequality: EU comparisons, 2008

Gini coefficient[1]

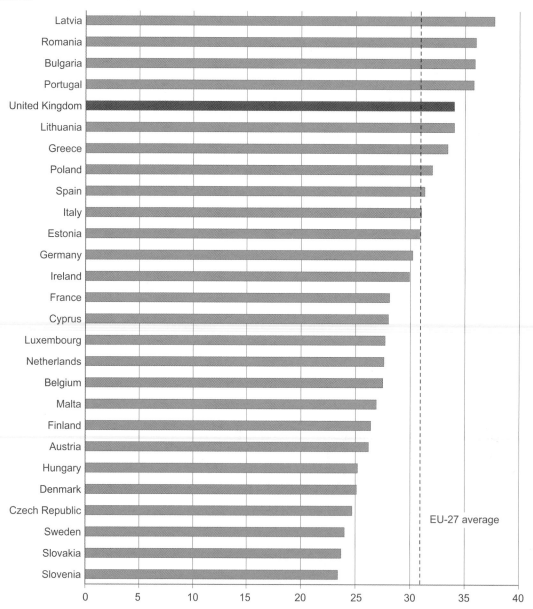

1 The Gini coefficient can take a value between 0 and 100.

Source: Eurostat (table ilc_di12)

The level of income inequality in the UK in 2008, at 34 per cent, was joint fifth highest in the EU (alongside Lithuania). In 2007 the UK had the eighth highest level, moving up to fifth in 2008 as a result of income inequality increasing in the UK and falling in both Greece and Estonia (Eurostat table ilc_di12).

It appears that the recession has had a mixed impact on income inequality in the EU with increases between 2007 and 2008 for 11 countries, including the UK with an increase of 1.2 percentage points indicating greater income inequality. There were decreases for 13 countries, with Estonia recording the biggest fall of 2.5 percentage points while three countries remained at the same level (Eurostat table ilc_di12).

There have been changes in the concerns of EU citizens over the course of the 2008–09 recession. In spring 2007, 20 per cent of people in the EU-27 and just 6 per cent of people in the UK identified the economic situation as one of the two most important issues facing their country (European Commission, 2007). By spring 2009 concern about the economic situation had increased to 42 per cent across the EU and 31 per cent in the UK (European Commission, 2009a). This proportion, increased again in the UK to reach 38 per cent in spring 2010, but fell to 40 per cent for the EU-27, as shown in **Figure 3**.

Figure 3	**Key concerns of citizens:** [1] **UK/EU comparison, spring 2010**

Percentages

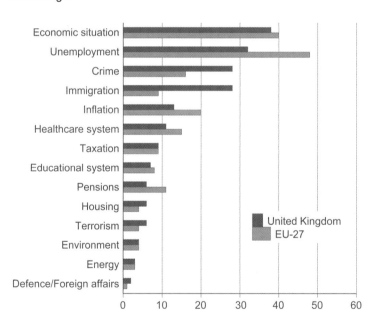

1 Respondents aged 15 or over were asked 'What do you think are the two most important issues facing (OUR COUNTRY) at the moment? (MAX. TWO ANSWERS)'.

Source: Eurobarometer 73, (European Commission, 2010a)

While the key concern for UK citizens in spring 2010 was the economic situation, the main concern of EU citizens as a whole in spring 2010 was unemployment, with 48 per cent of people identifying unemployment as one of the two most important issues facing the country.

Unemployment was the second most important concern in the UK at 32 per cent, an increase of 24 percentage points from spring 2007 (European Commission, 2007). The joint third highest concerns of UK citizens in spring 2010 were crime and immigration at 28 per cent each. The following sections will look at these concerns in turn, starting with unemployment.

Education and employment

During and after the recession annual average unemployment rates have increased in the UK and across the EU-27.

Figure 4   **Annual average unemployment rates: [1] UK/EU comparison**

Percentages

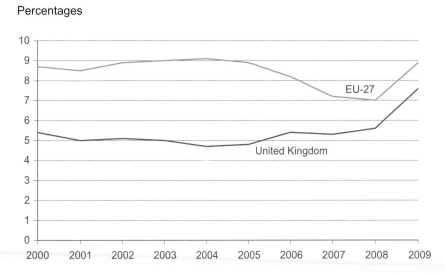

1 The unemployment rate is the number of people unemployed as a percentage of the labour force. The labour force is the total number of people employed and unemployed, where employed persons are those who worked at least one hour for pay during the reference week, or were temporarily absent from such work, and unemployed persons are those aged 15–74 (16–74 in Spain, Sweden and UK) who were not employed during the reference week.

Source: Eurostat (table tsiem110)

Between 2000 and 2007 the UK annual average unemployment rate remained relatively stable at around 5 per cent of the labour force, but between 2007 and 2009 it increased from 5.3 per cent to 7.6 per cent. The EU average rate of unemployment showed a slightly different pattern, remaining relatively stable at just under 9 per cent between 2000 and 2005 before falling from 8.9 per cent to 7.0 per cent between 2005 and 2008. However, this fall was reversed between 2008 and 2009, with the unemployment rate moving back to the 2005 level of 8.9 per cent. In comparison, the USA saw a rise of 5.3 percentage points between 2000 and 2009, to reach 9.3 per cent.
Between 2000 and 2009 Ireland saw the biggest rise in unemployment within the EU-27, increasing by 7.7 percentage points to 11.9 per cent. However, Spain recorded the highest unemployment rate in 2009 at 18.0 per cent (Eurostat table tsiem110).

Along with overall unemployment, a recent concern has been the number of young people not in education or employment.

Figure 5   **Youths aged 15 to 24 not in education or employment:** [1] **G7** [iii] **comparison**

Percentages

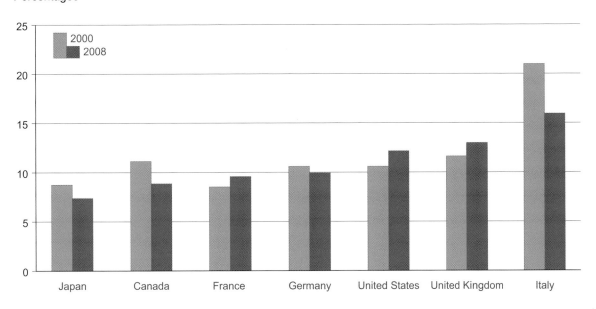

1 Youths in education include those attending part-time as well as full-time education, but exclude those in non-formal education and in educational activities of very short duration. Employment covers all those who have worked for pay for at least one hour in the reference week of the survey.

Source: OECD Education database

Between 2000 and 2008 the proportion of young people aged 15–24 not in education or employment increased in three of the G7 countries (**Figure 5**). The largest increase was in the USA with an increase of 1.6 percentage points, to 12.1 per cent, followed by the UK with an increase of 1.4 percentage points, to 13.0 per cent. However, Italy recorded the highest proportion of young people not in education or employment across the G7 in both 2000 and 2008, despite also experiencing the biggest fall of 5.0 percentage points over the period.

The charity the Prince's Trust has expressed concern about the number of young people not in education or employment saying that 'all too often unemployed young people face a downward spiral towards a loss of self-confidence, or even crime, homelessness and drug-use.' (Telegraph, 2010).

The following section will look at crime and criminal justice across Europe.

Crime and criminal justice

In spring 2010, 28 per cent of people in the UK selected crime as one of the two most important issues facing the UK, compared with 16 per cent of people across the EU-27 (**Figure 3**).

Table 2   Fear of violent crime: [1] European Social Survey
             participant country comparison, 2008

Percentages

	All or most of the time	Some of the time	Just occasionally	Never		All or most of the time	Some of the time	Just occasionally	Never
Croatia	0.5	5.6	17.9	76.1	Belgium	3.0	23.7	29.9	43.5
Turkey	2.7	16.7	6.5	74.1	Spain	4.3	21.8	33.4	40.5
Cyprus	0.9	10.5	19.4	69.3	Sweden	2.0	17.9	40.6	39.5
Switzerland	1.2	13.1	28.7	57.0	**United Kingdom**	**4.3**	**18.6**	**38.4**	**38.7**
Netherlands	0.9	14.0	28.7	56.5	France	3.8	25.8	34.0	36.4
Israel	3.2	15.6	25.6	55.7	Finland	1.0	17.3	46.4	35.4
Slovenia	0.6	4.7	39.3	55.4	Estonia	2.0	23.0	39.8	35.3
Norway	0.6	6.6	37.4	55.4	Slovakia	4.6	29.6	30.5	35.3
Denmark	1.1	9.1	36.8	53	Greece	6.9	33.5	24.7	34.9
Germany	1.6	12.3	34.0	52.1	Latvia	2.0	10.2	53.3	34.5
Romania	4.6	23.4	20.8	51.1	Russian Federation	3.5	12.6	50.0	34.0
Czech Republic	0.8	6.6	44.9	47.7	Bulgaria	13.0	26.8	31.0	29.3
Hungary	2.5	11.6	40.3	45.7	Ukraine	2.3	13.3	57.1	27.3
Portugal	5.1	23.3	25.9	45.7					
Poland	2.0	5.0	48.3	44.7					

1 Respondents aged 15+ asked 'How often do you worry about becoming a victim of violent crime?'
Source: European Social Survey 2008

In 2008 more than a fifth of UK residents stated that they feared becoming a victim of violent crime some (18.6 per cent) or all or most (4.3 per cent) of the time (**Table 2**). Of those countries participating in the European Social Survey, Croatia had the highest proportion of people stating they never feared violent crime at 76.1 per cent, compared with 38.7 per cent of people in the UK.

The relationship between fear of crime and crime rates is not straightforward as fear of crime in the UK has remained high despite falls in actual crime rates (Home Office, 2010). However, it is difficult to compare crime rates across countries because of differences in definitions of crime and traditions of policing. Also comparing crime data from societies that are fundamentally different may ignore cultural differences that affect levels of reporting.

While it is difficult to compare crime rates across countries, the Council of Europe does collect information on prison populations and staffing in Europe.

Figure 6   **Prison population: EU comparison, 2008[1]**

Prison population rate per 100,000 inhabitants

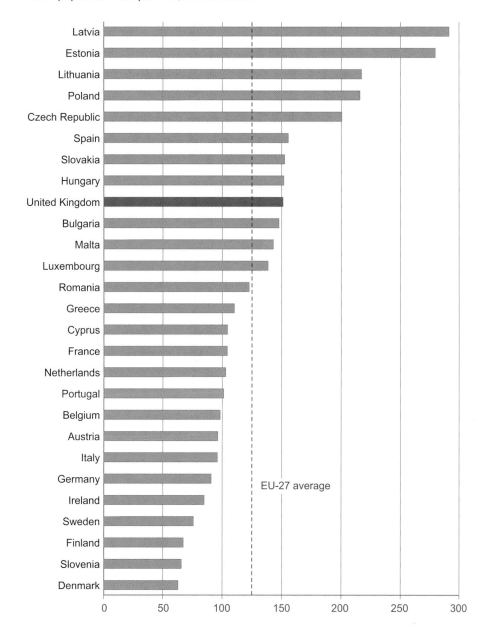

1 Data are point estimates with different countries taking estimates on different days of the year
Source: SPACE I (Council of Europe, 2010)

In 2008 the size of the prison population relative to the total population in the UK ranked ninth highest in the EU-27 and, at 151.2 prisoners per 100,000 population, higher than the EU-27 average of 125.4 (**Figure 6**). Prison population was highest in Latvia at 291.4 prisoners per 100,000 population. It should be remembered that countries may have different sentencing and remand policies which may affect the size of the prison population.

The Council of Europe also gather data on the main offences for which prisoners were sentenced. A higher proportion of prisoners in the UK in 2008 were sentenced for assault and battery (17.3 per cent) or rape and other sexual offences (10.8 per cent) than in most other EU countries, as shown in **Table 3**. However, in most countries shown in the table, including the UK, the highest proportion of the prison population in 2008 had been sentenced for robbery and other thefts. The only exceptions were Italy, Luxembourg and Sweden, where the highest proportion of the prison population had been sentenced for drug offences and Denmark and France, where the highest proportion were sentenced for assault and battery.

Table 3   **Sentenced prisoners by main offence: EU comparison,[1] 2008[2]**

Percentages

	Homicide[3]	Assault and Battery	Rape and other sexual offences	Robbery and other thefts	Drug offences		Homicide[3]	Assault and Battery	Rape and other sexual offences	Robbery and other thefts	Drug offences
Belgium	4.7	10.9	10.5	32.8	13.9	Malta	3.1	4.7	7.1	20.5	20.2
Bulgaria	12.1	1.6	6.8	56.9	5.5	Netherlands	14.0	3.6	2.8	23.7	19.8
Cyprus	9.0	2.1	8.6	31.8	20.7	Poland	6.7	..	3.6	40.8	..
Czech Republic	0.6	22.1	2.5	31.9	13.1	Portugal	12.7	1.6	5.0	26.9	21.3
Denmark	7.9	27.6	5.6	24.0	24.2	Romania	24.6	0.8	6.9	51.3	4.0
Estonia	23.3	..	3.5	37.2	15.2	Slovenia	11.8	6.9	12.9	34.1	10.3
Finland	20.1	19.6	2.9	22.1	16.1	Spain	5.6	5.2	6.3	41.5	27.1
France	7.1	22.9	16.2	18.0	14.2	Sweden	10.1	14.2	9.1	16.2	30.5
Germany	7.3	12.0	8.0	33.0	15.4	United Kingdom	10.7	17.3	10.8	28.7	15.7
Hungary	11.8	7.9	4.9	46.2	2.5						
Ireland	10.9	14.3	9.0	28.5	19.3						
Italy	22.7	0.3	10.3	25.3	36.1						
Latvia	9.2	6.9	7.3	58.3	12.0						
Lithuania	25.5	5.3	5.9	42.6	6.5						
Luxembourg	12.0	4.5	8.0	20.1	44.6						

1 Data not available for Austria, Greece and Slovakia.

2 Data are point estimates with different countries taking estimates on different days of the year.

3 Including attempted homicide.

Source: SPACE I (Council of Europe, 2010)

Population

Immigration was of equal concern to UK citizens as crime in the spring 2010 Eurobarometer (**Figure 3**). There are two components of population change: natural change, being the difference between births and deaths, and net migration, the difference between the numbers of people immigrating and emigrating. In the 10 years to 2009 net migration was the main driver of overall population change in the EU (Eurostat, 2009).

Figure 7   **Population change: EU comparison, 2004–2009[1]**

Average rates per 1,000 inhabitants per year

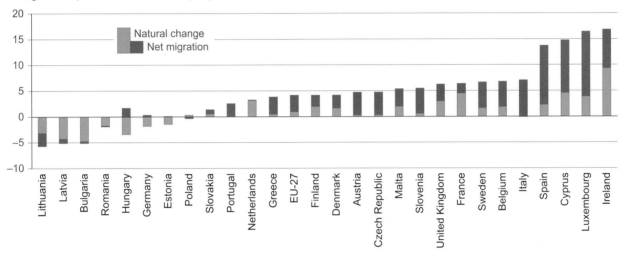

1 ONS publishes UK components of population change relating to mid-year population estimates. UK figures published by Eurostat relate to 1 January.

Source: Eurostat (table demo_gind: natgrowrt and cnmigratrt)

Between 2004 and 2009 net migration and natural population change contributed relatively equally to population change in the UK, averaging 3.4 and 3.0 people per 1,000 inhabitants per year respectively. The average rate of net migration in the UK was joint 11th highest in the EU (alongside Malta and Greece) and slightly higher than the EU average of 3.2. Averaged across the EU-27 the natural rate of population change was 0.9 people per 1,000 population per year.

Ireland had the highest level of population change at an average increase of 16.8 people per 1,000 inhabitants per year with the majority (9.3) resulting from natural change. Luxembourg had the highest average rate of net migration at 12.6 people per 1,000 population per year.

Over the period 2004 to 2009 eight EU countries saw negative rates of natural population change (that is, more deaths than births). Bulgaria had the lowest rate of natural population change averaging -4.8 people per 1,000 population per year.

Figure 8   Foreign citizens:[1] EU comparison, 2008

Proportion of total population

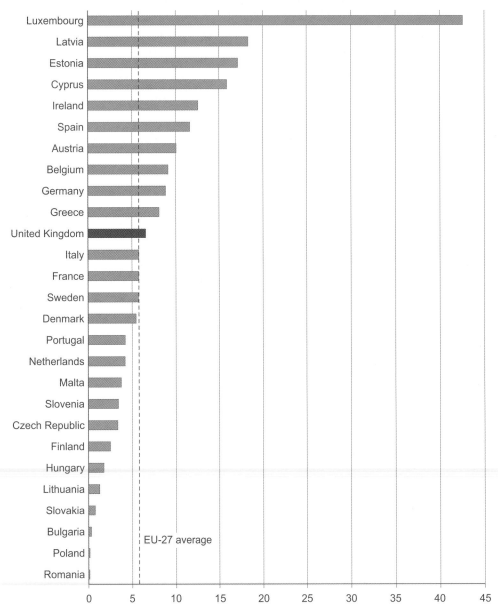

1 Total number of foreigners including citizens of other EU Member States and non-EU citizens, usually resident in the reporting country.

Source: Eurostat (table demo_gind: jan and tps00157)

The proportion of the UK population in 2008 that were foreign citizens was slightly higher than the EU-27 average at 6.6 per cent compared with 6.2 per cent (**Figure 8**). Population structures across the EU vary widely with 0.1 per cent of the population of Romania in 2008 being foreign citizens compared with 42.6 per cent of the population of Luxembourg.

Luxembourg is a small country with a long tradition of immigration, in particular labour migration that started with the first wave of German and Italian labour immigration during the early stage of industrialisation around 1875. Immigration has increased with the founding and expansion of the EU (European Commission, 2004).

Table 4   **World population**[1]

Percentages

	1950	1960	1970	1980	1990	2000	2010[2]
Asia	55.5	56.0	57.7	59.1	60.1	60.5	60.3
Africa	9.0	9.4	10.0	10.9	12.1	13.4	15.0
Europe	21.6	20.0	17.8	15.6	13.6	11.9	10.6
Latin America and the Caribbean	6.6	7.3	7.8	8.2	8.4	8.5	8.5
Northern America	6.8	6.8	6.3	5.7	5.3	5.2	5.1
Oceania	0.5	0.5	0.5	0.5	0.5	0.5	0.5
World (=100%) (millions)	**2,529**	**3,023**	**3,686**	**4,438**	**5,290**	**6,115**	**6,909**
United Kingdom (millions)	**50.6**	**52.4**	**55.7**	**56.3**	**57.2**	**58.9**	**61.9**

1 As of 1 July.

2 Data for 2010 are projections.

Source: World population prospects (United Nations, 2009)

Between 1950 and 2010 the world's population has more than doubled from 2.5 to 6.9 billion people (**Table 4**). The UK population also increased over this period, though at a much slower rate, from 50.6 million to 61.9 million. The total population in areas outside Europe grew at a much faster rate between 1950 and 2010 so that Europe's share of world population halved from 21.6 to 10.6 per cent. In 2010 Asia accounted for 60.3 per cent of world population and the country with the largest population was China with 1.4 billion people.

The United Nations estimates that world population will reach 7.7 billion in 2020 with the population of Europe remaining fairly stable and the population of Africa increasing by nearly a quarter and Asia by 10 per cent (United Nations, 2008).

The previous sections have compared the UK and other countries in terms of their economy, unemployment, crime and population structure, all of which were key concerns of UK respondents in the spring 2010 Eurobarometer survey. The following sections analyse two other components of societal wellbeing, namely health and political and social engagement.

Health

Life expectancy at birth is often used as a key indicator of population health. However, over recent years there has been growing interest in healthy life expectancy, the proportion of a person's life that they are expected to be free from illness. An increase in healthy life expectancy is one of the main goals for European health policy as this would not only improve the situation of individuals but would also result in lower levels of public healthcare expenditure (Eurostat, 2009).

Table 5   **Life expectancy and healthy life expectancy:[1] UK/EU comparison, 2007**

	Males		Females	
	UK	EU-27	UK	EU-27
Life expectancy at birth (years)	77.7	76.1	81.9	82.2
Life expectancy at 65 (years)	17.5	17	20.2	20.5
Health life expectancy at 65 - as a proportion of life expectancy at 65	58.8	51.1	56.9	43.2

1 The indicator Healthy Life Years (HLY) measures the number of remaining years that a person of a specific age is still expected to live in a healthy condition. A healthy condition is defined by the absence of limitations in functioning/disability.

Source: Eurostat (tables hlth_hlye)

Between 1997 and 2007 life expectancy increased for men and women in the UK (Eurostat table hlth_hlye). The increase in life expectancy was larger for men than women but life expectancy for women remains greater (81.9 years at birth for women in 2007 compared with 77.7 years at birth for men). In comparison with the EU-27 average, men could expect to live 1.6 years longer at birth in the UK in 2007 and women 0.3 years less (**Table 5**).

Turning to healthy life expectancy at 65, that is the proportion of life after 65 that individuals can expect to be free from illness, the UK performs better than the EU-27 average for both men and women. In 2007, women in the UK could expect to live 57 per cent of their life after the age of 65 in a healthy state, compared with 43 per cent for the EU on average. Men in the UK had a healthy life expectancy after the age of 65 of 59 per cent compared with 51 per cent for the EU average. In the UK healthy life expectancy increased between 1997 and 2007 by 1.3 percentage points for men and 5.2 percentage points for women.

Cancer was the second most common cause of death for both males and females in the UK in 2008 (ONS, 2009). The most recent data available for international comparisons are for 2007.

Figure 9   Deaths from cancer:[1] EU comparison,[2] 2007

Standardised death rate[3] by 100,000 inhabitants

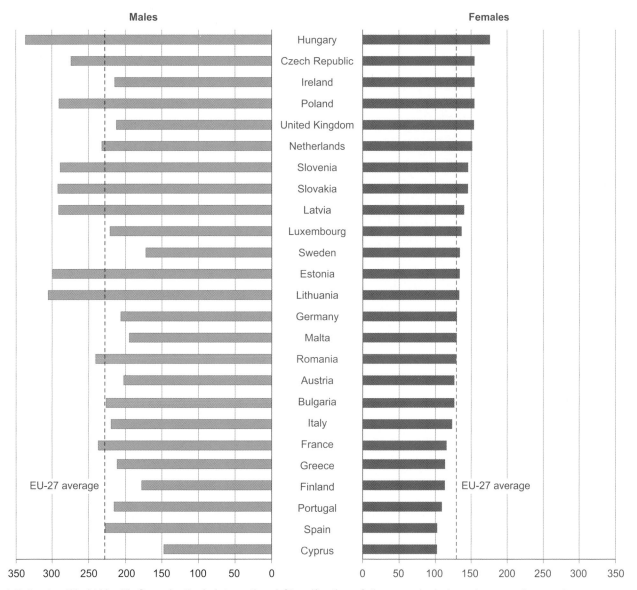

1 Following World Health Organisation's International Classification of diseases. Includes primary and secondary malignant neoplasm and malignant neoplasm of independent (primary) multiple sites.

2 Data not available for Belgium and Denmark.

3 The (age-) standardised death rate is a weighted average of age-specific mortality rates.

Source: Eurostat (table hlth_cd_asdr: C)

In the UK in 2007 the death rate from all cancers for men was lower than the average for the 25 EU countries for which data are available, at 212.3 deaths per 100,000 inhabitants compared with 228.7 (**Figure 9**). However, the opposite was true for women with the UK recording 153.7 deaths per 100,000 inhabitants for women from all cancers compared with an average of 131.5 deaths for the 25 EU countries for which data are available.

Breast cancer is the most common form of female cancer in England and Wales. It is also the second most common cause of cancer deaths in women, after lung cancer (ONS, 2009). Between 2000 to 2007 death rates from breast cancer in women have fallen in both the UK and the EU, by 3.7 and 3.2 deaths per 100,000 inhabitants respectively. However the death rate from breast cancer for women in the UK has remained higher than the EU in 2007 at an average at 26.8 deaths per 100,000 inhabitants compared with 23.6 (Eurostat table hlth_cd_asdr).

In most OECD countries, spending on health is a large and growing share of both public and private expenditure. Health spending as a share of GDP varies widely across countries, reflecting market and social factors as well as the diverse financing and organisational structures of the health system in each country (OECD, 2010a).

Figure 10   **Total expenditure on health as proportion of GDP: G7 countries, 2008**

Percentages

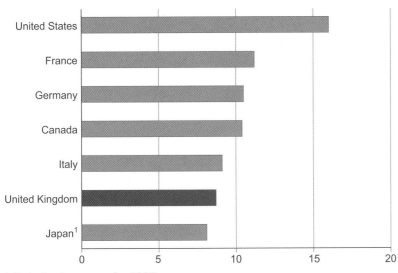

1 Data for Japan are for 2007.
Source: OECD Health Data 2010 (OECD, 2010b)

In 2008 health expenditure as a percentage of GDP in the UK was the second lowest among G7 countries at 8.7 per cent **(Figure 10)**. This compares with 16.0 per cent of GDP in the USA, which had the highest expenditure. Health expenditure as a percentage of GDP in the UK has grown from 7.0 per cent in 2000 (OECD, 2010b).

In 2008, 82.6 per cent of total healthcare expenditure in the UK came from public sources, the highest proportion of all G7 countries. The lowest public expenditure on healthcare as a proportion of the total was recorded by the USA at 46.5 per cent (OECD, 2010b). However, even though the public share of health spending is much lower in the USA than in the UK, public spending on health per head is substantially higher in the USA than in the UK.

A recent Special Eurobarometer[iv] survey asked EU citizens about their perceptions of healthcare quality.

Figure 11   **Satisfaction with healthcare quality:** [1] **EU comparison, autumn 2009**

Percentages

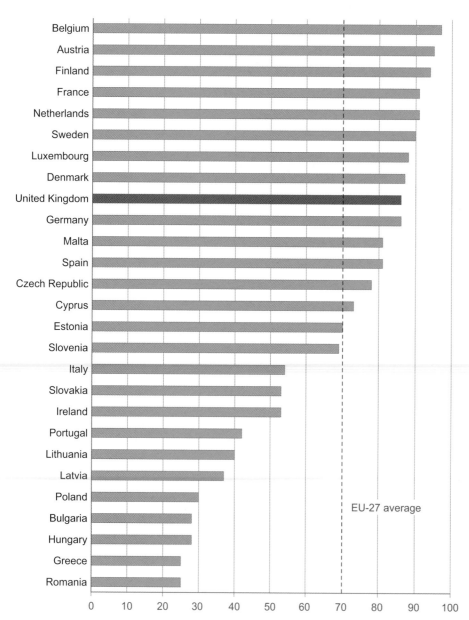

1 Percentage of respondents, aged 15 and over, who stated 'good' or 'very good' in response to the following question: 'How would you rate the overall quality of healthcare in OUR COUNTRY'.

Source: Special Eurobarometer 327, (European Commission, 2010)

When asked in autumn 2009, 47 per cent of UK and an average of 50 per cent of EU citizens thought it 'likely' that patients could be harmed by hospital care, on average 70 per cent of citizens across the EU rated the quality of healthcare in their country as 'good' or 'very good' **(Figure 11)**.

An average of 86 per cent of citizens in the UK rated healthcare as 'good' or 'very good' as compared with 97 per cent in Belgium and 25 per cent in Romania.

Political engagement

Figure 12   Trust in political parties:[1] EU comparison, autumn 2009

Percentages

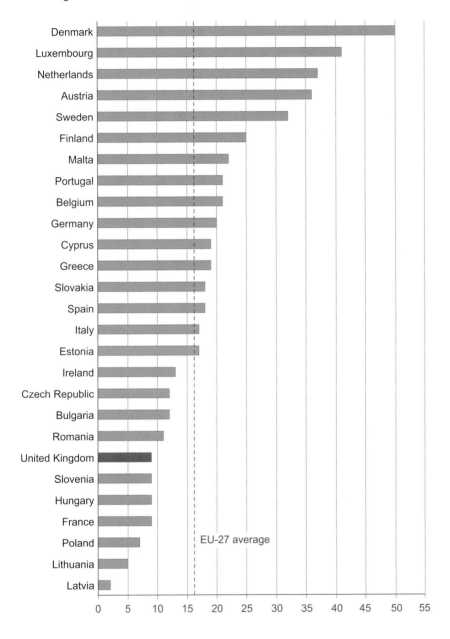

1 Respondents, aged 15 and over, who responded 'tend to trust' when asked 'I would like to ask you a question about how much trust you have in certain institutions. For each of the following institutions, please tell me if you tend to trust it or tend not to trust it. Political parties.'

Source: Eurobarometer 72 (European Commission, 2010c)

Trust in political parties in the UK fell from 18 per cent in autumn 2008 (European Commission, 2009a) to 9 per cent in autumn 2009. This is lower than EU average of 16 per cent for autumn

2009 (**Figure 12**). Trust by EU citizens as a whole in their political parties also fell but to a lesser extent, from 20 per cent in 2008. The steep fall in trust in the UK may in part have been prompted by public concern about the level and nature of claims for expenses made by Members of Parliament.

However, interest in politics in the UK has increased in the years leading up to the 2010 General Election, with 12.6 per cent of people saying they were 'very interested' in politics in 2008 compared with 10.9 per cent in 2006 (**Table 6**).

Table 6   **Interest in politics:** [1] **European Social Survey participant country comparison**

Percentages

	Very interested		Quite interested		Hardly interested		Not at all interested			Very interested		Quite interested		Hardly interested		Not at all interested	
	2006	2008	2006	2008	2006	2008	2006	2008		2006	2008	2006	2008	2006	2008	2006	2008
Austria	14.0	..	36.5	..	39.2	..	10.3	..	Latvia	..	4.7	..	31.2	..	49.2	..	14.9
Belgium	8.2	8.3	36.6	40.1	33.6	32.4	21.6	19.2	Netherlands	10.8	9.7	52.3	57.1	26.1	23.3	10.8	9.9
Bulgaria	7.5	9.5	39.2	36.4	27.5	28.7	25.8	25.4	Norway	9.4	10.0	38.5	37.1	44.3	45.1	7.7	7.
Croatia	..	6.9	..	23.9	..	33.6	..	35.5	Poland	6.4	6.5	32.2	35.0	43.8	39.1	17.6	19..
Cyprus	10.6	17.3	27.6	25.2	39.6	33.5	22.2	24.0	Portugal	5.0	4.0	23.4	25.0	33.4	32.2	38.2	38.8
Czech Republic	..	2.8	..	15.1	..	48.5	..	33.6	Romania	..	6.7	..	36.0	..	32.8	..	24.9
Denmark	18.7	21.7	49.1	50.1	25.9	24.5	6.2	3.7	Russian Federation	8.0	8.1	35.0	40.0	34.4	34.4	22.7	17.9
Estonia	6.9	8.4	34.3	36.7	44.3	42.3	14.4	12.6	Slovakia	6.5	8.5	31.2	33.2	48.4	43.6	14	14.
Finland	7.3	8.1	40.3	40.3	40.5	40.8	11.9	10.8	Slovenia	7.1	7.2	36.3	41.8	35.2	35.4	21.5	15.6
France	12.5	14.9	32.7	36.5	35.8	35.4	18.9	13.3	Spain	5.7	5.3	20.1	20.8	38.4	39.7	35.7	34.
Germany	16.1	18.3	37.7	43.4	36.0	32.8	10.2	5.6	Sweden	14.9	13.0	46.9	45.7	29.8	32.9	8.4	8.4
Greece	..	7.3	..	23.3	..	36.8	..	32.5	Switzerland	14.5	16.1	42.1	41.8	32.7	31.4	10.7	10.1
Hungary	9.7	8.3	32.2	29.0	35.4	37.1	22.8	25.6	Turkey	..	9.6	..	30.1	..	21.1	..	39.2
Ireland	9.9	..	35.6	..	29.2	..	25.4	..	Ukraine	11.0	9.9	36.2	35.4	38.7	38.5	14.1	16.2
Israel	..	13.9	..	34.3	..	25.6	..	26.2	United Kingdom	10.9	12.6	41.3	43.9	28.2	28.3	19.7	15.2

1 Respondents, aged 15 and over, asked 'How interested would you say you are in politics?'

Source: European Social Survey 2006 and 2008

Interest in politics was highest in Denmark in 2008, with 21.7 per cent of the population stating that they were 'very interested' in politics, while interest was lowest in the Czech Republic, at 2.8 per cent.

Environment

Only 4 per cent of people in the UK and across the EU-27 considered the environment to be one of the two most important issues facing their country in spring 2010 (see **Figure 3**). A recent Flash Eurobarometer[v] looked at the attitudes of Europeans towards sustainable production and consumption. **Figure 13** shows those actions which people believe would have the highest impact on solving environmental problems.

Figure 13   **Actions thought to solve environmental problems:[1] EU comparisons, April 2009**

Percentages

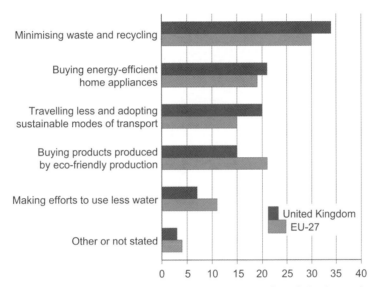

1 Respondents, aged 15 and over, were asked 'In your opinion, which one of the following actions would have the highest impact on solving environmental problems?'

Source: Flash Eurobarometer 256 (European Commission, 2009b)

In both the UK and across the EU-27 minimising waste and recycling was regarded as the action which would have the highest impact on solving environmental problems, with 34 per cent of people in the UK and 30 per cent of people across the EU-27 selecting this option in 2009.

The following items look at changes in waste generation and greenhouse gas emissions.

Figure 14   **Municipal[1] waste generation and treatment:[2] EU/UK comparison**

Kg per person per year (Index 1998 = 100)

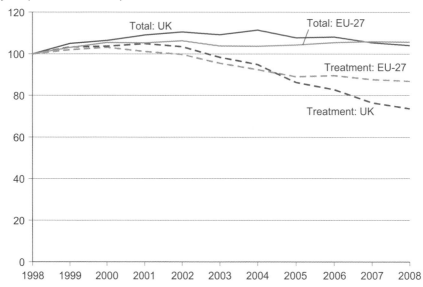

1 Municipal waste is mainly produced by households, though similar wastes from sources such as commerce, offices and public institutions are included.

2 Waste disposed of through landfill or incineration.

Source: Eurostat (tables tsien120 and tsien130)

Over the period 1998 to 2008 the quantity of municipal waste generated in kilograms per person had increased by 4.1 per cent in the UK and 5.6 per cent across the EU-27. However, the quantity of waste sent to landfill or incinerated had fallen by 26.4 per cent in the UK and 13.2 per cent in across the EU-27. Although this is an indication that a higher total quantity of waste is being recycled, the percentage of waste sent to landfill or incinerated in the UK was still higher than across the EU-27 in 2008. In the UK waste sent to landfill or incinerated had decreased from 90.8 per cent of all waste in 1998 to 64.2 per cent in 2008, compared with a decrease from 71.8 per cent in 1998 to 59.0 per cent in 2008 in the EU-27 (see Eurostat tables tsien120 and tsien130).

The EU's sixth environment action programme, adopted in 2002, is a 10-year policy for the environment. It identifies a number of key issues including four key priorities including increasing recycling and waste prevention and achieving the EU's target of reducing greenhouse gas emissions by 8 per cent by 2008–12 (Eurostat, 2010).

Figure 15   **Greenhouse gas emissions:[1] EU/UK comparison**

Index (100=1998)

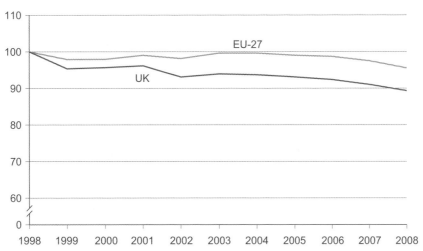

1 One thousand tonnes of CO2 equivalent, weighted according to the global warming potential of each gas.
Source: Eurostat (table env_air_gge: Tot_x_5)

Between 1998 and 2008 the quantity of greenhouse gas emissions has fallen both in the UK and across the EU-27. The fall in UK greenhouse gas emissions was larger than the fall across the EU-27, 10.7 per cent compared with 4.4 per cent.

Looking to the future, the Eurostat Yearbook 2010 sets out the policy aims for 2020:

International negotiations for reaching a global agreement related to reducing greenhouse gas emissions for the period after 2012, when key provisions of the Kyoto Protocol expire, have been at the forefront of policy activity in recent months. The EU formulated a policy response to help reduce greenhouse gas emissions in the shape of an integrated energy and climate change policy, which was adopted in December 2008 and includes the following three key targets:

- cut greenhouse gases by at least 20 per cent of their 1990 levels (30 per cent if other developed countries commit to comparable cuts) by 2020
- increase the use of renewables (wind, solar, biomass, etc.) to 20 per cent of total energy production by 2020, including a 10 per cent biofuel target for transport
- cut energy consumption by 20 per cent in relation to projected 2020 levels – by improving energy efficiency

(Eurostat, 2010: page 513).

References

Council of Europe (2010). Annual penal statistics - SPACE I. Available at
www.coe.int/t/e/legal_affairs/legal_co-operation/prisons_and_alternatives/statistics_space_i/PC-CP(2010)07_E%20SPACE%20Report%20I.pdf

European Commission (2004). Country report Luxembourg: On migration and asylum 2003. Available at
http://ec.europa.eu/home-affairs/doc_centre/asylum/docs/2003/country_reports/luxembourg.pdf

European Commission (2007). Eurobarometer 67: First results. Available at
http://ec.europa.eu/public_opinion/archives/eb/eb67/eb67_en.htm

European Commission (2009a). Standard Eurobarometer 71: Annex. Available at
http://ec.europa.eu/public_opinion/archives/eb/eb71/eb71_en.htm

European Commission (2009b). Flash Eurobarometer 256: Analytical report. Available at
http://ec.europa.eu/public_opinion/archives/flash_arch_269_255_en.htm

European Commission (2010a). Standard Eurobarometer 73: First results annex. Available at
http://ec.europa.eu/public_opinion/archives/eb/eb73/eb73_en.htm

European Commission (2010b). Special Eurobarometer 327: Full report. Available at
http://ec.europa.eu/public_opinion/archives/eb_special_339_320_en.htm

European Commission (2010c). Standard Eurobarometer 72: Full report annex. Available at
http://ec.europa.eu/public_opinion/archives/eb/eb72/eb72_anx_vol1.pdf

Eurostat (2009). Eurostat yearbook 2009. Available at
http://epp.eurostat.ec.europa.eu/portal/page/portal/publications/eurostat_yearbook

Eurostat (2010) Eurostat yearbook 2010. Available at
http://epp.eurostat.ec.europa.eu/cache/ITY_OFFPUB/KS-CD-10-220/EN/KS-CD-10-220-EN.PDF

Home Office (2010). Crime in England and Wales 2009/10: Statistical bulletin. Available at
http://rds.homeoffice.gov.uk/rds/pdfs10/hosb1210.pdf

OECD (2010a). OECD factbook 2010. Available at
www.oecd-ilibrary.org/economics/oecd-factbook_18147364

OECD (2010b). OECD health data 2010. Available at
www.irdes.fr/EcoSante/DownLoad/OECDHealthData_FrequentlyRequestedData.xls

ONS (2009). Mortality statistics: Deaths registered in 2008. Available at
www.statistics.gov.uk/downloads/theme_health/DR2008/DR_08.pdf

Telegraph (2010). Young people classed as NEETS. Available at
www.telegraph.co.uk/education/educationnews/7745421/900000-young-people-classed-as-Neets.html

United Nations (2008). World population prospects. Available at
 http://esa.un.org/unpp/

United Nations (2009). World population prospects. Available at
 http://esa.un.org/unpd/wpp2008/all-wpp-indicators_components.htm

Notes

[i]All item Harmonized Indices of Consumer Prices (HICP), a set of European Union consumer price indices (CPIs) calculated according to a harmonized approach and a single set of definitions to allow comparisons across countries.

[ii]The Gini coefficient can take a value between 0 and 100. A value of zero on the Gini coefficient indicates complete equality in the distribution of income (all people in the population receive exactly the same income), while a value of 100 indicates complete inequality (one person in the population receives all the income, others receive none).

[iii]The G7 is the meeting of the finance ministers from a group of seven industrialized nations. It was formed in 1976.

[iv]Special Eurobarometer reports are based on in-depth thematical studies carried out for various services of the European Commission or other EU Institutions and integrated in Standard Eurobarometer's polling waves.

[v]Flash Eurobarometers are ad hoc thematical telephone interviews conducted at the request of any service of the European Commission. Flash surveys enable the Commission to obtain results relatively quickly and to focus on specific target groups, as and when required.

Labour market

The labour market is a key part of the economy and long-term trends have major implications not only for the economy but also society more generally. There have been a number of changes in the UK labour market over recent decades including:

- growth in the size of the labour force as the population has increased

- an increase in the proportion of women in the labour market

- a reduction in the size of the manufacturing sector

- recessions in the 1970s, 1980s, 1990s and the recent recession in 2008–09

This Social Trends chapter provides an overview of the labour market in the UK. The majority of the data used come from the Labour Force Survey[i].

Key points:

Employment

- Between 1971 and 2011 there has been an upward trend in the proportion of women in employment and downward trend in employment rates for men

- The employment rate for women rose from 53 per cent in Q2 1971 to 66 per cent in Q1 2011, for men employment rates peaked in Q1 1971 at 92 per cent and decreased to 76 per cent in Q1 2011

- Over the last 15 years there has been a narrowing of the gap in employment rates for women with and without dependent children: the gap in employment rates has narrowed from 5.8 percentage points in Q1 1996 to 0.8 percentage points in Q4 2010

- Between Q2 1992 and Q1 2011 the age group with the largest increase in employment rates was the 50–64 year olds and the largest decrease was in the 16 to 17-year-old age group as an increasing number in this age group continue in education rather than entering employment

- While there was a decrease in employment as a result of the 2008–09 recession, the effect has not been equal across types of employment: there was a decrease in full-time and an increase in part-time employment

Unemployment

- Unemployment rates in the UK have varied considerably between 1971 and 2011, with high rates in the 1980s and 1990s during and following periods of recession

- During and after the 2008–09 recession unemployment rates were lower than earlier recessions having increased from 5.2 per cent in Q1 2008 to 7.7 per cent in Q1 2011

- While unemployment rates for men and women follow a similar long term pattern, the recessions of the early 1990s and 2008-9 resulted in a smaller increase in unemployment rates for women than for men

- The number of unemployed people per vacancy more than doubled from 2.3 unemployed people per vacancy in March 2008 to 5.1 unemployed people per vacancy in March 2011
- There has also been an increase in the number of households in the UK where no adult has ever worked in recent years: no adult had ever worked in 1.0 per cent of households in 1997 and this had risen to 1.7 per cent in 2010

Economic inactivity

- Between 1971 and 2011 there has been little change in the proportion of the population aged 16 to 64 in the UK who were economically inactive, varying between 22 and 26 per cent.
- The proportion of women who were economically inactive decreased considerably from 44.5 per cent in Q2 1971 to 29.3 per cent in Q1 2011, and the proportion of men who were economically inactive has increased from 4.9 per cent in Q2 1971 to Q2 17.1 per cent in 2011
- In 2011, men were more likely than women to be economically inactive because they were students (33.3 per cent compared to 19.2 per cent) or long term sick (33.5 per cent compared to 17.2 per cent)
- Women were more likely than men to be economically inactive because they were looking after the family or home in 2011 (35.4 per cent compared to 5.7 per cent)

The labour market

The labour market involves the interaction of labour demand (the amount of labour firms demand in order to produce goods and services) and labour supply (which is primarily determined by the size of the population). Within the labour market individuals can be classified as either economically active (those who are employed and those who are unemployed) or economically inactive. The definitions of employment, unemployment and economically inactive used by the Office for National Statistics (ONS) to calculate official UK rates and levels are based on the International Labour Organisation (ILO) definitions.

A person is considered to be employed if they are:

- in paid employment at work for at least one hour over the reference week (or temporarily not at work during the reference period but have a formal attachment to their job), or
- in self-employment at work for at least one hour over the reference week (or is a person with an enterprise who is temporarily not at work during the reference period for any specific reason)

A person is considered to be unemployed if they are:

- without a job, want a job, have actively sought work in the last four weeks, and are able to start work within the next two weeks, or
- out of work, have found a job and are waiting to start it in the next two weeks

Finally the economically inactive group consists of:

- those people who are out of work but who do not satisfy all of the ILO criteria for unemployment: this is often because they are either not seeking work or are unavailable to start work

As well as being important for the economy, labour market activity is an important part of people's lives. Donovan and Halpern (2002) found that there is a positive relationship between people's satisfaction with their job and their satisfaction with life overall and that unemployment can have a lasting negative impact on people's well-being.

Figure 1   Economic activity and inactivity rates[1]

United Kingdom

Percentages

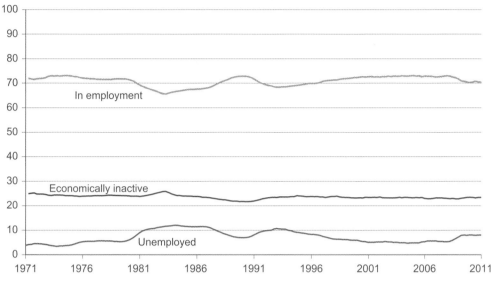

1 The headline employment and inactivity rates are based on the population aged 16 to 64 but the headline unemployment rate is based on the economically active population aged 16 and over. The employment and inactivity rates for those aged 16 and over are affected by the inclusion of the retired population in the denominators and are therefore less meaningful than the rates for those aged from 16 to 64. However, for the unemployment rate for those aged 16 and over, no such effect occurs as the denominator for the unemployment rate is the economically active population which only includes people in work or actively seeking and able to work.

Source: Labour Force Survey, Office for National Statistics[ii]

In Q1 2011:

- 70.7 per cent of people aged 16 to 64 were in employment
- 7.7 per cent of economically active people aged 16 and over were unemployed
- 23.2 per cent of people aged 16 to 64 were economically inactive

Figure 1 shows that over recent decades the proportion of people classified as economically active or economically inactive has been fairly stable (varying between 74 per cent and 78 per cent and 22 and 26 per cent respectively). However, there have been changes in patterns of employment and unemployment particularly during the recessions. These changes will be explored further below.

Employment

European comparisons

In Q4 2010 the employment rate in the UK was 70 per cent, the seventh highest employment rate amongst the EU-27 countries and 5.5 percentage points above the EU-27 average, as shown in **Table 1**.

Table 1   **Employment rates over the last four years (Q1 2007 to Q4 2010): EU comparison** [1]

Percentages

	Q4 2010	Lowest[2]		Highest[2]			Q4 2010	Lowest[2]		Highest[2]	
Austria	72	70	Q1 2007	73	Q3 2008	Lithuania	59	57	Q2 2010	66	Q3 2007
Belgium	63	61	Q3 2009	63	Q4 2007 Q4 2010	Luxembourg	65	63	Q4 2008	66	Q3 2010
Bulgaria	59	59	Q1 2010	65	Q3 2008	Malta	56	54	Q1 2007	57	Q3 2010
Cyprus	70	69	Q1 2010	72	Q4 2007	Netherlands	75	74	Q1 2010	78	Q4 2008
Czech Republic	66	64	Q1 2010	67	Q4 2008	Poland	60	55	Q1 2007	60	Q3 2008 Q4 2008 Q3 2010
Denmark	73	73	Q4 2010	79	Q3 2008	Portugal	65	65	Q4 2010	69	Q2 2008
Estonia	64	59	Q1 2010	70	Q3 2008	Romania	58	57	Q1 2010	61	Q3 2007 Q3 2008
Finland	68	67	Q1 2010	72	Q2 2008	Slovakia	59	58	Q1 2010	63	Q3 2008
France	64	64	Q4 2009	65	Q3 2008	Slovenia	66	66	Q4 2010	70	Q3 2008
Germany	72	68	Q1 2007	72	Q4 2010	Spain	58	58	Q1 2010	66	Q3 2007
Greece	58	58	Q4 2010	62	Q2 2008 Q3 2008	Sweden	73	71	Q1 2010	76	Q3 2007 Q3 2008
Hungary	56	55	Q1 2010	58	Q3 2007	**United Kingdom**	**70**	**69**	Q1 2010	**72**	Q4 2007
Ireland	59	59	Q4 2010	70	Q3 2007						
Italy	57	57	Q1 2010	59	Q2 2008						
Latvia	60	58	Q1 2010	70	Q4 2007	**EU-27 average**	**64**	**64**	Q1 2010	**66**	Q3 2008

1 Employment rates for 15 to 64-year-olds[iii].

2 Highest and lowest employment rates and the quarters in which they were observed.

Source: Eurostat[iv]

In Q4 2010, the highest rate of employment was seen in the Netherlands (75 per cent) and the lowest in Hungary (56 per cent). Over the last four years employment rates have varied both within and between countries. Across countries, rates have varied from a low of 54 per cent in Malta in Q1 2007 and a high of 79 per cent in Denmark in Q3 2008. The countries which have seen the largest changes in employment rates within the last four years were:

- Latvia with a high of 70 per cent in Q4 2007 and low of 58 per cent Q1 2010
- Estonia with a high of 70 per cent in Q3 2008 and low of 59 per cent Q1 2010
- Ireland with a high of 70 per cent in Q3 2007 and low of 59 per cent Q4 2010

The UK has seen less variation with a high of 72 per cent in Q4 2007 and low of 69 per cent in Q1 2010.

For people aged 16 to 64 employment rates in the UK have varied between 66 per cent and 73 per cent over recent decades, as shown in **Figure 2**. In Q1 2011 there were 28.4 million people aged 16 to 64 in employment, 71 per cent of that age group – a fall of 2.3 percentage points from Q1 2008 (the final quarter before the recent recession). Following the 2008–09 recession the lowest rate of employment was in Q1 2010, at 70 per cent: this was the lowest rate since Q3 1996.

Differences for men and women

Figure 2   **Employment rates:[1] by sex**

United Kingdom

Percentages

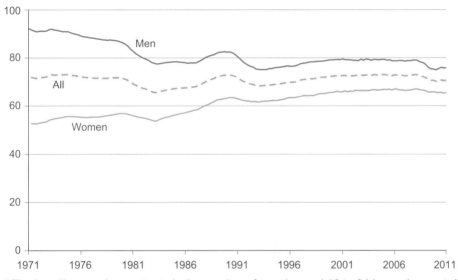

1 The headline employment rate is the number of people aged 16 to 64 in employment divided by the population aged 16 to 64. Data are seasonally adjusted.

Source: Labour Force Survey, Office for National Statistics[v]

There were sustained changes in employment rates for men and women aged 16 to 64 over the period, with an upward trend in the proportion of women in employment and downward trend in employment rates for men:

- the employment rate for women rose from 53 per cent in Q2 1971 to 66 per cent in Q1 2011, slightly below the peak of 67 per cent in Q1 2006
- for men employment rates peaked in Q1 1971 at 92 per cent with a low of 75 per cent in Q1 2010. In Q1 2011 the employment rate for men stood at 76 per cent

- while the overall trend in employment rates has been upward for women and downward for men, in 2010 the employment rate for men was still 10 percentage points higher than for women

Over the last 15 years not only has there been an increase in the employment rates for all women there has also been a narrowing of the gap in employment rates between women with and without dependent children[vi]. In Q4 2010 the employment rate for women with dependent children stood at 66.5 per cent, while the employment rate for women without dependent children stood at 67.3 per cent. The gap in employment rates has narrowed from 5.8 percentage points in Q1 1996 to 0.8 percentage points in Q4 2010. One factor which has contributed to this narrowing of the employment gap is a slight shift in the age of mothers, with more women having children later in life and older mothers more likely to be in employment (ONS, 2011d)[vii].

Employment by age group

Figure 3   **Employment rates:[1] by age group**

United Kingdom

Percentages

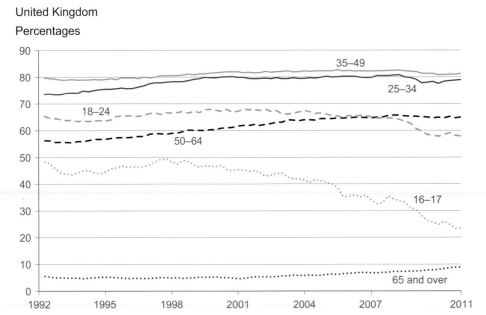

1 The headline employment rate is the number of people in each age group in employment divided by the population in that age group. Data are seasonally adjusted.

Source: Labour Force Survey, Office for National Statistics[viii]

Figure 3 shows that between Q2 1992 and Q1 2011 there were also changes in employment rates within different age groups, with the biggest changes being seen within the 16 to 17-year-old age group which saw a 24.9 percentage point fall in employment rates and within the 50 to 64-year-old age group, with a 8.7 percentage point increase in employment rates.

The large fall in the employment rates within people aged 16 to 24 may be because a higher proportion of this age group are remaining in education. The rise in employment rates for people aged 50 to 64 may be due in part to activities undertaken under a Public Service Agreement (PSA), agreed by the Labour Government in 2007 (HMT, 2007), to 'maximise employment opportunity for all'. People aged 50 to State Pension age[ix] were identified as a disadvantaged group[x] and a performance indicator for this PSA was to narrow the gap between the employment rates for disadvantaged groups and the overall rate for all people.

Disadvantaged groups

Barrett (2010) found that over the period Q1 1995 to Q4 2009 in the UK:

- employment rates for people aged 50 to State Pension age increased from 62.9 per cent to 71.0 per cent

- employment rates for people aged 25 to 49[xi] increased from 77.5 per cent to 80.2 per cent

- the gap between employment rates for these two age groups fell from 14.6 percentage points to 9.2 percentage points

Barrett (2010) also looked at the other disadvantaged groups in the UK (although start dates for comparison differ due to data availability) and found that gaps in employment rates fell for all disadvantaged groups except for those with low level or no qualifications:

- between Q2 1998 and Q4 2009 employment rates for disabled people increased from 38.3 per cent to 46.6 while for people who were not disabled employment rates fell from 79.6 per cent to 77.6 per cent

- the gap in employment rates between disabled people and people who were not disabled fell from 41.3 percentage points to 31.0 percentage points

- between Q2 1997 and Q4 2009 the employment rate for lone parents increased from 44.6 to 57.3 per cent while the employment rate for all other family types fell from 74.1 per cent to 73.8 per cent

- the gap in employment rates between lone parents and other family types fell from 29.5 percentage points to 16.5 percentage points

- between Q2 2001 and Q4 2009 the employment rate for ethnic minorities increased from 57.2 per cent to 59.6 per cent while for the white group employment rates fell from 75.8 per cent to 74.0

- the gap in employment rates between ethnic minorities and the white group fell from 18.6 percentage points to 14.5 percentage points

- between Q1 1995 and Q4 2009 the employment rate for people with low level or no qualifications fell from 60.1 per cent to 55.8 per cent while for people with higher qualifications employment rates increased slightly from 77.2 per cent to 77.4 per cent

- the gap in employment rates between people with low level or no qualifications and people with higher qualifications increased from 17.0 percentage points to 21.6 percentage points: however, over the same time period the proportion of people with low level or no qualifications fell from 36.6 per cent to 22.7 per cent

Working patterns and hours of work

ONS (2011a) suggested that despite the 2008–09 recession the labour market continues to show resilience in overall employment levels but that this masks differing situations between types of workers.

Figure 4   **Full- and part-time employment over the 2008–09 recession**

United Kingdom

Index (Q1 2008 =100)

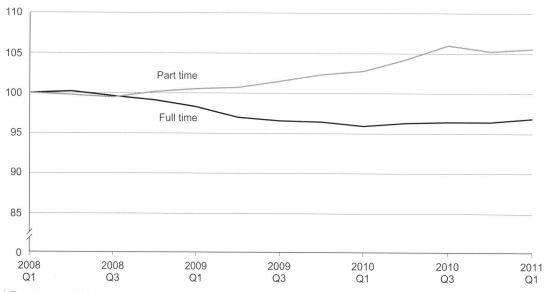

1 People aged 16 and over. Data are seasonally adjusted.

Source: Labour Force Survey, Office for National Statistics[xii]

For example employment numbers would mask the changing patterns in full-time and part-time employment over the recession as shown in **Figure 4**. Between Q1 2008 (the last quarter before the recession) and Q1 2011 the number of people in full-time employment fell by 3.1 per cent (689,000 people) but the number of people in part-time employment increased by 5.6 per cent (419,000). Data from the Labour Force Survey suggests that there was an increase over this period in the proportion of people working part-time who wanted to work full-time. Before the recession in Q1 2008, 9.5 cent of people in part-time work stated that they could not find full-time work. In Q1 2011 this stood at 15.2 per cent.

Stam and Coleman (2010) suggested that the number of hours worked is a more responsive measure of the state of the labour market than employment. In reaction to a fall in demand for their goods and services firms could either reduce the size of their workforce by making people redundant or adjust the number of hours employees work. Reducing hours rather than the number of people employed may be a more efficient way for firms to react to changes in demand, as there are costs associated with making people redundant and firms are likely to have invested in employees, for example through paying for training.

Figure 5 shows that during the recent recession total actual weekly hours worked by those in employment fell from a peak of 949 million hours in Q1 2008 (the last quarter before the recession) to reach 909 million hours in Q3 2009, a peak-to-trough fall of 4.2 per cent. Employment saw a smaller peak-to-trough fall during the most recent recession. For those aged 16 to 64, employment peaked at 28.8 million people in Q2 2008 (the first quarter of the recession) and fell to 28.0 million in Q1 2010, a fall of 2.7 per cent.

Figure 5   **Total and average weekly hours worked**[1]

United Kingdom
Millions/Units

1 All workers, main and second jobs. Data are seasonally adjusted.
Source: Labour Force Survey, Office for National Statistics[xiii]

Figure 5 also shows that the average actual weekly hours worked by individuals has generally shown a downward trend since 1996, reaching around 31 hours and 36 minutes in Q1 2011. This may reflect a rise in the proportion of people working part-time or an increase in the number of people choosing to or having to work fewer hours.

Industries and sectors

As mentioned in the introduction there has been a big change in the make up of the UK economy over recent decades and this is highlighted in **Table 2.**

Table 2   **Employee jobs:[1] by industry**

United Kingdom   Percentages

	1979	1989	1999	2008	2009	2010	Change 1979– 2010	Change 2008– 2010
Manufacturing	26.1	19.4	15.5	9.7	9.2	8.9	-17.2	-0.8
Construction	5.9	5.3	4.7	5.0	5.1	4.7	-1.2	-0.3
Total services	62.9	71.9	77.5	83.4	83.7	84.4	21.5	0.9
All industries (millions = 100 per cent)	24.6	24.1	25.1	27.6	27.2	26.7	2.1	-0.9

1 Data are at Q1 each year and are seasonally adjusted.

2 'All industries' covers: agriculture; mining and quarrying; electricity supply; water supply; waster management; manufacturing; construction; wholesale and retail; transport and storage; accommodation and food services; information and communication; finance and insurance; real estate; professional scientific and technological activities; administration; public administration and defence; education; health and social work; arts, entertainment and recreation; and other services.

Source: Short-term Employment Surveys, Office for National Statistics[xiv]

In Q1 1979 26.1 per cent of jobs were in the 'Manufacturing' industry but this proportion has fallen over the years to reach 8.9 per cent in Q1 2010, a fall of 17.2 percentage points. 'Total services' increased by 21.5 percentage points between Q1 1979 and Q1 2010.

Over the period 1979 to 2010 the total number of employee jobs increased from 24.6 million in 1979 to 26.7 million in 2010. However, between Q1 2008 (the last quarter before the latest recession) and Q1 2010 the number of employees jobs fell by 0.9 million. 'Manufacturing' saw its share of employees jobs fall over this period by 0.8 percentage point, a fall of 296,000 jobs. While 'Total services' saw an increase of 0.9 percentage points in its share of employee jobs it also saw a fall in the number of jobs (515,000).

Figure 6   **Annual change in public sector employment[1]**

United Kingdom

Thousands

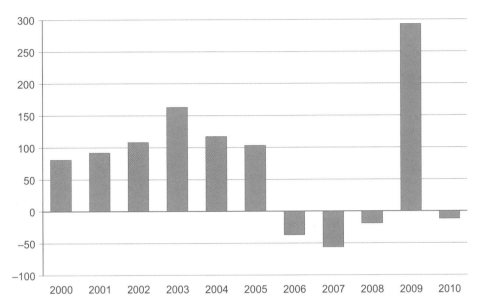

1 Annual changes in headcount of people aged 16 and over.

Source: Labour Force Survey, Office for National Statistics and returns from public sector organisations.[xv]

Figure 6 shows that initially there was an upward trend in public sector employment from 1999 to 2005 before falling slightly. Public sector employment reached a peak of 6.3 million (22 per cent of total employment) in 2009 primarily because of the reclassification of some banks from the private to the public sector (ONS, 2009). Public sector employment fell by 12,000 between 2009 and 2010.

Unemployment

Minimising unemployment is seen as a key goal of government economic policy. Rising unemployment has a number of economic costs (Anderton, 2008), including:

- consequences for government such as increased spending on benefits and a fall in income tax revenue

- costs to society as a whole such as rising inequality; increased risk of crime and family breakdown; and an increased burden on the welfare state which may require higher taxes

- consequences for individuals including loss of income; falls in real living standards; health risks including diet and mental health; and loss of marketable skills when unemployed for a long time.

Donovan and Halpern (2002: 3) found that 'being out of work is very damaging to your life satisfaction…' The loss of life satisfaction from the social effects of unemployment is far greater than the loss caused by loss of earnings. In recessions, rising unemployment also affects those who remain in their jobs, reducing their life satisfaction.'

Changes in unemployment over time

Figure 7 shows patterns of unemployment rates over recent decades. During the most recent recession the headline unemployment rate increased from 5.2 per cent in Q1 2008 (the last quarter before the recession) to a peak of 8.0 per cent in Q1 2010, an increase of 2.8 percentage points. In Q1 2011 the unemployment rate in the UK was 7.7 per cent.

Figure 7   **Unemployment rates:[1] by sex**

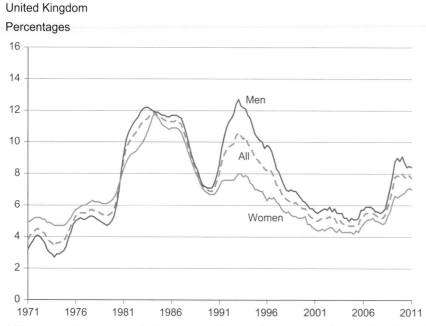

United Kingdom
Percentages

1 The unemployment rate is the number of unemployed people (aged 16 and over) divided by the economically active population (aged 16 and over). The economically active population is defined as those in employment plus those who are unemployed. Data are seasonally adjusted.

Source: Labour Force Survey, Office for National Statistics[xvi]

The recessions of the 1970s, 1980s, 1990s and the recent recession in 2008–09 had different impacts on unemployment. Following the recession in the early and mid 1970s unemployment reached a peak of 5.7 per cent in Q3 1977 and remained around this level until the 1980s recession during which unemployment increased from 5.5 per cent (Q4 1979, the last quarter before the recession) to a high of 11.9 per cent in Q2 1984 (13 quarters after the recession ended), an increase of 6.4 percentage points. Unemployment rates did not recover to the rate seen before the 1980s recession until more than 10 years later in Q2 2000. In the 1990s recession there was a smaller rise in unemployment, from 6.9 per cent (Q2 1990, the last quarter before the recession) to a high of 10.6 per cent in Q1 1993 (6 quarters after the recession ended). Unemployment rates recovered more quickly following this recession, reaching pre-recession levels four and a half years after the end of the recession in Q3 1997.

Differences for men and women

The impact of unemployment rates during the most recent recession has been different for men and women, as shown in Figure 7. For men the unemployment rate has increased from a pre-recession level of 5.6 per cent in Q1 2008 to a high of 9.1 per cent in Q1 2010 before falling again to 8.4 per cent in Q1 2011 while the unemployment rate for women continued to rise, from 4.8 per cent in Q1 2008 to 7.1 per cent in Q4 2010, falling slightly to 7.0 per cent in Q1 2011.

Unemployment by age

Unemployment rates also differ by age group.

Table 3   **Unemployment rates:[1] by age**

United Kingdom   Percentages

	1993	1996	1999	2002	2005	2008	2009	2010	2011
16–17	19.6	18.4	20.4	19.0	22.1	24.2	29.3	35.0	37.5
18–24	17.8	14.6	11.8	10.8	10.4	12.2	16.2	18.0	17.7
25–49	9.1	7.0	5.0	4.1	3.5	3.9	5.5	6.5	6.1
50 and over	8.7	6.3	4.3	3.1	2.8	2.8	4.2	4.6	4.6
16 and over	10.6	8.2	6.2	5.2	4.7	5.2	7.1	8.0	7.7

1 Data are Q1 and seasonally adjusted.
Source: Labour Force Survey, Office for National Statistics[xvii]

As can be seen in **Table 3**, in Q1 1993 people aged 16 to 17 had the highest rate of unemployment (19.6 per cent compared with 10.6 per cent for all those aged 16 and over), while those aged 50 and over had the lowest rate of unemployment (8.7 per cent). This has remained the case over the last two decades. Between 1993 and 2011 those aged 16 or 17 also saw the biggest rise in unemployment, an increase of 17.9 percentage points compared with a fall of 2.9 percentage points for all those aged 16 and over. The age group with the biggest fall in unemployment rates was those aged 50 and over, a fall of 4.1 percentage points between 1993 and 2011.

Unemployment rates increased for all age groups between Q1 2008 (the last quarter before the recession) and Q1 2011. Again the biggest increase was for those aged 16 to 17 (13.3 percentage points) and lowest for those aged 50 and over (1.8 percentage points).

Graduates and non-graduates

One group for which unemployment has been a particular concern following the recession is new graduates (those who graduated 0 to 2 years ago). ONS (2011b) showed that the unemployment rate for new graduates was 20 per cent in Q3 2010, the highest in over a decade and almost double the rate before the start of the recession. By the end of the recession the unemployment rate for new graduates was 2.3 times higher than for the UK as a whole (18.5 per cent in Q2 2008 compared with 7.9 per cent in Q3 2009). While unemployment rates for those aged 21 to 24 with a degree remained lower in Q3 2010 than for people of the same age without a degree (11.6 per cent compared with 14.6 per cent) the recession seems to have impacted on graduates aged 21 to 24 more than non-graduates aged 21 to 24. Unemployment rates increased by 6.3 percentage points (from 7.2 per cent in Q2 2008 to 13.4 per cent in Q3 2009) for graduates aged 21 to 24 while for non-graduates aged 21 to 24 unemployment rates increased by 5.3 percentage points (from 10.7 per cent in Q2 2008 to 16.0 per cent in Q3 2009)[xviii].

Unemployment and vacancies

Figure 8   Number of unemployed people per vacancy[1]

United Kingdom
People

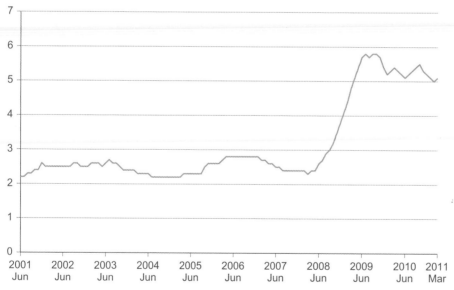

1 UK excluding Agriculture, Forestry & Fishing. Data are seasonally adjusted.
Source: Vacancy Survey and Labour Force Survey, Office for National Statistics[xix]

Over the course of the 2008–09 recession the number of unemployed people per job vacancy more than doubled, as shown in **Figure 8**. In March 2008 there were an average of 2.3 unemployed people per job vacancy; by July 2009 this had reached 5.8 people per vacancy. The number of unemployed people per vacancy decreased to 5.1 in March 2011.

Duration of unemployment

Stam and Long (2010) used Labour Force Survey data to analyse the effect that an individual's characteristics have on the length of their spell of unemployment and their likelihood of exiting a spell by becoming employed, for people aged 18 to State Pension age between 2006 and 2009. They found that, holding other things equal, the following are more likely to have a spell of unemployment:

- the youngest age group (18 to 24-year-olds)
- people who are not married
- men
- women with dependent children
- people from ethnic minority groups

In terms of the length of the spell of unemployment Stam and Long (2010) found that, compared with the average of 3.7 months:

- people in the youngest age group could expect a spell of unemployment to last 1.3 months less
- males could expect to experience a spell of unemployment to last 1.6 months less
- an individual claiming Job Seekers Allowance (JSA) could expect a longer spell of unemployment (3.8 months longer) than those not claiming JSA, all other things being equal

After controlling for other factors the length of unemployment was found to have a significant impact on the probability of ending the unemployment spell by moving into employment. Those who have the shortest duration of unemployment (six months or less) are most likely to exit unemployment into employment. All other things being held equal[xx]:

- the youngest age group are most likely to find employment
- unemployed men are less likely to find employment than unemployed women
- married people are more likely to find employment than those who are not married
- women with dependent children are less likely to find employment than women without dependent children
- when compared with individuals reporting low levels of qualification (below GCSE level) those with higher levels (at least a GCSE or equivalent) had a higher probability of finding employment
- those claiming JSA were more likely to find employment compared with those who were not. It may be that conditions connected with claiming JSA, such as attending interviews with Jobcentre Plus advisers, encourage unemployed individuals to remain 'attached' to the labour market

Unemployment and Households

Along with recent increases in unemployment rates there has also been an increase in the number of households in which no one has ever worked. Between Q2 1997 and Q2 2010 the number of households in which no one had ever worked almost doubled from 184,000 to 352,000 households (ONS, 2011c). The 352,000 households where no one had ever worked equated to 1.7 per cent of the households in the UK up from 1.0 per cent in 1997. Excluding student households, where everyone was aged 16 to 24 and in full-time education, there remain 269,000 households where no one has ever worked in Q2 2010. Across the country, the highest proportion was in Inner London at 6.5 per cent of all households, three times more than the next highest – Outer London at 2.2 per cent. The lowest percentage was in the East of England at 0.5 per cent, followed by 0.8 per cent in the South West and 0.9 per cent in the South East.

As can be seen in **Table 4** the majority of households where no one has ever worked were one-person households followed by lone-parent households (around 39 per cent and 35 per cent of households where no one has ever worked, respectively, increasing to 40 and 44 per cent respectively when student households are excluded). Only 29,000 of the 352,000 households where no one has ever worked were couple households (around 8.2 per cent).

Table 4   **Number of households[1,2] where no one has ever worked: by household type, 2010[3]**

United Kingdom   Thousands

	Households never worked	Excluding student households[4]
Total households where no one has ever worked	352	269
One-person households	138	107
Couple households	29	22
Lone-parent households	124	119
Other households[5]	61	22

1 Households including at least one person aged 16 to 64.

2 A household is defined as having never worked if all members aged 16 years and over are currently not in employment and state that they have never had paid work (apart from casual or holiday work, or the job that they are waiting to begin)
3 Data are Q2 and are not seasonally adjusted.

4 Student households are households where all adults are aged 16 to 24 and in education. Excludes households where all members are in education but some members are aged 25 years and over.

5 Other household types include households that contain more than one family unit.

Source: Labour Force Survey, Office for National Statistics (ONS, 2011c)

In Q2 2010 around 552,000 adults were living in households where no one had ever worked, with a third of these in student households not wanting to work because of their studies. Of the remaining 374,000 adults:

- 68 per cent were not seeking a job and would not like to work
- 16 per cent were not seeking a job but would like to work
- 13 per cent were unemployed, therefore looking for and available to work

There are also around a quarter of a million children under 16 years old, living in households where none of the adults has ever worked (265,000 in all households that have never worked and 258,000 in non-student households) (ONS, 2011c).

Economic inactivity

The final category of people to examine in this chapter are those who are economically inactive. Over recent decades the proportion of people aged 16 to 64 who were classified as economically inactive has been relatively stable, varying between a low of 22 per cent in 1990, and a high of 26 per cent in 1983, as shown in **Figure 9**.

Differences for men and women

Figure 9   **Economic inactivity rates:[1] by sex**

United Kingdom

Percentages

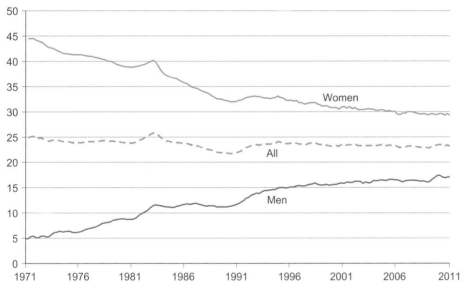

1 People aged 16 to 64. Data are seasonally adjusted.

Source: Labour Force Survey, Office for National Statistics[xxi]

While the overall proportion of people classified as economically inactive has been fairly stable the trend by sex is quite different. Between Q2 1971 and Q1 2011 the proportion of women classified as economically inactive fell, from 44.5 per cent to 29.3 per cent, while the trend was the opposite for men, increasing from 4.9 per cent to 17.1 per cent.

Reasons for inactivity

There have also been changes in the reasons for economic inactivity, as shown in **Table 5.**

Table 5   **Reasons for economic inactivity:[1] by sex**

United Kingdom   Percentages

	1994	1999	2004	2009	2010	2011
Men						
Students	27.7	25.0	28.0	32.9	34.4	33.3
Looking after family/home	4.7	6.0	6.1	6.2	6.3	5.7
Temporary sick	3.8	2.9	3.1	2.5	2.6	2.2
Long-term sick	39.9	42.8	37.7	34.6	32.5	33.5
Discouraged	3.4	1.6	0.7	1.0	1.2	1.5
Retired	11.1	12.1	12.9	13.2	13.3	13.5
Other	9.4	9.5	11.4	9.5	9.6	10.2
Does not want a job	68.2	67.9	71.0	72.1	69.8	70.1
Wants a job	31.8	32.1	29.0	27.9	30.2	29.9
Women						
Students	11.9	12.5	14.1	17.7	18.8	19.2
Looking after family/home	48.1	40.8	38.7	35.9	35.6	35.4
Temporary sick	1.9	1.9	1.7	1.6	1.5	1.5
Long-term sick	14.6	19.3	19.1	17.8	17.9	17.2
Discouraged	1.4	0.7	0.3	0.5	0.5	0.5
Retired	13.4	15.8	16.7	18.5	18.1	18.3
Other	8.7	9.0	9.4	8.0	7.7	7.8
Does not want a job	75.3	75.7	78.7	78.5	77.2	77.1
Wants a job	24.7	24.3	21.3	21.5	22.8	22.9

1 Data are Q1 and are seasonally adjusted.
Source: Labour Force Survey, Office for National Statistics[xxii]

Between 1994 and 2011 there has been a fall of 12.7 percentage points in the proportion of women who give 'looking after the family/home' as the prime reason for economic inactivity. Over the same period there was an increase of 7.3 percentage points in the proportion of women giving the reason for economic inactivity as 'student'; those who were retired increased by 4.9 percentage points; and those reporting long-term sickness increased by 2.6 percentage points. For men the biggest increase was in the proportion reporting being students (an increase of 5.6 percentage points); the proportion reporting that they were inactive due to looking after the family/home also increased slightly (by 1.0 percentage point). The proportion of men reporting long-term sickness as their main reason for economic activity fell by 6.4 percentage points and the proportion reporting that they were 'discouraged' fell by 1.9 percentage points. A discouraged worker is an individual who wants to work but is not looking for a job because of a perceived lack of demand.

References

Anderton, A (2008). Economics: Fifth edition. Pearson: Essex

Barrett (2010). Disadvantaged groups in the labour market. Available at www.statistics.gov.uk/CCI/article.asp?ID=2442

Donovan and Halpern (2002). Life satisfaction: the state of knowledge and implications for government. Available at www.cabinetoffice.gov.uk/media/cabinetoffice/strategy/assets/paper.pdf

HMT (2007). Public Service Agreements 2008-2011. Available at http://webarchive.nationalarchives.gov.uk/+/http://www.hm-treasury.gov.uk/pbr_csr07_psaindex.htm

ONS (2009). Public Sector Employment - Q3 2009. Available at www.statistics.gov.uk/mediareleases/findreleases.asp?releasetitle=Public+Sector+Employment&releaseorganisation=42&releasetheme=&daterange=3&sday=15&smonth=06&syear=2010&ShowHits=10&SortOrder=0&ShowYear=2010

ONS (2011a) GDP and the Labour Market

ONS (2011b). Graduates in the labour market. Available at www.statistics.gov.uk/cci/nugget.asp?id=1162

ONS (2011c). Data: Households that have never worked. Available at www.statistics.gov.uk/cci/nugget.asp?id=1163

ONS (2011d). Mothers in the labour market. Available at www.statistics.gov.uk/CCI/nugget.asp?ID=2124

Stam and Coleman (2010). The relationship between hours worked in the UK and the economy. Available at www.statistics.gov.uk/cci/article.asp?ID=2574

Stam and Long (2010). Explaining exits from unemployment in the UK, 2006-09. Available at www.statistics.gov.uk/cci/article.asp?ID=2573

Notes

i The Labour Force Survey (LFS) is a quarterly sample survey of about 53,000 households living at private addresses in the UK, representing about 0.2 per cent of the population. The survey asks respondents for information on their personal circumstances and labour market status. The LFS is weighted to provide information that is representative of the UK population. The LFS is conducted using rolling five quarter waves, with each sample household retained for five consecutive quarters, and a fifth of the sample replaced each quarter. The ability to track an individual across quarters produces a rich source of longitudinal data.

ii Data obtained from Labour Market Statistics Integrated FR available at
www.statistics.gov.uk/StatBase/TSDTimezone.asp?vlnk=md&Pos=&ColRank=1&Rank=-1

iii http://epp.eurostat.ec.europa.eu/portal/page/portal/employment_unemployment_lfs/methodology/definitions

iv Data obtained from table lfsi_emp_q on http://epp.eurostat.ec.europa.eu/portal/page/portal/statistics/search_database

v Data obtained from Labour Market Statistics Integrated FR available at
www.statistics.gov.uk/StatBase/TSDTimezone.asp?vlnk=md&Pos=&ColRank=1&Rank=-1

vi Dependent children are all those under 16 and those aged 16 to 18 who have never married and who are in full-time education.

vii A video explaining this story is available at www.youtube.com/user/onsstats?feature=mhum#p/u/0/D-AOq0ACups

viii Data obtained from Labour Market Statistics Integrated FR available at
www.statistics.gov.uk/StatBase/TSDTimezone.asp?vlnk=md&Pos=&ColRank=1&Rank=-1

ix State Pension age is the earliest age you can get your State Pension, but individuals do not have to retire at State Pension age. State Pension age is changing for both men and women. Currently, the State Pension age for men is 65. On 6 April 2010, the State Pension age for women started to increase gradually from 60 to 65, to match men's. The government has announced new proposals for increasing State Pension age which would mean women's State Pension age would increase more quickly to 65 between April 2016 and November 2018 and from December 2018 the State Pension age for both men and women would start to increase to reach 66 by April 2020. The Government is also considering the timetable for future increases to the State Pension age from 66 to 68.

x The disadvantaged groups identified in the Public Service Agreements (PSAs) were disabled people; lone parents; ethnic minorities; people aged 50 to state pension age (at the time this was 64 for men and 59 for women); the lowest qualified (those who have not obtained a minimum of a C grade at GCSE or equivalent); and those living in the most deprived wards (these have not been included here).

xi Due to a large fall in the employment rates for people aged 16 to 24 over the last six to seven years, partly through policies aimed at keeping this group in education, people aged 50 to state pension age will be compared to people aged 25 to 49.

xii Data obtained from Labour Market Statistics Integrated FR available at
www.statistics.gov.uk/StatBase/TSDTimezone.asp?vlnk=md&Pos=&ColRank=1&Rank=-1

xiii Data obtained from Labour Market Statistics Integrated FR available at
www.statistics.gov.uk/StatBase/TSDTimezone.asp?vlnk=md&Pos=&ColRank=1&Rank=-1

xiv Data obtained from www.statistics.gov.uk/STATBASE/tsdataset.asp?vlnk=341

xv Data obtained from Labour Market Statistics Integrated FR available at
www.statistics.gov.uk/StatBase/TSDTimezone.asp?vlnk=md&Pos=&ColRank=1&Rank=-1

xvi Data obtained from Labour Market Statistics Integrated FR available at
www.statistics.gov.uk/StatBase/TSDTimezone.asp?vlnk=md&Pos=&ColRank=1&Rank=-1

xvii Data obtained from Labour Market Statistics Integrated FR available at
www.statistics.gov.uk/StatBase/TSDTimezone.asp?vlnk=md&Pos=&ColRank=1&Rank=-1

xviii A video explaining this story is available at www.youtube.com/user/onsstats#p/u/8/TS9hwfkxGe0

xix Data obtained from Labour Market Statistics Integrated FR available at
www.statistics.gov.uk/StatBase/TSDTimezone.asp?vlnk=md&Pos=&ColRank=1&Rank=-1

xx Base categories were as follows:

Characteristic	Base category
Age	35 to 49
Sex	Female
Ethnicity	Not classified as an ethnic minority
Marital status	Unmarried with no dependent children
Education	Below GCSE
Housing	Renting privately
Region	'West Midlands Metropolitan County'
Previous occupation	'Elementary'

xxi Data obtained from Labour Market Statistics Integrated FR available at
www.statistics.gov.uk/StatBase/TSDTimezone.asp?vlnk=md&Pos=&ColRank=1&Rank=-1

xxii Data obtained from Labour Market Statistics Integrated FR available at
www.statistics.gov.uk/StatBase/TSDTimezone.asp?vlnk=md&Pos=&ColRank=1&Rank=-1

Income and wealth

The United Kingdom has experienced many changes to both its economy and society, and these two aspects are related. In this analysis, long and short-term trends in a number of aspects of household and individual economic circumstances are examined in relation to economic activity levels in the UK. Living standards depend on the level of economic activity and on the redistribution of economic resources within society as a whole, and have a major influence on social well-being. Income and wealth are generally analysed at the level of either the family or the household, because these are the units across which income and expenditure are considered to be pooled, so that the income of the family or household can be regarded as representative of the standard of living of each person living in it. However, for some purposes such as the analysis of income from employment, income is analysed for individuals.

Key Points:

Trends in the economy and household income

- During the recent recession (2008 to 2009) GDP per head decreased by 5.5 per cent while real household disposable income per head increased by 1.2 per cent

- The decrease in GDP per head between 2008 and 2009 was the largest annual percentage decrease in any year since 1949

- Unlike the 1970s and 1980s, real household disposable income per head grew almost continuously through the 1990s and 2000s, irrespective of recessions

Sources of household income

- On average, from 2006/07 to 2008/09 an estimated 73 per cent of household income was derived from wages, salaries and self-employed earnings

Household income distribution

- Pensioner households and lone parent households are more likely to be in the lower end of the income distribution

- Couples without children are more likely to be at the higher end of the income distribution

- In 2008/09 an estimated 18 per cent of individuals in the UK were from households with low income – below 60 per cent of contemporary median income. This is virtually unchanged since 1998/99

- In 2008/09 a higher proportion of pensioners and children lived in households with low income, although both percentages had decreased since 1998/99

- People living in households where income was below £20,000 per annum were considerably more likely to perceive their household financial situation as bad or very bad in 2009 than those living in households with higher incomes

Earnings growth

- Between 2008 and 2009 earnings growth was larger for part-time employees and smallest for male full-time employees
- Between 1998 and 2009 earnings grew on average at a faster rate than inflation

Household wealth

- Household net wealth more than doubled in real terms between 1987 and 2009, from £56,000 to £117,000 in 2008/09 prices
- Household net wealth was lower in 2009 than in 2007 largely because of the decrease in total property assets as a result of the fall in house prices during the 2008-2009 recession

Household savings

- Household saving as a percentage of household income increased from 2.0 per cent to 7.0 per cent between 2008 and 2009. This increase followed a decrease in 2008 to the lowest recorded value since 1970

Taxes

- H M Revenue & Customs (HMRC) estimated that income tax paid in 2010/11 would be 18.3 per cent of all income on average
- For those earning incomes between £6,475 and £7,499 income tax would be 1.3 per cent of overall income, and for those with an income of £1 million and over 44.4 per cent
- Indirect taxes, such as Value Added Tax, duties and levies, form a larger percentage of the disposable income of those who earn less, even though they may also spend less

Trends in the economy and household income

Gross domestic product (GDP) is the total value of output in the UK and is used to measure change in economic activity. Over long periods of time, change in GDP can be greatly affected by change in the size of the population. Therefore, GDP per head is the preferred measure for comparison over time. Between 1970 and 2009, GDP per head in the UK more than doubled in real terms although the annual rate of change varied over the period (**Figure 1**).

Figure 1   **Real household disposable income per head[1] and gross GDP per head[2]**

United Kingdom
Index numbers (1970=100)

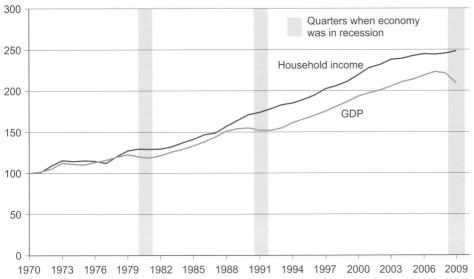

1 Adjusted to real terms using the expenditure deflator for the household sector.
2 Adjusted to real terms using the GDP deflator.
Source: Office for National Statistics

There was a period of continuous growth in GDP per head from 1992 until 2007, albeit with some year-on-year variation, followed by a slight decrease in 2008 at the start of the most recent recession. The generally accepted definition of recession is that GDP falls in at least two consecutive quarters. In **Figure 1**, which shows annual figures, the recessions of the 1980s, the 1990s and most recently between 2008 and 2009 are indicated by shading. Between 2008 and 2009, GDP per head dropped sharply by 5.5 per cent, falling to just below its 2004 level. This is the largest annual percentage decrease in GDP per head in any year since 1949.

When assessing material living standards within a society another important consideration is the level of household[i] income (Chiripanhura, 2010). Over the period 1970 to 2009 in the UK, GDP and real household disposable income per head grew on average by 1.9 and 2.4 per cent per year respectively. In the 1970s real household disposable income per head tended to increase more than GDP per head in times of economic growth, and decrease more than GDP per head in times of recession. This relationship changes in the 1980s, with real household disposable income per head continuing to rise during the recession in the early 1990s, albeit at a slower rate than the preceding few years. Since then, real household disposable income per head growth was more variable than growth in GDP per head up to 2001, varying between 1.1 per cent and 4.0 per cent. Growth slowed to 0.5 per cent in 2008 and 2009. This recent growth in real household disposable income per head during the recession is in part due to the fall in interest paid on mortgages and the fall in taxes and increase in social benefits.

Table 1   **Perceptions of the current economic climate[1] by income grouping, 2009[2]**

United Kingdom

Percentages

	Less than £20,000	£20,000– £39,999	£40,000– £59,999	£60,000– £99,999	£100,000 and over	All individuals
The economic situation in the world						
Good or very good	6	3	2	1	0	4
Neither good or bad	17	18	12	8	8	16
Bad or very bad	77	79	85	91	92	80
The economic situation in the UK						
Good or very good	8	5	4	4	0	6
Neither good or bad	17	15	13	4	11	15
Bad or very bad	76	80	83	92	89	80
The financial situation in your household						
Good or very good	28	44	54	64	63	40
Neither good or bad	47	42	35	36	34	43
Bad or very bad	25	14	11	1	3	18

1 Respondents aged 16 and over were asked 'How would you judge the current situation in each of the following?' regarding the aspects shown. Results are based only on those respondents who, in a separate question, provided information on their income.

2 Data were collected in February to March.

Source: 2009 Survey of Public Attitudes and Behaviours towards the Environment, Department for Environment, Food and Rural Affairs

As well as looking at objective measures of the economy and household income, subjective measures that look at people's views on the economic situation are also useful. Peoples' reported perception of the economic situation at an international, national and household level tends to vary by their actual standards of living. In 2009, 80 per cent of people in the UK thought that the current economic situation both in the world and the UK was bad or very bad (**Table 1**). Those with higher incomes were more likely to judge the economic situation as bad or very bad. However, in the same survey 18 per cent of respondents thought that the financial situation in their own household was bad or very bad with those with lower incomes more likely to report that the household situation was bad (25 per cent of those with incomes less than £20,000 compared with 3 per cent of those with incomes of £100,000 and over).

Sources of household income

On average, for 2006/07 to 2008/09, an estimated 73 per cent of all household income was derived from wages, salaries and self-employed earnings, 13 per cent came from state retirement and other pensions, 9 per cent from benefits and tax credits and 3 per cent from investments. The relative contribution of different sources of household income varies by characteristics such as household composition, region, and the occupation, age and ethnic group of the household reference person[ii].

Table 2	Sources of total weekly household income: by ethnic group of household reference person, 2006/07–2008/09

United Kingdom

Percentages

	Wages and salaries	Self-employed income	Investments	Tax credits	State retirement pension[1]	Other pensions	Social security disability benefits	Other social security benefits	Other sources
White	64	9	3	1	7	7	2	5	2
Mixed	71	8	1	2	2	2	1	8	4
Asian or Asian British	70	9	1	4	2	2	1	7	4
Indian	74	9	1	1	2	2	1	4	4
Pakistani and Bangladeshi	56	10	1	10	4	1	2	13	4
Black or Black British	69	7	0	3	3	1	1	10	4
Black Caribbean	70	5	1	3	5	2	2	10	2
Black non-Caribbean	69	8	0	4	1	1	1	11	5
Chinese or other ethnic group	70	8	1	2	2	3	1	5	7
All households	**64**	**9**	**3**	**2**	**6**	**7**	**2**	**5**	**2**

1 May include income support or pension credit.

Source: Family Resources Survey, (DWP, 2010a)

Averaged over the period 2006/07 and 2008/09, the composition of income for households with a reference person belonging to the White ethnic group was very similar to the overall average (**Table 2**). However, wages and salaries represented a higher proportion of total income for households with a reference person belonging to the Mixed, Indian, Black or Black British, and

Chinese or other groups. Households with a reference person in the Pakistani and Bangladeshi group and the Black or Black British group derived a higher than average proportion of their income from social security benefits – other than those for disability. Households where the household reference person was from any of the ethnic groups other than White derived a smaller proportion of their income from state retirement and other pensions. This could in part be because lower proportions of people with an ethnic background other than White are in older age groups compared with the White ethnic group, resulting in lower dependence on pensions (ONS, 2009a).

Household income distribution

Various sources of income differ in importance for different types of households, and levels of earnings vary between individuals. The result is an uneven distribution of total income between households. However, this inequality is reduced to some extent by the deduction of taxes and social contributions, and their subsequent redistribution to the households in the form of benefits from the government. For this reason disposable income is usually used in analysis of household income distribution. Disposable income is also adjusted for household size and composition. This takes into account that to achieve a comparable standard of living a household of, say, three adults will need a higher disposable income than a single person living alone. This adjustment is known as equivalisation[iii].

Figure 2   **Distribution of real[1] household disposable income[2]**

United Kingdom/Great Britain[3]
£ per week at 2008/09 prices

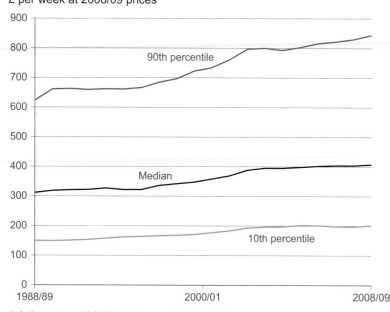

1 Adjusted to 2008/09 prices using the retail prices index less council tax/domestic rates.

2 Equivalised household disposable income before deduction of housing costs, using OECD equivalisation scale.

3 Data for 1994/95 to 2001/02 are for Great Britain only.

Source: Department for Work and Pensions (DWP)

Figure 2 shows disposable income in pounds per week, before deduction of housing costs, at the median, the 10th percentile (the income of one in ten of the population is below this level) and the 90th percentile (the income of one in ten of the population is above this level) for years between 1988/89 and 2008/09 at 2008/09 prices. Throughout this time period the level of income inequality remained fairly stable. Income at the 90th percentile was more than 4 times the income at the 10th percentile, both in 1988/89 and 2008/09.

Figure 3   **Distribution of weekly household disposable income,[1] 2008/09**

United Kingdom

Millions of individuals

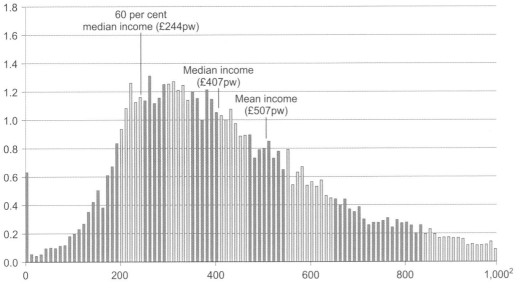

1 Equivalised household disposable income before deduction of housing costs (in £10 bands), using OECD equivalisation scale. The £10 bands are grouped into decile groups in alternating colours.

2 There were also an additional 3.6 million individuals with income above £1,000 per week.

Source: DWP (2010b)

Figure 3 shows a more detailed picture of income distribution in the UK for 2008/09. Disposable incomes, before housing cost deduction, are not distributed equally. There is a much greater concentration of people at lower levels of weekly income, with nearly two-thirds of individuals living in households with disposable weekly income lower than the mean. There is a long 'tail' of people at the higher end of the distribution with an estimated 6 per cent of individuals living in households with disposable incomes of £1,000 per week or more. This results in a much higher mean income per week, £507, compared with the median of £407.

Table 3   **Distribution of household disposable income[1] by household type, 2008/09**

United Kingdom

Percentages

	Bottom fifth	Second fifth	Middle fifth	Fourth fifth	Top fifth	All (millions)
Pensioner couple	20	24	21	18	16	**7.9**
Single pensioner	27	31	22	14	7	**4.7**
Couple with children	18	20	22	21	19	**20.7**
Couple without children	11	9	16	26	38	**11.3**
Single with children	39	31	18	9	4	**5.0**
Single without children	21	18	20	22	20	**10.6**
All individuals	**20**	**20**	**20**	**20**	**20**	**60.3**

1 Equivalised household disposable income before deduction of housing costs has been used to rank the individuals into quintile groups.
Source: DWP (2010b)

Household type can be related to position within the income distribution (**Table 3**). During 2008/09 people living in lone parent households and pensioners living alone were more concentrated at the lower end of the income distribution (39 per cent and 27 per cent respectively in the lowest fifth). A higher proportion of couples without children were concentrated at the top of the distribution (38 per cent in the highest fifth). Single people without children and people living in households consisting of couples with children or pensioner couples were more evenly spread across the income distribution.

Map 1   **Gross Disposable Household Income per head: by NUTS 2 area,[1] 2008**

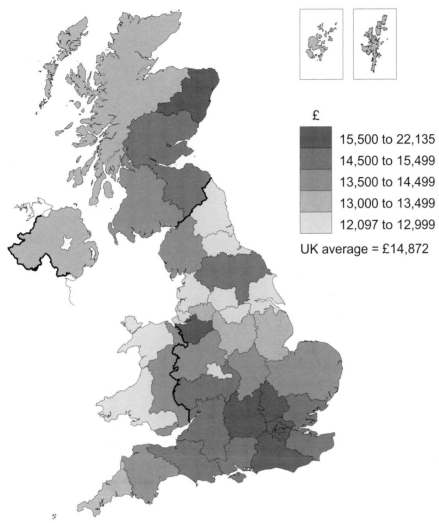

£

	15,500 to 22,135
	14,500 to 15,499
	13,500 to 14,499
	13,000 to 13,499
	12,097 to 12,999

UK average = £14,872

1 Nomenclature of Units for Territorial Statistics level 2 area.

There are also large differences in average gross disposable household income (GDHI) per head in different geographic areas of the UK. **Map 1** illustrates how household disposable income per head varied by local areas (NUTS 2 level[iv]) in 2008. It shows that GDHI per head was higher in London, the South East and parts of the East of England. Relatively lower incomes were recorded in parts of the West Midlands, the North East and West Wales and the Valleys. The main contribution to GDHI per head comes from compensation of employees, so is strongly influenced by an area's productivity and labour market outcomes. GDHI per head is also influenced by sources of income apart from work such as from property, pensions and social transfers (Oguz et al., 2010).

The incidence of low income, together with the factors contributing to low income and ways to reduce their effects, have been a focus of attention for government since the first Poor Laws were introduced in the 16th century. Having a low income is associated with being disadvantaged and excluded from many of the opportunities available to the average citizen, and thus affects the level of societal wellbeing.

Figure 4   **Individuals living in households below 60 per cent of median household disposable income[1]**

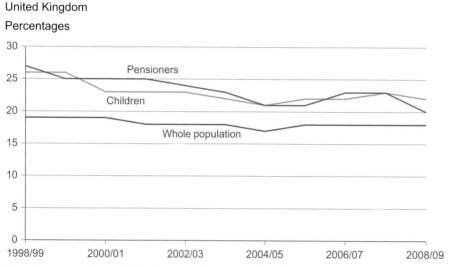

United Kingdom
Percentages

1 Contemporary household disposable income before deduction of housing costs, using OECD equivalisation scale.
Source: DWP (2010b)

The threshold generally used in the UK and other developed countries to define low income is 60 per cent of contemporary equivalised median household disposable income (before deduction of housing costs). In 2008/09 in the UK, 18 per cent of individuals were living in a household with income below this threshold, a proportion similar to that recorded in 1987 (DWP, 2010b). **Figure 4** shows that children and pensioners were at higher than average risk of living in a low income household. Between 1998/99 and 2008/09 however, the proportion of children and pensioners in low income households has decreased, from 26 per cent to 22 per cent, and from 27 per cent to 20 per cent, respectively.

Earnings growth

Figure 5   **Earning growth for full-time and part-time employees[1] and the retail prices index and consumer price index[2]**

United Kingdom

Percentage change over 12 months[3]

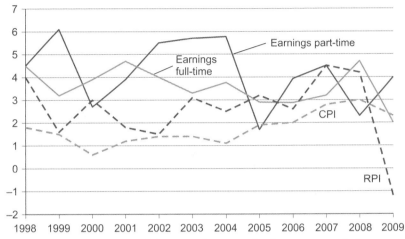

1 Full-time employees on adult rates whose pay for the survey period was unaffected by absence.

2 Further information about CPI[v] and RPI[vi] can be found in notes at the end of this section.

3 Data are at April each year.

Source: Office for National Statistics

Wages and salaries are the largest important components of household and individual incomes in the UK (64 per cent of household income for the years 2006/07 to 2008/09, see Table 2). Between 2008 and 2009 median earnings for both part-time and full-time employees in the UK grew, at 4.0 per cent and 2.0 per cent respectively (**Figure 5**). Over the same period the consumer price index (CPI[v]) increased by 2.3 per cent and retail price index (RPI[vi]) decreased by 1.2 per cent.

Between1998 and 2009 median earnings for part-time employees increased on average by 5.2 per cent per year, while the average growth in earnings for full-time employees was 4.2 per cent. On average, over this period the CPI increased by 1.9 per cent and the RPI by 2.8 per cent per year, meaning that earnings grew at a faster rate than inflation.

Table 4   **Gross weekly pay for full-time and part-time employees: by gender,[1] April 2008 and 2009**

United Kingdom

£ per week

	Median		
	2008	**2009**	**Percentage change**
Male			
Full-time	522.0	531.1	1.7
Part-time	136.6	143.6	5.1
Female			
Full-time	412.4	426.4	3.4
Part-time	149.9	155.6	3.8

1 Employees on adult rates whose pay for the survey pay-period was not affected by absence.
Source: Annual Survey of Hours and Earnings, ONS (2009c)

The level of earnings in 2008 and 2009 and the change between these two years show differences between the pay for men and women (**Table 4**). Median weekly earnings for full-time employees were higher for men than women in both years, but weekly earnings for part-time employees were higher for women than men. There was higher growth in median pay for females than males for those in full-time employment and lower growth for women than men for those in part-time work. The lowest growth in median pay was for men in full-time employment.

The difference in earnings growth between men and women can partially be explained by structural changes in employment. According to the Annual Population Survey, between 2008 and 2009 there was a fall in full-time employment rates and an overall increase in part-time employment rates for both men and women. Also men experienced the largest fall in both types of employment.

Household wealth

The terms wealth and income are often used interchangeably but they are different. Income represents a flow of resources over a specified period of time received either in cash or in kind, for example, earnings or state benefits. Wealth measures the value of assets owned at a particular point in time. People's ownership of assets contributes to their economic wellbeing as a source of financial security: for example, some assets can be sold to help maintain a stable standard of living when income is falling in real terms. Some forms of wealth can also provide a current income flow, for example, interest on savings.

Figure 6   **Real household net wealth per head[1]**

United Kingdom

Index number (1987=100)

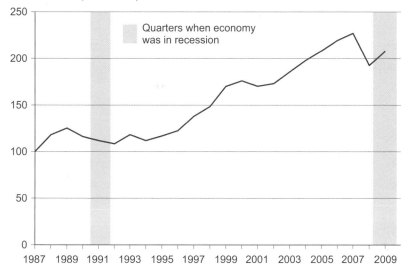

1 Adjusted to real terms using the expenditure deflator for the household sector.
Source: Office for National Statistics

Trends in the estimated total real household wealth per head in the UK between 1987 and 2009 are shown in **Figure 6**. In 2009 real household wealth was £117,000 per head, more than double that for 1987 (£56,000) and an increase from the 2008 figure of £109,000. The real household wealth per head in 2008 was the lowest since 2003, reflecting the effects of the recession.

Figure 7   Distribution of household wealth including pension wealth: by earned income per week,[1] 2006–08

Great Britain
£ per week

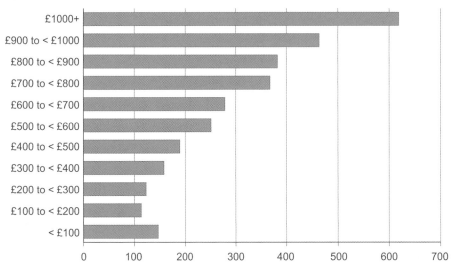

1 Earned income is income from employment and self-employment. It excludes income from pensions, benefits, and other sources such as interest and dividends.
Source: Wealth and Assets Survey, Office for National Statistics

The Wealth and Assets Survey collects information about earned income from employment and self-employment excluding any income from pensions, benefits and other sources. The analysis of total household wealth by grouped earned income for 2006 to 2008 is shown in **Figure 7**. As would be expected, higher total wealth is in general associated with the higher earned income bands. However, there is an exception for the lowest earned income band of less than £100, where median wealth is higher than those in the two income bands between £100 and less than £300. Those with very low earned incomes might well be expected to benefit from income from sources other than earnings such as benefits, pensions and investments. The total wealth of those in these groups may well fall into two categories: those who receive benefits and have very low levels of assets, and those who have wealth in the form of houses, pensions and investments from which they derive unearned income.

Ownership of wealth also varies between regions. In 2006/08 in Great Britain, median total household total wealth was lowest in Scotland (£150,600) and highest in the South East (£287,900) (ONS, 2009b).

Wealth can be held in different forms. Financial wealth is composed of assets such as saving accounts, which may provide sources of current income, and those such as pension rights which may provide entitlement to a future income flow. Ownership of non-financial wealth, such as property, does not necessarily provide an income flow but may provide financial security.

Table 5   **Composition of the net wealth[1] of the household sector, 2009**

United Kingdom

£ Billion at 2009 prices[2]

	2007	2008	2009
Non-financial assets			
Residential buildings	4,260	3,737	3,827
Other	881	776	796
Financial assets			
Life assurance and pension funds	2,266	1,892	2,192
Securities and shares	666	452	577
Currency and deposits	1,153	1,189	1,184
Other assets	173	197	199
Total assets	**9,399**	**8,243**	**8,776**
Financial liabilities			
Loans secured on dwellings	1,233	1,240	1,235
Other loans	230	230	209
Other liabilities	128	103	87
Total liabilities	**1,591**	**1,573**	**1,531**
Total net wealth	7,807	6,670	7,244

1 At end of each year.
2 Adjusted to 2009 prices using the expenditure deflator for the household sector.
Source: Office for National Statistics

The value of the stock of net wealth owned by a household equals the amount of accumulated assets (such as houses, pensions and life assurance) less liabilities (such as mortgages and other loans). In 2009 the total net wealth owned by the household sector in the UK was £7.2 trillion (**Table 5**). This was lower than 2007 but an increase relative to 2008. These changes are related to the effects of the recession in 2008–2009 on different parts of the UK economy. In the non-financial sector, house prices fell considerably between 2007 and 2008 but then began to recover in 2009, and these changes are reflected in the asset value of residential buildings. In the financial sector, changes in stock market prices have reduced the value of securities and shares, life assurance and pension funds. Total financial liabilities were very similar in all three years: about 80 per cent of all liabilities were loans secured on dwellings in each year.

Table 6   **Reason for not saving into a pension[1] 2006–2008**

Great Britain

	Percentages
Can't afford to contribute/low income/ not working/still in education	65
Not interested/ thought about it/got around to it	11
Prefer alternative forms of saving	9
Too many debts/bills/financial commitments	7
Don't know enough about pensions	6
Too early to start a pension	6
Don't trust pension companies/schemes	6
Not eligible/employer doesn't offer a pension scheme	3
Too late to start a pension	2
Not staying with employer/looking for a new job/recently changed jobs	2
Past pension arrangements are adequate	1
Don't think I will live that long	1
Employer scheme not attractive/generous	1
Other	2
Don't know (spontaneous only)	-

1 Individuals aged under 60 not paying into a pension and not receiving a pension.

Source: Wealth and Assets Survey, ONS (2009b)

Money set aside for future retirement is also an important form of household wealth, as it will affect a person's living standards in the future. Averaged over the period 2006 to 2008, 55 per cent of people under the age of 60 in Great Britain were neither saving for a pension nor already receiving income from one (ONS, 2009b). Nearly two-thirds attributed this to having a low income, being out of employment or being in education (**Table 6**).

Household savings

The household saving ratio is defined as household saving as a percentage of total resources, comprising disposable income and the change in the net equity of households in pension funds. It is a key indicator of households' willingness and ability to purchase goods and services.

Figure 8   **Household saving ratio[1]**

United Kingdom
Percentages

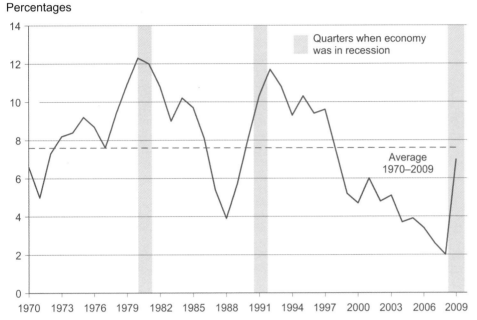

1 Household saving ratio is household saving expressed as a percentage of total resources.
Source: Office for National Statistics

In 2009 the household saving ratio was at a similar level to that in1998 (**Figure 8**). The household saving ratio peaked either during or soon after the recessions in the 1980s and 1990s, and appears to be following the same pattern in the most recent recession of 2008-09. The trend in household saving ratio since 1992 has been variable, but generally downwards from a peak of 11.7 per cent to a low point of 2.0 per cent in 2008. However, there was an increase in 2009 to 7.0 per cent which reflected the effects of the most recent recession.

Taxes

Taxes are the main means by which governments raise revenue. In earlier centuries tax liabilities were typically based on a variety of measures of the value of property. Taxes on income were first raised in Great Britain by William Pitt the Younger[vii] in the 1790s to finance the Napoleonic Wars. Today the major taxes paid by individuals are income tax, social contributions and taxes on expenditure. The income tax system in the UK is progressive, meaning that people with higher incomes are subject to higher rates of tax and so pay higher proportions of their income in taxes.

Table 7   Income tax payable:[1] by annual income,[2] 2010/11

United Kingdom

	Number of taxpayers (thousands)	Total tax liability after tax reductions[3] (£ million)	Average rate of tax (percentages)	Average amount of tax (£)
£6,475–£7,499	939	86	1.3	91
£7,500–£9,999	2,620	1,000	4.3	382
£10,000–£14,999	6,440	6,150	7.7	956
£15,000–£19,999	5,210	10,200	11.3	1,960
£20,000–£29,999	6,910	23,100	13.7	3,350
£30,000–£49,999	5,680	33,000	15.4	5,800
£50,000–£99,999	2,050	30,000	22.3	14,600
£100,000–£149,999	342	12,200	29.8	35,700
£150,000–£199,000	145	8,120	33.1	55,900
£200,000–£499,999	143	15,500	37.8	109,000
£500,000–£999,999	26	7,340	41.4	281,000
£1,000,000 and over	13	12,700	44.4	1,010,000
All incomes	**30,500**	**159,000**	**18.3**	**5,220**

1 Based on projections in line with the March 2010 Budget and subsequent changes (June 2010) to the income tax personal allowance and basic rate limit.

2 Total income of the individual for income tax purposes including earned and investment income. Figures relate to taxpayers only.

3 In this context tax reductions refer to allowances given at a fixed rate, for example the married couple's allowance.

Source: HMRC (2010)

For 2010/11 the personal allowance (below which no tax is payable) is £6,475 and there are three rates of income tax: taxable income up to £37,400 charged at 20 per cent, between £37,401 and £150,000 charged at 40 per cent, and over £150,000 charged at 50 per cent. Taking into account the personal allowance and any other tax relief to which an individual may be entitled, and the variable rates of taxation, the estimated actual proportion of income payable as tax varies by income group (**Table 7**). The average tax rate projected for 2010/11 was 18.3 per cent. This compares with the projected rate of 1.3 per cent for those with earnings between £6,475 and £7,499 and 44.4 per cent per cent for those with earnings of over £1million (HMRC, 2010). The average amount payable during the year also varies considerably, from £91 for individuals earning between £6,475 and £7,499, to £1.01 million for those earning over £1 million.

Table 8   **Indirect taxes as a percentage of disposable income: by expenditure[1] and income[2] grouping of households, 2008/09**

United Kingdom

Percentages

	Expenditure distribution	Income distribution
Bottom fifth	12.3	28.2
Second fifth	15.8	21.0
Middle fifth	17.2	17.9
Fourth fifth	16.8	16.8
Top fifth	18.2	12.8
All households	16.7	16.7

1 Households are ranked by equivalised expenditure.

2 Households are ranked by equivalised income.

Source: Office for National Statistics

Indirect taxes are those such as VAT, duties, and levies which are paid on the purchase of goods and services. Overall, indirect taxes amounted to 16.7 per cent of disposable household income in 2008/09. The amount of indirect tax that each household pays is determined by their expenditure rather than their income. Therefore it is useful to study their effects on household material living standards, referring to both the distribution of household income and household expenditure. As would be expected, when households are ranked and grouped based on their level of expenditure, indirect taxes constitute a lower proportion of income for those with expenditure in the bottom fifth of all expenditure than for those in the top fifth (12.3 per cent and 18.2 per cent respectively). Therefore indirect taxes can be regarded as progressive with respect to expenditure; that is the more you spend, the higher the proportion paid in indirect taxes (**Table 8**).

When analysed (by ranking households based on their income rather than expenditure) indirect taxes represent a higher proportion of income for those households with incomes in the bottom fifth of all incomes when compared to households in the highest fifth (28.2 per cent and 12.8 per cent respectively). This is because, although households in lower income groups spend smaller amounts, the indirect taxes paid make up a higher percentage of their income. Therefore indirect taxes can be regarded as regressive with respect to income; that is the less you earn, the higher the proportion you pay in indirect taxes. Indirect taxation forms a larger percentage of the income of lower income households, even though they may also spend less.

References

Chiripanhura (2010). Measures of economic activity and their implications for societal wellbeing. Available at www.statistics.gov.uk/elmr/07_10/downloads/ELMR_Jul10.pdf

DWP (2010a). Family Resources Survey: United Kingdom 2008-09. Available at http://statistics.dwp.gov.uk/asd/frs/2008_09/index.php?page=intro

DWP (2010b). Households Below Average Income: An analysis of the income distribution 1994/95–2008/09. Available at http://statistics.dwp.gov.uk/asd/hbai/hbai_2009/index.php?page=contents

HMRC (2010). Table 2.5: Income tax liabilities, by income range. Available at www.hmrc.gov.uk/stats/income_tax/menu.htm

Oguz and Knight (2010) Regional Economic indicators with a focus on gross disposable household income Available at www.statistics.gov.uk/elmr/05_10/downloads/ELMR-May10-Knight.pdf

ONS (2009a). ST40: Population. Available at www.statistics.gov.uk/cci/nugget.asp?id=2311

ONS (2009b). Wealth in Great Britain: Main Results from the Wealth and Assets Survey 2006/08. Available at www.statistics.gov.uk/StatBase/Product.asp?vlnk=15074&Pos=1&ColRank=1&Rank=192

ONS (2009c). 2009 Annual Survey of Hours and Earnings (ASHE): Analysis by All Employees. Available at www.statistics.gov.uk/downloads/theme_labour/ASHE-2009/2009_all_employees.pdf

Notes

[i] The household sector covers people living in households and institutions and also sole traders, and charities and universities. Disposable income is the amount of money that households have available for consumption expenditure or savings and is calculated by taking total income from all sources and deducting expenditure on taxes, social contributions and other expenses such as insurance premiums.

[ii] The household reference person is the person responsible for the accommodation, be it through ownership, renting, having the accommodation as part of a job or a relationship to an owner who is not part of the household. For joint householders, the reference person is taken to be the one with the highest income or, if their income is equal, the oldest person.

[iii] The analysis in Households Below Average Income (HBAI) uses household disposable incomes, adjusted for household size and composition, as a proxy for the material living standards of individuals or, more precisely, for the level of consumption of goods and services that people could attain given the disposable income of the household in which they live. This is known as equivalisation and allows the comparison of incomes between households of different sizes and compositions.

[iv] Nomenclature of Units for Territorial Statistics (NUTS) is a hierarchical classification of areas that provides a breakdown of the EU's economic territory. For further information go to www.statistics.gov.uk/geography/nuts.asp

v The Consumer Price Index (CPI) is the main UK measure of inflation for macroeconomic purposes and forms the basis for the Government's inflation target. It is also used for international comparisons. The CPI is the measure adopted by the Government for monitoring inflation and indexing benefits and tax credits.

vi The Retail Prices Index (RPI) is the most familiar general purpose domestic measure of inflation in the UK. It is available continuously from June 1947. Until 2010 the government used it to uprate state pensions, social security benefits and index-linked gilts.

[vii] In his budget of December 1798 William Pitt introduced a new graduated income tax. Beginning with a 120th tax on incomes of £60 and rising by degrees until it reached 10 per cent on incomes of over £200. Pitt believed that this income tax would raise £10 million but in fact in 1799 the yield was just over £6 million.

Housing

The housing market in the UK includes owner occupiers – people who either own their home outright or are buying with it with a mortgage – and tenants, either renting from the social sector (local authorities or housing associations) or renting privately. Some people in the UK live in poor living conditions such as homes that are in serious disrepair or homes that are energy inefficient, while many households live in temporary accommodation. The recent credit freeze and economic recession has made it more difficult to get finance either to move house or to purchase a home for the first time. The likelihood of falling behind with rent or mortgage payments is a real risk to some households and the number of repossessions of homes has increased.

Key points:

Housing stock

- The number of dwellings in Great Britain increased substantially from 7.7 million at the start of the 20th century to 26.2 million in 2008

- In 2008 there were around 22.4 million dwellings in England of which around four-fifths (81.5 per cent) were houses or bungalows and 19 per cent were flats or maisonettes

- The number of new permanent dwellings completed in the UK as a whole in the last 20 years peaked in 2006/07 at 219,000

Tenure and accommodation

- In 2009, 37 per cent of households in Great Britain were buying their homes with a mortgage: almost a third (32 per cent) of homes were owned outright and 31 per cent were rented either from the social sector (18 per cent) or privately (13 per cent)

- Almost two-thirds (65 per cent) of lone parents with dependent children rented their home in Great Britain in 2009 while over a third (35 per cent) lived in owner-occupied accommodation

- As of October 2009, there were 316,000 vacant dwellings in England, with the highest proportion (22 per cent) situated in the North West

Homelessness

- In England in 2009/10 40,000 households were accepted as being owed a main homelessness duty by local authorities, a fall of 25 per cent since 2008/09 and 70 per cent since the peak of 135,000 in 2003/04

- The most common reason for loss of their last settled home for those accepted as homeless was the inability, or unwillingness, of friends or relatives to accommodate them, with just over a third (34 per cent) homeless for this reason

- At the end of 2009/10, there were around 51,000 households in temporary accommodation in England, a fall of 49 per cent from a peak of around 101,000 at the end of 2004/05

Housing conditions and energy efficiency

- In 2008, 44 per cent of privately rented homes were deemed to be non decent compared with 21 per cent of those rented from a registered private landlord.
- In 2008, 36 per cent of households in the lowest fifth of the income distribution lived in a non-decent home compared with 31 per cent of those in the highest fifth; while 20 per cent of the lowest income households lived in poor quality environments compared with 14 per cent of the highest income group
- In 2008, 10 per cent of dwellings in England achieved the highest Energy Efficiency Ratings Bands A to C, equivalent to 2.3 million dwellings, compared with 7 per cent, equivalent to 1.6 million dwellings in 2006

Household mobility

- In 2008/09, 9 per cent of all households in England (2.0 million) had moved to their current homes within the previous 12 months, the smallest number of moves in any year since 1994/95 when data were first collected
- In 2008/09 the average (median) length of time that households in England had lived in their home was 8 years. Owner-occupiers had been in their current home on average the longest at 11 years, followed by social-renters at 7 years

Housing market and finance

- Between 2007 and 2008 the number of property transactions with a value of £40,000 or more in the UK fell by 44 per cent from 1.6 million to 900,000
- In 2009 the average price paid for a dwelling (based on a mix-adjusted methodology) in the UK was £194,235, a decrease of 8.1 per cent since 2008
- Since 1998 the number of loans approved for house purchase (seasonally adjusted) in the UK peaked in March 2002 at 92,912, compared with a low of 17,421 in November 2008
- The majority of adults in the UK (57 per cent) felt that there was no risk at all of falling behind with either rent or mortgage payments, while 37 per cent felt that there was either a low or moderate risk and just 6 per cent a high risk
- Since 2004, the number of properties taken into repossession increased nearly six-fold to 47,900 in 2009

Housing stock

Figure 1   **Dwelling stock[1] and households[2,3]**

Great Britain

Millions

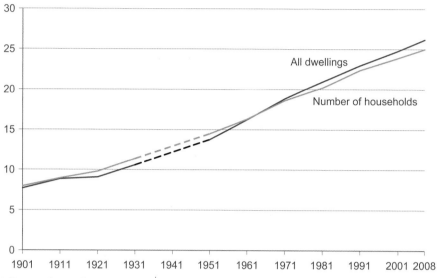

1 See endnote: Dwelling stock[i]

2 Data for number of households for 2001 and 2008 are Q2 (April to June) Labour Force Survey data and are not seasonally adjusted.

3 No census was undertaken in 1941, so data for this year is plotted as the mid-point between 1931 and 1951.

Source: English Housing Survey, Communities and Local Government (DCLG, 2010a); Census, Labour Force Survey, Office for National Statistics

The increase in the population over the past century has increased demand for accommodation. The number of dwellings[ii] in Great Britain increased substantially, from 7.7 million at the start of the 20th century to 26.2 million in 2008 **(Figure 1)**. In 1901, and in all subsequent censuses up to and including 1961, there were fewer dwellings than households therefore some houses accommodated more than one household.[iii] However from 1971 onwards there were more separate dwellings than households. Some surplus dwellings are necessary to allow for mobility in the housing market (see vacant dwellings later in this chapter). The family formation of the population has also influenced accommodation requirements. The number of households tripled in Great Britain during the 20th century, partly a result of increasing population together with decreasing average household size. In the latter part of the century the change in household size was influenced by the increase in the numbers of people living on their own.

Between 1901 and 2008 the number of dwellings in England increased over three and a half times, from nearly 6.3 million to around 22.4 million. The rate of increase was smaller in the other UK countries. In Wales the number of dwellings increased three times from 433,000 to 1.3 million, while in Scotland the number of dwellings more than doubled from 986,000 to 2.5 million over the same period. In Northern Ireland the number of dwellings doubled from 354,000 in 1951 (the earliest data available) to 737,000 in 2008 (DCLG 2010b).

Table 1   Dwelling stock: by region and type of accommodation, 2008

England and Wales   Percentages

	House or bungalow			Flat or maisonette		All dwellings (=100) (thousands)
	Detached	Semi-detached	Terrace	Purpose-built	Conversion	
England	22.5	29.2	29.9	14.9	3.6	22,398
North East	12.6	37.3	34.6	13.8	1.7	1,152
North West	18.0	35.0	35.5	9.8	1.7	3,076
Yorkshire and the Humber	20.9	34.4	32.3	9.8	2.7	2,258
East Midlands	33.3	35.1	23.1	7.1	1.5	1,923
West Midlands	25.3	32.1	30.0	11.2	1.4	2,325
East	28.3	29.6	28.3	12.1	1.7	2,466
London	4.5	15.1	32.3	38.7	9.4	3,248
South East	28.8	28.0	25.4	13.4	4.4	3,606
South West	31.9	24.8	28.1	10.7	4.5	2,345
Wales	27.0	30.0	32.0	8.0	2.0	1,287

Source: 2008 English Housing Survey, Department for Communities and Local Government; Welsh Assembly Government

In 2008 there were around 22.4 million dwellings in England of which around four-fifths (81.6 per cent) were houses or bungalows and 18.5 per cent were flats or maisonettes **(Table 1)**. Around three in ten (29.2 per cent or around 6.5 million dwellings) were semi-detached and a further three in ten (29.9 per cent or around 6.7 million dwellings) were terraced houses. Around 5 million dwellings were detached (22.5 per cent). Around four-fifths (80.7 per cent) of all flats and maisonettes were purpose built equivalent to around 3.3 million dwellings, while the remaining 0.8 million were conversions.

The composition of the dwelling stock varied by region, with over nine in ten (91 per cent) of dwellings in the East Midlands being houses or bungalows compared with 52 per cent in London. In London purpose built flats or maisonettes and terraced houses were most common (39 per cent and 32 per cent respectively).

According to the 2008 Living in Wales survey, nearly a third (32 per cent) of the dwelling stock consisted of terraced housing. Semi-detached and detached houses or bungalows made up 30 per cent and 27 per cent of the dwelling stock respectively. According to the 2009 Scottish House Condition Survey, 22 per cent of dwelling stock consisted of terraced housing, with tenement flats making up a further 23 per cent. The 2009 Northern Ireland House Condition Survey showed that nearly a third (31 per cent) of the dwelling stock was terraced houses and 22 per cent bungalows. Around two in ten dwellings were semi-detached houses or detached houses (20 per cent and 19 per cent respectively).

As well as estimates of the stock of housing in the UK, estimates of the number of new builds are also available. The number of new permanent dwellings completed in the UK as a whole in the last 20 years peaked at 219,000 in 2006/07. The peak in England occurred in 2007/08 (just under 169,000 completions) but the pattern varied in the other UK countries. In Wales the completion of new dwellings peaked in 1989/90 with 11,000 completions: in Scotland the peak was in 2004/05 when around 26,500 dwellings were completed while in Northern Ireland the completion of new permanent dwellings peaked in 2006/07 with around 18,000 dwellings. In 2009/10 there were 114,000 new permanent dwellings completed in England, 6,000 in Wales and around 17,500 in Scotland (DCLG, 2010c).

Tenure and accommodation[iv]

Table 2   Housing tenure: EU comparison 2009

Percentage of households

	Owned outright or with a mortgage	Tenant paying at market price	Tenant paying a reduced price or free accommodation		Owned outright or with a mortgage	Tenant paying at market price	Tenant paying a reduced price or free accommodation
Romania	96.5	0.8	2.7	Ireland	73.7	11.3	15.0
Lithuania	91.0	2.1	6.9	Belgium	72.7	18.5	8.8
Hungary	89.8	2.2	8.0	Italy	72.5	13.3	14.2
Slovakia	89.5	8.8	1.7	Luxembourg	70.4	22.3	7.2
Latvia	87.1	6.3	6.6	**United Kingdom**	**69.9**	**12.5**	**17.6**
Estonia	87.1	2.5	10.4	Sweden	69.7	29.8	0.5
Bulgaria	86.8	2.0	11.2	Poland	68.7	2.2	29.1
Spain	83.2	8.2	8.6	Netherlands	68.4	31.1	0.5
Slovenia	81.3	4.1	14.5	Denmark	66.3	33.7	0.0
Malta	79.2	1.4	19.4	France	63.0	19.7	17.3
Czech Republic	76.6	5.4	17.9	Austria	57.5	27.7	14.8
Greece	76.4	17.9	5.7	Germany	56.2	..	..
Portugal	74.6	10.9	14.5				
Finland	74.1	10.4	15.4	**EU-27**	**73.5**	**13.0**	**13.5**
Cyprus	73.8	10.3	15.9				

Source: Eurostat, (SILC ilc_lvho02)

Housing tenure varies across the EU. In all EU-27 countries in 2009, the majority of households owned their own homes, either outright or with a mortgage or loan (**Table 2**). This is particularly true of countries in Central and Eastern Europe, where most households acquired possession of the housing that they occupied when their country became a market economy. Overall, the proportion of households owning their own home in the EU ranged from 96.5 per cent in Romania to 56.2 per cent in Germany compared with the EU-27 average of 73.5 per cent. In the UK, 69.9 per cent of households lived in a home either owned outright or owned with a mortgage or loan. The remaining households either rented their accommodation at market value or at a reduced rate or they lived in rent free accommodation which in some cases was tied to their job. In Denmark, the Netherlands, and Sweden, around three in ten households reported that they paid rents at the market price, while in the UK just 12.5 per cent reported doing so, very similar to the EU-27 average of 13.0 per cent.

Table 3   **Tenure of household reference person:[1] by household composition, 2009**

Great Britain   Percentages

	Owned outright	Owned with mortgage	Privately rented[2]	Rented from social sector
One person households				
Under state pension age[3]	18.9	36.6	18.7	25.8
Over state pension age[3]	59.5	4.4	7.9	28.2
One family households				
Couple[4]				
No children	48.5	33.6	9.9	8.0
Dependent children[5]	8.3	65.9	12.5	13.2
Non-dependent children only	36.2	49.8	4.6	9.5
Lone parent[4]				
Dependent children[5]	5.0	30.3	23.6	41.0
Non-dependent children only	31.1	31.7	10.2	27.0
Other households[6]	20.3	28.2	37.9	13.6
All households	31.9	37.1	12.9	18.1

1 See endnote: Household reference person.[v]
2 Includes tenants in rent-free accommodation and squatters.
3 State pension ages in 2009 is 65 for men and 60 for women.
4 Other individuals who were not family members may also be included.
5 May also include non-dependent children.
6 Comprising two or more unrelated adults or two or more families or a small number of same-sex couples.
Source: General Lifestyle Survey (Longitudinal), Office for National Statistics (ONS 2011)

In 2009, 37 per cent of households in Great Britain were buying their homes with a mortgage **(Table 3)**. Almost a third (32 per cent) owned their home outright and 31 per cent rented their homes either from the social sector (18 per cent) or privately (13 per cent).

Tenure varies according to the size and composition of the household. Lone parent households with dependent children were more likely to rent property rather than own it compared with all other types of household. Almost two-thirds (65 per cent) of lone parents with dependent children rented their home, mostly from the social sector, while over a third (35 per cent) lived in owner-occupied accommodation. In contrast just under three-quarters (74 per cent) of couple households with dependent children were owner-occupiers, with two-thirds (66 per cent) buying their property with a mortgage. The majority of one-person households owned their property either outright or with a mortgage. Six in ten (60 per cent) of one person households with the household reference person over state pension age owned their property outright, while 37 per cent of one-person households under state pension age owned their property with a mortgage

In Northern Ireland in 2009, two-thirds (66 per cent) of households owned and occupied their own property either outright or with a mortgage, a similar proportion to that for Great Britain. The pattern of tenure in relation to household type was also similar to Great Britain with three-quarters (75 per cent) of lone parents with dependent children either privately renting or living in social housing and a quarter (25 per cent) owning their accommodation. In contrast, over three-quarters (78 per cent) of couple households with dependent children owned their own property.

Long-term vacant dwellings[vi] which are often referred to as empty homes may be an indicator of low housing demand and the decline of particular neighbourhoods. As of October 2009, around 1.4 per cent of all dwellings were deemed to be long-term vacant (not including second homes) in England, amounting to 316,000 vacant dwellings. Nearly a quarter of these vacant dwellings (22 per cent) were situated in the North West, where there were just over 71,000 dwellings. The next highest proportions of vacant dwellings were situated in Yorkshire and The Humber and London at 13 per cent and 12 per cent respectively. In Scotland in 2009 there were just under 71,000 vacant dwellings, just under 3 per cent of all dwellings. In Northern Ireland in 2009, 6 per cent of all dwellings were vacant, around 43,000 dwellings.

Another reason for a dwelling to be vacant some of the time is that it may be a second home. A second home is defined for council tax purposes as a privately-owned habitable accommodation that is not occupied by anyone as their main residence. It will usually be occupied some of the time, for example as a holiday home or by someone working away from their household's main home. In 2008/09, there were 651,000 properties classified as second homes, which were either owned or rented by a total of 563,000 households (for second homes abroad see Lifestyles and social participation chapter) (DCLG, 2010d).

The local authority with the largest number of second homes reported for council tax purposes in England in 2009 was Cornwall with around 14,000 second homes, followed by Westminster with around 7,500 homes, and Kensington and Chelsea, and Birmingham, both with around 7,000 homes.

Homelessness

A person not having their own home could be defined as being homeless, but this does not necessarily mean that they are sleeping rough. For example, people may be legally classed as homeless if they are sleeping on a friend's sofa, staying in a hostel or suffering from overcrowding.

Figure 2   **Opinions of why people become homeless:[1] EU comparison, 2009**

Percentages

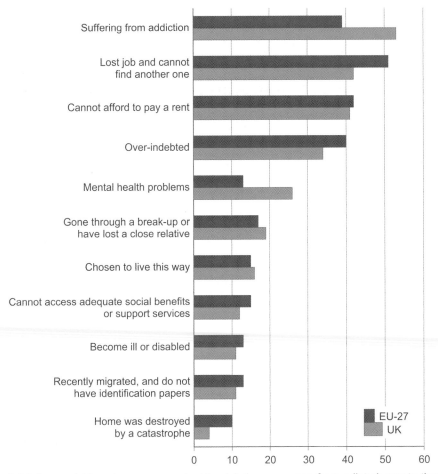

1 Adults aged 15 and over were asked to pick three reasons from a list shown to them that best explain why people are homeless.

Source: Special Eurobarometer 321 (European Commission, 2010a)

In a Special Eurobarometer report in 2009, people aged 15 and over across the EU were asked to pick three reasons from a list shown to them that best described their views of why people became homeless. The most common reason picked by just over half (51 per cent) of people in the EU was losing a job and not being able to find another one, and the second most common was not being able to afford to pay a rent (42 per cent) **(Figure 2)**. Other common reasons among EU citizens were that the homeless person was over-indebted (40 per cent) or that they were suffering from an addiction (39 per cent) such as alcohol or drugs. There was a some differences between responses by adults in the UK and in the EU: the two most common reasons picked in the UK were suffering from an addiction (53 per cent), and losing a job and not being able to find another one

(42 per cent). Twice as many people in the UK as in the EU overall chose mental health problems as a reason for being homeless (26 per cent and 13 per cent respectively).

In England in 2009/10 there were 40,000 households accepted as being owed a main homelessness duty by local authorities[vii]. This was a fall of 25 per cent since 2008/09 and 70 per cent since the peak of 135,000 in 2003/04. The most common reason for loss of their last settled home for those accepted as homeless was the inability, or unwillingness, of friends or relatives to accommodate them, with just over a third (34 per cent) homeless for this reason. In one in five households the reason for homelessness was a relationship breakdown (20 per cent) and 17 per cent had become homeless because their private rented accommodation (including that tied to a job) had come to an end. Mortgage or rent arrears were the reason for homelessness for 6 per cent of households (DCLG, 2010e).

Figure 3   **Homeless households in temporary accommodation**[1]

England

Thousands

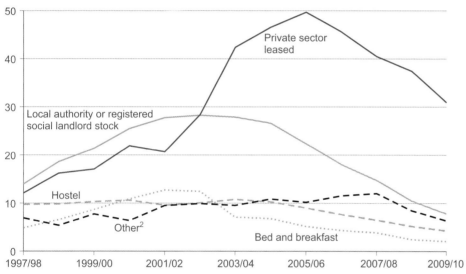

1 Households in accommodation arranged by local authorities pending enquiries or after being accepted as homeless under the 1996 Act. Excludes cases where a duty is owed but accommodation has been secured. Data are at the end of March each year.

2 Includes mobile homes (such as caravans and portacabins) or being accommodated directly with a private sector landlord.

Source: P1E Homelessness Returns, Department for Communities and Local Government (DCLG, 2010f)

At the end of 2009/10, there were around 51,000 households in temporary accommodation in England, a fall of 49 per cent from a peak of around 101,000 at the end of 2004/05. Around 31,000 of these households were in temporary accommodation leased from the private sector by local authorities or housing associations **(Figure 3)**. This was a fall of 38 per cent from the peak of around 50,000 households in 2005/06. A further 8,000 households were in housing stock owned by the local authority or registered social landlord, a fall of 72 per cent from a peak of around 28,000 in 2002/03. The number of households in hostels and women's refuges fell 61 per cent from a peak of around 11,000 in 2003/04 to around 4,000 in 2009/10, while those in bed and breakfast hotels fell by 84 per cent from a peak in 2001/02 of 13,000 to just 2,000 in 2009/10.

In Wales there were around 2,500 households in temporary accommodation at the end of 2009/10, with 42 per cent living in accommodation leased from the private sector, equivalent to around 1,000 households. The remainder were accommodated in hostels, social housing, bed and breakfast or classed as 'Homeless at Home'[viii] and were in some other sort of temporary accommodation. In Scotland at the end of 2009/10 there were just under 11,000 households in temporary accommodation. This was the highest number of households in temporary accommodation on record. Over six in ten (63 per cent) of households at the end of 2009/10 were living in social sector accommodation including housing association stock while 17 per cent were living in bed and breakfast accommodation. The remainder were either living in a hostel (12 per cent) or in other accommodation (9 per cent) which was mainly rented from private landlords.

The most extreme manifestation of homelessness is rough sleeping. According to experimental Official Statistics from the Department for Communities and Local Government, in the 70 local authorities with suspected high numbers 440 rough sleepers were counted in 2010, with more than half being found in the London area. A total estimate of 807 rough sleepers was made by the other 256 local authorities in June 2010 (DCLG, 2010g).

Housing conditions and energy efficiency

To be considered 'decent' a dwelling must satisfy four criteria: it must meet the statutory minimum standard for housing; be in a reasonable state of repair; have reasonably modern facilities and services; and have a reasonable degree of thermal comfort.ix In 2008 a third (33 per cent) of all dwellings in England (7.4 million) were considered to be non-decent (DCLG, 2010h).

Figure 4   Poor living conditions:[1] by tenure, 2008

England

Percentage of households

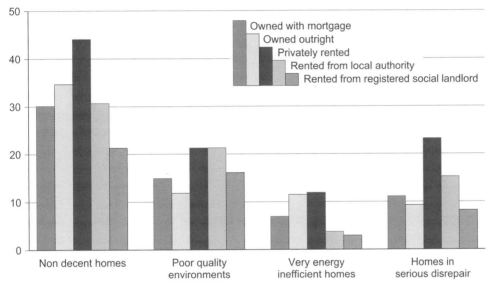

1 For information on non-decent homes, poor quality environments, very energy inefficient homes and homes in serious disrepair see endnote[x]

Source: English Housing Survey 2008, Department for Communities and Local Government

The likelihood of experiencing poor living conditions, including living in a non-decent home; having a poor quality environment; living in a home which is very energy inefficient; or is in serious disrepair, differs according to tenure. In 2008, households in England renting their home privately were more likely than households in other tenures to have poor living conditions (Figure 4). Households renting privately were more than twice as likely to live in a non-decent home as those who rented from a registered social landlord, 44 per cent and 21 per cent respectively. Private renters were also four times more likely than those who rented from a registered social landlord to live in a very energy inefficient home (11.9 per cent and 2.9 per cent respectively) and nearly three times as likely to live in a home in serious disrepair (23.2 per cent and 8.2 per cent respectively).

In Scotland housing quality is defined by the Scottish Housing Quality Standard (SHQS). The five higher-level criteria are that the dwelling must be above the statutory Tolerable Standard; free from serious disrepair; energy efficient; have modern facilities and services; and be healthy, safe and secure. In 2009, 62 per cent of dwellings in the private sector (both owner occupied and rented) and 62 per cent of dwellings in the social sector failed the SHQS, equivalent to just over 1 million and 396,000 dwellings respectively (Scotland, 2010a).

Table 4   **Poor living conditions:[1] by household income quintile group,[2] 2008**

England   Percentages

	Non decent homes	Poor quality environments	Energy inefficient homes	Homes in serious disrepair
Lowest 5th	36.4	19.6	9.1	17.4
2nd	33.2	16.9	9.5	14.1
3rd	33.6	14.3	7.6	11.9
4th	29.8	13.3	6.7	10.1
Highest 5th	30.8	13.6	9.0	8.2
All households	32.8	15.5	8.4	12.3

1 For information on non-decent homes, poor quality environments, very energy inefficient homes and homes in serious disrepair see endnote[x]

2 Household incomes have been 'equivalised' on a Before Housing Cost (BHC) income measure. Equivalisation adjusts income to reflect household size and composition, enabling comparisons to be made of the standard of living achieved by different types of household.

Source: 2008 English Housing Survey, household sub sample, Department for Communities and Local Government

There is also an association between poor living conditions and household income. Living in a non-decent home is more likely as household income decreases. In England in 2008, 36.4 per cent of the poorest fifth of households lived in a non-decent home compared with 30.8 per cent of the fifth of households with the highest incomes, while 19.6 cent of the poorest households lived in poor quality environments compared with 13.6 cent of the highest income group (Table 4). The poorest households were more than twice as likely as the richest households to live in a home in serious disrepair, 17.4 per cent and 8.2 per cent respectively. However there was little difference between the proportions of the poorest and richest households living in energy inefficient homes (9.1 per cent and 9.0 per cent respectively).

In recent years there has been an increasing focus on making homes energy efficient. In the 2009 Environmental Attitudes and Behaviour Survey run by the Department for Environment, Food and Rural Affairs, adults aged 16 and over in England were asked for their attitudes about saving energy at home. Only 14 per cent strongly agreed or tended to agree that they 'don't give much thought to saving energy in their home' while over three-quarters (77 per cent) strongly or tended to disagree with the statement (Defra, 2009).

 The energy efficiency of a home is based on the Government's Standard Assessment Procedure (SAP)[xi]. This rates properties on a scale of 1 (highly energy inefficient) to 100 (highly energy efficient). The average energy efficiency of the housing stock in England improved between 1996 and 2008 by 9 SAP points from 42 to 51. The social sector (local authority and housing association dwellings) saw the greatest improvement, with an average SAP rating increasing by 12 SAP points from 47 to 59. This compared with an increase for the private sector (owner occupied and privately rented dwellings) from 41 SAP points to 50 SAP points over the same period (DCLG, 2010i).

Figure 5   Energy efficient dwellings: by rating[1]

England

Percentages

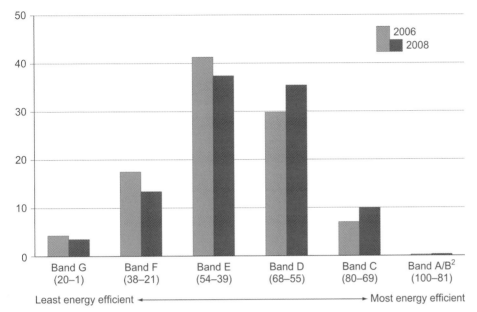

1 Energy Efficiency Ratings are grouped into bands (EER Bands) and based on Standard Assessment Procedure (SAP) ratings which are shown in brackets.[xii]

2 EER Bands A and B are grouped because of insufficient numbers of properties in Band A.

Source: English House Condition Survey 2006, English Housing Survey 2008, Department for Communities and Local Government

Whenever a building is built, sold or rented out, there is also a requirement for each dwelling to have an Energy Performance Certificate (EPC) which, among other things, rates its energy efficiency. For the purposes of EPCs the Energy Efficiency Rating (EER) is presented in a banding system, with Band A containing the most energy efficient properties and Band G the least energy efficient. Between 2006 and 2008 there were increases in the proportion of dwellings achieving the higher EER Bands **(Figure 5)**. In 2006, 7.2 per cent of dwellings in England achieved the highest EER Bands A to C, which was equivalent to 1.6 million dwellings. In 2008 this had increased to 10.3 per cent, or 2.3 million dwellings. In contrast the number of dwellings in the lowest EER Bands F and G fell by around a million over the same period (DCLG, 2010i).

According to the 2008 Living in Wales survey, the overall average SAP rating increased by 4 SAP points between 2004 and 2008 from 46 to 50. In 2008 the most common SAP rating band was band E with 38 percent of dwellings in this band. Bands C and D showed the largest increase, by 5 and 7 percentage points respectively. According to the 2009 Scottish House Condition Survey, the largest proportions of homes were in Band D (46 per cent), with 23 per cent and 22 per cent of homes in Bands E and C respectively. According to the 2009 Northern Ireland House Condition Survey, the largest proportion of homes (42 per cent) were in Band D, an increase of 4 percentage points since 2006.

There are a range of things that households can do to make a home more energy efficient for example fitting a condensing boiler or fitting insulation. In 1996 the majority of dwellings (51 per cent, 10.4 million dwellings) in England had a standard boiler but by 2008 this had decreased to 36 per cent (8.1 million dwellings). In contrast the number of dwellings with a more efficient boiler doubled over the same period from around 2.8 million dwellings to 6.1 million dwellings. Between 1996 and 2008 the number of dwellings with insulated cavity walls had more than doubled from 2.9 million to 7.4 million dwellings, while over the same period, the number of dwellings with 200mm or more of loft insulation had increased from 0.6 million to 4.7 million. Double glazing on the entire dwelling more than doubled from 6.2 million to 15.7 million dwellings between 1996 and 2008 (DCLG, 2010i).

Household mobility

In 2008/09, 9 per cent of all households in England (2.0 million) had moved to their current homes within the previous 12 months. This was the smallest number of moves in any 12-month period since 1994/95 when data were first collected. Overall, movement within each of the three most common tenure groups in 2008/09 was more likely than movement between them. For example, 77 per cent of private renters who had moved were still renting privately and 75 per cent of households who had rented in the social sector continued to do so. Of all the households who moved, 57 per cent were renting privately, showing how important this sector is in creating mobility within the housing market (DCLG, 2010d).

Figure 6   **New households:[1] by tenure**

England

Percentages

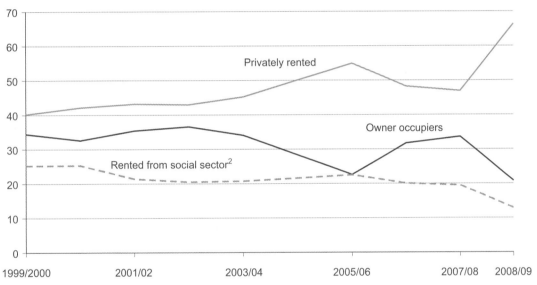

1 New heads of household resident less than one year.

2 Includes local authority and housing association tenants.

Source: English Housing Survey, Department for Communities and Local Government

In 2008/09, of the households who had moved to their current home in the previous 12 months, 345,000 were newly formed households, an 11 per cent decrease from 2007/08. Of these households, 66 per cent were renting from the private sector and 21 per cent moved into owner-occupation, including shared ownership **(Figure 6)**. The proportion of new households renting in the private sector increased from 40 per cent in 1999/2000 to 66 per cent in 2008/09. The largest year-on-year rise was between 2007/08 and 2008/09 (19 percentage points). Conversely there was a large fall in new owner occupier households over the same period (13 percentage points). The change in tenure for new households formed in 2008/09 is mainly related to the difficulty in securing mortgage finance and the high deposits required by lenders which lead many people to rent rather than to buy (DCLG, 2010d).

Table 5 — Length of residence in current accommodation: by tenure, 2008/09

England   Percentages

	Less than 1 year	1 year but less than 2 years	2 years but less than 3 years	3–4 years	5–9 years	10–19 years	20–29 years	30 years or more	Average number of years
Owner-occupiers	3.7	4.2	7.4	10.2	19.8	21.5	16.0	17.2	11
Social renters	8.0	7.1	8.7	13.6	22.0	21.6	10.2	8.8	7
Private renters	36.5	17.5	12.4	12.7	10.3	5.2	2.1	3.4	1
All tenures	9.1	6.6	8.3	11.2	18.8	19.2	13.0	13.7	8

Source: English Housing Survey, Department for Communities and Local Government (DCLG, 2010d)

In 2008/09 the average (median) length of time that households in England had lived in their current home was eight years (Table 5). Owner-occupiers were the least mobile, having been in their current home on average the longest at 11 years, followed by social-renters at seven years. Private renters were much more mobile with an average length of residence of around one year; 36.5 per cent had lived in their home for less than a year and a further 17.5 per cent for more than a year but less than two years. Only one in ten (10.7 per cent) private renters had lived in their home 10 years or more. In contrast, 3.7 per cent of owner occupiers and 8.0 per cent of social renters had lived in their homes for less than a year. Over half (54.7 per cent) of owner occupiers and 40.6 per cent of social renters lived in their homes for 10 years or more.

The picture of housing mobility is very similar within the UK. According to the 2008 Living in Wales survey 41 per cent of all households who were living in their current address for less than a year were renting from the private sector. Around 64 per cent of households who rented from the social sector were living in their current address for up to 10 years. Owner occupied households were more likely to live at the same address for longer with over a third (38 per cent) living at their current address for more than 20 years and 20 per cent for between 11 and 20 years. In Scotland in 2009, almost a half (47 per cent) of households who had been living for less than a year at their current address were renting from the private sector. Around 62 per cent of all households renting from the social sector had been living at their current address for up to 10 years. Owner occupied households were the least mobile, with two-thirds (66 per cent) of those living at their current address for between three and four years being owner occupiers, increasing to 80 per cent for those residing at the same address for more than 10 years (Scotland 2010b). According to the 2009 Northern Ireland House Condition Survey, 65 per cent of households who had been living for less than a year at their current address were renting from the private sector, and nearly two-thirds (64 per cent) of all owner occupier households had lived in their homes for 10 years or more.

Housing market and finance

Table 6   Residential property transactions:[1] by region

United Kingdom   Thousands

	2007	2008	2009
England	1,361	750	737
North East	60	31	27
North West	167	89	79
Yorkshire and The Humber	128	70	63
East Midlands	117	65	64
West Midlands	124	70	65
East	166	91	96
London	192	102	95
South East	253	142	151
South West	153	88	96
Wales	66	36	33
Scotland	148	99	75
Northern Ireland	38	15	14
United Kingdom	1,613	899	859

1 Property transactions with a value of £40,000 or more.[xiii]

Source: HM Revenue and Customs (HMRC, 2010)

Between 2007 and 2008 the number of property transactions with a value of £40,000 or more in the UK fell by 44 per cent from 1.6 million to 900,000; reflecting the effect of the recent economic recession **(Table 6)**. There was a further, smaller decrease in the number of transactions between 2008 and 2009 to 859,000 a fall of 4.4 per cent. Between 2007 and 2008 the picture was similar across the English regions and Wales with property transactions falling by between 42 per cent and 48 per cent. However, the number of transactions in Scotland fell by less (33 per cent) while in Northern Ireland they fell by more (61 per cent). Between 2008 and 2009 the number of property transactions continued to fall in six English regions but rose in three. The largest decreases in England between 2008 and 2009 were in the North East (13 per cent), the North West (11 per cent) and in Yorkshire and the Humber (10 per cent). The number of transactions increased in the South West (9 per cent), the South East (6.3 per cent) and the East (5.5 per cent). In Wales and Northern Ireland the number of transactions fell by 8.3 per cent and 6.7 per cent respectively, while in Scotland the number of transactions fell by a much larger proportion than the other regions of the UK, by just under a quarter (24 per cent).

In 2009 the average price paid for a dwelling (based on a mix-adjusted methodology[xiv]) in the UK was £194,235, a decrease of 8.1 per cent since 2008. Changes in the average price paid for a dwelling over the same period varied very little between England and Wales, at 8.4 and 8.2 per cent respectively. However, Scotland saw a smaller decrease at around 2.6 per cent while Northern Ireland a much larger one at 15.7 per cent (DCLG, 2010j & DCLG 2010k).

Figure 7   Annual house price change[1,2]

United Kingdom
Percentages

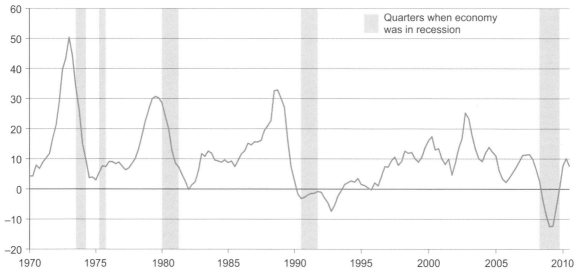

1 Based on mix-adjusted house prices for completed mortgages. See endnote [xiv] about average dwelling prices.
2 Data are annual house price changes for each quarter, up to Q3 (Jul-Sep) 2010. Data are not seasonally adjusted.
Source: Regulated Mortgage Survey, Department for Communities and Local Government (DCLG, 2010j)

In the past four decades there have been large decreases in annual house prices around the times that the UK economy has been in recession **(Figure 7)**. During the recession in the early 1970s, although house prices did not fall the annual rate of increase slowed down. The annual increase in house prices fell from 50.4 per cent in the first quarter of 1973 to just 3.0 per cent in the first quarter of 1975. However the next three recessions in the early 1980s, 1990s and 2000s did produce house price falls. In the first quarter of 1980, house prices rose by around 28.6 per cent year-on-year but by the first quarter of 1982 there was a slight fall of 0.2 per cent year on year. House prices rose by an annual rate of around 2.9 per cent in the first quarter of 1990 but by the fourth quarter of 1992 the year-on-year change represented a fall of 7.4 per cent. In the latest recession, house prices fell by 12.5 per cent between the first quarter of 2008 and the first quarter of 2009, the largest annual decline since the series began. The first quarter of 2009 was the third consecutive quarter to show a decrease, and this decline continued for another two quarters. Annual house prices started to rise beginning in the fourth quarter of 2009 (0.4 per cent) and had risen to 10.1 per cent in the second quarter of 2010, but then fell back to 7.5 per cent in the third quarter of 2010.

Although the average house price has declined between 2008 and 2009, and the UK base interest rate has dropped to its lowest level in three centuries, these changes have not necessarily been reflected in people's perceptions of home affordability. According to a 2009 Special Eurobarometer report, over two-thirds (68 per cent) of adults aged 15 and over in the EU considered the affordability of housing in their country as bad. Only 2 per cent judged the affordability of housing to be very good in their country. In the UK, just under a quarter (24 per cent) of adults felt that the affordability of housing was good and 70 per cent thought it was bad (European Commission, 2010b).

Figure 8   Loans approved for house purchase[1]

United Kingdom

Numbers

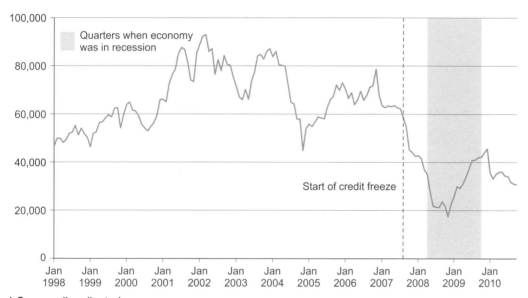

1 Seasonally adjusted.

Source: British Bankers' Association (BBA, 2010)

The decline in house prices has been accompanied by reduced mortgage availability and stricter lending criteria, and this is a major reason in the UK for the continuing low level of housing transactions illustrated in Table 6. Data shown in **Figure 8** are from the British Bankers' Association which represents the main high street banking groups who account for around two-thirds of all UK mortgage lending. In the last 12 years the number of loans approved for house purchase (seasonally adjusted) peaked in March 2002 at 92,912. The number of loans approved in July 2007, the month before the credit freeze began was 62,363, however approvals fell rapidly to reach a low of 17,421 in November 2008. Since November 2008, the number of loans approved increased in nearly every month to reach 45,562 in December 2009, but then started to fall again to reach 30,766 in October 2010.

The average value of a loan for house purchase (not seasonally adjusted) peaked in June 2007 in the UK at £159,600 before decreasing to a low of £116,100 in December 2008. This was partly due to house prices falling and partly to the higher deposits required before a loan could be approved. The average value of a loan for house purchase was £144,900 in October 2010, around 2.0 per cent higher than a year previously (BBA, 2010).

Table 7   **Likelihood of falling behind with rent or mortgage payments:[1] EU comparison, 2010**

Percentages

	No risk at all	Low risk	Moderate risk	High risk		No risk at all	Low risk	Moderate risk	High risk
Romania	21	21	27	26	Slovenia	53	16	19	9
Cyprus	27	19	26	25	Hungary	38	29	22	8
Greece	25	18	33	24	**United Kingdom**	**57**	**25**	**12**	**6**
Latvia	27	20	30	20	Belgium	69	15	4	6
Portugal	25	28	29	17	France	56	22	17	5
Bulgaria	26	18	22	17	Luxembourg	70	16	10	3
Lithuania	26	21	30	16	Germany	69	17	10	2
Italy	41	20	22	16	Netherlands	79	12	5	2
Poland	36	25	22	14	Austria	77	15	4	2
Malta	37	18	25	13	Finland	75	19	5	1
Spain	49	19	18	13	Sweden	81	14	3	1
Estonia	32	27	26	11	Denmark	85	10	3	1
Slovakia	32	39	17	11					
Czech Republic	28	30	28	9	**EU–27 average**	**55**	**20**	**15**	**8**
Ireland	46	22	23	9					

1 Adults aged 15 and over who provided an answer to the question 'looking at the next 12 months, would you say that there is a high risk, a moderate risk, a low risk or no risk at all of falling behind with your rent or mortgage payments?' Does not include those who answered 'don't know'. Fieldwork carried out in May 2010.

Source: Flash Eurobarometer 289 (European Commission, 2010c)

According to a Flash Eurobarometer report in 2010, over half (55 per cent) of all adults aged 15 and over in the EU felt that was no risk at all of them falling behind with rent or mortgage payments over the 12 months following their interview (Table 7). Over a third (35 per cent) felt there was a low or moderate risk and 8 per cent a high risk of falling behind. The majority of adults in the UK (57 per cent) felt that there was no risk at all of falling behind with either rent or mortgage payments, while 37 per cent felt that there was either a low or moderate risk and just 6 per cent a high risk. Around a quarter of adults in Romania (26 per cent), Cyprus (25 per cent) and Greece (24 per cent) felt that there was a high risk of falling behind with either rent or mortgage payments. In contrast around eight in ten adults living in Denmark (85 per cent), Sweden (81 per cent) and the Netherlands (79 per cent) felt there was no risk at all.

Figure 9   Properties taken into repossession[1]

United Kingdom

Thousands

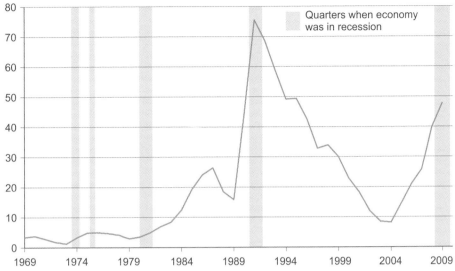

1. From Quarter 1 2009 figures are grossed up to be representative of the entire first-charge market mortgage market. Reporting lenders accounted for around 92 per cent of the estimated total first-charge market in January to March 2010.[xv]

Source: Council of Mortgage Lenders

When people fall behind with their mortgage payments and are unable to reach an alternative arrangement with their lender, a county court possession summons may be issued. This may result in the mortgage lender repossessing the property if repayments cannot be made. The number of repossessions reached its peak in 1991 when 75,500 properties were repossessed **(Figure 9)**. However, mainly due to lower interest rates, repossessions began to fall and reached a low point in 2004 when 8,200 homes were repossessed. Since 2004 repossessions have increased nearly six-fold to 47,900 in 2009.

In December 2008 the Government announced proposals aimed at limiting repossessions by reducing the pressure on homeowners who have difficulty meeting their mortgage repayments. Two schemes were introduced in 2009:

- a Mortgage Rescue Scheme (MRS), which provides a structured exit from homeownership for vulnerable households who would otherwise have been entitled to homelessness assistance. The scheme was launched in January 2009

- the Homeowners Mortgage Support (HMS) that provides support to lenders to encourage greater levels of forbearance for up to two years for borrowers unable to access other support. This was launched in April 2009

Over the 15 months to March 2010 a total of 20,254 households in England approached local authorities for help with mortgage arrears. Of these, 1,230 were selected for a housing options interview to complete an application for MRS. Just under three-quarters (72 per cent or 14,634 households) received general advice, money advice, or were referred to their lender to seek greater forbearance to help sustain homeownership. Of the remaining households, 682 were supported to make an application for homelessness assistance as they were threatened with eviction within 28 days. A further 2,823 cases (14 per cent) were provided with advice and assistance in an attempt to prevent homelessness, since options with their lenders had been exhausted but their cases fell outside the MRS criteria. From April 2009 to March 2010 HMS had achieved a total of just 32 borrower registrations (DCLG, 2010l).

References

BBA, 2010 October figures for the main high street banks, available at
www.bba.org.uk/media/article/october-figures-for-the-main-high-street-banks3

DCLG, 2010a Table 102: Dwelling stock: by tenure, GB (historical series), available at
www.communities.gov.uk/housing/housingresearch/housingstatistics/housingstatisticsby/stockincludingvaca
nts/livetables/

DCLG, 2010b Table 104: Dwelling stock by tenure, (UK countries), available at
www.communities.gov.uk/documents/housing/xls/table-104.xls
www.communities.gov.uk/documents/housing/xls/table-106.xls
www.communities.gov.uk/documents/housing/xls/table-107.xls
www.communities.gov.uk/documents/housing/xls/table-108.xls

DCLG, 2010c Table 209 House building: permanent dwellings completed, by tenure and country, available
at www.communities.gov.uk/documents/housing/xls/1473507.xls

DCLG, 2010d English Housing Survey, Household report 2008–09, available at
www.communities.gov.uk/documents/statistics/pdf/1750765.pdf

DCLG, 2010e Table 774 Statutory homelessness: households accepted by local authorities, as owed a main
homelessness duty, by reason for loss of last settled home, England, 1998/99 - 2009/10, available at
www.communities.gov.uk/documents/housing/xls/141488.xls

DCLG, 2010f Table 775 Statutory homelessness: households in temporary accommodation, by type of
accommodation, at the end of each quarter, England, 1998 – 2010, available at
www.communities.gov.uk/documents/housing/xls/141755.xls

DCLG, 2010g Rough Sleeping England - Total Street Count and Estimates 2010, available at
www.communities.gov.uk/publications/corporate/statistics/roughsleepingcount2010

DCLG, 2010h Housing and planning key facts, England, available at
www.communities.gov.uk/documents/statistics/pdf/1760666.pdf

DCLG, 2010i English Housing Survey, Headline Report 2008-09, available at
www.communities.gov.uk/documents/statistics/pdf/1479789.pdf

DCLG, 2010j Table 502 Housing market: house prices from 1930, annual house price inflation, United
Kingdom, from 1970, available at
www.communities.gov.uk/documents/housing/xls/141272.xls

DCLG, 2010k Table 507 Housing market: mix-adjusted house prices, by new/other dwellings, type of buyer
and region, United Kingdom, from 1993, available at
www.communities.gov.uk/documents/housing/xls/141377.xls

DCLG, 2010l Evaluation of the Mortgage Rescue Scheme and Homeowners Mortgage Support, Interim report, available at
http://www.communities.gov.uk/documents/housing/pdf/1648140.pdf

Defra, 2009 Environmental Attitudes and Behaviours, available at
www.defra.gov.uk/evidence/statistics/environment/pubatt/download/data-tables2009.pdf

European Commission, 2010a Special Eurobarometer 321, Poverty and Social Exclusion, available at
http://ec.europa.eu/public_opinion/archives/ebs/ebs_321_en.pdf

European Commission, 2010b Special Eurobarometer 315, Social Climate, available at
http://ec.europa.eu/public_opinion/archives/ebs/ebs_315_en.pdf

European Commission, 2010c Flash Eurobarometer 289, monitoring the social impact of the crisis: public perceptions in the European Union, available at
http://ec.europa.eu/public_opinion/flash/fl_289_en.pdf

Eurostat, 2010 available at
http://epp.eurostat.ec.europa.eu/statistics_explained/images/a/a0/Housing_statistics_2011.xls

HMRC, 2010 Property Transactions in the United Kingdom, available at
www.hmrc.gov.uk/stats/survey_of_prop/menu.htm

ONS, 2011, General Lifestyle Survey 2009, available at
www.statistics.gov.uk/downloads/theme_compendia/GLF09/GeneralLifestyleSurvey2009.pdf

Scotland, 2010a Scottish House Condition Survey: Key Findings for 2009, available at
www.scotland.gov.uk/Publications/2010/11/23125350/5

Scotland, 2010b Scotland's People Annual report: Results from 2009 Scottish Household Survey, available at www.scotland.gov.uk/Publications/2010/08/25092046/4

Notes

[i] The definition of a dwelling follows the census definition applicable at that time. Currently the 2001 Census definition is used, which defines a dwelling as 'structurally separate accommodation'. This was determined primarily by considering the type of accommodation, as well as separate and shared access to multi-occupied properties. In all dwelling stock figures, vacant dwellings are included but non-permanent dwellings are generally excluded. For house building statistics, only data on permanent dwellings are collected.

Estimates of the total dwelling stock, stock changes and the tenure distribution in the UK are made by the Department for Communities and Local Government for England, the Scottish Government, the Welsh Assembly Government, and the Northern Ireland Department for Social Development. These are primarily based on census output data for the number of dwellings (or households converted to dwellings) from the censuses of population for the UK. Adjustments are carried out if there are specific reasons to do so. Census year figures are based on outputs from the censuses. For years between censuses, the total figures are obtained by applying gains and losses for each successive year. The increment is based on the annual total number of completions plus the annual total net gain from other housing statistics, that is, conversions, demolitions and changes of use.

Estimates of dwelling stock by tenure category are based on other sources where it is considered that for some specific tenure information, these are more accurate than census output data. In this situation it is assumed that the other data sources also contain vacant dwellings, but it is not certain and it is not expected that these data are very precise. Thus the allocation of vacant dwellings to tenure categories may not be completely accurate and the margin of error for tenure categories is wider than for estimates of total stock.

For local authority stock, figures supplied by local authorities are more reliable than those in the 2001 Census. Similarly, it was found that the Housing Corporation's own data are more accurate than census output data for the registered social landlord (RSL) stock. Hence only the privately rented or with a job or business tenure data were taken directly from the Census. The owner-occupied data were taken as the residual of the total from the Census. For non-census years, the same approach was adopted except for the privately rented or with a job or business, for which Labour Force Survey results were used (see Appendix, Part 4: Labour Force Survey).

For further information on the methodology used to calculate stock by tenure and tenure definitions for the UK, see Appendix B Notes and Definitions in the Communities and Local Government annual volume *Housing Statistics* or the housing statistics page of the Communities and Local Government website at: **www.communities.gov.uk/housing/housingresearch/housingstatistics/**

[ii] For dwelling stock data, unless specifically stated, the definition used follows the census' definition applicable at that time. The census' definition has changed several times. For example, the 1991 Census defined a dwelling as structurally separate accommodation. This was determined primarily by considering the type of accommodation, as well as separate and shared access to multi-occupied properties. The 2001 Census defined dwellings as either containing a single household space or several household spaces sharing some facilities.

A household's accommodation (a household space) is defined as being in a shared dwelling if it has accommodation type that is part of a converted or shared house, not all the rooms (including bathroom and toilet, if any) are behind a door that only that household can use and there is at least one other such household space at the same address with which it can be combined to form the shared dwelling. If any of these conditions are not met, the household space forms an unshared dwelling. Therefore a dwelling can consist of one household space (an unshared dwelling) or two or more household spaces (a shared dwelling).

In recent years (since 2001) a dwelling is defined (in line with the 2001 Census definition) as a self-contained unit of accommodation. Self-containment is where all the rooms (including kitchen, bathroom and toilet) in a household's accommodation are behind a single door which only that household can use. Non-self contained household spaces at the same address should be counted together as a single dwelling. Therefore a dwelling can consist of one self-contained household space or two or more non-self-contained household spaces at the same address.

Ancillary dwellings (for example former granny annexes) are included provided they are self-contained, pay separate council tax from the main residence, do not share access with the main residence (for example a shared hallway) and there are no conditional restrictions on occupancy.

Communal establishments, that is establishments providing managed residential accommodation, are not counted in overall housing supply. These cover university and college student accommodation, hospital staff accommodation, hostels/homes, hotels/holiday complexes, defence establishments (not married quarters) and prisons. However, purpose-built (separate) homes (for example self-contained flats clustered into units with four to six bedrooms for students) should be included. Each self-contained unit should be counted as a dwelling.

Non permanent (or temporary) dwellings are included if they are the occupant's main residence and council tax is payable on them as a main residence. These include caravans, mobile homes, converted railway carriages and houseboats. Permanent Gypsy and Traveller pitches should also be counted if they are, or likely to become, the occupants' main residence.

In all stock figures, vacant dwellings and second homes are included. House building statistics collect data on permanent dwellings only that is dwellings that have a design life of over 60 years.

[iii] The National Statistics harmonised survey definition of a household is:

One person or a group of people who have the accommodation as their only or main residence AND (for a group)

- either share at least one meal a day, or
- share the living accommodation, that is, a living room or sitting room.

The occupant(s) of a bedsit who do not share a sitting or living room with anyone else comprise a single household.

[iv] There are four tenure categories available for dwelling stock and household figures. These are:

- owner-occupied (or private enterprise in the case of house building statistics, that is dwellings financed and built by private developers for owner-occupiers or private landlords, whether persons or companies). This includes accommodation that is owned outright or is being bought with a mortgage

- rented privately, defined as all non-owner-occupied property other than that rented from local authorities and registered social landlords (RSLs) plus that rented from private or public bodies by virtue of employment. This includes property occupied rent-free by someone other than the owner. New build privately rented dwellings will be included in the house building private enterprise figures

- rented from RSLs, but for stock figures non-registered housing associations are excluded and subsumed within owner-occupied as are RSL shared ownership and shared equity dwellings; for house building figures the RSL tenure includes social rent, intermediate rent and low cost home ownership RSL new build dwellings

- rented from local authorities. In Scotland dwellings rented from local authorities include those rented from Communities Scotland, formerly Scottish Homes

[v] The Household Reference Person (HRP) is identified during the interview and is defined as the member of the household who:

- owns the household accommodation, or

- is legally responsible for the rent of the accommodation, or

- has the household accommodation as an emolument or perquisite, or

- has the household accommodation by virtue of some relationship to the owner who is not a member of the household

For joint householders, the HRP will be the householder with the highest income. If two or more householders have exactly the same income the HRP is the eldest.

[vi] Long-term empty homes are those dwellings which have been unoccupied and substantially unfurnished for over six months and, at local authority discretion, can be subject to a discount of between 0 per cent and 50 per cent.

Substantially unfurnished is not defined in the legislation; many local authorities regard a dwelling as substantially unfurnished if there are insufficient furnishings to enable someone to live in the dwelling, but in any case judgment has to be made on each individual case.

[vii] Under the Housing Act 1996, local housing authorities have a duty to secure settled accommodation for applicant households who are eligible for assistance, unintentionally homeless and who fall within a priority need group. Priority need groups include households with dependant children, pregnant women and people who are vulnerable in some way, for example because of mental illness or physical disability. Where a main duty is owed, the authority must ensure that suitable accommodation is available for the applicant and their household until a settled home becomes available for them.

[viii] Homeless at home refers to any arrangements where a household remains in, or returns to, the accommodation from which they are being made homeless, or in other accommodation found by the applicant. This includes any households who moved from accommodation arranged by the authority into this type of arrangement.

ix The definition of a decent home is one that meets all of the following criteria:

- meets the statutory minimum standard for housing. This was the Fitness Standard up to April 2006 when it was replaced by the Housing Health and Safety Rating System (HHSRS). More information on HHSRS is available here www.communities.gov.uk/publications/housing/hhsrsoperatingguidance. In Northern Ireland the current minimum standard is the Fitness Standard set out in Schedule 5 of the Housing (Northern Ireland) Order 1992

- it is in reasonable state of repair

- has reasonably modern facilities and services

- provides a reasonable degree of thermal comfort (adequate heating and effective thermal insulation)

x A decent home is one that meets the HHSRS statutory minimum standard for housing; is in a reasonable state of repair (assessed from the age and condition of a range of building components); has reasonably modern facilities and services; and provides a reasonable degree of thermal comfort.

A poor quality environment is one with (surveyor-assessed) significant problems in the neighbourhood with: the upkeep, management or misuse of the private and public space and buildings; road traffic and other forms of transport; or utilisation, that is abandonment or non residential use of property.

A very energy inefficient home is one with a rating of less than 35 under the SAP 2001 methodology (and equivalent to SAP less than 31.49 under the SAP 2005 methodology). For survey purposes this threshold is taken to indicate homes with a HHSRS Category 1 excess cold hazard, that is it poses a threat to health to vulnerable people arising from sub-optimal indoor temperatures.

A home in serious disrepair is one with standardised basic repair costs of more then £25/m^2 at 2001 prices.

xi The Government's Standard Assessment Procedure (SAP) is an index based on calculated costs per m^2 of floor area for space and water heating, ventilation and lighting, less cost savings from energy generation technologies based on a standard heating regime for a dwelling. It is expressed on a scale of 1 (highly energy inefficient) to 100 (highly energy efficient, with 100 representing zero energy cost). The detailed methodology for calculating the SAP to monitor the energy efficiency is periodically updated to reflect developments in the energy efficiency technologies and knowledge of dwelling performance. The rating scale underpinning figures reported here is based on the SAP 2005 methodology.

xii The Energy Efficiency Rating (EER) is presented in an A to G banding system by way of an Energy Performance Certificate, where Band A rating represents low energy costs (the most efficient band) and Band G rating represents high energy costs (the least efficient band). The break points in the SAP scale (see above) used for the EER bands are:

- Band A (92–100)
- Band B (81–91)
- Band C (69–80)
- Band D (55–68)
- Band E (39–54)
- Band F (21–38)

- Band G (1–20)

[xiii] In April 2008 changes were made to the way in which property transactions were counted. Under the new system, transactions are based on actual completions instead of the number of stamp duty land tax certificates issued. Properties valued at less than £40,000 are excluded from the data. Removing transactions at the very bottom end of the market means that data is closer to showing the sales of residential dwellings, as non dwellings such as small pieces of land, will tend to be in the excluded transactions.

[xiv] Information on dwelling prices at national and regional levels are collected and published by Communities and Local Government on a monthly basis. Until August 2005 data came from a sample survey of mortgage completions, the Survey of Mortgage Lenders (SML). The SML covered around 50 banks and building societies that are members of the Council of Mortgage Lenders (CML). From September 2005 data come from the Regulated Mortgage Survey (RMS), which is conducted by BankSearch and the CML.

There are two main methods of calculating house prices; simple average prices and mix-adjusted prices. Simple average prices are more volatile as they will be influenced by changes in the mix of properties bought in each period. This effect is removed by applying fixed weights to the process at the start of each year to create mix-adjusted house prices, based on the average mix of properties purchased during the previous three years, and these weights are applied to prices during the year.

The RMS sample provided to DCLG covers around 60 per cent of UK mortgage completions for house purchase. In the 6 months to July 2010 there were an average of 42,000 loans per month for house purchase and the RMS sample provided around 24,000 records per month from 32 lenders. The annual change in price is shown as the average percentage change over the year and is calculated from the house price index. The mix-adjusted average price excludes sitting tenant (right-to-buy) purchases, cash purchases, remortgages and further loans.

[xv] Figures are estimates of arrears on all first-charge loans held by Council of Mortgage Lenders (CML) members, both regulated and unregulated, and include buy-to-let. A first charge loan is the first mortgage on a property. Any additional loans secured against the property on top of this are not first charge loans. The lender with the first charge has the first call on the property if the borrower defaults on the loan. Figures presented here do not include arrears relating to other secured lending, or to firms that are not CML members. These estimates are based on reporting by a sample of CML members, which are then grossed up to represent the lending undertaken by CML members as a whole. In the first quarter of 2010 these accounted for about 92 per cent of the estimated total first-charge market.

Figures are revised as better information about rates of growth and performance in different parts of the market becomes available, so care should be taken when looking at changes over time as lenders newly reporting figures may distort comparisons. Trends in the number of months' arrears data may also be distorted by changes in mortgage rates. When rates change this may alter the contractual mortgage repayments due and so affect the number of months that a given arrears amount represents. In the case of variable rate products, with lower mortgage rates a given amount of arrears represents a higher number of monthly payments. Properties in possession are not counted as arrears. Buy-to-let mortgages, where a receiver of rent has been appointed, are also not counted as arrears.

Expenditure

There have been substantial changes in the patterns of household expenditure over the last 40 years. Trends in household expenditure provide an insight into changes in consumer preferences, the growth in choices available to consumers and their increased purchasing power, standards of living and wider changes in society. There have also been developments in the way that purchases are made, for example the use of different methods of payment and credit.

Key points:

Household and family expenditure

- In 2009 the volume of consumption of goods and services by UK households was more than two-and-a-half times the consumption in 1971

- Average weekly expenditure by households in the North East, between 2006 and 2008, was the lowest in the UK at £386.10, more than £73 less than the UK average of £459.70

- In 2008/09, for children aged 7 to 15 in the UK, the average total expenditure per child was £10.52

Consumer credit

- Between 1987 and 2009 total household debt, as a percentage of household disposable income, rose from 103 per cent to 161 per cent, slightly lower than the peak of 173 per cent in 2007

- In Q2 2010 there were 34,743 individual insolvencies, of which 14,982 were bankruptcies

Transactions

- The volume of consumer payments made by cheque has fallen by 64 per cent to 0.6 billion in 2009 from 1.8 billion in 1985

- Debit card payments accounted for the largest volume (49 per cent) of non-cash payments in 2009 with 5.8 billion transactions

- In 2009 the volume of retail sales in Great Britain was approximately 54 per cent higher than in 1996

- Retail sales peaked in November and December in the period up to and immediately after Christmas, accounting for 20 per cent of retail sales in 2009

Prices

- Between 2008 and 2009 the only category of goods and services for which prices fell was clothing and footwear, which decreased by 7.7 per cent

Household and family expenditure

This section gives an overview of the patterns and trends of household spending on goods and services, starting with the volume of domestic household expenditure. **Figure 1** shows the growth in the volume of consumption of goods and services by UK households over the last four decades.

Changes in the pattern of expenditure can be the result of changes in prices, in the volume of goods or services purchased or a combination of the two. Volume indices are useful for analysing time trends in consumption as they remove the effect of price changes which can differ depending on the category of expenditure.

Figure 1   Volume of domestic household expenditure

United Kingdom

Index numbers (1971=100)

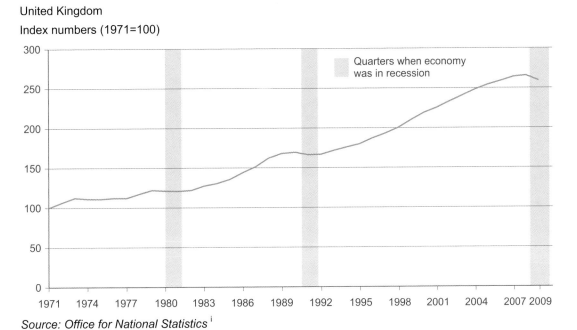

Source: Office for National Statistics [i]

In 2009 the volume of consumption of goods and services by UK households was more than two-and-a-half times the consumption in 1971 (£810 million compared with £312 million at 2006 prices). The volume of spending increased every year over the period, except 1974, 1975, 1980, 1981, 1991 and 2009. These years correspond to periods of contraction in the UK economy (see Social Trends: Income and wealth). Between 2008 and 2009 the volume of domestic household expenditure in the UK fell by 2.3 per cent from £829 million to £810 million (at 2006 prices).

There have been substantial changes over the last 40 years in the way households in the UK allocate expenditure between different goods and services. **Table 1** shows that the rise in volume of expenditure has not been the same for all categories of goods and services.

Table 1   Volume of household expenditure:[1] by purpose

United Kingdom

Index numbers (1971=100)

	1971	1981	1991	2001	2009	£ billions (current prices) 2009
Food and non-alcoholic beverages	100	105	117	137	151	84
Alcoholic beverages and tobacco	100	99	92	88	90	31
Clothing and footwear	100	120	187	344	553	48
Housing, water and fuels[2]	100	117	139	152	160	193
Furnishings, household equipment and maintenance	100	117	160	262	263	44
Miscellaneous goods and services	100	121	240	336	377	105
Restaurants and hotels[3]	100	126	167	193	185	89
Recreation and culture	100	158	279	545	869	99
Transport	100	128	181	246	273	125
Communication	100	190	306	790	1126	19
Health	100	125	182	188	229	14
Education	100	160	199	255	222	13
Total domestic household expenditure	100	121	166	225	259	863
Total goods	100	117	156	227	285	412
Total services	100	128	184	231	245	452
UK tourist expenditure abroad	100	193	298	699	576	29
less foreign tourist expenditure	100	152	187	222	258	20
Household final consumption expenditure[4]	**100**	**121**	**168**	**232**	**265**	**873**

1 Constant prices

2 Excludes mortgage interest payments, water charges, and council tax and Northern Ireland domestic rates. These are included in 'Other expenditure items'.

3 Includes purchases of alcoholic drinks in restaurants and hotels.

4 Includes expenditure by UK households in the UK and abroad.
Source: Office for National Statistics [i]

Over the period 1971 to 2009 the category with the strongest growth in volume was communication which increased by more than 11 times. The communication category includes mobile phone equipment and services, and Internet subscription charges, the estimates for which first became available in 1996 and 1998 respectively. Household ownership of mobile phone equipment and services has risen from 27 per cent in 1998/99 to 79 per cent in 2008, while the number of households with Internet access has risen from 10 per cent to 66 per cent over the same period (ONS, 2009).

Recreation and culture showed the next largest growth in volume expenditure between 1971 and 2009 increasing by over eight times, followed by UK tourist expenditure abroad which increased over five times. Alcoholic drinks and tobacco was the only category where the volume of expenditure fell.

The volume of spending by UK tourists abroad in 2009 was nearly six times that in 1971, this corresponds to an increase in the number of UK residents making holiday trips abroad over the same period (ONS, 2010a). Expenditure by foreign tourists in the UK increased much less, by just over two-and-a-half times over the same period. In 2009 the largest category of expenditure (at current prices) was spending on housing, water and fuel at £193 billion, followed by expenditure on transport at £125 billion.

Figure 2 shows how the level of household expenditure varied across the different regions and countries of the UK. These differences may arise because of differences in price levels between regions and countries, or differences in the volume of consumption of the various categories, or a combination of the two factors.

Figure 2   **Total average weekly expenditure per household:[1] by country and Government Office Region, 2006–2008**

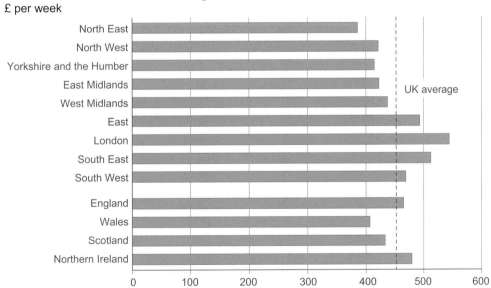

1 Total expenditure is based on COICOPs definition of total expenditure.
Source: Living Costs and Food Survey, (ONS, 2009)

Total household expenditure varies across the UK. Averaged over the period 2006–2008 total average weekly household expenditure in the UK was £459.70. In four regions household expenditure was higher than this; London (£544.70), South East (£512.30), East (£493.40) and the South West (£469.20). Average weekly household expenditure in Northern Ireland and England was also higher than the UK average at £479.70 and £465.20 respectively. The North East had the lowest average weekly household expenditure at £386.10, more than £73 per week less than the UK average. This was followed by Wales at £406.70 per week, £53 less than the UK average.

On average, expenditure of households in rural areas was higher than of those in urban areas, £505.40 compared with £446.70. Proportionately, rural areas spent more per week on transport compared with urban households, while urban households spent more per week on housing (excluding mortgage interest payments), fuel and power. In absolute terms, rural expenditure on transport was higher compared with urban expenditure (£76.10 per week compared with £58.10 per week) as was rural expenditure on recreation and culture (£67.40 per week compared with £56.00 per week).

The Living Costs and Food Survey collect information about the expenditure patterns of children in the UK. Children aged 7 to 15 are asked to keep diaries in which they record their expenditure over a two-week period. **Figure 3** shows children's weekly average spending on selected items.

Figure 3   **Children's expenditure on selected items:[1,2] by sex, 2008/09**

United Kingdom
Percentages

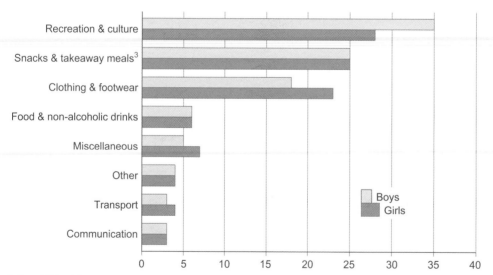

1 Aged 7 to 15.

2 From children's income, recorded by Living Costs and Food Survey as being wages, cash gifts and pocket money.

3 Expenditure item 'Snacks and takeaway meals' reflect the COICOP category 'Restaurants and hotels'. For children, hotel expenditure is negligible.

Source: Living Costs and Food Survey, Office for National Statistics

In 2008/09 the average expenditure on selected items by children aged 7 to 15 was £13.52 per week and the average total expenditure per child was £10.52 per week. Children's spending patterns in 2008/09 were very similar to those in 2001/02 with the bulk of their weekly spending going on recreation and culture, snacks and takeaway meals and clothing and footwear. However, there were differences between boys and girls. While expenditure on snacks and takeaway meals was similar, boys spent more than girls on recreation and culture (£4.74 compared with £3.89) while girls spent more than boys on clothing and footwear (£3.11 compared with £2.46).

Income and expenditure patterns are reflected in the ownership of goods, or in some cases, the inability of families to afford some goods and services. **Figure 4** shows that in 2008, households in the lowest 10th of the income distribution (the lowest decile group) had the lowest rate of ownership of durable goods.

Figure 4   **Household ownership of selected durable goods: by gross household income decile group, 2008**

United Kingdom
Percentages

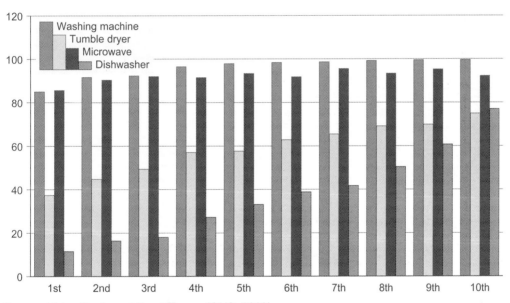

Source: Living Costs and Food Survey (ONS, 2009)

In 2008, 37 per cent of households in the lowest income decile group owned a tumble dryer compared with 75 per cent in the highest income decile group. Seventy-seven per cent of households in the highest income decile group owned a dishwasher in 2008 compared with just 11 per cent of households in the lowest income decile group. Household ownership of a microwave and washing machine was high across all of the income decile groups with 100 per cent of households in the highest income decile group owning a washing machine.

Consumer credit

In response to the Special Eurobarometer[ii] 321 survey, people reported different experiences of their ability to keep up with bills and credit commitments.

Figure 5   **Ability to keep up with bills and credit commitments: [1] EU/UK comparison, 2009**

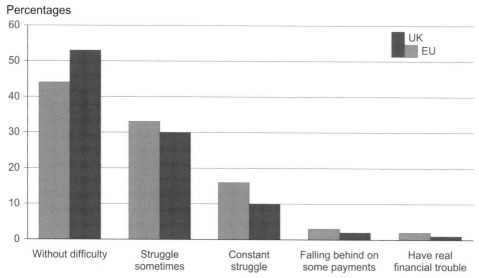

Percentages

1 Respondents were asked "Which of the following best describes how your household is keeping up with bills and credit commitments at present?" and shown above options. Excludes those who responded 'don't know'.
Source: Special Eurobarometer 321 (Eurostat, 2010)

Figure 5 shows that in December 2009, people in the UK reported having less difficulty in keeping up with bills and credit commitments when compared with respondents across the EU-27. However, only 53 per cent of respondents in the UK and 44 per cent of respondents across the EU-27 reported no difficulty.

Thirty per cent of UK citizens stated that their households struggle sometimes to keep up with bills and credit commitments; 10 per cent said that keeping up with bills and credit commitments had been a constant struggle; 2 per cent had fallen behind on some payments and 1 per cent had experienced real financial trouble. In the EU-27 as a whole, 33 per cent of citizens said that keeping up with bills and credit commitments was a struggle sometimes; 16 per cent said it was a constant struggle; 3 per cent had fallen behind on some payments and 2 per cent have experienced real financial trouble.

Total net lending to individuals by banks, building societies and other lenders is a measure of the value of new loans, less repayments, over a given period. **Figure 6** shows flows of net lending to individuals over the past 23 years.

Figure 6   Net lending to individuals[1]

United Kingdom

£ billion per quarter at 2009 prices [2]

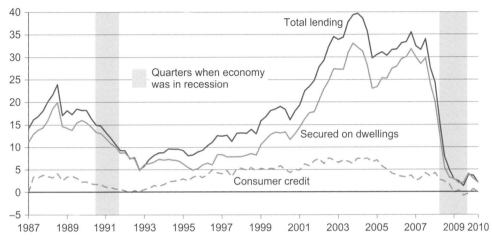

1 Lending secured on dwelling and consumer credit. Also includes lending to housing associations, seasonally adjusted.

2 Adjusted to 2009 prices using retail prices index.

Source: Bank of England; Office for National Statistics

The increase in total net lending between 1993 and 2004, adjusted for inflation, was driven primarily by growth in new loans for house purchases secured against those dwellings. The flow of net lending secured against dwellings fell in the recession of the early 1990s, and then started to gradually increase after 1996, and more rapidly from 2000 onwards with the acceleration in house prices. In Q4 2003 the flow of net lending secured on dwellings peaked at £33.1 billion, followed by a decline and subsequently another peak at a similar level in Q4 2006. It then decreased again, with the pace of decline increasing sharply at the beginning of the economic downturn which began in 2008; falling to £2.0 billion in Q2 2009, increasing to £4 billion in Q4 2009 and falling again to reach £2.1 billion in Q2 2010. The flow of total net lending reached a low point of £1.4 billion in Q3 2009, increasing slightly to £2.3 billion in Q2 2010. Although the flow of net secured lending in real terms remained positive during the recent financial crisis, the real stock of loans outstanding has fallen since Q1 2008. ST41: Housing, which will be published in February 2011, covers housing market and finances in more detail.

Consumer credit consists of credit card lending, overdrafts and non-secured loans and advances to individuals, less repayments of such lending. This type of lending has not shown the same level of volatility as net lending secured on dwellings. The net flow of consumer credit lending showed an upward trend from 1992, stabilising at around £7 billion between Q4 2001 and Q1 2005. Consumer credit then fell to -£0.8 billion in Q3 2009 (in other words, repayments were £0.8 billion larger that the amounts loaned). Consumer credit was also negative in Q4 2009 (-£0.3 billion) before rising to £0.2 billion in Q2 2010.

High levels of borrowing over a long period can lead to an increase in household debt relative to household disposable income. **Figure 7** shows how UK household debt has risen to historically high levels in recent years as consumers have borrowed to raise spending levels relative to income.

Figure 7   **Household debt¹ as a percentage of household income**

United Kingdom
Percentages

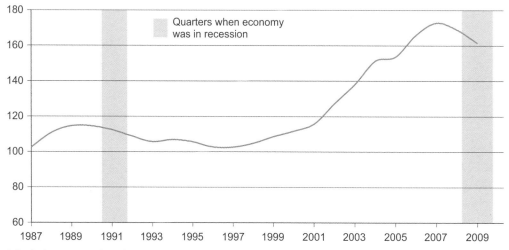

1 Includes secured and unsecured debt.
Source: Office for National Statistics [iii]

In 1987 total household debt (both secured and unsecured) as a percentage of household disposable income, known as debt ratio, was just over 100 per cent. In other words, household debt and household income were almost equal. Between 1997 and 2007 the debt ratio rose from 103 per cent to 173 per cent. This was the result of an increase of 159 per cent in household debt over the period while household income only increased by 54 per cent. The debt ratio fell by 11 percentage points between 2007 and 2009 to reach 161 per cent, though this was still over one-and-a-half times higher than the ratio seen in 1987.

In the UK in 2009 (in current prices) household debt was £1.5 billion.

Homeowners are likely to have access to better credit than non-homeowners, as they are able to use the value of their property as security for their borrowing. Housing equity withdrawal is defined as new borrowing secured on homes that is not used for house purchase or home improvements. This form of borrowing can represent a substantial supplement to a household's income and can be used to increase consumption expenditure, pay off debts, or invest in financial assets. **Figure 8** shows the pattern of household equity withdrawal over the last 40 years.

Figure 8   **Household equity withdrawal[1] as a percentage of post-tax income[2]**

United Kingdom
Percentages

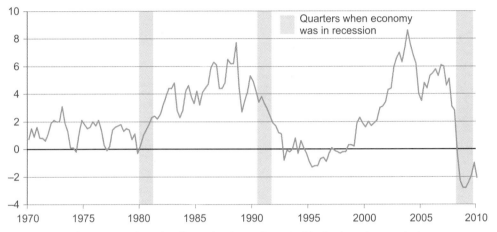

1 New borrowing secured on dwellings that is not invested in the housing market.

2 Post-tax income is household's total income less direct and indirect taxes.
Source: Bank on England; Office for National Statistics

During the 1980s housing equity withdrawal, defined as net borrowing secured on dwellings that is not invested in the housing market (for example, not used for house purchase or home improvements), in the UK began to increase from around 0.3 per cent of post-tax income in Q1 1980 to peak at 7.7 per cent in Q3 1988.

Housing equity withdrawal fell in the 1990s and remained below 2 per cent of post-tax income until 1999. Between 2000 and 2004 housing equity withdrawal rose again to peak at 8.6 per cent of post-tax income in Q4 2003 before falling sharply to 3.5 per cent of post-tax income in Q1 2005. Between Q1 2005 and Q1 2007 housing equity withdrawal rose again but began to fall in Q2 2007, becoming negative in Q2 2008, falling to its lowest level of -2.8 per cent in Q4 2008. Housing equity withdrawal remained negative into 2010 but has increased to -2.5 per cent in the second quarter. Low interest rates, as well as people's fears over future debt and job losses, may have caused individuals repayments of these loans to exceed new borrowing.

Individuals in financial trouble may keep up with bills and credit commitments by running down savings, selling assets or borrowing money. High levels of borrowing have been accompanied by an increase in the number of individual insolvencies as debtors found themselves unable to keep up with repayments. **Figure 9** shows how the number of individual insolvencies in England and Wales has risen over time.

Figure 9   **Individual insolvencies**

England and Wales

Thousands

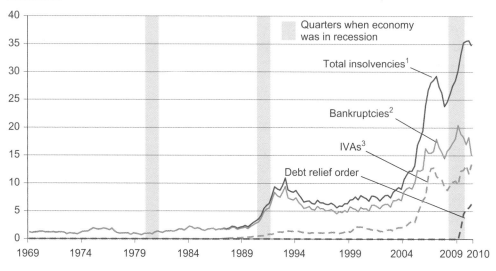

1 Data for 2009 include debt relief orders.

2 Individuals declared bankrupt by a court.

3 Individual Voluntary Agreements. Individuals who make a voluntary agreement with their creditors. Includes Deeds of Agreement, which enable debtors to come to an agreement with their creditors.

Source: The Insolvency Service

Some of the statutory insolvency instruments available to individuals experiencing financial difficulty in England and Wales include bankruptcy, individual voluntary arrangements (IVAs) and debt relief orders. The number of bankruptcies and IVAs in England and Wales remained generally stable from 1970 until the recession period in the early 1990s when they started to rise. Bankruptcies were the first to increase, starting in 1991 followed closely by an increase in IVAs from 1992. Total insolvencies did not go down to pre-recession levels again but stabilised in the 1990s before rising rapidly to peak at 35,682 in Q1 2010. There was then a slight fall to 34,743 in Q2 2010, an increase of 33.8 per cent compared with Q2 2008 (the first quarter of the recent recession), of which 14,982 were bankruptcies (a fall of 8.5 per cent compared with Q2 2008), 13,466 were IVAs (an increase of 40.4 per cent compared with Q2 2008) and 6,295 were debt relief orders.

Transactions

The ways in which transactions are carried out in the UK has changed dramatically over the last decade, **Figure 10** shows how the use of debit cards and automated payments has increased and the use of cheques and cash has declined.

Figure 10   **Non-cash transactions:[1] by method of payment**

United Kingdom

Billions

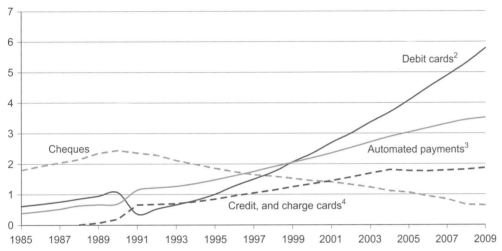

1 Figures are for payments made by households. Cheque encashment and cash withdrawals from cash machines and branch counters using credit, charge and debit cards are not included. Based on data supplied by UK card issuers.

2 Visa Debit and Switch cards in all years; includes Electron cards from 1996 and Solo cards from 1997.

3 Direct Debits, standing orders, direct credits and inter-branch automated items.

4 Visa, MasterCard, travel/entertainment cards and store cards.

Source: The Payments Council; The UK Cards Association

An increase in the use of electronic payment methods for regular payments such as mortgages, and of plastic cards for face-to-face, online and telephone retail payments has led to a decline in the use of cheques. Since 1985, the volume of consumer payments made by cheque has fallen by 64 per cent to 0.6 billion in 2009. The volume of transactions using credit and charge cards rose steadily between 1988 and 2004, but has stabilised since 2005 at 1.8 billion, increasing slightly in 2009 to approximately 1.9 billion.

Debit card payments accounted for the largest volume of non-cash payments (49 per cent) in 2009 with 5.8 billion transactions, followed by automated payment transactions (3.5 billion) and credit and charge card transactions (1.9 billion).

Figure 11   Volume of retail sales [1][iv]

Great Britain

Index numbers (2006=100)

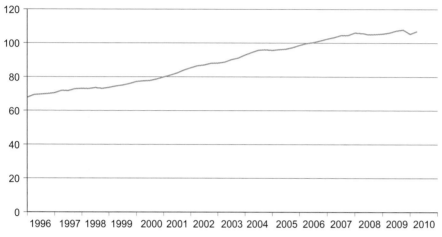

1 Includes sales of automotive fuel

Source: Retail Sales Inquiry (ONS, 2010b)

Purchases from businesses classified as retailers forms a considerable part of household expenditure. The retail sales index reflects the trends in overall consumer expenditure and, to a certain extent, the level of consumer confidence at the time. The retail sales index is a monthly measure of the turnover of retail businesses in Great Britain and is used as a key economic indicator. **Figure 11** shows how the volume of retail sales has increased steadily over the last decade. In 2009 the volume of retail sales in Great Britain was approximately 54 per cent higher than in 1996.

The volume of retail sales varies considerably over the course of the year and sales increase sharply in the run-up to Christmas. In 2009 November and December sales made up 20 per cent of the total sales for the year, a proportion that has shown little change since 1998 (ONS, 2010b).

Prices

The way people choose to spend their money is affected by the prices of goods and services. There are two main measures of UK consumer price inflation – the consumer price index (CPI) and the retail price index (RPI). The RPI was introduced in 1947 and is the longest standing measure of inflation in the UK. The CPI was launched in 1996 (although estimates are available from 1988), and since December 2003 has been the main domestic measure of UK inflation for macroeconomic purposes. The CPI excludes a number of items mainly related to housing costs – council tax, mortgage interest payments and housing depreciation.

Figure 12   **Percentage change in consumer price index: [1v] by purpose of expenditure, 2009**

United Kingdom
Percentage change over 12 months

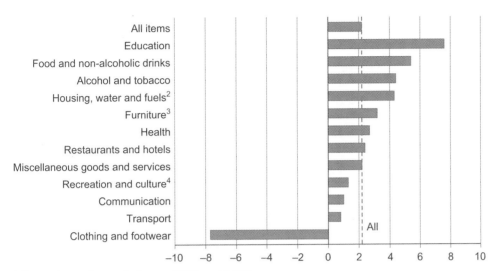

1 Percentage change between 2008 and 2009.

2 Excludes mortgage interest payments.

3 Includes household equipment and routine home repairs.

4 Includes personal care, personal effects (for example jewellery and watches), social protection, insurance and financial services.

Source: *Consumer Price Index (ONS, 2010c)*

While the overall rate of inflation has been low over the last decade, at around 2 per cent per year measured by the consumer price index, the prices for some categories of goods and services have increased more than others. Between 2008 and 2009 expenditure on education recorded the highest rate of price increase at 7.6 per cent **(Figure 12).** The second highest rate of price increase was for food and non-alcoholic drinks at 5.4 per cent, followed by alcohol and tobacco at 4.4 per cent. The only category of goods and services for which prices fell was clothing and footwear, which decreased 7.7 per cent between 2008 and 2009.

References:

Eurostat (2010). Special Eurobarometer 321. Available at:
www.ec.europa.eu/public_opinion/archives/eb_special_en.htm

ONS (2009). Family Spending: A report on the 2008 Living Costs and Food Survey. Available at
www.statistics.gov.uk/statbase/product.asp?vlnk=361

ONS (2010a). ST40: Income and wealth. Available at

www.statistics.gov.uk/socialtrends/stissue/

ONS (2010b), Retail sales index. Available at

www.statistics.gov.uk/statbase/Product.asp?vlnk=870

ONS (2010c). Available at

www.statistics.gov.uk/statbase/tsdtables1.asp?vlnk=mm23

Notes

i Underlying data are available at
www.statistics.gov.uk/StatBase/TSDTables1.asp?RELEASEID=ct&GLOBALRELEASEPOSITION=9

ii Special Eurobarometer reports are based on in-depth thematical studies carried out for various services of the European Commission or other EU Institutions and integrated in Standard Eurobarometer's polling waves.

iii Underlying data area available at
www.statistics.gov.uk/StatBase/TSDTimezone.asp?vlnk=bb&Pos=2&ColRank=1&Rank=-1

iv The retail sales index (RSI) is a measurement of monthly movements in the average weekly retail turnover or retailers in Great Britain. All retailers selected for the Retail Sales Inquiry are asked to provide estimates of total retail turnover, including sales from stores, e-commerce (including the Internet), mail order, stalls and markets, and door-to-door sales. Retail turnover is defined as the value of sales of goods to the general public for personal and household use. For further details see retail sales at: www.statistics.gov.uk/rsi

v The consumer price index (CPI) is the main measure of inflation used within the Government's monetary policy framework. Prior to 10 December 2003, this index was published as the harmonised index of consumer prices. For further details see consumer prices at: www.statistics.gov.uk/cpi

Transport

Most people use some form of transport in their everyday lives, whether they are escorting children to school, travelling to and from work, going shopping, visiting friends or family or participating in leisure activities.

This chapter looks at travel patterns, discussing the distances travelled, modes of travel and changes in the reason for travel by individuals in recent years. There is also analysis of the number and type of motor vehicles and of those with a licence to drive them. Changes in the cost to households of motoring and of public transport are also reported, together with trends in the use of public transport.

The movement towards more sustainable forms of transport such as walking, cycling or using public transport is also examined, together with people's accessibility to services by public transport. Throughout this chapter, where appropriate, the effects of the economic downturn in 2008 and 2009 are discussed.

We have also reintroduced a section on freight, looking at how its movement by various modes has changed over time.

Key points:

Travel patterns

- In 2009 an average of 973 trips were made per person in Great Britain a decrease of 1.9 per cent since 2008

- The highest proportion of trips made in 2009 were for shopping, at 20 per cent, followed by visiting friends (16 per cent) and commuting (15 per cent)

- In 2009 in Great Britain, 46.6 per cent of trips made by those living in a single parent family household were made by car. In contrast 63.5 per cent of trips made by those living in households with two or more adults and one of more children were by car.

- The number of air passengers at UK civil airports has seen substantial growth over the last 30 years. Between 1980 and 2009 the number of international passengers more than quadrupled, from 42.9 million to 176.4 million, and domestic passengers increased from 7.5 million to 20.9 million

Motor vehicles

- At the end of 2009 there were a total of 34 million vehicles licensed in Great Britain, an increase of 4.2 million (14 per cent) since the end of 2001

- In 2009, 52 per cent of households in Great Britain in the bottom fifth of the income distribution (or the lowest income quintile group) did not have a car or van, compared with only 10 per cent in the top income quintile group

- Overall there were 113,000 hybrid, electric or gas/LPG powered cars licensed at the end of 2009 in Great Britain although cars powered by these means were still less than half of one per cent of all licensed cars

Motoring Costs

- In 2009 motoring costs accounted for 13 per cent of all household expenditure in the UK

- In January 2011 UK petrol and diesel prices reached their all time high to date at 127.9 pence per litre for premium unleaded petrol and 132.3 pence per litre for diesel, double the prices at January 1999

Travel and public transport

- The number of journeys made on Great Britain's national railway network in 2009/10 was 1.3 billion, 434 million higher than in 1970, while there were 1.1 billion journeys on the London Underground, 387 million higher than 1970

- A total distance of 504 billion motor vehicle kilometres was travelled on Great Britain's roads in 2009. Car travel (including taxis) accounted for the largest share of overall distance travelled, making up 80 per cent of all vehicle kilometres travelled in 2009 (401 billion kilometres)

- During the recession of 2008 to 2009 pedal cycles and motorcycles were the only modes of transport in Great Britain which had an increase in the number of kilometres travelled at 6.4 per cent and 2.0 per cent respectively

- In 2009, 50 per cent of primary school aged children and 38 per cent of secondary school aged children walked to school

Access to services

- In England in 2009, 84 per cent of the target population in urban areas and 76 per cent in rural areas were able to reach their place of work by public transport or walking in a reasonable time

Transport safety

- In 1981 there were a total of 5,846 people killed on the roads in Great Britain; by 2009 this had fallen to 2,222 people, a 62 per cent decrease

- In 2009 95 per cent of car drivers observed were wearing a seatbelt, an increase on the 1999 rate of 91 per cent

Freight

- In 2009 around 1.9 billion tonnes of freight was lifted within Great Britain, over 80 per cent of which was by road. Between 2008 and 2009 total freight lifted decreased by 15 per cent

- UK ports handled 501 million tonnes of freight in 2009 of which 132 million tonnes was domestic freight. Between 2008 and 2009 overall freight decreased by 10.9 per cent

- In 2009 UK airports moved a total of 2.0 million tonnes of freight, a decrease of 10 per cent from 2008

Travel patterns

The results of the National Travel Survey[i] (NTS) show that travel patterns in Great Britain have been changing (**Table 1**).

Table 1   **Trips per person[1] per year: by purpose**

Great Britain   Trips per person

	2007	2008	2009
Shopping	186	198	193
Visiting friends[2]	158	156	157
Commuting	162	156	147
Education[3]	106	105	105
Personal business	98	103	103
Entertainment/public activity	48	43	44
Holiday[4]	39	41	41
Business	33	30	30
Sport: participate	18	20	20
Other[5]	124	140	134
All purposes	972	992	973

1 People of all ages.

2 Includes visiting friends at private home or elsewhere.

3 Includes escort education (ie: a trip made to take a child to school).

4 Includes day trips.

5 Includes other escort (ie: escorting someone from home to work or from work to home) and just walking.

Source: National Travel Survey, Department for Transport

In 2009 an average of 973 trips were made per person in Great Britain. This was a decrease of 1.9 per cent since 2008 and a return to the 2007 number. As in previous years the highest proportion of trips made in 2009 were for shopping, at 20 per cent, followed by visiting friends (16 per cent) and commuting (15 per cent).

Between 2007 and 2009 there was a 9.6 per cent decrease in the number of business trips and a 9.1 per cent decrease in the number of commuting trips made. Trips made for participation in sports increased by 8.9 per cent and trips made for personal business increased by 5.1 per cent.

Overall females made more trips in 2009 than males (998 compared to 947), and their travel patterns also differed. Males made more trips for commuting purposes (165 trips per male or 17 per cent of trips by males) compared with females (129 trips per female or 13 per cent of trips by females). More shopping trips were made by females at 212 trips per female per year (21 per cent) compared with 174 trips per male (18 per cent) (DfT2009).

Females were more likely to take children to school than males: 63 trips per female per year (6.3 per cent) compared with 24 trips per male per year (2.6 per cent) (DfT2009).

The results of the 2007–2009 Travel Survey for Northern Ireland show that an average of 914 trips were made per person per year, less than three trips on average per person per day. The average trip length was 6.6 miles and each person in Northern Ireland travelled an average of 6,002 miles per year of which 81 per cent were by car as a driver or a passenger (a total of 4,840 miles). Of the total distance travelled 7.5 per cent was on public transport (448 miles), while walking accounted for 2.4 per cent (144 miles).

In Northern Ireland 22 per cent of all journeys were made for leisure purposes (visiting friends, entertainment, sports, holidays and day trips) over the period 2007 to 2009, with shopping accounting for 20 per cent and commuting accounted for 16 per cent. The distance travelled for these purposes were 1,867 miles, 844 miles and 1,203 miles on average per person per year respectively (DRDNI2007–2009).

There are differences in how people travel as well as the distance they travel depending on the type of household in which they live. In 2009 in Great Britain, 38.8 per cent of trips made by those living in a single parent family household were made on foot and 46.6 per cent of trips were made by car (25.7 per cent as a car passenger and 21.0 per cent as a car driver). In contrast, 25.7 per cent of trips made by those living in households with two or more adults and one or more children were made on foot and 63.5 per cent were made by car (33.8 per cent as a car driver and 29.7 per cent as a car passenger) (**Table 2**).

Table 2   Trips by household type: by main mode, 2009

Great Britain   Percentages

	Single adult	2 or more adults	Single parent family	2 or more adults, 1 or more children	All households
Car driver	40.4	48.8	21.0	33.8	40.5
Walk	26.5	19.0	38.8	25.7	23.4
Car passenger	11.4	17.7	25.7	29.7	22.3
Bus and coach	13.3	6.8	10.0	5.3	7.0
Rail	2.9	3.4	1.0	1.9	2.6
Bicycle	1.6	1.7	1.0	1.5	1.6
Other public transport[1]	2.3	1.5	2.0	0.9	1.3
Other private transport[2]	1.4	1.2	0.5	1.3	1.2
All modes (=100%) (trips)	854	948	1,015	1,034	973

1 Includes taxi/minicab and other public transport (air and ferries).

2 Motorcycle and other private transport (mostly private hire bus).

Source: National Travel Survey, Department for Transport

Those who made the highest proportion of trips by bus and coach were those who lived in single adult households at 13.3 per cent, followed by those living in single parent family households at 10.0 per cent.

People in single parent family households travelled an average distance of 4,025 miles in 2009: 1,812 miles of which were as a car passenger, 409 miles by bus or coach and 261 miles of which were travelled on foot. People in households with two or more adults and one or more children travelled the furthest distance at 6,531 miles: 2,819 miles of which were by household members driving a car (DfT2009a).

A total of 58.6 million trips were made abroad by UK residents in 2009, and although this is an increase of 8.7 per cent compared with 1999 it is a decrease of 15.1 per cent on the total number of trips abroad in 2008 (**Table 3**). The total number of trips made by air decreased by 16.6 per cent between 2008 and 2009, with travel by the Channel Tunnel decreasing by 8.3 per cent and travel by sea decreasing by 6.2 per cent. These falls could be attributed to the recession between April 2008 and September 2009.

Table 3   **International travel by UK residents: by mode of travel and purpose of visit**

United Kingdom   Percentages

	1999				2008				2009			
	Air	Sea	Channel Tunnel	All modes	Air	Sea	Channel Tunnel	All modes	Air	Sea	Channel Tunnel	All modes
Holiday	67.4	65.6	48.8	65.0	65.6	69.7	64.5	66.0	65.3	68.8	64.3	65.7
Visiting friends and relatives	13.3	10.3	9.3	12.2	19.1	15.3	9.8	18.0	20.6	18.7	13.3	19.8
Business	17.1	8.4	14.9	15.1	13.2	7.8	18.2	12.9	12.1	6.6	17.4	11.7
Other	2.3	15.7	27.0	7.6	2.2	7.2	7.5	3.1	2.1	5.9	5.0	2.8
All purposes (=100%) (millions)	37.5	10.4	5.9	53.9	56.0	8.1	4.8	69.0	46.7	7.6	4.4	58.6

Source: International Passenger Survey, Office for National Statistics

Between 1999 and 2009 business trips as a percentage of all trips by air decreased by 5.0 percentage points, while holiday trips decreased by 2.1 percentage points. However, trips made by air to visit friends and relatives increased by 7.3 percentage points over this period. More information on holiday trips abroad is provided in the Lifestyles and social participation chapter.

The proportion of holiday trips made by UK residents through the Channel tunnel increased by 15.5 percentage points between 1999 and 2009 while over the same period the largest increase of trips by sea were for visiting friends and relatives (8.4 percentage points).

While air travel increased by 25 per cent between 1999 and 2009 travel by sea decreased by 27 per cent and through the Channel Tunnel by 25 per cent.

Although travel by air decreased between 2008 and 2009 the number of air passengers at UK civil airports has seen substantial growth over the last 30 years. Between 1980 and 2009 the number of international passengers more than quadrupled, from 42.9 million to 176.4 million, and domestic passengers increased from 7.5 million to 20.9 million (**Figure 1**).

Figure 1   Air passengers at UK civil airports

United Kingdom

Millions

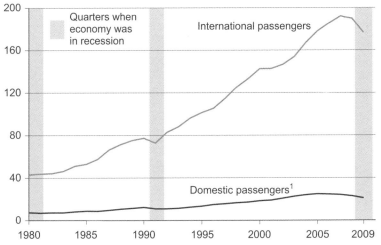

1 Numbers have been halved as domestic traffic is counted both at the airport of departure and at the airport of arrival.

Source: Civil Aviation Authority

The number of international passengers decreased from a high of 192 million in 2007 to 176 million in 2009. The largest part of this decrease (13 million passengers or 7.1 per cent) was between 2008 and 2009. The number of domestic passengers has fallen from a high of 25 million passengers in 2005 to 21 million in 2009. Again, the largest fall (of 8.4 per cent) was between 2008 and 2009. Both of these decreases may, in part, be because of the recession – a similar decrease can be seen in the recession of the early 1990s.

Motor vehicles

Another effect of the most recent recession can be seen in the decrease in the number of new vehicle registrations in 2008 and 2009 (**Table 4**).

Table 4   **Cars and motorcycles[1] currently licensed[2] and new registrations**

Great Britain   Thousands

	Currently licensed		New registrations	
	Cars	Motorcycles	Cars	Motorcycles
2001	25,126	1,010	2,586	180
2002	25,782	1,070	2,682	166
2003	26,240	1,135	2,646	161
2004	27,028	1,191	2,599	137
2005	27,520	1,206	2,443	136
2006	27,609	1,210	2,340	135
2007	28,000	1,248	2,390	146
2008	28,161	1,275	2,112	142
2009	28,246	1,276	1,968	115

1 Includes scooters and mopeds.
2 At 31 December each year by body type.
Source: Department for Transport

At the end of 2009 there were a total of 34 million vehicles licensed in Great Britain, an increase of 4.2 million (14 per cent) since the end of 2001 (DfT2009b).

The number of licensed cars on Britain's roads has continued to increase, reaching over 28 million in 2009, an increase of 12 per cent from 2001. The number of new registrations of cars fell by 24 per cent (618,000 cars) between 2001 and 2009. New registrations peaked at 2.7 million in 2002 and have since been declining, with the exception of 2007 when there was an increase of 2.1 per cent from 2006. The highest year-on-year decline was between 2007 and 2008 at 11.6 per cent, followed by 2008 and 2009 at 6.8 per cent.

Although the number of licensed motorcycles has increased by 26 per cent since 2001, from just over 1 million to nearly 1.3 million, there was little increase in the number licensed between 2008 and 2009. New registrations of motorcycles have declined each year from 2001, apart from in 2007 when there was an 8.3 per cent increase compared with 2006. The largest year-on-year decrease was in 2009 when new registrations declined by 19.1 per cent.

In April 2009 a voluntary discount scheme was announced whereby motor dealers would give vehicle owners a discount of £2,000 or more towards the purchase cost of a new vehicle if they traded in a car or van over 10 years old. The aim of the scheme was to provide a boost to demand and immediate support on a short-term basis to the new car industry and its supply chain in the wake of falling sales.

The scheme also aimed to remove older vehicles from the road and encourage motorists to invest in new, safer and potentially more environmentally friendly models[ii] Between May 2009 and January 2010 a total of 316,210 vehicle registrations were made through the scrappage scheme; 311,159 cars and 5,051 vans (SIS2010).

The average age of cars licensed at the end of 2009 was 7.1 years, similar to earlier years. The largest proportion of cars registered in 2009 were first registered between 6 and 13 years ago at 44 per cent (12.5 million cars), followed by those first registered between 4 and 6 years ago, 16 per cent (4.6 million cars) (DfT2009b).

The average age of motorcycles licensed at the end of 2009 was 10.8 years, an increase from 10.3 years in 2008. As with cars, the largest proportion of motorcycles registered in 2009 were first registered 6 to 13 years ago at 31 per cent (399,000 motorcycles) followed by those registered between 4 and 6 years ago, 11 per cent (146,000 motorcycles) (DfT2009b).

The availability of a car in a household is closely related to income: households with lower incomes are much more likely to not have a car (**Figure 2**).

Figure 2   **Household car availability: by household income quintile group,[1] 2009**

Great Britain
Percentages

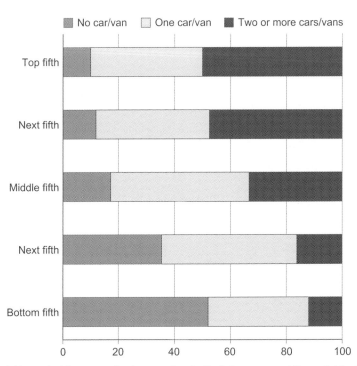

1 Households are ranked according to their income and then divided into five groups of equal size. The bottom fifth, or bottom quintile group is then the 20 per cent of households with the lowest incomes.

Source: National Travel Survey, Department for Transport

In 2009, 52 per cent of households in Great Britain in the bottom fifth of the income distribution[iii] (or the lowest income quintile group) did not have a car or van, compared with only 10 per cent in the top income quintile group. Almost a half of households in the second lowest and middle income quintile groups had one car or van (48 and 49 per cent respectively) compared with 36 per cent of households in the lowest and around 40 per cent in the highest income quintile groups. The proportion of households with two or more cars or vans increases as income increases from 12 per cent of households in the bottom income quintile group to 50 per cent of households in the highest income quintile group.

There has been a change in cars available to households over time: in 1951, 86 per cent of households in Great Britain did not have access to a car or van but by 2009 this had fallen to 25 per cent (DfT2009c).

Less than three-quarters of adults aged 17 and over in Great Britain held a full driving licence in 2009, a total of 35 million full car driving licence holders (DfT2009d). The proportion of men aged 17 and over holding a licence has remained relatively stable over the period 2002 to 2009 at around 80 per cent, while for women it has risen from 61 per cent in 2002 to 65 per cent in 2009 (**Figure 3**).

Figure 3   **Full car driving licence holders: by age and gender**

Great Britain

Percentages

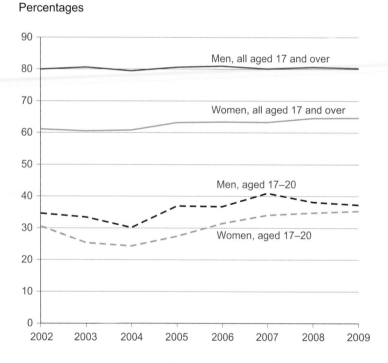

Source: National Travel Survey, Department for Transport

The proportion of younger men, aged 17 to 20, holding a full driving licence has fluctuated between 2002 and 2008, from a low of 30 per cent in 2004 to a peak in 2007 of 41 per cent, falling to 37 per cent in 2009. For women of the same age, the proportion holding a licence has roughly followed the same pattern as men over the same period, reaching a low of 24 per cent in 2004 to a peak of 35 per cent in 2009.

In the 2009 National Travel Survey, the main reasons given by those aged 17 to 20 for not holding a full driving licence or not currently learning to drive were the cost of learning to drive (57 per cent), the cost of buying a car (39 per cent) and the cost of insurance (33 per cent) (DfT2009e).

Non licence holders were also asked the likelihood of them learning to drive in the future. For those aged 17 to 20, 49 per cent said they would probably learn to drive within the next 5 years and 39 per cent said they would probably do so within the next year. Seven per cent of individuals within this age group answered that they would never learn to drive (DfT2009f).

In Northern Ireland 81 per cent of men and 66 per cent of women aged 17 and over held a driving licence between 2007 and 2009, very similar to the proportions for Great Britain.

The proportion of younger drivers in Northern Ireland, aged 17 to 20, holding a driving licence has increased from 36 per cent in the period 2006 to 2008 to 39 per cent between 2007 and 2009. The proportion of men in this age group holding a licence was 43 per cent in 2007 to 2009 compared with 36 per cent of women (DRDNI2007-2009).

Although petrol cars licensed in Great Britain dominate the market the proportion of the total number of petrol cars is decreasing. Between 2000 and 2009 the number of petrol cars licensed decreased by 3.5 per cent (741,000 petrol cars). While petrol cars accounted for 87 per cent of all licensed cars in 2000 by 2009 they accounted for 73 per cent (**Table 5**).

Table 5   Cars licensed by fuel type[1]

Great Britain   Thousands

	Petrol	Diesel	Petrol/Gas	Gas[2]	Electric	Hybrid Electric	Total
2000	21,233	3,153	19	1	-	-	24,406
2001	21,641	3,460	21	3	-	1	25,126
2002	21,839	3,912	23	6	-	1	25,782
2003	21,805	4,400	24	10	-	1	26,240
2004	21,977	5,011	25	13	-	3	27,028
2005	21,876	5,596	26	14	1	8	27,520
2006	21,466	6,083	27	16	1	17	27,609
2007	21,264	6,657	27	18	1	32	28,000
2008	20,899	7,164	27	23	1	47	28,161
2009	20,491	7,641	25	25	1	61	28,246

1 At 31 December each year by body type.
2 Includes gas, gas bi-fuel and gas-diesel.
Source: Department for Transport

The number of cars using all other types of fuel have increased in Great Britain between 2000 and 2009, with the number of licensed cars fuelled by diesel increasing by 142 per cent to 7.6 million cars.

Overall there were 113,000 hybrid, electric or gas/LPG powered cars licensed at the end of 2009 in Great Britain although cars powered by these means were still less than half of one per cent of all licensed cars. Hybrid electric cars comprised the largest number of these less 'traditional' cars in 2009 at 61,000.

In Northern Ireland there were a total of 1.0 million vehicles licensed at the end of 2009, an increase of 43 per cent from the year 2000 when there were a total of 731,000 vehicles licensed. Of the total licensed in 2009, 84 per cent were within the private and light goods taxation class (874,000).

Of the 874,000 private and light goods licensed in 2009, 53 per cent were diesel (460,000) and 47 per cent were petrol (412,000). In 2009, 909 private and light goods were of an 'other fuel' type, an eight-fold increase on the year 2000 figure of 109 vehicles by this fuel type (DRDNItransport2009-10 and DRDNItransport2000-01).

Motoring Costs

In 2009 motoring costs accounted for 13 per cent of all household expenditure in the UK. **Table 6** shows that after taking into account the effects of inflation there was considerable change in household expenditure on motoring between 2006 and 2009, showing a 9.5 per cent decrease.

Table 6   **Household expenditure on motoring in real terms[1]**

United Kingdom

£ per week

	2006[2]	2007	2008	2009
Cars, vans and motorcycle purchase	24.70	23.60	21.00	19.50
Repairs, servicing, spares and accessories	8.40	8.30	8.50	7.90
Motor vehicle insurance and taxation[3]	11.20	10.50	10.70	11.10
Petrol, diesel and other oils	19.30	18.90	20.90	19.20
Other motoring costs	2.50	2.50	2.10	2.20
All motoring expenditure	**66.20**	**63.90**	**63.30**	**59.90**

1 At 2009 prices deflated by the 'all items' retail prices index. Expenditure rounded to the nearest 10 pence.

2 From this version of 2006, figures are shown based on weighted data, including children's expenditure. Weighting is based on the population figures from the 1991 and 2001 Censuses.

3 Excludes boat insurance.

Source: Living Costs and Food Survey, ONS

The largest percentage decrease between 2006 and 2009 was on the purchase of motor vehicles at 21 per cent (£5.20 per week) followed by other motoring costs at 12 per cent (£0.30 per week). Table 5 shows that the number of cars licensed in Great Britain has been increasing, while Table 7 shows that the cost of purchasing a vehicle has decreased, therefore the decrease in household expenditure on vehicle purchases appears to have been driven by falling prices rather than falling demand.

Between 2008 and 2009 other motoring costs increased by 4.8 per cent (£0.10 per week) and motor vehicle insurance and taxation increased by 3.7 per cent (£0.40). The largest decreases in household expenditure on motoring over the same period were for petrol, diesel and other oils, decreasing by 8.1 per cent (£1.70 per week), the purchases of cars, vans and motorcycles, at 7.1 per cent (£1.50 per week) and the cost of repairs, servicing, spares and accessories at 7.1 per cent (£0.60 per week).

Consumer price indices[iv] measure the change in the general level of prices charged for goods and services bought for the purpose of household consumption in the UK. The index for the purchase of vehicles fell by 6.8 per cent between 2000 and 2009. This downward movement was entirely due to a 26.4 per cent fall in the index for second hand cars, though some of this fall was offset by rises of 11.3 per cent and 4.8 per cent in the indices for motorcycles and bicycles and new cars respectively (**Table 7**).

Table 7　　**Transport prices**

United Kingdom   Index numbers (2005=100)

	2000	2001	2002	2003	2004	2005	2006	2007	2008	2009
Purchase of vehicles	105.9	102.4	101.5	100.9	101.1	100	99.5	99.5	97.4	98.7
New cars	100.2	95.7	95.4	96.1	98.3	100	100.9	102.4	103.7	105.0
Second hand cars	117.9	115.9	113.5	110.0	106.0	100	97.1	94.5	87.6	86.8
Motorcycle and bicycles	101.6	102.0	101.8	100.3	102.6	100	98.9	99.3	101.4	113.1
Operation of personal transport equipment	84.0	83.7	84.3	88.5	93.4	100	105.5	109.4	120.0	116.9
Insurance	85.2	92.9	95.4	100.7	101.8	100	100.0	103.2	105.0	115.8
Spare parts and access	95.8	94.5	95.5	96.8	98.2	100	102.7	103.1	105.5	109.2
Fuels and lubricants	91.5	86.8	84.1	87.1	92.0	100	105.5	108.6	124.7	114.9
Maintenance and repairs	72.8	77.7	82.0	87.7	93.7	100	106.2	111.5	117.5	121.1
Other services	79.0	82.1	86.4	91.9	95.5	100	104.3	109.5	112.2	114.6
All items	93.1	94.2	95.4	96.7	98.0	100	102.3	104.7	108.5	110.8

Source: Consumer Prices Index, Office for National Statistics

Prices for the operation of personal transport equipment rose considerably between 2000 and 2009, with all components rising: the largest increases were for maintenance and repairs (66 per cent) and other services (45 per cent).

Between 2008 and 2009 prices for the purchase of vehicles increased by 1.3 per cent although there was still a slight decrease in the price of second hand cars (0.9 per cent). Over the same time period prices for the operation of personal transport decreased by 2.6 per cent, driven by a fall of 7.9 per cent in the price for fuels and lubricants, the only sub-index that showed a fall. The cost of insurance had the largest increase, rising 10.3 per cent.

There is considerable volatility in the prices of petrol and diesel, reflecting the market for crude oil which in turn is influenced by world events. On 1 January 2011 a government fuel duty change resulted in petrol and diesel prices increasing by 0.76p per litre. This, together with the increase of VAT from 17.5 per cent to 20 per cent on the 4 January 2011, has meant further rises in the cost of fuel. In January 2011 UK prices reached their all time high to date at 127.9 pence per litre for premium unleaded petrol and 132.3 pence per litre for diesel, double the prices at January 1999.

Figure 4   **Premium unleaded[1] and diesel pump prices[2]**

United Kingdom

Pence per litre

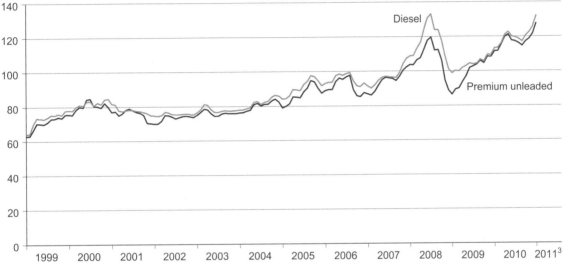

1 Unleaded petrol that is rated at 95 Research Octane Number. Does not include super unleaded petrol.

2 Including tax and duties.

3 Data for 2011 are to January only and are provisional.

Source: Department for Environment and Climate Change

Between January 1999 and January 2011, the average pump prices of both premium unleaded and diesel (including tax and duty) first reached a peak in July 2008, at 119.6 pence per litre and 133.0 pence per litre respectively (**Figure 4**). Prices then began to fall and in January 2009 were at 86.3 pence per litre for premium unleaded and 98.7 pence per litre for diesel.

These lower prices were relatively short-lived, with premium unleaded petrol returning to over £1.00 per litre in June 2009 (101.8 pence per litre) while diesel returned to over £1.00 per litre in February 2009 (100.3 pence per litre). In May 2010 another peak in prices was reached, with premium unleaded costing 121.2 pence per litre and diesel costing 122.8 pence per litre.

In December 2010 prices of premium unleaded petrol across the EU-27 ranged from 91.9 pence per litre in Bulgaria to 132.7 pence per litre in Greece. The UK was the eighth most expensive country in which to buy premium unleaded petrol at 121.6 pence per litre.

For diesel, the UK was the most expensive country in the EU-27 at 125.8 pence per litre, 36.7 pence more expensive than Luxembourg where diesel was the cheapest within the EU-27 at 89.1 pence per litre (DECC2010).

Taxes and duties form a major component of petrol prices, ranging from 46.7 per cent in Cyprus to 62.7 per cent the UK in December 2010 (DECC2010).

The UK also had the largest tax and duty on diesel throughout the EU-27 in December 2010 at 61.2 per cent. Sweden had the second largest component of tax on diesel at 54.8 per cent and Lithuania had the lowest component at 42.1 per cent (DECC2010).

Travel and Public transport

In 2009 fares and travel costs other than motoring accounted for 2.1 per cent of all household expenditure in the UK. After taking into account the effects of inflation there was little change overall in household expenditure on fares and other travel costs between 2006 and 2008, but a decrease of 7.7 per cent between 2008 and 2009 (**Table 8**).

Table 8   Household expenditure on travel costs in real terms[1]

United Kingdom

£ per week

	2006[2]	2007	2008	2009
Rail and tube fares	2.30	2.60	2.40	2.50
Bus and coach fares	1.40	1.30	1.40	1.30
Taxi, air and other travel costs[3]	6.90	6.60	6.60	5.90
All fares and other travel costs[4]	**10.70**	**10.40**	**10.40**	**9.60**

1 At 2009 prices deflated by the 'all items' retail prices index. Expenditure rounded to the nearest 10 pence.

2 Figures are shown based on weighted data, including children's expenditure. Weighting is based on the population figures from the 1991 and 2001 Censuses.

3 Includes combined fares.

4 Includes expenditure on bicycles and boats – purchases and repairs.

Source: Living Costs and Food Survey, ONS

The decrease in household expenditure on travel between 2008 and 2009 was largely because of a reduction in expenditure on taxis, air and other travel. One reason for this is the decrease in air travel as shown in Figure 1, but the fall is also related to the costs of fares. Between 2008 and 2009 air fares fell by 0.3 per cent, as measured by the consumer prices index (CPI)[iv].

There has been a considerable change in the use of local buses. In 2009/10 a total of 5.2 billion local bus journeys were made in Great Britain a decrease of 1.1 per cent since 2008/09. This is part of a long term trend: since 1985/86 the number of local bus journeys decreased by 7.9 per cent. However, the change is not evenly spread across Great Britain: bus journeys made in London nearly doubled between 1985/86 and 2009/10, from 1.2 billion to 2.2 billion, those made in Scotland decreased by 30 per cent over the same period, and those made in Wales decreased by 28 per cent (671,000 to 467,000 for Scotland and 163,000 to 117,000 for Wales) (DfT2010).

The proportion of people, in Great Britain, aged 60 and over who said they used a local bus at least once a week increased from 28 per cent in 2005 to 39 per cent in 2009 (**Figure 5**).

Figure 5   **Frequency of bus use: for those aged 60 years and over**

Great Britain
Percentages

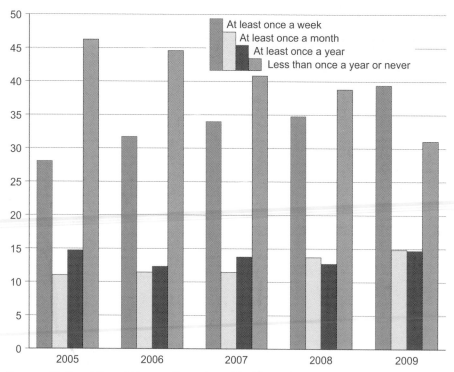

Source: National Travel Survey, Department for Transport

Between 2005 and 2009 the proportion of people in this age group who said they use a bus less than once a year or never decreased, from 46 per cent to 31 per cent

The increase in bus use by people aged 60 and over could be linked to the increase in the take-up of concessionary fare schemes[v]. Overall, in Great Britain, the take-up rate increased 20 percentage points between 2005 and 2009, from 56 per cent to 76 per cent and by 2.7 percentage points between 2008 and 2009. Take up rates remain highest in the London Boroughs but the largest increases in take up rates are outside London, particularly in rural areas (DfT2009g).

The number of journeys made on Great Britain's national railway network in 2009/10 was 1.3 billion, 434 million higher than in 1970, while there were 1.1 billion journeys on the London Underground, 387 million higher than 1970 (**Figure 6**).

Figure 6   **Passenger rail journeys**

Great Britain

Millions

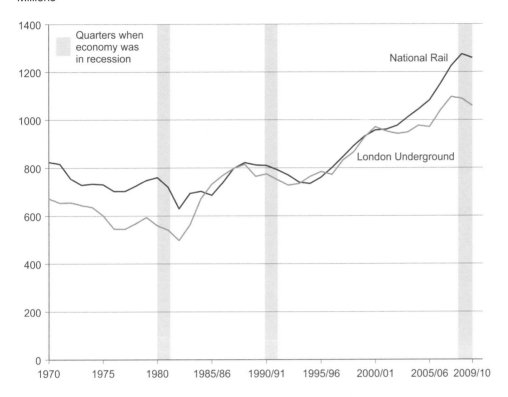

Source: Department for Transport

National rail passenger journeys fell in most years between 1970 and the early 1980s, with the sharpest decrease during the recession of the 1980s. Rail travel then rose to reach 822 million journeys in 1988/89 followed by a further fall in the 1990s to reach another low of 735 million in 1994/95. After the recession in the 1990s rail passenger journeys increased steadily each year to peak at 1.3 billion in 2008/09. London Underground passenger journeys followed a similar pattern dropping to 498 million in 1982, then rising to 815 million in 1988/89 and falling in the early 90s before rising to a peak of 1.1 billion in 2007/08.

Between 2008/09 and 2009/10 there was a slight decline in the number of journeys made on the national rail network and the London Underground of 1.3 per cent and 2.8 per cent respectively which could reflect the economic downturn between April 2008 and September 2009.

In Northern Ireland a total of 10 million passenger journeys were made by rail in 2009–2010, a slight decrease from the 10.2 million passenger journeys made in 2008–2009. However, passenger journeys have increased by 61 per cent from 1996–1997 (DRDNItransport2009-10 and DRDNItransport2000-01).

A total distance of 504 billion motor vehicle kilometres was travelled on Great Britain's roads in 2009. Car travel (including taxis) accounted for the largest share of overall distance travelled, making up 80 per cent of all vehicle kilometres travelled in 2009 (401 billion kilometres).

Figure 7   Traffic on public roads:[1] by vehicle type

Great Britain

Index numbers (1993=100)

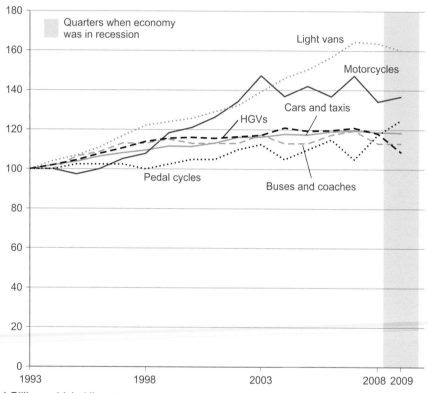

1 Billion vehicle kilometres.

Source: Department for Transport

Between 1993 and 2009 the total distance travelled on Great Britain's roads increased by 22.2 per cent (**Figure 7**). The largest increase of 60.1 per cent was in the number of kilometres travelled by light vans. Distance travelled by cars and taxis increased by 18.5 per cent and the smallest increase of 8.6 per cent was in the distance travelled by heavy goods vehicles. The distance travelled by pedal cycles increased by 25.0 per cent

During the recession of 2008 to 2009 pedal cycles and motorcycles were the only modes of transport in Great Britain which had an increase in the number of kilometres travelled at 6.4 per cent and 2.0 per cent respectively. Not unexpectedly the largest decrease over the same period was for the distance travelled by heavy goods vehicles, at 8.0 per cent.

By promoting more sustainable transport it is believed that environmental and social impacts of travel will be minimised. Increasing proportions of sustainable transport will reduce transport emissions that contribute to local pollution problems and climate change. Increases in walking or cycling, use of public transport and low carbon vehicles are some of the ways which could contribute to minimising the effects of transport on the environment.

In *Social Trends 40* we reported that traffic in the local area has been the most common problem reported by householders since 2003/04 with more that half (52 per cent) of householders stating this was a problem in their area in 2007/08 (please see Table 10.12 in the following link: http://www.statistics.gov.uk/cci/article.asp?ID=2520&Pos=8&ColRank=1&Rank=224).

How children travel to and from school varies by age as well as by the distance they live from their school. Between 2002 and 2009 walking was the most commonly reported method of getting to and from school. The proportion of primary aged school children aged 5 to 10 walking to school has remained relatively stable over this period at around 50 per cent. For secondary school aged children aged 11 to 16, the proportion walking to school was more variable and ranged between 38 per cent and 44 per cent. In 2009, 50 per cent of primary school aged children and 38 per cent of secondary school aged children walked to school (**Table 9**).

Table 9   **Trips[1] to and from school: by age of child and selected mode[2]**

Great Britain   Percentages

			Age 5–10			
	Walk	Car/van	Bus	Bicycle	Rail	Other[3]
2002	51	41	6	1	0	1
2003	51	41	7	1	0	1
2004	49	43	7	1	0	1
2005	49	43	6	1	..	1
2006	52	41	6	1	..	1
2007	51	41	7	1	0	1
2008	48	43	7	2	0	..
2009	50	42	6	1	..	1

			Age 11–16			
	Walk	Car/van	Bus	Bicycle	Rail	Other[3]
2002	38	24	33	2	1	2
2003	40	23	32	2	1	2
2004	43	22	29	3	1	2
2005	44	22	29	2	1	2
2006	41	20	31	3	2	2
2007	43	22	30	2	1	3
2008	40	21	33	2	1	2
2009	38	22	33	3	2	2

1 Trips of less than 80 kilometres (50 miles) only.

2 Due to methodological changes short walks were under-recorded in 2002 and to a lesser extent in 2003. Under-recording of short walks affects the average time and length of trips, especially for walking and school trips.

3 All other modes of transport.

Source: National Travel Survey, Department for Transport

For primary school children the second most popular method of transport in 2009 was by car or van at 42 per cent while for secondary school children it was by bus at 33 per cent.

The average lengths of journey to school for primary and secondary aged school children in 2009 were 1.5 miles and 3.3 miles respectively (DfT2009h).

Access to services

For those without their own transport, access to employment, educational establishments, medical facilities and shops (key services[vi]) by public transport or on foot in a reasonable time is very important. In England in 2009, access to employment centres was the highest with 84 per cent of the target population in urban areas and 76 per cent in rural areas being able to reach their place of work by public transport or walking (**Figure 8**).

Figure 8   **Percentage of the target population[1] with access[2] to key services by public transport/walking: by rural and urban areas,[3] 2009**

England
Percentages

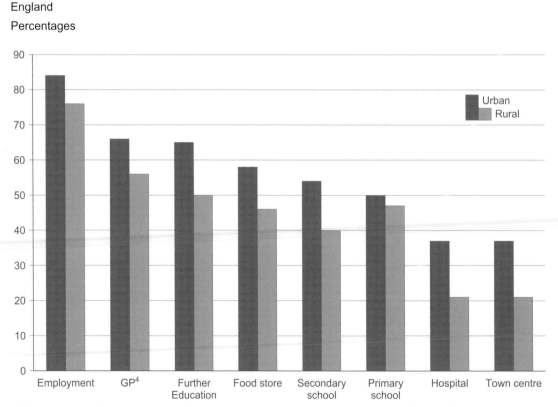

1 Target populations are the populations of the local area for the relevant service, eg: for primary schools, the target population is children aged 5–10 years old.

2 The percentage of the population that can access a given service within a reasonable time. Please see the Guidance note for further information on methods:
http://www.dft.gov.uk/adobepdf/162469/221412/221692/639263/cai2009guidance.pdf

3 Defra's Rural Definition and Local Authority Classification has been used. For further information see:
http://www.defra.gov.uk/evidence/statistics/rural/rural-definition.htm

4 General Practitioner.

Source: Department for Transport

The largest differences between rural and urban areas in people's access to key services were for reaching a hospital and town centre, with both having a 16 percentage point difference. Access to a primary school was almost the same, with 47 per cent of the target population in rural areas and

50 per cent in urban areas being able to access this service within a reasonable time by public transport or by foot.

Overall[vii], 60 per cent of the target population in urban areas could access all eight key services within a reasonable time by public transport or on foot compared with 48 per cent in rural areas. The average minimum travel time was 15 minutes by public transport or on foot, 17 minutes by cycling and 5 minutes by car. Access to all services was highest by car (76 per cent) and lowest by bicycle (50 per cent) (DfT2009i).

Transport safety

Although traffic on public roads has increased over the last thirty years the number of fatalities has decreased. In 1981 there were a total of 5,846 people killed on the roads in Great Britain, a rate of 20.7 fatalities per billion vehicle kilometres. By 2009 this had fallen to 2,222 people, a 62 per cent decrease, and a rate of 4.4 people per billion vehicle kilometres. The largest decreases over this period were fatalities of children at 86 per cent, followed by pedestrian fatalities at 73 per cent (**Table 10**).

Table 10   Reported fatalities: by road user

Great Britain   Number of fatalities

	1981	1991	2001	2008	2009
Car users	2,287	2,053	1,749	1,257	1,059
Pedestrians	1,874	1,496	826	572	500
Motorcycle users	1,131	548	583	493	472
Pedal cyclists	310	242	138	115	104
Other road users	224	204	140	95	73
Bus/coach users	20	25	14	6	14
All road users	5,846	4,568	3,450	2,538	2,222
of which children	571	377	219	124	81

Source: Department for Transport

In 2009 there were a total of 163,554 reported accidents on Great Britain's roads, just over 7,000 less than in 2008. The largest proportion of accidents, 39 per cent (64,086 accidents) occurred on B, C or unclassified roads with a speed limit of 30mph. The second largest proportion of accidents, 25 per cent (41,180 accidents), occurred on A roads with a speed limit of 30mph (Dft2009j).

A total of 298,687 vehicles were involved in the 163,554 reported accidents in 2009. Most were cars, with 227,244 involved, followed by motorcycles at 21,590. There were a total of 17,599 pedal cycles involved in reported accidents and 13,214 light goods vehicles (DfT2009j).

The long term trends in Northern Ireland are similar to those in Great Britain. The total number of reported road fatalities decreased by 38 per cent between 1991 and 2009, the largest decrease being pedal cycle users falling from nine fatalities in 1991 to zero in 2009, followed by pedestrians at 47 per cent. Over the same period reported fatalities of car users decreased by 38 per cent. The total number of child fatalities on Northern Ireland's roads decreased by 82 per cent between 1991 and 2009.

In December 2003 legislation was introduced making it illegal to use a hand-held mobile phone while driving, with a penalty of a £30 fixed penalty notice. Although more than 75,000 penalty notices were given out in 2004, some drivers continued to ignore the law. Thus from February 2007 the fixed penalty notice doubled to £60 and a driver found guilty was also given 3 penalty points on their licence[viii].

Figure 9 shows trends in observation of mobile phone use by drivers in England. The use of a hand-held phone decreased immediately after legislation changes were introduced, but then increased again. The use of hands free phones by drivers – which is not illegal – is more variable although there was a slight increase after the introduction of legislative changes (DfT2009k).

Figure 9   **Mobile phone use by driver:[1] by vehicle type**

England[2]

Percentages

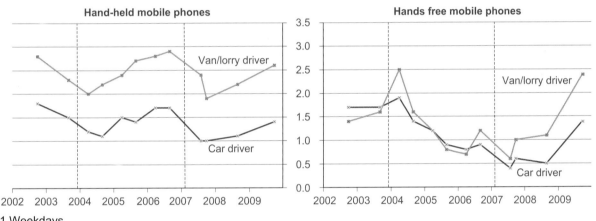

1 Weekdays.

2 Observational surveys at 30 sites in South East England.

Note: vertical lines indicate legislative changes (December 2003 and February 2007). Points are shown for the month survey was undertaken.

Source: Department for Transport

In September 2006, before the amendment to the penalty for using a hands free phone while driving in February 2007, 1.7 per cent of car drivers were observed using a hand held mobile phone, this decreased to 1.0 per cent in October 2007. However, by October 2009 the proportion of car drivers observed using a hand held device had increased to 1.4 per cent.

The proportion of van/lorry drivers observed using a hand held mobile phone is higher throughout this time period but follows a similar pattern, decreasing from 2.9 per cent in September 2006 to 1.9 per cent in October 2007 and then increasing to 2.6 per cent in October 2009.

Since 1983 it has been a legal requirement to wear a seatbelt in a car as a driver or passenger; on the rear seat, belt use was made compulsory in 1989 for children and in 1991 for adults in cars with restraints fitted. In September 2006 new regulations were introduced governing the wearing of seatbelts in cars, vans and good vehicles. The changes in 2006 largely related specifically to children and how they are to be secured within a vehicle. There are also various exemptions from wearing a seat belt[ix].

Figure 10 shows the overall rate for car occupants in England wearing a seat belt or restraint.

Figure 10   **Car occupant seatbelt wearing rates:[1] by position**

England[2]

Percentages

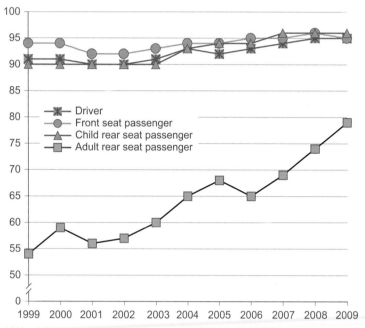

1 Weekdays.

2 Observational surveys in two areas centred around Crowthorne and Nottingham.

Source: Department for Transport

Virtually all car drivers wear a seatbelt. In 2009, 95 per cent of car drivers observed were wearing a seatbelt, an increase on the 1999 rate of 91 per cent. The use of a restraint by front seat passengers fluctuated between 92 per cent and 96 per cent over the period 1999 to 2009. The proportion of children in the rear seats of a car using some form of restraint has increased from 90 per cent in 1999 to 96 per cent in 2009. The proportion of adults in the rear seats of a car using a restraint is lower, but has nevertheless increased 25 percentage points over the same period, from 54 per cent to 79 per cent.

In 2009, of those car occupants who were classified as unrestrained, 8 per cent of unrestrained drivers and 9 per cent of unrestrained passengers were wearing a seatbelt or child restraint incorrectly. Overall, female drivers were more likely to use a seatbelt/restraint than males (98 per cent compared with 93 per cent of male drivers). However, the rate of seatbelt wear among rear seat passengers was virtually the same with 90 per cent of females wearing a seatbelt compared with 89 per cent of males.

Freight

In 2009 around 1.9 billion tonnes of freight was lifted within Great Britain, over 80 per cent of which was by road (**Table 11**). Between 2008 and 2009 total freight lifted decreased by 15 per cent, which is more than likely because of the recession that occurred between April 2008 and September 2009.

Table 11   Domestic freight lifted: by mode

Great Britain   Million tonnes

	1981	1991	2001	2008	2009[1]
Road	1,299	1,600	1,682	1,868	1,556
Rail[2]	154	136	94	103	87
Water	129	144	131	123	110
Pipeline[3]	75	105	151	147	147
All modes	1,657	1,985	2,058	2,241	1,900

1 Pipeline figures for 2009 are not available. Figures for 2008 have been used to provide a total for all modes.
2 Data for rail is for financial years.
3 Data for pipeline are for oil pipelines only (excluding offshore pipelines).
Source: Department for Transport

Between 1981 and its peak in 2008, the tonnage of freight lifted by road increased by 44 per cent, from 1.3 to 1.9 billion tonnes. Freight lifted by pipeline nearly doubled over the same period, from 75 to 147 million tonnes. However, the amount of freight lifted by rail fell by 33 per cent and rail transport fell from being the second greatest mode of freight transport in 1981 to the least used method in 2008. Between 2008 and 2009 freight lifted fell: road fell by 17 per cent, rail by 16 per cent and water by 11 per cent.

Domestic freight is also moved through ports in the UK. UK ports handled 501 million tonnes of freight in 2009 of which 132 million tonnes was domestic freight. Between 2008 and 2009, which was the period of the economic recession, overall freight decreased by 10.9 per cent, imports decreased by 13.5 per cent, exports by 10.9 per cent and domestic traffic fell by 5.9 per cent (**Figure 11**).

Figure 11   **Sea freight at UK ports: foreign or domestic**

United Kingdom
Million tonnes

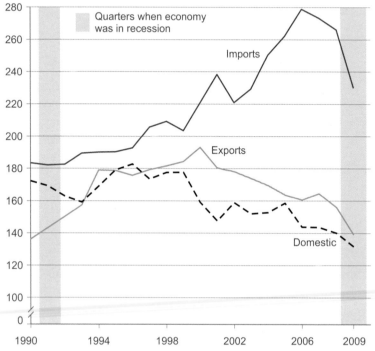

Source: Maritime Statistics 2009, Department for Transport

During the early 1990's imports remained relatively stable at around 183 million tonnes and started to gradually rise from 1993 onwards to reach a peak in 2006 of 279 million tonnes, which has since fallen by 18 per cent to reach 230 tonnes in 2009.

Exports rose during the early 1990's to reach a peak in the year 2000 of 193 million tonnes, since this peak exports have declined by 28 per cent, falling to 139 million tonnes in 2009.

Domestic traffic declined during the early 1990's to a low of 159 million tonnes in 1993 before rising by 15 per cent to reach a peak in 1996 of 183 million tonnes. Since this peak domestic traffic has decreased by 28 per cent to a low of 132 million tonnes in 2009.

Overall, between 1990 and 2009 imports have increased by a quarter, from 183 million tonnes to 230 million tonnes, while exports have increased by 2.1 per cent, from 136 million tonnes to 139 million tonnes. Domestic traffic declined by 24 per cent over the same period from 172 million tonnes to 132 million tonnes.

Between 2008 and 2009 the only port group to increase the weight of imported goods handled was West and North Wales[x], at 12.4 per cent while the port group with the largest decrease was the Bristol Channel[xi] at 27.4 per cent. For exports over the same time period, Haven[xii] saw the only increase at 1.8 per cent and the West Country[xiii] saw the largest decrease at 26.2 per cent (DfT2009l).

Looking at a longer timescale, between 2000 and 2009 the port group that experienced the largest increase in imports was Scotland West Coast[xiv] at 75 per cent and the largest decrease was for Scotland East Coast[xv] at 52 per cent. For exports the port group with the largest increase was Northern Ireland[xvi] at 17 per cent while the West Country saw the largest decrease at 46 per cent (DfT2009l).

Airports in the UK also handle international and domestic freight. In 2009 UK airports moved a total of 2.0 million tonnes of freight, a decrease of 10 per cent from 2008. International freight was 98 per cent of all freight moved through airports. From 2008 to 2009 international freight handled decreased by 10.4 per cent while domestic freight handled decreased by 6.7 per cent (**Table 12**).

Table 12   **Freight handled[1] at UK airports:[2] International or domestic**

Thousand tonnes

	1999	2000	2001	2002	2003	2004	2005	2006	2007	2008	2009
International[3]	2,088	2,204	2,034	2,086	2,091	2,247	2,226	2,179	2,220	2,191	1,963
Domestic[4]	49	54	55	54	58	61	67	68	53	45	42
All traffic[4]	**2,137**	**2,258**	**2,089**	**2,140**	**2,148**	**2,308**	**2,294**	**2,247**	**2,272**	**2,237**	**2,005**

1 Includes freight set down and picked up. Excludes mail and passengers' luggage.
2 Excludes air-taxi operations, the Channel Islands and Isle of Man.
3 Includes traffic to/from oil rigs.
4 Adjusted to avoid double counting.
Source: Department for Transport

Over the period 1999 to 2009, the largest year on year increase for international freight handled at UK airports was between 2003 and 2004 at 7.5 per cent. For domestic freight handled the largest increase was between 2004 and 2005 at 10.2 per cent. International freight handled at airports varied between 1999 and 2008 from a low of 2.0 million tonnes in 2001 to a peak in 2004 at 2.2 million tonnes before falling to under 2.0 million tonnes in 2009, the lowest amount moved during the time period, reflecting the effects of the economic downturn. Domestic freight moved through airports increased from 49 thousand tonnes in 1999 to 68 thousand tonnes in 2006 and then decreased to 42 thousand tonnes in 2009.

References

DECC2010, International comparisons, premium unleaded petrol/diesel prices in the EU (QEP 5.1.1 and 5.2.1), available at
http://decc.gov.uk/en/content/cms/statistics/source/prices/prices.aspx

DfT2009, Purpose of travel, by age and gender, table NTS0611, available at
http://www.dft.gov.uk/pgr/statistics/datatablespublications/nts/

DfT2009a, Travel by car availability, income, ethnic group and household type, table NTS0706, available at
http://www.dft.gov.uk/pgr/statistics/datatablespublications/nts/

DfT2009b, Vehicle licensing statistics, table 19 and table 28, available at
http://webarchive.nationalarchives.gov.uk/+/http://www.dft.gov.uk/pgr/statistics/datatablespublications/vehicles/licensing/vehiclelicensingstatistics2009

DfT2009c, Car and motorcycle availability, table NTS0205, available at
http://www.dft.gov.uk/pgr/statistics/datatablespublications/nts/

DfT2009d, Driving licence holding, table NTS0201, available at
http://www.dft.gov.uk/pgr/statistics/datatablespublications/nts/

DfT2009e, Driving licence holding, table NTS0203, available at
http://www.dft.gov.uk/pgr/statistics/datatablespublications/nts/

DfT2009f, Driving licence holding, table NTS0204, available at
http://www.dft.gov.uk/pgr/statistics/datatablespublications/nts/

DRDNItransport2009–10 and DRDNItransport2000–01, Northern Ireland transport statistics, available at
http://www.drdni.gov.uk/index/statistics/stats-catagories/ni_transport_statistics.htm

DfT2009g, Concessionary bus travel, table NTS0619, available at
http://www.dft.gov.uk/pgr/statistics/datatablespublications/nts/

DfT2009i, Core accessibility indicators, available at
http://www.dft.gov.uk/pgr/statistics/datatablespublications/ltp/coreaccessindicators2009

DfT2009h, School travel, table NTS0613, available at
http://www.dft.gov.uk/pgr/statistics/datatablespublications/nts/

DfT2009j, Reported road casualties, table 3, available at
http://www.dft.gov.uk/pgr/statistics/datatablespublications/accidents/casualtiesgbar/rrcgb2009

DfT2009k, Seatbelt and mobile phone usage survey, available at
http://www.dft.gov.uk/adobepdf/162469/221412/221549/564852/seatbeltphoneusage.pdf

DfT2009l, Maritime statistics, available at
http://www.dft.gov.uk/pgr/statistics/datatablespublications/maritime/compendium/maritimestatistics
2009

DfT2010, Coaches, buses and taxis, table BUS0103, available at
http://www.dft.gov.uk/pgr/statistics/datatablespublications/tsgb/

DRDNI2007–2009, Travel Survey for Northern Ireland, available at
http://www.drdni.gov.uk/index/statistics/stats-catagories/stats-catagories-travel_survey.htm

DRDNI2007-2009, Driving licence holders by age and sex (Northern Ireland), available at
http://www.drdni.gov.uk/index/statistics/stats-catagories/stats-catagories-travel_survey.htm

SIS2010, Registrations through the scrappage scheme, available at
http://www.smmt.co.uk/articles/article.cfm?articleid=21212

Notes

[i] The National Travel Survey (NTS) is designed to provide a databank of personal travel information for Great Britain. It has been conducted as a continuous survey since July 1988, following ad hoc surveys since the mid-1990s. Further information is available at http://www.dft.gov.uk/pgr/statistics/datatablespublications/nts/technical/nts2009notes.pdf

[ii] see http://www.bis.gov.uk/Policies/business-sectors/automotive/vehicle-scrappage-scheme, for more information

[iii] The main method of analysing income distribution is to rand units (households, individuals or adults) by a given income measure and then to divide the ranked units into groups of equal size. Groups containing 20 per cent of units are referred to as 'quintile groups' or 'fifths'. Thus the 'bottom quintile group' of income is the 20 per cent of units with the lowest incomes.

[iv] The Consumer Price Index (CPI) is the main UK measure of inflation for macroeconomic purposes andforms the basis for the Government's inflation target. It is also used for international comparisons. Further information is available at http://www.statistics.gov.uk/StatBase/Product.asp?vlnk=62&Pos=2&ColRank=2&Rank=272
Data for 2010 is now available at
http://www.statistics.gov.uk/StatBase/Product.asp?vlnk=868&Pos=2&ColRank=2&Rank=272

[v] Concessionary bus fares scheme offer discounted travel on local public transport for older and disabled people. Further information is available at http://www.dft.gov.uk/pgr/regional/buses/concessionary/

[vi] Accessibility is the extent to which individuals and households can access day to day services, such as employment, education, healthcare, food stores and town centres. Accessibility Indicators will reflect both the current transport network and land use planning. Further information is available at
http://www.dft.gov.uk/pgr/statistics/datatablespublications/ltp/coreaccessindicators2009

[vii] Overall access is calculated by averaging the values for each of the 8 key services at output area level. More local area information can be found here
http://www.dft.gov.uk/pgr/statistics/datatablespublications/ltp/coreaccessindicators2009

[viii] See http://www.nopenaltypoints.co.uk/TheLawAndUsingYourMobilePhoneWhileDriving.html and
http://www.parliament.uk/briefingpapers/commons/lib/research/briefings/snbt-00366.pdf

[ix] See http://www.legislation.gov.uk/uksi/1993/176/contents/made and
http://www.lawontheweb.co.uk/Road_Traffic_Law/Seat_Belts.

[x] Ports included in the West and North Wales port group are: Milford Haven; Fishguard; Holyhead; Mostyn, Llanddulas and Port Penrhyn

[xi] Ports included in the Bristol Channel port group are: Bridgwater; Bristol; Gloucester and Sharpness; Newport; Cardiff; Barry; Port Talbot; Neath; Swansea and Bideford.

[xii] Ports included in the Haven port group are: Felixstowe; Ipswich; Mistley Quay and Harwich.

[xiii] Ports included in the West Country port group are: Poole; Teignmouth; Plymouth; Fowey; Par; Falmouth; Weymouth & Portland, Torbay; Truro; Penryn; Dean Point; Penzance; Newlyn; Padstow and Porthoustock.

[xiv] Ports included in the Scotland West Coast port group are: Stranraer; Cairnryan; Ayr; Clyde; Glensanda; Troon; Ardrishaig & Corpach; Lochaline and Stornoway.

[xv] Ports included in the Scotland East Coast port group are: Orkney; Lerwick; Sullom Voe; Cromarty Firth; Inverness; Peterhead; Aberdeen; Montrose; Dundee; Perth; Forth; Wick; Scrabster; Buckie; Macduff; Burghead; Fraserburgh; Inverkeithing.

[xvi] Ports included in the Northern Ireland port group are: Londonderry; Coleraine; Larne; Carrickfergus; Belfast; Warrenpoint and Ballylumford & Kilroot.

Education and training

Education is an essential part of any society and helps with economic, social and political growth as well as the development of society in general. Increasingly in the UK people's experience of formal education is no longer restricted to their years at school. There has been an expansion in further and higher education as more people in the UK continue in full-time education. Qualifications achieved at school are increasingly supplemented by further education and job-related training to equip people with the skills required by a modern labour market. This chapter discusses educational expenditure, the qualifications of the workforce and the stock of human capital. This is followed by sections which examine education and educational achievement from early years through compulsory and post-compulsory education to adult learning and training.

Key points:

Introduction

- UK public expenditure on education and training has doubled in real terms over the last 24 years, from £43 billion in 1987/88 to a planned spend of £87 billion in 2010/11

- UK expenditure on education and training as a proportion of GDP increased from 4.8 per cent in 1987/88 to 6.3 per cent in 2009/10; in 2010/11 planned expenditure is 6.0 per cent of GDP

- Three quarters of working age adults in the UK were qualified to at least NVQ level 2 in 2010

- The economic value of the UK's stock of human capital was £16,700 billion in 2009, approximately three times the value of the physical assets of the UK

Early years education

- The proportion of children aged under five enrolled in all schools in the UK has increased from approximately 21 per cent in 1970/71 to 62 per cent in 2009/10

Compulsory education

- In 2009/10 there were over 33,000 schools in the UK a decrease of nearly 1000 since 2005/06

- Although they still form a small proportion of the total number, academies have increased to 203 in 2009/10, 176 more than in 2005/06 when there were just 27

- In 2008/09, 88,270 appeals against non-admission to maintained primary and secondary schools in England were lodged by parents, of which 63,720 were heard by a panel and 19,060 (29.9 per cent) were decided in favour of the parents

- Pupil to teacher ratios in maintained nursery, primary and secondary schools have varied over the last three decades, although they are lower in 2010 compared with 1978 in all school types

- Key Stage assessments have shown improvements in performance of both sexes over the last five years, but the proportion of girls reaching the required standard was generally higher than that for boys

- While 70 per cent of pupils in England achieved five or more GCSE grades A* to C in 2008/09, only 51 per cent achieved five or more GCSE grades A* to C including English and mathematics

Post-compulsory education

- Between 2008/09 and 2009/10 the number of apprenticeships started in England increased by 17 per cent from 239,900 to 279,700 the number of completed apprenticeships also increased by 20 per cent from 143,000 to 171,500

- In 2008/09 958,000 NVQ/SVQs were awarded in the UK compared with 153,000 in 1991/92 the majority of which (67.5 per cent) were at Level 2

- In 2009/10 there were approximately 2.6 million students in higher education in the UK compared with 827,000 in 1980/81

- Nearly six in ten UK higher education students in 2008/09 were women

- In 2009/10 there were 351,000 first degrees obtained by UK and overseas domiciled students in higher education institutions in the UK

- In 2008/09 of the 227,180 students who left higher education with a first degree 60 per cent moved into employment either in the UK or overseas

Adult training and learning

- A higher proportion of employees in professional, personal and associate professional and technical occupations reported receiving job-related training in 2010 compared with other types of occupation

- In 2009/10 4.6 million adult learners participated in some form of government-funded further education, a decrease of 4.5 per cent compared with 2008/09

- In 2009/10 11 per cent of employers in the hotel and catering industry reported that their employees lacked at least some of the skills required to be fully proficient at their jobs

Introduction

UK public expenditure on education and training has doubled in real terms over the last 24 years; from £43 billion in 1987/88 to a planned spend of £87 billion in 2010/11. Spending levels increased through the late eighties and early nineties to £53 billion in 1994/95 before decreasing to £51 billion in 1997/98. Spending then began to rise again reaching its highest recorded level of £88 billion in 2009/10 before falling slightly in 2010/11 to £87 billion.

Figure 1   **Public expenditure on education and training as a proportion of GDP[1,2,3]**

United Kingdom

Percentages

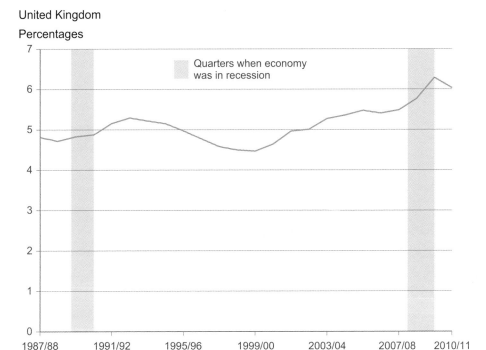

1 Total managed expenditure to 1987/88, total expenditure on services thereafter.
2 Data from 2000/01 onwards calculated on resource basis and may not be directly comparable with earlier years which were calculated on a cash basis.
3 Data are outturn to 2008/09, estimates for 2009/10 and planned for 2010/11.
Source: House of Commons Library (HC, 2010)

Figure 1 shows public spending on education and training expressed as a proportion of economic output measured by GDP, this varies less than real spending levels. Following the generally upward trend in the late 1980s, spending fell as a proportion of GDP for most of the 1990s. The level increased from 5.0 per cent of GDP in 2002/03 to 6.3 per cent in 2009/10 the highest level in the period covered. Planned expenditure on education and training in 2010/11 is slightly lower at 6.0 per cent of GDP.

There are considerable differences between public education expenditure as a proportion of GDP across the 27 European Union countries (EU-27). In 2007 in the UK it was 5.4 per cent of GDP, just above the EU-27 average of 5.0 per cent. On this measure education expenditure was highest in Denmark at 7.8 per cent, followed by Cyprus at 6.9 per cent and Sweden at 6.7 per cent. Slovakia and Luxembourg had the lowest proportions of expenditure at 3.6 per cent and 3.2 per cent respectively[i].

Education is devolved across the UK with education systems differing between countries. While the education systems in England, Wales and Northern Ireland are similar, the Scottish system is quite different. The devolution of education in the UK means that each county is responsible for setting its own educational funding policy.

Figure 2   Local authority education expenditure[1] per pupil

England and Wales

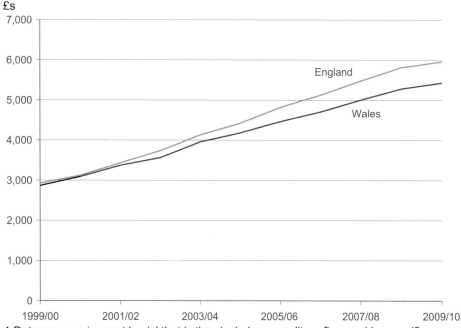

1 Data are on a 'current basis' that is they include expenditure financed by specific government grants. Data also include expenditure on school services, LEA central costs, mandatory student awards, inter-authority education recoupment, nursery schools and adult and youth education. Expenditure figures are based on outturn data, with the exception of 2009/10 which are budgeted.
Source: Welsh Assembly Government (WAG, 2010)

Although the education systems in England and Wales are similar, data from the Welsh Assembly Government show that there are differences in expenditure per pupil. In 2009/10 the average budgeted spend on local authority education in England was £5,956 per pupil, a rise of 2.4 per cent on the previous year. This compares with £5,429 per pupil in Wales in 2009/10, an increase of 2.8 per cent on the previous year. In 2009/10 the public education funding gap (£527) between England and Wales was more than eight times higher than in 1999/2000 (£61) (**Figure 2**).

Data from Eurostat show that spending per pupil varies among the EU-27 member states. In 2007 the UK ranked third in the annual amount spent on public and private educational institutions at €7,972 PPS (Purchasing Power Standard)[ii] per pupil, €1,721 PPS higher than the EU-27 average of €6,251 PPS per pupil. Austria topped the table with an annual spend of €8,695 PPS per pupil while Bulgaria had the lowest annual spend at €2,290 PPS per pupil[iii].

Figure 3   **Highest qualification held by working-age adults:[1] by country, 2010**

United Kingdom

Percentages

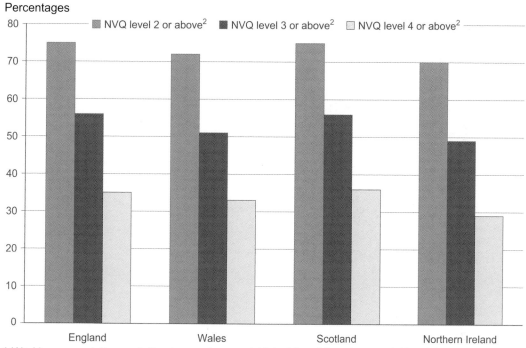

1 Working-age adults are defined as males aged 19 to 64 and females aged 19 to 59.
2 See note[iv].
Source: Department for Education (DfE, 2010)

In Q2 (April to June) 2010, 75 per cent of working-age adults in the UK were qualified to NVQ level 2 or above, with 76 per cent of men and 73 per cent of women achieving this level. **Figure 3** shows that qualification levels were lower in Northern Ireland. In 2010 75 per cent of working-age adults in England and Scotland were qualified to NVQ level 2 or above compared with 72 per cent in Wales and 70 per cent in Northern Ireland. Attainment levels also varied by age with 81 per cent of those aged 25 to 29 in the UK being qualified to NVQ level 2 or above compared with 69 per cent of those aged 50 to 64.

Human capital is the knowledge and skills of individuals that facilitate the creation of personal, social and economic well-being. Measures of human capital provide an important indication of the productive capacity of the UK economy. Estimates released by ONS in November 2010 (*Jones and Chiripanhura, 2010*), showed that the economic value of the stock of human capital in the UK, was £16,686 billion in 2009. This is approximately three times the value of all the physical assets in the UK such as buildings and machinery.

The estimates of the stock of human capital were derived using information on the earnings of individuals of different ages, gender and levels of educational attainment, taken from the UK Labour Force Survey and measured in 2009 prices.

Figure 4   Human capital stock

United Kingdom

£ billion

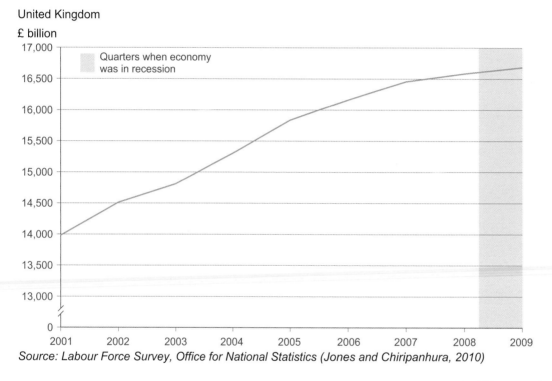

Source: Labour Force Survey, Office for National Statistics (Jones and Chiripanhura, 2010)

Figure 4 shows that the stock of human capital stood at £14,000 billion in 2001 and increased to £16,700 billion in 2009. Between 2001 and 2007 the stock of human capital grew by an average of £300 billion per year. The slowing of earnings growth and increases in unemployment during the economic downturn meant that growth in the stock of human capital slowed between 2007 and 2009.

In 2009 the average human capital stock per head of working-age population was £419,300. This was an increase of £46,800 compared with 2001 but only £717 more than in 2007. Less time in paid employment over their lifetime and lower average labour market earnings means that the total market value of women's human capital (£6,500 billion) was around 64 per cent of men's (£10,200 billion). In 2009, one-third of the human capital stock was embodied in 22 per cent of the working-age population whose highest educational attainment is a degree or equivalent (see **Figure 3**).

Early years education

Some form of free early years education[v] aimed at developing young children's learning is available in all of the countries of the UK although delivered under different strategies and in different settings.

Figure 5   **Children under five[1] in schools**

United Kingdom
Percentages

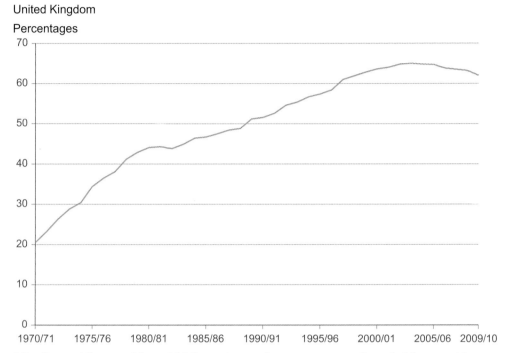

1 Pupils aged three and four at 31 December each year as a proportion of all three and four-year-olds, with the exception of Scotland where census data differ over the years.
Source: Department for Education

Since records began in the early 1970s, there has been an expansion in early year's education provided in all settings[vi] in the UK. The proportion of children under five enrolled in schools rose from approximately two in ten (21 per cent) in 1970/71 to over six in ten (62 per cent) in 2009/10. Further information on the change in population of those aged under 16 can be found in the Population chapter[vii] (**Figure 5**).

Data from the Childcare and Early Years Providers Survey (DfE, 2010a) show that between 2008 and 2009 there was a decline in the number of children attending all childcare provider types in England, with the exception of full-day care[viii] providers. The number of children enrolled in sessional care saw the largest decrease of 9.8 per cent between 2008 and 2009, while the number of children enrolled in full-day care increased by 0.1 per cent from 873,000 to 874,000. Over the same period the number of childcare providers in maintained schools in England, which shows the number of providers offering full-day care, increased from 13,800 in 2008 to 14,100 in 2009. This has been accompanied by a fall in the number of providers offering sessional care[ix], from 8,500 in 2008 to 7,800 in 2009, a fall of 8.2 per cent.

Compulsory education

Table 1   Schools:[1] by type of school

United Kingdom   Number of schools

	2005/06	2006/07	2007/08	2008/09	2009/10
Public sector mainstream schools[2]					
Nursery	3,349	3,326	3,273	3,209	3,166
Primary	22,156	21,968	21,768	21,568	21,427
State-funded secondary	4,244	4,232	4,209	4,183	4,149
of which, specialist schools[3]	2,381	2,611	2,799	2,981	2,857
of which, admissions policy					
Comprehensive	3,424	3,398	3,304	3,247	3,156
Selective	233	233	233	233	233
Modern	115	113	172	169	160
City technology colleges	11	10	5	3	3
Academies	27	46	83	133	203
Not applicable	434	432	412	398	394
All public sector mainstream schools	29,749	29,526	29,250	28,960	28,742
Non-maintained schools	2,455	2,486	2,527	2,547	2,570
Special schools[4]	1,416	1,391	1,378	1,378	1,373
Pupil referral units	481	489	506	511	452
All schools	34,101	33,892	33,661	33,396	33,137

1 See note[x]: Main categories of educational establishments.
2 Excludes special schools and pupil referral units (PRUs).
3 Numbers of specialist schools in England, operational from September of each academic year shown.
4 For children with special educational needs. Includes maintained (the majority) and non-maintained sectors.
Source: Department for Education (DfE, 2008; 2010)

Table 1 shows that in 2009/10 there were 33,137 schools in the UK a fall of 964 since 2005/06. In 2009/10 9.1 million pupils (94 per cent of all pupils) attended public sector schools and 621,200 (6.4 per cent of all pupils) attended one of the 2,570 non-maintained mainstream schools. There were around 452 pupil referral units (PRUs) attended by 13,000 pupils in the UK. PRUs provide suitable alternative education on a temporary basis for pupils who have been excluded from mainstream schools and children with medical problems (DfE, 2010a)

Although they still form a small proportion of the total number of schools in the UK, academies are growing in number. In 2009/10 there were 203 academies in the UK compared with 27 in 2005/06 an increase of 176. The academies programme was introduced in 2000 to promote publicly funded independent schools managed by sponsors from a range of backgrounds including universities, businesses, faith communities and voluntary groups. Most academies are located in areas of disadvantage and either replaced existing schools or were established where there was a need for additional places.

Choosing the right school for their children is one of the most important things a parent can do. However, sometimes schools do not have enough places for the number of children who have applied. If a child does not get a place at their preferred school parents have the legal right to appeal[xi].

Table 2   Appeals against non-admission to maintained primary and secondary schools

England   Number

	2004/05	2005/06	2006/07	2007/08	2008/09
Admissions[1]	1,491,370	1,483,250	1,484,320	1,488,870	1,467,820
Admission appeals lodged by parents[2]	83,410	78,670	80,010	86,020	88,270
Appeals heard by appeals panel	59,330	56,590	56,610	61,950	63,720
Appeal decided in parents' favour	21,040	20,540	19,450	19,150	19,060

1 Figures relating to admissions are calculated from School Census for all schools.
2 Some appeals are resolved before they reach a panel hearing and the number of appeals heard by an appeals panel is deemed to be the more reliable and critical indicator.
Source: Department for Education (DfE, 2010b)

Table 2 shows that over the last five years, although the number of admission appeals lodged by parents and the number of appeals heard by a panel has risen, the number of appeals decided in parents favour has decreased.

In 2008/09 in England, parents lodged 88,270 appeals against non-admission to maintained primary and secondary schools of which 24,550 were resolved before reaching a panel hearing. Of the 63,720 appeals heard by a panel 19,060 (29.9 per cent) were decided in the parents favour. This compares with 83,410 appeals lodged in 2004/05 of which 59,330 were heard by an appeals panel and 21,040 (35.5 per cent) were decided in the parents favour.

Pupil to teacher ratio is calculated by dividing the number of full-time equivalent pupils who attend a school by the number of full-time equivalent teachers in the school. A low pupil to teacher ratio is often used as a selling point to those choosing a school.

Figure 6   **Pupil to teacher ratio:[1] by type of school**

England

Pupil: teacher ratio

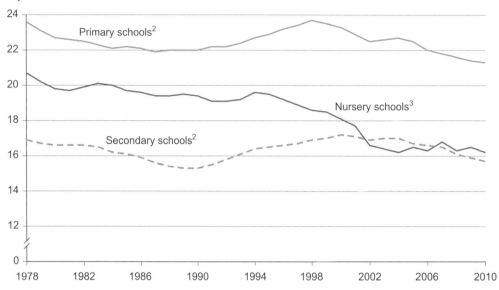

1 Data are at January.
2 Includes middle schools as deemed and from 1978 to 1982 also include immigrant centres (centres for teaching English as an additional language).
3 Includes two Direct Grant Nursery schools.
Source: Department for Education (DfE, 2010c)

Figure 6 shows that the pupil to teacher ratio in maintained nursery, primary and secondary schools has varied over the last three decades. However, it is lower in 2010 than in 1978 in all three types of schools. The pupil to teacher ratio in nursery schools[xii] decreased from 21 pupils in 1978 to 16 pupils per teacher in 2010. Over the same period the pupil to teacher ratio in primary schools decreased from 24 pupils to 21 pupils per teacher. The downturn in pupil to teacher ratio in primary schools from 1998 coincides with the introduction of legislation to reduce all infant class sizes to no more than 30 pupils for each teacher by 2002[xiii]. The secondary school pupil to teacher ratio has also decreased over the same period but at a slower rate decreasing from 17 pupils per teacher in 1978 to 16 pupils per teacher in 2010.

Class size is calculated by dividing the number of pupils in classes being taught at the time of the school census by the number of classes. The average class size in maintained primary schools in England in January 2010 was 26.4 up from 26.2 per class in January 2009. The average size of classes in state-funded secondary schools fell slightly in January 2010 to 20.5 compared with 20.6 in January 2009 (DfE, 2010d). Since 2000/01, average class sizes in primary schools in Wales have also decreased from 25.2 to 24.4 in 2009/10. The average number of children per class in secondary schools in Wales has fluctuated between a high of 21.3 in 2000/01 and a low of 20.1 in 2009/10 (WAG, 2010b).

The *Education Act of 1944* made it an entitlement for every pupil to receive a free school meal. In 1980 the act was amended so that Local Authorities are only obliged to provide a meal to those pupils who are eligible[xiv].

In January 2010 17 per cent of pupils in maintained nursery and primary schools in England were known to be eligible for free school meals, as were 14 per cent of pupils attending state-funded secondary schools (DfE, 2010d). The corresponding figures for Wales were 18 per cent and 16 per cent (WAG, 2010c). In Northern Ireland in 2009/10 23 per cent of nursery pupils, 19 per cent of primary pupils and 17 per cent of post-primary pupils were entitled to free school meals (DENI, 2011). In Scotland in 2010 20 per cent of primary and 14 per cent of secondary pupils were registered for meals (SG, 2010).

Assessment at Key Stages forms part of the *National Curriculum* in England and is carried out through a combination of teacher assessments and tests which measure pupils' attainment against the levels set by the *National Curriculum*. Wales, Scotland and Northern Ireland each have their own guidelines for assessing attainment against the curriculum.

Table 3   **Pupils reaching or exceeding expected standards:[1] by Key Stage and sex**

England   Percentages

	2005		2010	
	Boys	**Girls**	**Boys**	**Girls**
Key Stage 1[2]				
English				
Reading	81	89	81	89
Writing	77	88	76	87
Mathematics	90	92	88	91
Science	88	91	87	90
Key Stage 2[3]				
English	70	81	76	86
Mathematics	76	76	81	82
Science	82	84	84	86
Key Stage 3[4]				
English	64	78	73	86
Mathematics	74	77	79	81
Science	70	73	79	82

1 By teacher assessment.
2 Pupils achieving level 2 or above at Key Stage 1.
3 Pupils achieving level 4 or above at Key Stage 2.
4 Pupils achieving level 5 or above at Key Stage 3.
Source: Department for Education (DfE, 2007; 2010)

Table 3 shows that in 2005 and 2010 the proportion of girls reaching the required standard by teacher assessment was generally higher than that for boys at all key stages. In particular girls did better than boys in English (at all key stages) and differences between boys and girls were smallest for mathematics. Between 2005 and 2010 improvements in attainment were largest for boys in Key Stage 3 English and science and Key Stage 2 English. For girls the biggest improvements were also seen in Key Stage 3 English, science and mathematics with slight falls in attainment in Key Stage 1 writing, mathematics and science.

In June 2010 figures for Wales show that as in England, girls out performed boys at all key stages with the gap in performance highest for Key Stage 3 Welsh and English. Differences were smallest for Key Stage 1 science and Key Stages 2 and 4 mathematics (WAG, 2010d).

Figure 7   **Pupils achieving five or more GCSE grades A* to C or equivalent:[1,2] by sex**

United Kingdom

Percentages

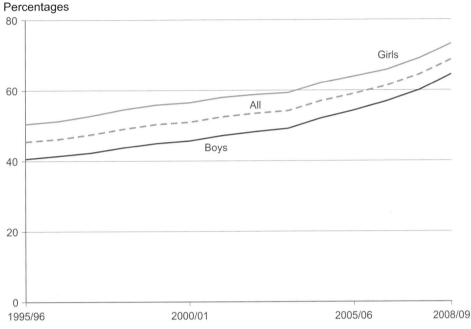

1 For pupils in their last year of compulsory education. Pupils aged 15 at the start of the academic year; pupils in year S4 in Scotland. From 20004/05, pupils at the end of Key Stage 4 in England.
2 From 1990/91, National Qualifications[xv] were introduced in Scotland but are not included until 2000/01.
Source: Department for Education

There is also a difference in overall performance between boys and girls at GCSE level. In 2008/09, 73 per cent of girls in the UK in their last year of compulsory education achieved 5 or more GCSEs at grades A* to C or equivalent, compared with 65 per cent of boys (**Figure 7**). Overall there has been a steady increase in the proportion of all pupils in the UK achieving five or more GCSEs at grades A* to C from 46 per cent in 1995/96 to 69 per cent in 2008/09.

A different measure of pupils academic achievement focussing more on core skills is the proportion of pupils achieving at least five or more GCSEs at grades A* to C including English and mathematics. In England 51 per cent of pupils in their last year of compulsory education achieved this measure in 2008/09 compared with 70 per cent achieving five or more GCSEs at grades A* to C in any subject. A higher proportion of girls (54 per cent) than boys (47 per cent) achieved five or more GCSE grades A* to C including English and mathematics (DfE 2010e).

Post-compulsory education

For those students who decide to stay in education post age 16, there are a wide range of subjects and qualifications available to choose from. As well as A levels, students can choose from a growing range of work-related qualifications and selected schools and colleges offer diploma qualifications for 14 to 19-year-olds. Depending on the subject to be studied students can decide to stay on at school (in sixth form), go to a sixth form college, a specialist college or a further education college.

While many young people opt for further education or higher education, some choose the opportunity to work and study at the same time through an apprenticeship[xvi]. Apprentices are able to gain valuable on-the-job training while earning a minimum of £80 per week and can achieve a variety of nationally recognised qualifications such as an NVQ (National Vocational Qualification), BTEC (Business and Technology Education Council) or City and Guilds certificate.

Table 4   Apprenticeship programme starts:[1] by level and age[2,3]

England

People starting apprenticeships

	2005/06	2006/07	2007/08	2008/09	2009/10
Apprenticeship (level 2)					
Under 19	77,100	80,800	82,000	74,200	89,400
19–24	45,600	46,500	55,200	52,600	72,800
25 and over	100	100	14,600	31,700	28,400
Total	122,800	127,400	151,800	158,500	190,600
Advanced and Higher (levels 3 and 4+)					
Under 19	22,400	24,800	25,500	25,100	27,300
19–24	29,500	32,100	34,800	32,100	41,000
25 and over	200	100	12,600	24,200	20,700
Total	52,100	57,000	73,000	81,500	89,200
All Apprenticeships					
Under 19	99,500	105,600	107,600	99,400	116,800
19–24	75,200	78,600	90,100	84,700	113,800
25 and over	300	300	27,200	55,900	49,100
Total	175,000	184,400	224,800	239,900	279,700

1 Numbers are a count of the number of starters at any point during the year. Learners starting more than one framework will appear more than once.
2 Based on age at start of programme.
3 Due to rounding figures may not always add up to total.
Source: Department for Business Innovations and Skills (BIS, 2010)

In February 2011, Vince Cable[xvii] the Business Secretary announced government plans to create an extra 100,000 apprenticeships and to increase apprenticeship funding by an extra £222 million to £1.4 billion.

Table 4 shows that the number of apprenticeships which were started in 2009/10 was 279,700, an increase of 17 per cent compared with 2008/09 (239,900). Of these 190,600 were level 2 starts (a 20 per cent increase compared with 2008/09) and 89,200 were level 3 and 4 or above (an increase of 9 per cent compared with 2008/09). While the numbers of learners starting apprenticeships have generally increased in all age groups, the most noticeable change is in those aged 25 and over, where there was a considerable increase from 300 apprenticeship starts in 2005/06 to 55,900 in 2008/09 before the numbers fell by 12 per cent to 49,100 in 2009/10.

The number of completed apprenticeships in 2009/10 was 171,500, an increase of 20 per cent compared with 2008/09. Of these, 111,900 were at level 2, an increase of 14 per cent compared with 2008/09. There were 59,400 at level 3 and 4 or above, an increase of 31 per cent compared with 2008/09. Learners aged 19 and under achieved 73,100 apprenticeship frameworks, an 8.0 per cent increase on 2008/09 while 64,200 19 to 24-year-olds achieved apprenticeship frameworks, an 11 per cent increase on 2008/09. Again the largest change was in those aged 25 and over where almost double the number achieved apprenticeship frameworks, 34,300 compared with 17,900 in 2008/09 (BIS, 2010).

National Vocational Qualifications (NVQs) and Scottish Vocational Qualifications (SVQs) are alternatives to more traditional academic qualifications as they are generally aimed at a particular occupation or group of occupations.

Figure 8   NVQ/SVQs awarded:[1] by level of qualification

United Kingdom

Thousands

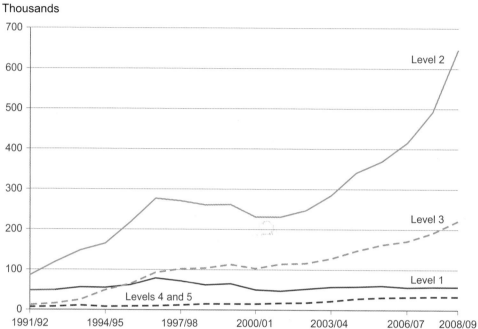

1 National Vocational Qualifications (NVQs) and Scottish Vocational Qualifications (SVQs)[xviii], data for 2000/01 are NVQ awards only.
Source: Department for Education

Figure 8 shows that in 2008/09 958,000 NVQ/SVQs were awarded in the UK compared with 153,000 in 1991/92. The majority (67.5 per cent) of NVQ/SVQs awarded in 2008/09 were at level 2, a further 23.1 per cent of awards were at level 3 and 5.9 per cent were at level 1.

Higher education courses are generally attended by those who have undertaken some sort of post-compulsory education such as A levels or NVQ/SVQs. There has been considerable growth in the numbers attending higher education institutions in the UK; the total number of home and overseas students on all types of education courses in 2008/09 was more than three times the number in 1980/81.

Table 5   **Students in higher education:[1] by type of course and sex**

United Kingdom   Thousands

	Men				Women			
	1980/81	1990/91	2000/01	2008/09	1980/81	1990/91	2000/01	2008/09
Higher education								
Undergraduate								
Full-time	277	345	510	593	196	319	602	735
Part-time	176	148	224	262	71	106	320	424
Postgraduate								
Full-time	41	50	82	137	21	34	81	132
Part-time	32	46	118	114	13	33	123	160
All higher education	526	588	934	1,106	301	491	1,126	1,451

1 Home and overseas students attending higher education institutions.
Source: Department for Education

Table 5 shows there were around 2.6 million students in higher education in the UK in 2008/09 compared with 827,000 in 1980/81, of this number nearly six in ten (57 per cent) were women. In 2008/09 there were around 1.5 million female higher education students, 29 per cent more than in 2000/01 and around 1.1 million male students, 18 per cent more than in 2000/01. The growth in the number of higher education students between 1980/81 and 2008/09 is larger for women than for men; for undergraduate courses the number of men nearly doubled (from 453,000 to 855,000) while there were over four times as many women in 2008/09 as in 1980/81 (from 267,000 to 1.2 million).

Table 6   **Higher Education qualifications attained:[1] by class of qualification and sex, 2009/10**

United Kingdom   Percentages

	Men	Women	All
First Degree			
First class	13.7	13.0	13.3
Upper second	41.7	47.0	44.7
Lower second	29.0	26.6	27.6
Third class/Pass	8.5	5.8	7.0
Unclassified	6.9	7.6	7.3
All (=100%) (thousands)	152	199	351
Higher degree			
Doctorate	12.7	11.0	11.9
Other higher degree	87.3	89.0	88.1
All (=100%) (thousands)	81	77	158
Other postgraduate			
Postgraduate certificate in education	25.6	36.2	32.3
Other post graduate	74.5	63.8	67.7
All (=100%) (thousands)	25	43	68
Other undergraduate			
Professional graduate certificate in education	4.7	5.7	5.3
Foundation degree	18.7	17.3	17.8
HND/DipHE[2]	14.4	18.9	17.2
Other undergraduate	62.3	58.1	59.7
All (=100%) (thousands)	53	87	140

1 Full-time and part-time, home and overseas student.
2 Higher National Diplomas or Diploma in Higher Education.
Source: Higher Education Statistics Agency (HESA, 2011)

In 2009/10, there were 351,000 first degrees obtained by UK and overseas domiciled students at higher education institutions in the UK. Of these 92.7 per cent were classified degrees and 7.3 per cent were unclassified (certain qualifications obtained at first degree level are not subject to classification, for example medical degrees). Of those classified first degrees, 13.3 per cent were graded first class with 13.7 per cent of men and 13.0 per cent of women achieving this level. A higher proportion of women than men achieved upper second class first degrees (47.0 per cent compared with 41.7 per cent), while a higher proportion of men than women achieved lower second first degrees (29.0 per cent compared with 26.6 per cent) (**Table 6**).

The labour market status of former students six months after they have left higher education in the UK varies according to the type of qualification obtained. Those with postgraduate qualifications are more likely to be in employment compared with those with a first degree or other undergraduate qualification.

Table 7   Destination of students leaving higher education:[1] by type of qualification, 2008/09

United Kingdom   Percentages

	1st degree	Other undergraduate[2]	Postgraduate[3]
UK employment only[4]	57.9	51.4	69.4
Overseas employment only[4]	2.3	0.5	6.7
Work and further study	8.3	18.2	8.6
Further study only	17.2	23.1	6.4
Assumed to be unemployed	9.2	3.7	5.1
Not available for employment	3.9	2.0	2.5
Other	1.3	1.1	1.3
All (=100%) (thousands)	227,180	44,455	83,090

1 Destination of UK and other European Union domiciled full-time and part-time students after leaving higher education institutions approximately six months after graduation. Excludes those where destination was not known.
2 Includes foundation degrees and undergraduate diplomas and certificates.
3 Includes Post Graduate Certificates of Education (PGCEs).
4 Includes self-employed and voluntary or unpaid work.
Source: Higher Education Statistics Agency (HESA, 2010)

Table 7 shows that of the 227,180 students who left with a first degree in 2008/09, 57.9 per cent moved into UK employment while a small proportion (2.3 per cent) gained overseas employment. Around 8.3 per cent went on to combine employment with some form of studying, while 17.2 per cent continued with their studies only. Of those who had gained undergraduate qualifications other than a first degree, 51.4 per cent moved into UK employment, 23.1 per cent continued studying and 18.2 per cent combined study with employment. Those who left with postgraduate qualifications were the most likely to move into employment either in the UK (69.4 per cent) with a further 8.6 per cent combining work with further study.

Adult training and learning

Whether looking for a job or looking to progress in a career, improving skills for work can open up new opportunities. Work-based learning is often necessary in order for workers to keep their skills up-to-date and to be able to satisfy the demands of the modern day labour market. Keeping the skills of the workforce current is vital to the economy in order to help retain competitiveness through increased productivity. There are also wider social benefits to people engaging in learning, both in terms of individual development and through social and civic engagement.

Figure 9   **Employees receiving job-related training:[1] by sex and occupation, 2010[2]**

United Kingdom

Percentages

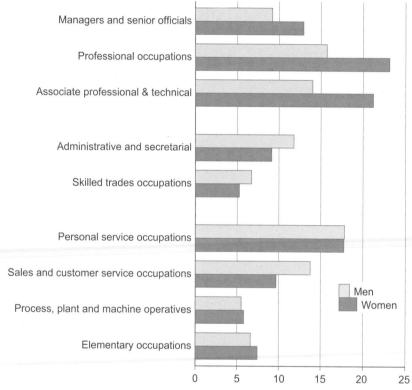

1 In the four weeks prior to interview.
2 Data are at Q2 (April to June) and are not seasonally adjusted.
Source: Labour Force Survey, Office for National Statistics (ONS, 2011)

Figure 9 shows information from the Labour Force Survey about job-related training received in the previous four weeks by employed men and women in the UK in Q2 (April to June) 2010. Training varied by occupation, those in professional, associate professional and technical and personal service occupations were more likely to report receiving training in the last four weeks. The proportions receiving training were lower for those in skilled trades, working with process plant and machines and in elementary occupations.

While in some occupations very similar proportions of men and women reported having training in the last four weeks, there were considerable differences between the sexes in others. Men were more likely than women to have had training in sales and customer services (13.8 per cent compared with 9.7 per cent) and in administrative and secretarial occupations (11.8 per cent compared with 9.1 per cent). More than one in five women (23.1 per cent) in professional and associate professional and technical occupations (21.2 per cent) had received job-related training in the last four weeks. This compares with 15.7 per cent and 14.0 per cent respectively for men in these occupations.

Table 8   Adult further education and skills participation: by level[1]

England   Thousands

	2005/06	2006/07	2007/08	2008/09[2]	2009/10
Below level 2	1,366	905	865	788	746
Skills for life	1,478	1,298	1,312	1,450	1,431
Full level 2	749	817	1,042	1,264	1,287
Full level 3	597	611	686	795	867
Level 2[3]	1,797	1,676	1,882	2,125	2,045
Level 3[3]	968	945	1,002	1,106	1,115
Level 4 and above	69	61	55	59	51
No level assigned	1,446	1,277	1,269	1,493	1,558
All learners	5,022	4,232	4,361	4,837	4,636

1 See note[xix]: Qualifications.
2 Data are not directly comparable with earlier years as the introduction of demand-led funding changed how data were collected and how funded learners were defined.
3 Includes all those studying for a full level 2 or 3 and those studying for a part level 2 or 3.
Source: The Department for Business Innovations and Skills (BIS, 2010)

Table 8 shows that 4.6 million adult learners participated in some form of government-funded further education in 2009/10; this is a decrease in learner participation of 4.5 per cent compared with 2008/09. The main reduction has been in the number of learners participating in Below level 2 and non-full Level 2 courses.

Approximately 3.4 million learners achieved a government-funded further education qualification in 2009/10 an increase of 0.5 per cent compared with 2008/09. Of these 1.3 million learners achieved a level 2 qualification and increase of 2.7 per cent compared with 2008/09 and 674,600 achieved a level 3 qualification an increase of 7.4 per cent compared with 2008/09.

Further education and job-related training can be used to help employees develop all the skills they need for their jobs. Employers report skills gaps[xx] within their businesses through the *National Employers Skills Survey*.

Figure 10   **Percentage of Employers reporting skills gaps:[1] by sector,[2] 2009**

England
Percentages

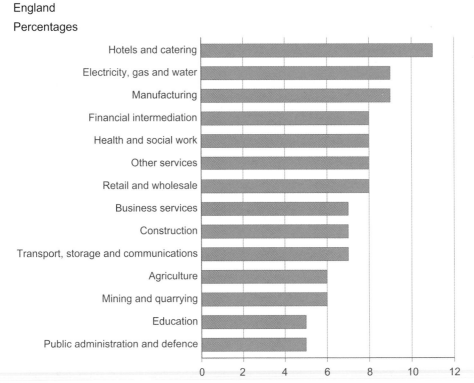

1 Skills gaps exist where employers consider that employees are not fully proficient at their job. Data show the proportion of employees considered to have skills gaps as a proportion of all employees in each sector.
2 Sectors according to their Standard Industrial Classification (SIC2003) [xxi].
Source: UK Commission for Employment and Skills (UKES, 2010)

The 2009 *National Employer Skills Survey* for England showed that the industry for which employers were most likely to report that their employees had skills gaps was hotels and catering[xxii], with 11 per cent of businesses in this group reporting that staff lacked at least some of the skills required to be fully proficient at their jobs. This group was closely followed by those in the electricity, gas and water and manufacturing and industry with 9 per cent of employers reporting skills gaps. Employers in education and public administration and defence reported the lowest level of employees with skills gaps at 5 per cent (**Figure 10**).

There are various reasons why staff may lack skills. In 2009, 71 per cent of employers reported that the main cause of skills gaps in their business was lack of experience in recently recruited staff, followed by a lack of staff motivation (29 per cent), failure to train and develop staff (25 per cent) and the failure to keep staff up-to-date with changes (25 per cent). High staff turnover and recruitment problems are also quite common at 13 per cent and 11 per cent respectively.

References:

BIS (2010). Current SFR, Post 16 Education: March 2011: All March 2011 SFR Files. Available at www.thedataservice.org.uk/statistics/statisticalfirstrelease/sfr_current/

DENI (2011). Percentage pupils entitled to free school meals 2001/02 - 2010/11 Excel 33kb. Available at www.deni.gov.uk/index/32-statisticsandresearch_pg/32-statistics_and_research_statistics_on_education_pg/32_statistics_and_research-numbersofschoolsandpupils_pg/32_statistics_and_research-northernirelandsummarydata_pg.htm

DfE (2007). Education and Training Statistics for the United Kingdom 2007 (Internet only). Available at www.education.gov.uk/rsgateway/DB/VOL/v000761/index.shtml

DfE (2008). Education and Training Statistics for the United Kingdom: 2008. Available at www.education.gov.uk/rsgateway/DB/VOL/v000823/index.shtml

DfE (2010). Education and Training Statistics for the UK, 2010. Available at: www.education.gov.uk/rsgateway/DB/VOL/v000992/index.shtml

DfE (2010a). Childcare and Early Years Providers Survey 2009. Available at: www.education.gov.uk/publications/standard/publicationdetail/page1/DFE-RR012

DfE (2010b). Admission appeals for maintained primary and secondary schools in England, 2008/09. Available at www.education.gov.uk/rsgateway/DB/SFR/s000934/index.shtml

DfE (2010c). Pupil teacher ratios. Available at www.education.gov.uk/rsgateway/DB/TIM/m002005/index.shtml

DfE (2010d). Schools, Pupils and their Characteristics: January 2010. Available at www.education.gov.uk/rsgateway/DB/SFR/s000925/index.shtml

DfE (2010e). GCSE and equivalent attainment by pupil characteristics in England, 2009/10. Available at www.education.gov.uk/rsgateway/DB/SFR/s000977/index.shtml

HC (2010). Education Spending in the UK (02.11.2010). Available at: http://www.parliament.uk/topics/SchoolsArchive.htm#SN

HESA (2010). Leavers table 1 and 2. Available at www.hesa.ac.uk/index.php?option=com_content&task=view&id=1899&Itemid=239

HESA (2011). Students and qualifiers data tables; qualifications obtained 2009/10. Available at www.hesa.ac.uk/index.php/component/option,com_datatables/Itemid,121/task,show_category/catdex,3/#quals

Jones and Chiripanhura (2010) Measuring the UK's human capital stock. Available at: www.statistics.gov.uk/CCI/article.asp?ID=2607&Pos=&ColRank=1&Rank=240

Understanding the National Curriculum. Further information available at:
http://www.direct.gov.uk/en/Parents/Schoolslearninganddevelopment/ExamsTestsAndTheCurriculu
m/DG_4016665

National Employers Skills Survey for England 2009: Key findings report available at:
http://www.ukces.org.uk/tags/report/national-employer-skills-survey-for-england-2009-key-findings-
report

ONS (2011). Table 12: Percentage of employees receiving job-related training. Available at
www.statistics.gov.uk/downloads/theme_labour/LFSHQS/2010/Table12.xls

SG (2010). Pupils registered for free school meals by sector, 2006 to 2010. Available at
www.scotland.gov.uk/Publications/2010/07/06095048/0

Skills for Life qualifications are designed to help adults (over 16s) develop skills used in everyday
life, such as reading, writing or maths. Further information available at:
http://www.direct.gov.uk/en/EducationAndLearning/QualificationsExplained/DG_10039031

The Education Act of 1944. Further information available at: http://www.parliament.uk/about/living-
heritage/transformingsociety/livinglearning/school/overview/educationact1944/

UKES (2010), National Employer Skills Survey for England, 2009: Key findings report. Available at:
http://www.ukces.org.uk/publications-and-resources/browse-by-
title/*/Module%5B48%5D%5BrestrictRange%5D/M-O/

WAG (2010). Local Authority Budgets for Education: Wales and England Comparisons, 2009–10.
Available at http://wales.gov.uk/topics/statistics/headlines/localgov2010/0127/?lang=en

WAG (2010b), Class Sizes in Primary Schools, September 2010. Available at:
http://wales.gov.uk/topics/statistics/headlines/schools2010/101130/?lang=en

WAG (2010c), Schools Census, 2010: Final results; Table 9 Provision of Meals and Milk. Available
at http://wales.gov.uk/topics/statistics/headlines/schools2010/1006291/?lang=en

WAG (2010d), National Curriculum Assessments of 7, 11 and 14-year-olds, 2010. Available at:
http://wales.gov.uk/topics/statistics/headlines/schools2010/100818/?lang=en

Notes:

[i] Data obtained from table educ_figdp available at
http://epp.eurostat.ec.europa.eu/portal/page/portal/statistics/search_database

[ii] The Purchasing Power Standard (PPS) is a unit of measurement calculated by scaling Purchasing Power Parities (PPPs) so that the aggregate for the EU-27 as a whole is the same whether expressed in Euros (ECUs) or in PPS. Purchasing Power Parities are conversion factors, which make it possible to eliminate the combined effect of price level differences and other factors from a comparison of economic aggregates and thereby obtain a real volume comparison between countries

[iii] Data obtained from table tps00067 available at
http://epp.eurostat.ec.europa.eu/portal/page/portal/statistics/search_database

[iv] The following table outlines what is included in each NVQ level equivalent or above category

NVQ Level 2 or above	In addition to Level 3 and above, includes 5 or more GCSE/SCE/O-level grades at A to C, CSE grade 1, 1 A level pass or 2 or 3 AS levels and the equivalent in vocational qualifications
NVQ Level 3 or above	In addition to Level 4 and above, includes 2 or more A level passes, 4 or more AS levels and the equivalent in vocational qualifications
NVQ Level 4 or above	Includes Higher degrees and other qualifications at Level 5. First degree and teaching qualifications

See http://www.gos.gov.uk/497745/docs/379399/428699/469541/qualificationsguidance

[v] Early year's education refers to education provided before the age at which compulsory education starts for children, currently the age of five in the UK

[vi] Settings include nursery schools, private nurseries and other childcare providers but excludes childminders

[vii] Social Trends 41: Population available at - http://www.statistics.gov.uk/socialtrends/stissue/

[viii] Full-day care provides day care for children under eight for a continuous period of 4 hours or more in any day, in premises which are not domestic premises e.g. day nurseries and children's centres, and some family centres

[ix] Sessional care providers, day care for children under eight, for a session which is less than a continuous period of 4 hours in any day in premises which are not domestic premises. Where two sessions are offered in any one day, individual children must not attend more than five sessions a week. There must be a break between sessions with no children in the care of the setting

[x] Main categories of educational establishments. Educational establishments in the UK are administered and financed in several ways. Most schools are controlled by Local Authorities (LAs), which are part of the structure of local government, but some are 'assisted', receiving grants direct from central government sources and being controlled by governing bodies that have a substantial degree of autonomy. Completely outside the public sector are non-maintained schools run by individuals, companies or charitable institutions.

Up to March 2001, Further Education (FE) courses in FE sector colleges in England and Wales were largely funded through grants from the respective Further Education Funding Councils (FEFCs). In April 2001 the

Learning and Skills Council (LSC) took over the responsibility for funding the FE sector in England, and the National Council for Education and Training for Wales (part of the Education and Learning Wales – ELWa) did so for Wales. The LSC in England is also responsible for funding provision for FE and some non-prescribed Higher Education in FE sector colleges; in addition, it funds some FE provided by LA maintained and other institutions referred to as 'external institutions'. From April 2006 FE funding in Wales, became the responsibility of the Welsh Assembly Government. The Scottish Further and Higher Education Funding Council (SFC) fund FE colleges in Scotland, while the Department for Employment and Learning funds FE colleges in Northern Ireland.

Higher Education (HE) courses in HE establishments are largely publicly funded through block grants from the HE funding councils in England and Scotland, the Higher Education Funding Council in Wales, and the Department for Employment and Learning in Northern Ireland. In addition, some designated HE, mainly Higher National Diplomas (HND)/Higher National Certificates (HNC) is funded by these sources. The FE mentioned above fund the remainder

[xi] More information about admission and appeals can be found at:
http://www.education.gov.uk/publications/eOrderingDownload/Primary%20and%20Secondary%20School%20Admissions.pdf

[xii] Nursery schools and classes have a minimum ration of two adults to 20 to 26 children. One must be a qualified teacher, the other a qualified nursery assistant

[xiii] In its 1997 election manifesto, the Labour Party pledged to cut class sizes to 30 or under for 5, 6 and 7 year-olds. After its election in 1998 the Government put this requirement on a statutory footing: Clause 1 of the Schools Standards and Framework Act 1998 placed a duty on Local Education Authorities (LEAs) and schools to restrict class sizes to 30 in Key Stage 1 classes from September 2002

[xiv] Free school meals. Local Authorities that maintain schools are responsible for providing free school meals to those that are eligible. Further information on the eligibility for free school meals is available at:
http://www.direct.gov.uk/en/Parents/Schoolslearninganddevelopment/SchoolLife/DG_4016089

[xv] National Qualifications. In Scotland, National Qualifications (NQs) are offered to students, these include Standard Grades, National Courses and National Units. Further information on National Qualifications can be found at: http://www.scotland.gov.uk/Topics/Education/Schools/curriculum/qualifications

[xvi] More information on apprenticeships can be found at:
http://www.direct.gov.uk/en/EducationAndLearning/AdultLearning/TrainingAndWorkplaceLearning/DG_4001327

[xvii] Announcement can be seen at: http://www.bis.gov.uk/news/topstories/2011/Feb/national-apprenticeship-week-2011

[xviii] Vocational Qualifications were initially split into three groups, National Vocational Qualifications (NVQs), General National Vocational Qualifications (GNVQs) and Vocationally Related Qualifications (VRQs), however GNVQs were phased out between 2005 and 2007. Further information on Vocational Qualifications can be found at:
http://www.direct.gov.uk/en/EducationAndLearning/QualificationsExplained/DG_181951

xix Qualifications. Includes Learning and Skills Council (LSC) funded training in England at different levels. The following table provides explanatory notes for each level.

Below level 2	This is activity funded by the LSC which is below level 2. This excludes any Skills for Life qualifications.	
Skills for Life	This is measured by the number of adults aged 16 and over who improve their skills by at least one level through one of the following nationally approved qualifications:	
	• Certificates in adult literacy, innumeracy or English for speakers of other languages (ESOL) Skills for Life at entry level 3, level 1 or level 2	
	• Key Skills in communication or application of number at level 1 or level 2 (partial achievement of key skills qualification counts where there is an achievement of a test)	
	• GCSEs in English or mathematics (grades A* to C = level 2, grades D to G = level 1)	
Full level 2	The width of the level 2 aims is summed up to establish whether a learner is taking a full level 2 programme. This would include qualifications shown below in the table. Learners only count if the total width of their aims is 100 per cent or more - part level 2 learners are excluded, for example those taking 4 GCSEs.	
	Aim type	Percentage of full level 2
	NVQ level 2	100 per cent
	GNVQ Intermediate (part GNVQ constitute 40 per cent)	80 per cent
	GCSE Double awards (including vocational GCEs)	40 per cent
	GCSE (including vocational GCEs)	20 per cent
	GCSE short course	10 per cent
	Other Vocationally Related Qualifications which are 80 per cent or more of a full level 2 (325 guided learning hours or more)	100 per cent
Full level 3	The width of the level 3 aims is summed up to establish whether a learner is taking a full level 3 programme. This would include qualifications shown below in the table. Learners only count if the total width of their aims is 100 per cent or more - part level 3 learners are excluded, for example those taking 2 AS level qualifications.	
	Aim type	Percentage of full level 3
	AS Levels (including VCEs)	25 per cent
	A/A2 levels (including VCEs)	50 per cent
	Advanced GNVQ	100 per cent
	Advanced pilot 6 unit GNVQ	100 per cent
	NVQ level 3 or above	100 per cent
	Other Vocationally Related Qualifications which are 80 per cent or more of a full level 2 (595 guided learning hours or more)	100 per cent
	Advanced apprenticeships and Higher Level Apprenticeships are counted as full level 3	
Level 2	LSC-funded level 2 qualifications. This includes all learners that are doing full level 2 programmes as well as those that are doing part level 2 qualifications, for example 1 GCSE.	
Level 3	LSC-funded level 3 qualifications. This includes all learners that are doing full level 2 programmes as well as those that are doing part level 2 qualifications, for example 1 AS level.	
Level 4 and above	LSC-funded level 4 and above qualifications	

xx Skills gap: skills gaps exist where employers report having employees who are not fully proficient at their job.

xxi Standard Industrial Classification (SIC2003). A Standard Industrial Classification (SIC) was first introduced into the UK in 1948 for use in classifying business establishments and other statistical units by the type of economic activity in which they are engaged. The classification provides a framework for the collection, tabulation, presentation and analysis of data and its use promotes uniformity. In addition, it can be used for administrative purposes and by non-government bodies as a convenient way of classifying industrial activities into a common structure.

Since 1948 the classification has been revised in 1958, 1968, 1980, 1992 and 2003. **Figure 10** uses SIC2003. Revision is necessary because over time new products and the new industries to produce them emerge, and shifts of emphasis occur in existing industries. It is not always possible for the system to accommodate such developments and so the classification is updated.

For further information about SIC see:
www.statistics.gov.uk/methods_quality/sic/downloads/UK_SIC_Vol1(2003).pdf

[xxii] Much of the hotel and catering industry is part of the tourism sector. The article at this link suggest that employment in these industries is more likely to be part-time, self-employed or temporary and have a younger age profile than in other industries: http://www.statistics.gov.uk/cci/article.asp?id=2626

04 August 2011

Correction Notice

Crime and Justice

ST41

Due to a production error, data in the key points under Prisons and sentencing (bullet point 1) and the units used in Table 5 (page 17) and the associated text were incorrect.

Text for Table 6 has been amended as it should refer to people sentenced for indictable offences not people in prison as previously stated.

ONS apologises for any inconvenience caused.

Issued by:
Office for National Statistics
Government Buildings
Cardiff Road
Newport NP10 8XG

Telephone:
Media Office   0845 604 1858
Contact Centre   0845 601 3034

Crime and justice

This chapter reports on data about crimes recorded by the police in the United Kingdom. We also report on information about crime levels, types of offence and victims of crime and how residents of England and Wales perceive changes in levels of crime both nationally and locally. The chapter then discusses statistics on offenders, prisons, sentencing and the police.

Key Points

Crime levels

- Of the 9.6 million crimes in England and Wales in 2010/11, almost two-thirds (5.9 million) were household crime and the remainder 3.8 million offences, were personal crime

- In 2009/10 in England and Wales, crime levels were at their historically lowest levels since the survey began in 1981

- In 2009/10 across the UK, there were 4.8 million crimes recorded by the police a fall of 8 per cent from 5.2 million offences in 2008/09

Offences and victims

- There were 7,006 offences in England and Wales, in which a firearm was reported to have been used and reported to the police in 2010/11. This was a decrease of 36 per cent from the peak of 11,088 in 2005/06

- In England and Wales in 2009/10, 619 deaths were recorded as homicide, a decrease of 4 per cent compared with 644 in 2008/09

- In England and Wales in 2009/10 males aged 16 to 20 in England and Wales were most at risk of being victims of homicide, with a rate of 34 homicides per million people in this age group

- In 2010/11 in England and Wales, repeat victimisation for the main crime types remained at around their lowest level since the first British Crime Survey results for 1981

Perceptions of crime

- The proportion of adults aged 16 and over who thought crime nationally had increased in England and Wales fell from 66 per cent in 2009/10 to 60 per cent in 2010/11

- At a local level in England and Wales, adults aged 16 and over believe that crime is not going up, while at a national level people believe that it is

Offenders

- Criminal justice figures based on administrative data collected by the police and courts in England and Wales, show that in 2010 1.6 million offenders were found guilty of, or cautioned for indictable and summary (including motoring) offences

- In 2010 in England and Wales, the total number of offenders found guilty of or cautioned for indictable offences had increased by 0.8 per cent for males and decreased by 8.0 per cent for females when compared with 2009

- Over four fifths of persons convicted of, or cautioned for indictable offences in England and Wales in 2010 were males (82 per cent)

Prisons and sentencing

- There were 140,800 Public Notice Disorders issued in England and Wales in 2010, of which 13,900 (10 per cent) were for possession of cannabis
- Between 1 June 2000 and 31 December 2009, nearly half (49 per cent) of adults aged 21 and over in England and Wales with an ASBO breached it at least once while 38 per cent breached it more than once
- In 2010, there were 384 prisoners sentenced to life imprisonment in England and Wales, a decrease of 9 per cent when compared with 421 in 2009

Resources

- In 2009/10 in England and Wales, police funding was at its highest recorded level of £12.6 billion, 44 per cent higher than 1995/96 when it was £8.8 billion

Crime levels

This section discusses the incidence of crime[i], while the victims of crime are covered in the offences and victims section.

Table 1   Crime in England and Wales; British Crime Survey[1]

Millions

	All household crime	All personal crime	All crime
1981	7.0	4.1	11.1
1991	10.4	4.7	15.1
1995	12.2	6.9	19.1
1997	10.3	6.1	16.5
2001/02	7.8	4.7	12.5
2002/03	7.5	4.7	12.3
2004/05	6.6	4.1	10.7
2005/06	6.6	4.1	10.7
2006/07	6.9	4.2	11.1
2007/08	6.2	3.8	10.0
2008/09	6.5	3.9	10.4
2009/10	5.9	3.6	9.5
2010/11	5.9	3.8	9.6

1 Prior to 2001/02, BCS estimates relate to crimes experienced in a given calendar year. From 2001/02 onwards the estimates relate to crimes experienced in the last 12 months based on interviews in the given financial year.
Source: Crime in England and Wales 2010/11 (HO, 2011)

The British Crime Survey (BCS) is a sample survey which collects information for England and Wales. It shows that the estimated number of crimes in England and Wales began to rise steadily from 11.1 million in 1981 and continued to rise through the early 1990s to peak at 19.1 million in 1995 (**Table 1**). Subsequently, the number of crimes fell to 9.5 million in 2009/10, the lowest since the survey began, and increased slightly in 2010/11 to 9.6 million. Of these 9.6 million crimes in 2010/11, almost two-thirds (5.9 million) were household crime and 3.8 million crimes, were personal crime. The number of personal crimes increased by 3 per cent between 2009/10 and 2010/11 while there was no noticeable change in the number of household crimes.

The Scottish Crime and Justice Survey (SCJS) estimated that there were 945,000 crimes committed against adults living in private households in Scotland in 2009/10, compared with 1.04 million in 2008/09, a decrease of 10 per cent. Of the 945,000 crimes committed in 2009/10, 679,000 (72 per cent) were property crimes, a decrease of 51,000 (7 per cent) compared with 2008/09. The remaining 266,000 (28 per cent) crimes were violent crimes of assault and robbery, a decrease of 54,000 (16 per cent) compared with 2008/09.

The Northern Ireland Crime Survey (NICS) estimated that there were 189,000 crimes committed against adults living in private households in the 12 months prior to interview in 2009/10, an increase of 7 per cent compared with 2008/09 (176,000), but more than a third (36 per cent) lower than the peak of 295,000 in 2003/04.

The BCS estimates of crime are considerably higher than the number of offences recorded by the police. Many crimes included in responses to the BCS are not reported to the police for a variety of reasons. For example, people may consider that the crime was too trivial or that it was not worthwhile reporting because there was no loss involved. Police recorded crime statistics provide a good measure of trends in well-reported crimes. They are an important indicator of police workload and can be used for local crime-pattern analysis. They do not, however, include crimes that have not been reported to the police or that the police decided not to record.

Table 2   Offences recorded by the police: by type of offence[1], 2009/10

United Kingdom   Percentages

	England & Wales	Scotland	Northern Ireland	United Kingdom
Theft and handling stolen goods	35.3	34.6	24.4	35.1
Theft from vehicles	7.8	3.0	3.7	7.4
Theft of vehicles	2.7	2.8	2.7	2.7
Criminal damage	18.6	27.6	24.2	19.4
Violence against the person [2]	20.1	3.3	27.4	19.1
Burglary [3]	12.5	7.0	11.5	12.1
Drug offences	5.4	11.7	2.9	5.8
Fraud and forgery	3.5	2.6	3.1	3.4
Robbery	1.7	0.7	1.2	1.6
Sexual offences	1.3	0.8	1.8	1.2
Other offences [4]	1.6	12.4	3.6	2.3
All notifiable offences (=100%) (thousands)	4,339	338	109	4,786

1 See note[ii]: Types of offences.
2 In Scotland, violence against the person includes robbery.
3 In Scotland, burglary is recorded as housebreaking which includes dwellings, non dwellings and other premises.
4 Northern Ireland includes 'offences against the state'. Scotland excludes 'offending while on bail'. Also includes offences against vehicle and other thefts.
Source: Home Office; Scottish Government; Police Service of Northern Ireland

In 2009/10 in the UK there were 4.8 million crimes recorded by the police (**Table 2**), a fall of 8 per cent from 5.2 million offences in 2008/09. Of the 4.8 million offences recorded in the UK in 2009/10, 4.3 million (91 per cent) were in England and Wales. Of these 35 per cent were for theft and handling stolen goods followed by 20 per cent for violence against the person.

Police in Scotland recorded 338,000 crimes in 2009/10, the most common was theft and handling stolen goods (35 per cent) followed by criminal damage (28 per cent). Police in Northern Ireland recorded 109,000 crimes in 2009/10 of which, 27 per cent were for violence against the person and 24 per cent for theft and handling stolen goods.

Offences and victims

Firearms are defined as having been used in an incident if they are fired, used as a blunt instrument against a person or used as a threat.

Figure 1   **Firearm offences (excluding air weapons):[1] by type of weapon**

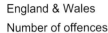

England & Wales
Number of offences

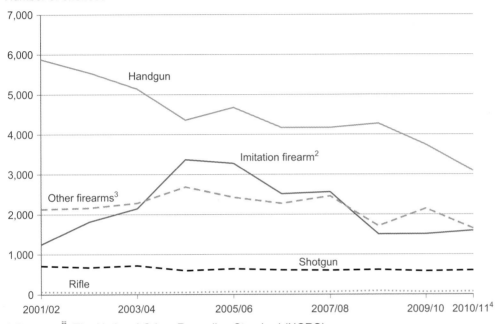

1 See note[iii]: The National Crime Recording Standard (NCRS).
2 Imitation handguns, which are converted to fire bullets like handguns, are counted as handguns.
3 Other firearms include unidentified firearms, CS gas, disguised firearms, machine guns, pepper spray, stun guns and other specified weapons (the majority being paintball guns).
4 Year 2010/11 includes the 12 victims of Derrick Bird. Data for police recorded firearms offences are provisional and are submitted via an additional detailed return. Final data are due for publication in January 2012.
Source: Crime in England and Wales 2010/11 (HO, 2011)

There were 7,006 offences in England and Wales, in which a firearm was reported to have been used and reported to the police in 2010/11. This was a decrease of 36 per cent from the peak of 11,088 in 2005/06 and a decrease of 13 per cent compared with 2009/10. This decrease is largely driven by a reduction in the number of offences involving the use of handguns which has fallen 17 per cent from 3,744 offences in 2009/10 to 3,090 offences in 2010/11 (**Figure 1**).

The term 'homicide' covers the offences of murder, manslaughter and infanticide. The offence infanticide was created by the *Infanticide Act 1922*[iv] and refined in 1938.

Figure 2   Offences currently recorded as homicide: by sex of victim and apparent method of killing, England and Wales, 2009/10

Percentage of all homicides

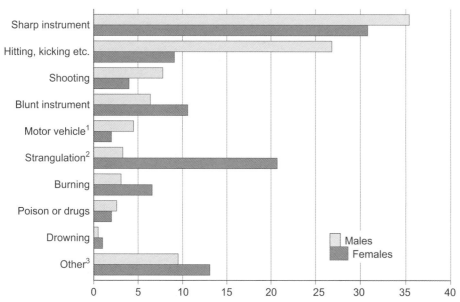

1 Motor Vehicle excludes death by careless/dangerous driving and aggravated vehicle taking.
2 Includes asphyxiation.
3 'Other' includes all other apparent methods and where the method is unknown.
Source: Homicides, Firearm Offences and Intimate Violence 2009/10 (HO, 2010)

In England and Wales in 2009/10, 619 deaths were recorded as homicide, a decrease of 4 per cent compared with the previous year when 644 homicides were recorded. Over two thirds of victims of homicide were men in 2009/10 (68 per cent of all victims).

Figure 2 shows that in 2009/10, as in previous years, the most common method of killing was by a sharp instrument[v], used in 35 per cent of homicides where the victim was male and 31 per cent of those where the victim was female. The second most common method of killing men was hitting, kicking, etc. (27 per cent). The second most common homicide method for female victims was strangulation used in 1 in 5 (21 per cent) of these homicides.

According to the Home Office, Homicides 'Firearm Offences and Intimate Violence 2009/10' (HO, 2010) supplementary report when data for the three years 2007/08 to 2009/10 is combined, males aged 16 to 20 were found to be most at risk of being victims of homicide, with a rate of 34 homicides per million people in this age group. The second most at risk age group were males aged under one year at a rate of 31 per million (although this is the smallest population analysed and involves very small numbers of homicides) followed by males aged 21 to 29 at a rate of 30 per million.

The risk of becoming a victim of crime varies according to personal characteristics with men more likely to be at risk than women except in cases of domestic violence.

Figure 3   Adults who were victims of crime:[1] by personal characteristic, 2010/11

England & Wales
Percentages[2]

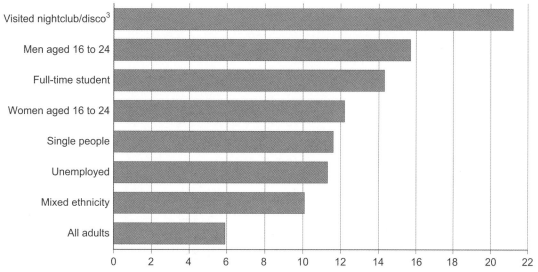

1 Adults aged 16 and over who reported being a victim of crime one or more times in the 12 months prior to interview.
2 Percentage of all those who reported being a victim of crime.
3 Visited nightclub/disco once a week or more in the last month.
Sources: Crime in England and Wales 2010/11 (HO, 2011)

The 2010/11 BCS reported that just over a fifth (21 per cent) of adults aged 16 and over in England and Wales who reported being a victim of crime had visited a nightclub once a week or more prior to interview (**Figure 3**). As with previous years, men aged 16 to 24 also had a high occurrence of being a victim of crime followed by full time students and women aged 16 to 24. Similarly, the Northern Ireland Crime Survey (NICS) for 2009/10 also reports that men aged between 16 and 24 were more likely to be victims of a crime.

There are also differences in the rates of being a victim of crime according to the respondent's occupation. For example, the proportion of victims who were full-time students was two and a half times higher than the proportion in managerial and professional occupations: this could be related to the differences in age groups for these two occupations.

According to the 2010/11 BCS, offences with injury in England and Wales accounted for just over half (55 per cent) of all violent incidents and nearly half (45 per cent) of all police recorded violence against the person offences.

Repeat victimisation is defined as being a victim of the same type of crime (e.g. vandalism) more than once in the last 12 months. Levels of repeat victimisation account for differences between incidence rates and prevalence rates.

Figure 4   Repeat victimisation:[1] by type of offence, England and Wales, 2010/11

Percentages[2]

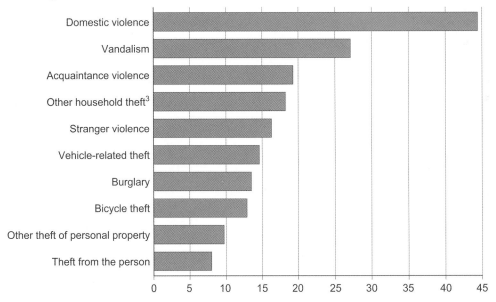

1 Proportion of victims victimised more than once, in the 12 months to interview.
2 Percentages of all those who reported being a victim of the specific offence.
3 Excludes burglaries. Includes theft from both inside and outside a dwelling and from garages, sheds and outbuildings not directly linked to the dwelling.
Sources: Crime in England and Wales 2010/11 (HO, 2011)

BCS data shows that levels of repeat victimisation vary by offence type (**Figure 4**). In 2010/11, the most common repeat victimisation was 'domestic violence' with 44 per cent of victims of this offence reporting that they had been victimised more than once in the last year. One reason for this may be that victims are able to take more preventative measures against repeat victimisation for some crime types such as theft from the person. It is likely to be more difficult for a victim of domestic violence to avoid repeat victimisation.

Repeat victimisation for the main crime types remain at around their lowest level since the first BCS results for 1981. Since BCS crime peaked in 1995 (see **Table 1**), the proportion of victims who reported being victimised more than once has fallen for most crime types, notably acquaintance violence (from 37 per cent to 19 per cent), vehicle-related theft (from 28 per cent to 15 per cent) and stranger violence (from 24 per cent to 16 per cent).

Perceptions of crime

The BCS also asks respondents whether they think that crime has increased nationally and in their local area. In contrast to responses to the 2008/09 BCS, when there was a marked increase compared to the previous year, in 2010/11 there was a fall in the proportion of people who thought crime nationally had increased from 66 per cent in 2009/10 to 60 per cent in 2010/11, returning to similar levels seen in 2004/05 and 2005/06. Similarly, the perception of crime at local level also fell from 31 per cent in 2009/10 to 28 per cent in 2010/11.

Table 3   Perceptions of changing crime levels: by type of crime,[1,2] 2009/10

England & Wales   Percentages

	National level		Local level	
	Gone up a lot	Gone up a little	Gone up a lot	Gone up a little
Knife crime	69	21	7	20
Bank/credit card fraud	65	25	19	31
Gun crime	51	30	3	10
People getting beaten up	47	34	8	24
Mugging/street robberies	40	37	5	21
Vandalism	35	35	7	25
Homes broken into	30	38	7	26
Cars being broken into	30	34	7	23
Cars being stolen	28	32	5	18

1 British Crime Survey respondents were asked if they thought specific crimes had increased locally or nationally. Data are the proportion of people who answered 'increased a lot' or 'increased a little'.
2 BCS estimates for 2010/11 are based on face to face interviews with 46,654 adults aged 16 and over.
Source: Crime in England and Wales 2009/10 (HO, 2010a)

The published 2010/11 BCS data about perceptions of crime does not give the same detailed breakdown as shown for 2009/10 in **Table 3**. In response to the BCS questions about specific crimes at national level, an estimated 69 per cent of people living in private households in England and Wales in 2009/10 believed that knife crime had gone up a lot nationally over the last two years, while 21 per cent believed it had gone up a little. Perceptions of an increase in bank/credit card fraud were also quite high at a national level in 2009/10, with 65 per cent of people believing it has gone up a lot and a quarter (25 per cent) of people believing it has gone up a little. This may be a reflection of media concerns at the time of the survey about these two types of crime.

There is a considerable contrast between people's perceptions of crime at a local level and national level: at local level a lower proportion of people believe that crime is going up compared to their beliefs of crime at a national level. For specific crimes at local level 7 per cent of people believed that knife crime had gone up a lot and one in five (20 per cent) of people thought it had gone up a little. Perceptions of bank/credit card crime were also believed to have increased at local level with 19 per cent of people stating that they thought bank/credit card crime fraud had gone up a lot in their area and 31 per cent thinking it had gone up a little.

Figure 5   Perceived and actual likelihood of being a victim of crime:[1,2] by crime type

England and Wales
Percentages

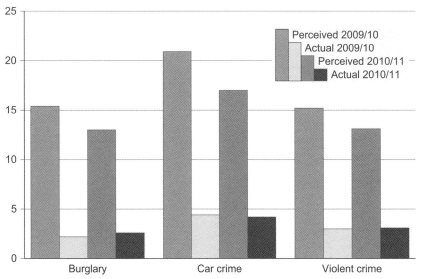

1 Percentages are of households/car-owning households and adults.
2 BCS estimates for 2010/11 are based on face to face interviews with 46,654 adults aged 16 and over.
Sources: Crime in England and Wales 2010/11 (HO, 2011)

In addition to questions on perceptions of crime, BCS also asks how likely people think it would be that they would be a victim of crime in the next 12 months. As can be seen in **Figure 5**, the perception of the rates of victimisation by burglary, car crime and violent crime are a lot higher than the actual rates.

Between 2009/10 and 2010/11 there was very little difference in the actual rates of victims of burglary, car crime and violent crime. However, the perception of the likelihood of being a victim has decreased for all three types of crime. The largest change was in the perceived likelihood of being a victim of car crime which reduced by four percentage points from 21 per cent in 2009/10 to 17 per cent in 2010/11. The perception of being a victim of violent crime decreased from 15 per cent to 13 per cent and the perceived likelihood of being a victim of burglary also decreased from 15 per cent in 2009/10 to 13 per cent in 2010/11.

Although there is disparity between people's perceptions and their actual risk of crime, people were more likely to perceive they would be a victim of crime in more common types of crime, such as car crime than less common crimes such as violent crime. However, in 2010/11 people overestimated the risk of being a victim of burglary (5 times), violent crimes (4 times) and vehicle crimes (4 times).

Offenders

Figure 6   Persons convicted or cautioned for indictable offences:[1,2] by age

England and Wales

Thousands

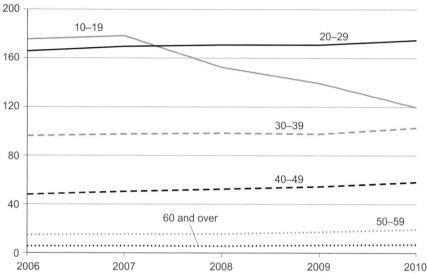

1 People found guilty of, or cautioned for, indictable offences. Excludes persons where sex 'Not Stated' and other offenders, i.e. companies, public bodies, etc
2 For motoring offences only persons found guilty are included; these offences may attract written warnings, which are not included in this figure.
Source: Criminal Justice Statistics, England and Wales 2010 (MOJ, 2011)

Criminal justice statistics based on administrative data collected by the police and courts show that in 2010 1.6 million offenders were found guilty of or cautioned for indictable and summary (including motoring) offences in England and Wales.

Figure 6 shows that the highest number of persons convicted of, or cautioned for indictable offences in England and Wales in 2010 were those aged 20 to 29 and 10 to 19 (174,800 and 119,600 respectively). The most noticeable change over the time period shown is a reduction for those 10 to 19 since 2007 (178,400 in 2007 to 119,600 in 2010).

Over four fifths (82 per cent) of persons convicted of, or cautioned for indictable offences in England and Wales in 2010 were males. Overall the recorded figure in 2010 is the lowest in five years, at 481,400, a decrease of 1 per cent compared with 2009.

Figure 7   Persons found guilty of, or cautioned for, indictable offences:[1] by sex[2] and type of offence 2010

England and Wales

Thousands

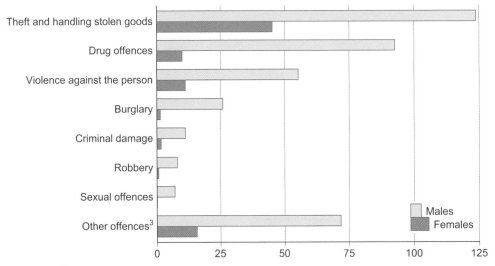

1 See note[vi] : Types of offence in England and Wales.
2 Excludes persons whose sex was not recorded
3 Includes fraud and forgery and indictable motoring offences
Source: Criminal Justice Statistics, England and Wales 2010 (MOJ, 2011)

Figure 7 shows that in 2010, the most common type of indictable offence for which males and females were found guilty or cautioned was theft and handling of stolen goods, 123,700 (31 per cent of all offences) for males and 45,200 (53 per cent of all offences) for females.

For males the second most common type of crime was drug offences at 92,500 (23 per cent) followed by violence against the person 55,400 (14 per cent). The second most common offence type for females was violence against the person 11,200 (13 per cent).

The total number of offenders found guilty of or cautioned for indictable offences increased 0.8 per cent for males and decreased 8.0 per cent for females in 2010 compared with 2009. The biggest increase was for male offenders in the 'sexual offences' category from 6,400 to 7,000 (9.4 per cent) whilst the biggest decrease was for female offenders in the 'robbery' category from 800 to 700 (12.5 per cent).

Prisons and sentencing

The majority of offenders in Britain will go on to commit another crime, with almost half of all offences committed by people that have already been through the system. A re-conviction is defined as any offence committed in the one-year follow up period proven by a court conviction. It should be noted that any offences committed in the one-year follow up period are not necessarily of the same offence type as the initial offence.

Figure 8   **Percentage of reconviction rate: by offence[1]**

England & Wales

Percentages

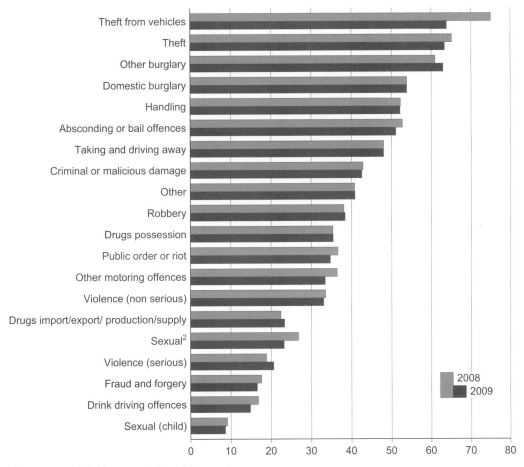

1 Data are at Q1 (January to March) in each year.
2 Does not include soliciting or prostitution also excludes offences against a child.
Source: Adult re-convictions: results from the 2009 cohort (MOJ, 2011a)

Theft from vehicles showed the lowest proportional differences in reconvictions between 2008 and 2009, from 75 per cent of all offences in Q1 2008 to 64 per cent in Q1 2009, a fall of 11 percentage points **Figure 8** The next largest decrease was sexual reconvictions which decreased from 27 per cent in 2008 to 23 per cent in 2009, a fall of 4 percentage points. The biggest increase was in serious violence which includes offences involving grievous bodily harm (GBH), where reconvictions increased by 2 percentage points from 19 per cent to 21 per cent.

The Ministry of Justice has an executive agency known as the National Offender Management Service (NOMS) which brings together HM Prison Service and the Probation Services to deliver sentences and other orders of the courts in custodial and community settings in England and Wales to protect the public and reduce re-offending by helping offenders to reform their lives.

Information from the National Offender Management Service Annual Report and Accounts 2009 to 2010 shows that offenders entering the system present a range of challenges which need to be addressed; 48 per cent have a reading age at or below the expected level of an 11-year-old and 82 per cent have a writing level at or below that expected of an 11-year-old, 62 per cent of newly sentenced prisoners report using an illegal drug during the four-week period before custody (28 per cent using heroin and 25 per cent using crack cocaine), 44 per cent need help with alcohol misuse and 22 per cent want help with mental health problems.

Figure 9   Drug treatment programme completions while in prison: by age[1], 2009/10

England & Wales

Numbers

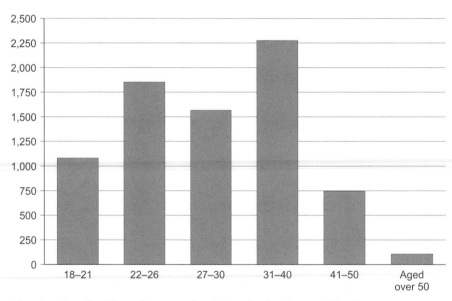

1 Age bands reflect those in use on the data collection forms at the time.
Source: HM Prison Service

In 2009/10, 75 per cent of prisoners who started the NOMS Drug Treatment Programme in England and Wales successfully completed it. Prisoners completing the programme were more likely to be aged 31 to 40 years, followed by those aged 22 to 26 years (**Figure 9**).

Apart from custodial and community sentences, offenders can also receive cautions for some offences, penalty notices and civil notices such as Anti-Social Behaviour Orders[vii] (ASBOs). The number of fixed penalty notices for motoring offences detected by camera, Penalty Notices for Disorder[viii] (PNDs) and ASBOs are discussed below.

Table 4   Fixed penalties for motoring offences detected by cameras:[1] by type of offence

England and Wales   Thousands

	Speeding offences	Traffic light offences	All offences
2000	599	52	651
2001	878	46	924
2002	1,135	71	1,206
2003	1,670	115	1,785
2004	1,787	113	1,900
2005	1,824	124	1,948
2006	1,689	120	1,808
2007	1,296	109	1,406
2008	1,048	100	1,147
2009	935	92	1,027

1 Includes paid, fixed penalties only. Offences where the fixed penalty was not paid are not counted, as further action was taken.
Source: Police Powers and Procedures England and Wales 2009/10 (HO, 2011a)

There were a little over 1 million fixed penalty notices for traffic light and speeding offences detected by camera in 2009, a decrease of 120,000 (10 per cent) compared with 2008 (**Table 4**). This followed the larger decrease of 259,000 (18 per cent) between 2008 and 2009. There were 935,000 fixed penalties for speeding offences in 2009 which accounted for 91 per cent of all fixed penalties for motoring offences in 2009. This is the lowest number of fixed penalties for speeding since 2001 when there were 878,000 fixed penalties.

Fixed penalties paid for traffic light offences in 2009 were at their lowest level of 92,000 since a peak of 124,000 offences in 2005. Cameras are also used to provide evidence for other offences, such as unauthorised use of a bus lane but these data are not collected separately by the Home Office.

Penalty Notices for Disorder (PNDs) more commonly known as 'on the spot fines' were introduced under the *Criminal Justice and Police Act 2001* as part of the strategy to tackle low-level, anti-social and nuisance offending. PNDs were initially piloted in four police-force areas in 2002 and rolled out to all police forces in England and Wales in 2004.

Table 5   Number of Penalty Notices for Disorder (PNDs) issued: by offence

England and Wales   Number issued

	2005	2006	2007	2008	2009	2010
Causing harassment, alarm or distress	64,007	82,235	77,827	57,773	43,338	32,317
Drunk and disorderly	37,038	43,556	46,996	44,411	43,570	37,119
Criminal damage (under £500)	12,168	20,620	19,946	13,427	10,145	6,253
Retail theft	21,997	38,772	45,596	45,616	48,161	40,170
Possession of cannabis[1]	..	..	..	..	11,491	13,916
Other	11,271	16,014	17,629	14,937	13,688	10,994
Total	**146,481**	**201,197**	**207,544**	**176,164**	**170,393**	**140,769**

1 PNDs for possession of cannabis were only issued from 2009 onwards. Offence added with effect from 27 January 2009.
Source: Criminal Justice Statistics, England and Wales 2010 (MOJ, 2011)

There were 140,800 Penalty Notices for Disorder (PNDs) issued in 2010 a decrease of 30,000 (17 per cent) compared with 2009. Of the 140,800 PNDs issued, 13,900 were for possession of cannabis[ix] (10 per cent of all PNDs issued). Retail theft (40,200), drunk and disorderly (37,100) and behaviour likely to cause harassment, alarm or distress (32,300) accounted for a further 78 per cent of all PNDs issued (**Table 5**).

The largest decrease in the number of PNDs issued between 2009 and 2010 was for the criminal damage (under £500), which decreased by 38 per cent from 10,100 in 2009 to 6,300 in 2010, down from a peak of 21,000 in 2006. The only increase was in the issue of PNDs for cannabis possession which increased by 21 per cent to 13,900 from 11,500 in 2009.

Anti-social behaviour orders (ASBOs) were introduced in England and Wales under the *Crime and Disorder Act (1998).*

Figure 10   Anti-social behaviour orders (ASBOs) issued and proven to have been breached

England and Wales

Numbers

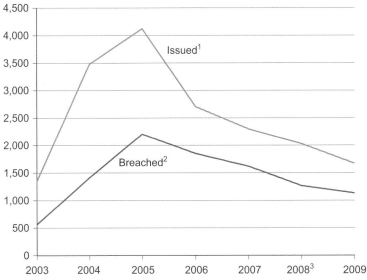

1 Includes ASBOs issued on application by magistrates and county courts and ASBOs made following conviction for a relevant criminal offence at the Crown Court and at magistrates' courts.
2 ASBOs may be issued in one area and breached in another and may be breached more than once and in more than one year.
3 Excludes data for Cardiff magistrates' court for April, July, and August.
Source: Anti-social behaviour order statistics, England and Wales 2009 (HO, 2010b)

Figure 10 shows the total number of ASBOs issued increased in England and Wales from 1,300 in 2003 to a peak of 4,100 in 2005, but have since decreased steadily to reach 1,700 in 2009. In 2009 1,100 ASBOs were breached, equivalent to 68 per cent of the number which were issued in that year (although the breaches may relate to ASBOs issued in previous years). The ratio of breached ASBOs to ASBOs issued was relatively low in 2003 and 2004 (42 and 41 per cent respectively), the highest ratio of breached to issued ASBOs was in 2007 at 70 per cent.

There were differences between age groups in breaches of ASBOs. Between 1 June 2000 and 31 December 2009, nearly half (49 per cent) of adults aged 21 and over with an ASBO breached it at least once and 38 per cent breached it more than once. A much larger proportion of juveniles breached their ASBOs at least once; 73 per cent of 12 to 14-year-olds, 71 per cent of those aged between 10 and 11 and 65 per cent of those aged between 15 and 17.

Table 6   Persons sentenced for indictable offences: by type of offence and sex, 2010

England & Wales   Numbers

	Males	Females	All[1]
Violence against the person	39,057	5,325	44,458
Drug offences	56,532	4,723	61,435
Sexual offences	5,694	73	5,772
Robbery	7,816	680	8,514
Other offences[2]	50,790	6,781	58,139
Burglary	22,571	976	23,599
Theft and Handling	94,913	25,939	121,230
Fraud and Forgery	14,090	6,280	20,865
Motoring offences	3,232	169	3,410
Total	**294,695**	**50,946**	**347,422**

1 All persons includes persons whose sex was not recorded and excludes organisations such as companies and public bodies.
2 Other offences include criminal damage.
Source: Criminal Justice Statistics, England and Wales 2010 (MOJ, 2011)

There were 347,422 people sentenced for indictable offences in England and Wales as at December 2010; of these 294,695 (85 per cent) were male and 50,946 (5 per cent) were female (**Table 6**). The indictable offence type for which both males and females were most commonly sentenced was theft and handling, 94,913 (32 per cent of all male offences) and 25,939 (51 per cent of all female offences).

The second next most common offence for males was drug offences, 56,532 (19 per cent of all offences by males) while the second most common offence for females was other offences including criminal damage, 6,781 (13 per cent of all offences by females).

Life imprisonment, or its equivalent, must be imposed on all persons aged 10 and over convicted of murder. This sentence may also be imposed for a number of the most serious crimes including manslaughter, robbery, rape, assault with intent to do grievous bodily harm, aggravated burglary and certain firearms offences.

Table 7   People sentenced to life imprisonment:[1] by sex

England & Wales   Numbers

	Males	Females	All people
2000	446	21	467
2001	484	19	503
2002	536	19	555
2003	489	24	513
2004	548	22	570
2005	594	31	625
2006	531	16	547
2007	471	21	492
2008	495	28	523
2009	401	20	421
2010	364	20	384

1 See note[x]

Source: Criminal Justice Statistics, England and Wales 2010 (MOJ, 2011)

In 2010, 384 persons were sentenced to life imprisonment in England and Wales, a decrease of 9 per cent compared with 421 persons in 2009 (**Table 7**). Of the 384 persons sentenced to life imprisonment, 364 were male and 20 female. The number of persons sentenced in 2010 is the lowest figure during the eleven year period.

Resources

Figure 11   **Police revenue funding, in real terms**[1]

England & Wales

£ Millions

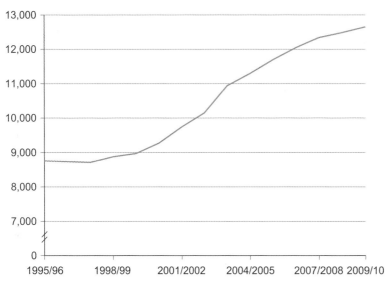

1 Adjusted for inflation using Gross Domestic Product (GDP) deflators.
Source: Central government police revenue funding 1995/96 to 2009/10 (HO, 2010c)

Figure 11 shows that between 1995/96 and 2009/10, police funding[xi] increased by 44 per cent from £8.8 billion in 1995/96 to £12.6 billion in 2009/10. The highest year-on-year increase was between 2002/03 and 2003/04 when funding increased 8 per cent from £10.2 billion in 2002/03 to £10.9 billion in 2003/04.

Table 8   Police Officer strength: English Regions and Wales[1]

Numbers

	2009 [2]	2010 [2]
North East	7,388	7,301
North West	19,922	19,306
Yorkshire and the Humber	12,339	12,102
East Midlands	9,412	9,246
West Midlands	14,315	13,853
Eastern	11,416	11,318
London	34,185	33,778
South East	17,129	16,897
South West	10,899	10,701
Wales	7,349	7,349
Total of all 43 forces	**144,353**	**141,850**
Central service secondments	480	513
British Transport Police	2,686	2,652
Total police officer strength[3]	**147,519**	**145,015**

1 Based on full-time equivalent figures rounded to the nearest whole number. Because of rounding there may be an apparent discrepancy between the totals and the sums of the constituent items.
2 Data are as at 30th September in each year.
3 Including British Transport Police Officers in England and Wales only.
Source: Police Service Strength England and Wales, 30 September 2010 (HO, 2011b)

In 2010 there were 145,015 full time equivalents (FTE) Police Officers in England and Wales of which 2,652 were British Transport Police (these are additional to the 43 forces of England and Wales) and 513 were Central Service secondments (**Table 8**). While the number of Police Officer remained the same in Wales, there were decreases in the size of the police force in all English regions.

The West Midlands saw the largest percentage decrease in Police Officers between September 2009 and September 2010 of 3.2 per cent (14,315 in September 2009 to 13,853 in September 2010). The next largest decrease was in the North West which decreased by 3.1 per cent (19,922 in September 2009 to 19,306 in September 2010).

There were 16,376 FTE Police Community Support Officers (PCSO's), in the 43 English and Welsh police forces on 30 September 2010, a decline of 2.6 per cent (438) since September 2009.

References:

(HO, 2010) Homicide, Firearm Offences and Intimate Violence 2009/10. Available at
http://search.homeoffice.gov.uk/search?q=Firearm%2C+Offences+and+Intimate+Violence+&entqr
=0&ud=1&sort=date%3AD%3AL%3Ad1&output=xml_no_dtd&oe=UTF-8&ie=UTF-
8&client=default_frontend&proxystylesheet=default_frontend&site=default_collection

(HO, 2010a) Crime in England and Wales 2009/10. Available at:
http://webarchive.nationalarchives.gov.uk/20110218135832/http://rds.homeoffice.gov.uk/rds/a-
zsubjects.html

(HO, 2010b) Anti-social behaviour order statistics - England and Wales 2009. Available at:
http://www.homeoffice.gov.uk/publications/science-research-statistics/research-statistics/crime-
research/asbo-stats-england-wales-2009/

(HO, 2010c) Central government police revenue funding 1995/96 to 2009/10. These documents
are part of a series of consistent police revenue funding numbers from 1995/96-2009/10. They are
designed to allow for funding levels to be compared over time. Available at:
http://www.homeoffice.gov.uk/publications/police/

(HO, 2011) Crime in England and Wales 2010/11. The findings from the latest *British Crime
Survey (BCS)* and police recorded crime report is available at:
http://www.homeoffice.gov.uk/publications/science-research-statistics/research-statistics/crime-
research/hosb1011/

(HO, 2011a) Police Powers and Procedures England and Wales 2009/10. Available at:
http://www.homeoffice.gov.uk/publications/science-research-statistics/research-statistics/police-
research/hosb0711/

(HO, 2011b) Police Service Strength England and Wales, 30 September 2010. Available at:
http://homeoffice.gov.uk/science-research/research-statistics/police/

(MOJ, 2011) Criminal Justice Statistics, England and Wales 2010. Available at:
http://www.justice.gov.uk/publications/statistics-and-data/criminal-justice/criminal-justice-
statistics.htm

(MOJ, 2011a) Adult re-convictions: results from the 2009 cohort. Available at:
http://www.justice.gov.uk/publications/statistics-and-data/reoffending/adults.htm

National Offender Management Service (NOMS). For more information on NOMS see:
http://www.justice.gov.uk/about/noms/index.htm

National Offender Management Service Annual Report and Accounts 2009 to 2010. Available at
http://sitesearch.justice.gov.uk.openobjects.com/kb5/justice/justice/results.page?ha=&qt=national+
offender+management+service+annual+report

The Scottish Crime and Justice Survey. Latest report available at:
http://www.scotland.gov.uk/Publications/2010/11/01090437/0

The Northern Ireland Crime Survey. Latest report available at:
http://www.dojni.gov.uk/index/statistics-research/stats-research-
publications/current_publications.htm

Notes:

ⁱ Features of the British Crime Survey and police recorded crime. Police recorded crime statistics reflect those crimes reported to the police and so they provide data at a local as well as national level, and they can provide a good measure of the more serious types of crime. However, many crimes are not reported to the police, and for some crimes, for example drug offences, the statistics can be seen as a measure of police activity rather than of crime.

The British Crime Survey (BCS), being a survey of the population, provides a measure of crime that includes incidents that are unreported to the police and unrecorded by the police, and thus provides a good measure of the long term trends in the more common types of crime against individuals or households. On the other hand, it does not cover homicide, commercial crime or 'victimless' crimes.

British Crime Survey	Police Recorded Crime
Sample survey of 46,000 nationally representative households in England and Wales	Uses administrative records
Supports crime statistics and Home Office and Ministry of Justice research	Notifiable crime governed by the National Crime Recording Standard and the Home Office Counting Rules (HOCR)
Good measure of long-term trends	Local data available
Excludes homicides, children, victimless crimes, homeless and communal establishments	Linkage possible with other data in the criminal justice system
Sample size does not support local breakdown	Trends sensitive to changes in the Notifiable Offence List: recording practice: operational decisions on policing: changes in the HOCR

ⁱⁱ **Types of offence in England and Wales**. The figures are compiled from police returns to the Home Office and the Ministry of Justice or directly from court computer systems.

Indictable offences in England and Wales cover those offences that can only be tried at the Crown Court and include the more serious offences.

Summary offences are those for which a defendant would normally be tried at a magistrate's court and are generally less serious – the majority or motoring offences fall into this category.

Triable-either-way offences are triable either on indictment or summarily.

Types of offence in Scotland. In Scotland the term 'crime' is reserved for the more serious offences (broadly equivalent to 'indictable' and 'triable-either-way' offences in England and Wales) while less serious crimes are called 'offences'. The seriousness of an act is *generally* based on the maximum sentence that can be imposed.

Types of offence in Northern Ireland. In recoding crimes, the Police Service of Northern Ireland (PSNI) broadly follows the Home Office rules for counting crime. As from 1 April 1998 notifiable offences are recorded on the same basis as those in England and Wales. Before the revision of the rules, criminal damage offences in Northern Ireland excluded those where the value of the property damaged was less than £200.

[iii] The National Crime Recording Standard (NCRS) was introduced in April 2002, although some forces adopted NCRS practices before the standard was formally introduced. Figures before and after that date are not directly comparable. The introduction of NCRS led to a rise in recording in 2002/03 and, particularly for violent crime, in the following years as forces continued to improve compliance with the new standard.

[iv] Infanticide is an offence in its own right. *The Infanticide Act 1938* provides that when a mother kills her child, when the child is under 12 months old, and at the time the balance of the mother's mind was disturbed as a result of her not having fully recovered from the effect of giving birth or due to the effect of lactation, the mother will be guilty of infanticide rather than murder.

[v] Includes knives and other sharp instruments.

[vi] Types of offence in the UK. The figures for England and Wales are compiled from police returns to the Home Office and the Ministry of Justice or directly from court computer systems. **Indictable offences** in England and Wales cover those offences that can only be tried at the Crown Court and include more serious offences. **Summary offices** are those for which a defendant would normally be tried at a magistrates' court and are generally less serious – the majority of motoring offences fall into this category. **Triable-either-way offences** are triable either on indictment or summarily.

[vii] An ASBO is a civil order made against a person who has been shown to have engaged in anti-social behaviour. Anti-social behaviour describes a range of everyday nuisance, disorder and crime, from graffiti and noisy neighbours to harassment and street drug dealing. It is sometimes dismissed as trivial, but anti-social behaviour has a huge impact on victims' quality of life, and it is the public's number one concern when it comes to local crime issues.

Breach of an ASBO is a criminal offence, which is arrestable and recordable. The ASBO will usually last for a minimum of 2 years. An ASBO does not indicate that a criminal offence has taken place. This means that an ASBO will not appear on your criminal record. However, if you break the terms of the ASBO this is a criminal offence and could result in up to 5 years in prison and a fine. The case could be taken to the magistrate's court, but in some cases could be referred to the Crown Court.

viii A penalty notice for disorder (PND) is a type of fixed penalty notice that can be issued for a specified range of minor disorder offences. The PND scheme was introduced under the Criminal Justice and Police Act 2001 and implemented in all 43 police forces in England and Wales in 2004. Under the scheme the police may issue anyone aged 16 years or over who has committed a specified penalty offence with a fixed penalty and to those aged 10-15 in seven pilot police forces. http://www.homeoffice.gov.uk/police/penalty-notices/

ix A new PND for the offence of possession of cannabis was introduced in 2009. Revised statutory guidance on PNDs published in July 2009 limited the use of PNDs for cannabis possession to offenders age 18 and over.

x Those sentenced to life imprisonment or an indeterminate sentence of imprisonment for Public Protection (IPP) has no automatic right to be released. Instead such prisoners must serve a minimum period of imprisonment to meet the needs of retribution and deterrence. This punitive period is announced by the trial judge in open court and is known commonly as the 'tariff' period.

The courts must impose a life sentence on any individual convicted of murder. This is the only sentence available for such a conviction.

The maximum sentence that can be awarded by the Courts for a number of other types of offences, for example, rape, manslaughter and arson is life imprisonment.

Under Section 225 of the Criminal Justice Act 2003, the courts will impose an indeterminate sentence of IPP (Imprisonment for public protection) when the offender is aged 18 or over, is convicted of a serious specified violent or sexual offence committed on or after 4 April 2005-for which the maximum penalty is 10 years or more and who in the court's opinion poses a significant risk of harm to the public.

xi There are four main sources of funding from central government to the police. Two are from the Home Office; Police Main Grant and Specific Grants. The other two are from the Department for Communities and Local Government (DCLG) and Welsh Assembly Government (WAG); Revenue Support Grant and Redistributed Business Rates.

The Police Allocation Formula (PAF) is essentially a calculation that uses various data sources (such as population density) to share money between police authorities in England and Wales. It is not a calculation of absolute needs that is it does not estimate how much each force needs independently of other forces. Instead it shares out the amount of money designated for police funding between forces based on their relative needs compared with each other.

Designing a system to fund 43 police forces in England and Wales is complex. The PAF is a way to measure the need for policing in areas relative to each other. It uses a range of indicators that are available on a consistent basis for all police authorities.

The first step of the PAF is to divide everything the police services has to do to police the country into 11 categories (tasks). Seven of these relate to reducing/investigating different types of crime including violence/sexual offences, robbery, vehicle crime, burglary, other crime (high cost) and other crime (low cost). The other four categories are providing reassurance to the public, providing assistance at or reducing road traffic accidents, assistance with non-crime incidents and policing special events such as a protest march or football match.

The PAF is important because it is used to divide the majority of the money available for the total police funding between forces. Consequently, the results of the PAF have a significant impact on how much a force will receive in order to police it.

Environment

The environment in which we live has changed considerably over the last 200 years. The move from rural, agricultural communities into industrial towns has led to increasing pressures being put on the land, wildlife, atmosphere and water. The environment around us has a significant impact on the quality of our lives, for example, the cleanliness of our streets, air and water quality, energy consumption, climate change and access to green space. Individuals can demonstrate concern for the environment by undertaking personal environment protection activities, such as recycling and reducing their energy consumption. In addition households contribute the majority of UK environmental tax revenue.

Key points

Environmental attitudes and lifestyles

- After the economy and unemployment, the environment and pollution was the third most important issue that adults aged 16 and over in England felt the government should address when asked in 2009 (35 per cent)
- Around a third (32 per cent) of adults aged 16 and over in England reported in 2010 that they were environmentally-friendly in most or everything they did.

Energy

- Domestic energy consumption in the UK increased by 18 per cent between 1970 and 2009, from 37 to 44 million tonnes of oil equivalent
- Space heating accounted for over half (58 per cent) of all final domestic energy consumption in the UK in 2008, while cooking accounted for just 3 per cent
- In 2008, 5.6 per cent of gross electricity consumption in the UK was generated by renewable sources, compared with the EU-27 average of 16.7 per cent

Waste management

- Households in England generated around 24 million tonnes of waste in 2009/10, equivalent to around 460 kilograms per person
- In 2009/10, 40 per cent of household waste per person in England was recycled, composted or reused, compared with less than 1 per cent in 1983/84
- Local authorities in England dealt with nearly 947,000 incidents of fly-tipping in 2009/10, with nearly half (49 per cent) occurring near the highway

Pollution

- There were 22 days of moderate or higher air pollution in rural areas in the UK in 2010, the lowest since 1987. For urban areas there were 8 days of moderate or higher air pollution in 2010, the lowest since records began in 1993
- In 2009 there were 770 recorded serious (Category 1 or 2) pollution incidents in England and Wales, around half of the 1,500 serious incidents that were reported in 2002

Climate change

- Approximately half (46 per cent) of adults aged 16 and over in England disagreed with the statement 'the effects of climate change are too far in the future to worry me', while 37 per cent agreed with the statement.

- In 2009, UK emissions of the basket of greenhouse gases were estimated to be 566.3 million tonnes carbon dioxide equivalent, 8.7 per cent lower than in 2008 and 27.2 per cent lower than in 1990

- Since 1987 yearly average temperature in Central England has been consistently above the 1961–1990 average at 0.42°C in 2010

- Summer rainfall in the UK since 2006 has been at least 22 per cent higher than the 1961–1990 average and in 2010 was higher than it has been since 1892 (32.3 per cent higher than the 1961–1990 average)

Local environment, countryside and wildlife

- Over 8 in 10 (85 per cent) of adults aged 16 and over in England in 2011 felt that being proud of their local environment was important

- Dog fouling was considered to be the most problematic local environment quality issue to just over 4 in 10 (41 per cent) adults in England aged 16 and over in 2009, while just over a third (34 per cent) felt that litter was a problematic issue to some extent

- Over 6 in 10 (63 per cent) of adults aged 16 and over in England in 2011 reported that it was very important to have public gardens, commons or other green space nearby. Just over 7 in 10 (71 per cent) reported that the most important reason for visiting a green space was fresh air

- Wild bird populations remained relatively stable between 1970 and 2009, however breeding populations of some common farmland and woodland birds have decreased, while the seabird population has risen over the period

Environmental taxes

- Just over half (51 per cent) of adults aged 15 and over in Great Britain in 2007 supported 'green' taxes in principle, while just under a third (32 per cent) opposed them

- In 2008, UK households paid £20.9 billion in environmental taxes, over half (53.7 per cent) of total environmental tax revenue

Environmental attitudes and lifestyles

The environment and pollution was the third most important issue that adults aged 16 and over in England felt that the government should address according to the 2009 Survey of Public Attitudes and Behaviours towards the Environment carried out by the Department for Environment, Food and Rural Affairs (Defra). Over a third (35 per cent) felt that environment and pollution issues were important compared with 57 percent for the economy in general and 37 per cent for unemployment (Defra, 2011a).

Table 1   **Attitudes towards current lifestyle and the environment,[1] 2010**

England   Percentages[2]

	Agree[3]	Neither agree or disagree	Disagree[3]
The so-called 'environmental crisis' facing humanity has been greatly exaggerated	38	19	39
Being green is an alternative lifestyle it's not for the majority	36	17	44
I find it hard to change my habits to be more environmentally friendly	28	15	56
It's not worth me doing things to help the environment if others don't do the same	25	10	64
It's only worth doing environmentally friendly things if they save you money	23	11	64
It would embarrass me if my friends thought my lifestyle was purposefully environmentally friendly	11	13	74

1 1,712 adults aged 16 and over were asked in March 2010 how much they agreed or disagreed with the statements in the table.

2 Percentages do not sum to 100 as the table excludes those who responded 'Don't know'.

3 Strongly or tend to agree or disagree.

Source: 2010 Omnibus Survey on Public attitudes and behaviours towards the environment, Department for Environment, Food and Rural Affairs (Defra, 2011a)

Adults aged 16 and over in England were asked to agree or disagree with statements on the environment in 2010 **(Table 1)**. Nearly 4 in 10 (38 per cent) agreed that the 'environmental crisis' facing humanity had been greatly exaggerated. Over a third (36 per cent) agreed that being green was an alternative lifestyle and was not for the majority of people. Similar proportions (39 per cent and 44 per cent) disagreed with these statements.

Just under 3 in 10 (28 per cent) agreed that it was hard to change their habits that so that they could be more environmentally friendly. Around a quarter of adults agreed that it was not worth doing things to help the environment if other people didn't do the same or if they didn't save money doing so (25 per cent and 23 per cent respectively). Just over 1 in 10 (11 per cent) agreed that they would feel embarrassed if their friends thought that their lifestyle was purposefully environmentally friendly. The majority of respondents disagreed with each of these four statements, however.

Table 2   **Environmentally friendly lifestyle, 2010[1]**

England   Percentages

	All aged 16 and over
I do one or two things or quite a few things that are environmentally-friendly	64
I'm environmentally-friendly in most things or everything I do	32
I don't really do anything that is environmentally-friendly	3

1 1,712 adults aged 16 and over in March 2010 were shown a list and asked 'Which would you say best describes your lifestyle?'

Source: 2010 Omnibus Survey on Public attitudes and behaviours towards the environment, Department for Environment, Food and Rural Affairs (Defra, 2011a)

In 2010 when adults in England were asked what best described their lifestyle, just under a third (32 per cent) agreed that they were environmentally-friendly in most or everything they did **(Table 2)**. Just under two-thirds (64 per cent) reported they had performed at least one environmentally-friendly task, while only 3 per cent reported that they didn't do anything environmentally-friendly.

Energy

The amount of energy consumption in domestic homes is important. Increased energy use depletes non-renewable resources. Further impacts can be climate change and rising energy bills.

Domestic energy consumption in the UK increased by 18 per cent between 1970 and 2009, from 37 to 44 million tonnes of oil equivalent. This change was affected by a number of factors such as the increase in number of households, changes in energy efficiency and external temperatures. In each year over the period 1970 to 2008, around 60 per cent of energy was consumed for heating purposes. This energy use shapes the total domestic energy consumption trend and makes it sensitive to year–on–year winter temperature fluctuations.

Figure 1   **Domestic energy consumption: by household and per person**

United Kingdom
Index numbers (1971=100)

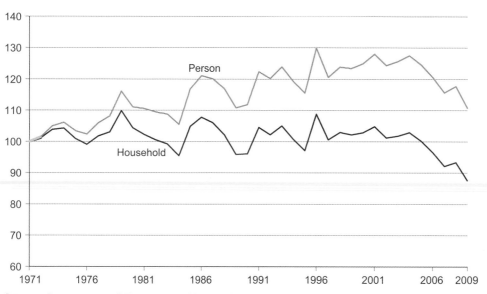

Source: Department of Energy and Climate Change (DECC, 2010a)

Since total energy consumption depends on the population and number of households, it is useful to analyse the changes in energy use per person and per household in order to capture the energy efficiency changes occurring. The energy consumption per household decreased by 13 per cent (from 1.87 to 1.64 tonnes of oil equivalent) between 1971 and 2009, and by 9 per cent (from 1.79 tonnes of oil equivalent) from 1990 **(Figure 1)**. This fall was accompanied by an increase in loft insulation, cavity walls insulation and double glazing. However, domestic energy consumption per person rose by 11 per cent from 637 to 705 kilograms of oil equivalent per person between 1971 and 2009.

The major factors affecting domestic energy consumption are:

- Household size: For example, the amount of energy required by two people living in two households is greater than the amount of energy required by two people living in the same household. The proportion of one-person households in Great Britain increased from 18 per cent in 1971 to 29 per cent in 2010 (ONS, 2011)

- Housing stock: In Great Britain in 2007, 36 per cent of the housing stock was built before 1939, 38 per cent between 1939 and 1975, and 26 per cent after 1975. Newer houses have to conform to much higher energy efficiency standards than previous building stock. However, considerable improvements in insulation standards in existing homes have offset some of the energy losses that would have otherwise been incurred. For example, the number of households with loft insulation increased by nearly a third (32.7 per cent) between 1976 and 2008, while the proportion of housing stock with double glazing increased by 31.2 per cent between 1976 and 2007. (DECC, 2010a)

- External temperature: When it is cold outside, more energy is used in the home for space heating.

- Internal temperature: Households are also kept warmer than they were in 1970, but more households have central heating which has made internal temperatures easier to manage. In 1971, 6.4 million homes were centrally heated; this had increased to 23.5 million by 2007, accounting for over 90 per cent of all households in Great Britain. Average internal temperatures in centrally heated homes increased from 14°C in 1971 to 17°C in 2008 (DECC, 2010a)

Table 3   Domestic energy consumption: by final use

United Kingdom   Million tonnes of oil equivalent

	1970	1980	1990	2000	2007	2008
Space heating[1]	22.1	23.8	23.7	28.7	24.9	26.5
Water heating	9.9	10.0	10.1	10.7	11.4	10.9
Lighting and appliances	2.7	4.1	5.5	6.1	7.2	7.3
Cooking	2.2	2.0	1.5	1.3	1.3	1.3
Total	36.9	39.8	40.8	46.9	44.9	46.0

1 The heating of a space, usually enclosed, such as a house or room.
Source: Department of Energy and Climate Change; Building Research Establishment (DECC, 2010a)

Most domestic energy consumption is used for space heating, which accounted for 58 per cent (26.5 million tonnes of oil equivalent) of final domestic energy use in the UK in 2008 **(Table 3)**. Water heating accounted for almost a quarter (24 per cent) of total domestic energy consumption. While the amount of domestic energy increased, the proportion of energy used for domestic space and water heating each year remained fairly steady over the period 1970 to 2008.

The other major areas of domestic energy consumption are lighting and appliances and cooking. In 1970, the energy used for household lighting and appliances accounted for 7 per cent of total domestic energy consumption, compared with 16 per cent in 2008 (2.7 compared to 7.3 million tonnes of oil equivalent). Energy use for cooking in the home fell from 6 per cent to 3 per cent of total domestic energy consumption over the same period, perhaps partly explained by changes in lifestyle with the greater availability of convenience food.

In 1970, nearly half (48.7 per cent) of domestic energy came from solid fuels such as coal, coke and breeze, while just under a quarter came from natural gas (24.2 per cent). Electricity and petroleum supplied 18.0 per cent and 9.1 per cent respectively. However, by 2009, two-thirds (66.0 per cent) of domestic energy came from natural gas with solid fuels supplying just 1.7 per cent. Electricity and petroleum supplied 24.2 per cent and 6.9 per cent respectively. Renewable sources and waste supplied 1.1 per cent of domestic energy (DECC, 2010a).

Renewable energy is used to describe a source of energy or power that has the capacity to replenish itself. In June 2009, the UK signed up to the EU Renewable Energy Directive, which includes a target whereby the UK has to provide 15 per cent of energy by 2020 (for electricity, heat and transport) from renewable sources. This target is equivalent to a seven-fold increase in UK renewable energy consumption from 2008 levels (DECC, 2010b).

In 2009, renewable energy accounted for 6.7 per cent of all electricity generated in the UK. This was equivalent to 2.2 million tonnes of oil equivalent, an increase of around 17 per cent since 2008 and more than three times the level in 1990. Biomass[i] accounted for the largest proportion of electricity generated from renewable sources (0.9 million tonnes of oil equivalent) followed by wind and wave power (0.8 million tonnes of oil equivalent) and hydroelectricity (0.5 million tonnes of oil equivalent). Over recent years, wind and wave power has been the fastest growing major renewable source, with its use in electricity generation increasing by nearly 10 times since 2000 (DECC, 2010c).

At the end of 2009, the UK had 1,648 sites generating electricity from renewable sources. 939 sites were in England, 436 in Scotland, 143 in Wales and 130 in Northern Ireland. The sites consisted of 536 wind and wave, 421 landfill gas, 400 hydro, 177 sewage gas and 114 other biofuel sites (DECC, 2010d).

Table 4   **Proportion of gross electricity consumption generated by renewable sources:[1] EU comparison**

Percentages

	1990	1998	2007	2008		1990	1998	2007	2008
Austria	65.4	67.9	60.5	62.0	Greece	5.0	7.9	6.8	8.3
Sweden	51.4	52.4	52.0	55.5	Bulgaria	4.1	8.1	7.5	7.4
Latvia	43.9	68.2	36.4	41.2	**United Kingdom**	**1.7**	**2.4**	**5.1**	**5.6**
Finland	24.4	27.4	26.0	31.0	Hungary	0.5	0.7	4.6	5.6
Slovenia	25.8	29.2	22.1	29.1	Belgium	1.1	1.1	4.2	5.3
Denmark	2.6	11.7	29.0	28.7	Czech Republic	1.9	3.2	4.7	5.2
Romania	23.0	35.0	26.9	28.4	Lithuania	2.5	3.6	4.6	4.6
Portugal	34.5	36.0	30.1	26.9	Poland	1.4	2.1	3.5	4.2
Spain	17.2	18.6	19.7	20.6	Luxembourg	2.0	2.5	3.7	4.1
Italy	13.9	15.6	13.7	16.6	Estonia	0.0	0.2	1.5	2.0
Slovakia	6.4	15.5	16.6	15.5	Cyprus	0.0	0.0	0.1	0.3
Germany[2]	3.8	4.8	14.8	15.4	Malta	0.0	0.0	0.0	0.0
France	14.8	14.4	13.3	14.4					
Ireland	4.8	5.5	9.3	11.7	**EU-27 average**	**11.9**	**13.4**	**15.5**	**16.7**
Netherlands	1.4	3.4	7.5	8.9					

1 Electricity produced from renewable energy sources comprises the electricity generation from hydro plants (excluding pumping), wind, solar, geothermal and electricity from biomass/wastes. Gross national electricity consumption comprises the total gross national electricity generation from all fuels (including autoproduction), plus electricity imports, minus exports.

2 Germany 1990 does not include former GDR.

Source: Eurostat, table tsdcc330 (Eurostat, 2011)

In the EU-27, 16.7 per cent of gross electricity consumption was generated by renewable sources in 2008 (the latest data available), nearly one and a half times more than in 1990 and nearly three times higher than the UK **(Table 4)**. The proportion of renewable sources used to generate electricity varied greatly across the EU-27. Austria generated the most electricity from renewable sources at around 62.0 per cent, followed by Sweden and Latvia at 55.5 per cent and 41.2 per cent respectively. All three of these countries have significant hydropower. Just under half of all the countries in the EU-27 generated less than 10 per cent of electricity from renewable sources in 2008.

Waste Management

Recycling prevents waste of materials and reduces the consumption of new raw materials and the use of energy. It also reduces air pollution and water pollution from incineration and landfill respectively. According to the Defra 2010 Omnibus Survey, 86 per cent of adults in England agreed that people have a duty to recycle their waste (Defra, 2011a).

In 2009/10, households in England generated around 23.7 million tonnes of waste which was 457 kilograms per person. Just under half (48.3 per cent) of the waste came from regular household collections; 39.7 per cent from household recycling; 7.5 per cent from civic amenity sites; and 4.5 per cent from other household sources not collected as part of the ordinary waste collection service. (Defra, 2010a).

Figure 2   **Household waste and recycling[1]**

England
Kilograms per person

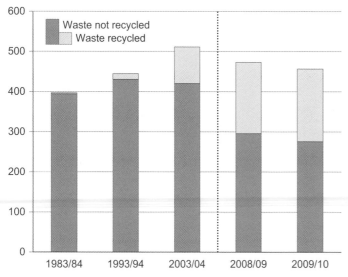

1 Recycling includes composting and reused waste.
Source: Department for Environment, Food and Rural Affairs (Defra, 2010a)

In 2009/10, 40 per cent (181 kilograms per person) of household waste was recycled, composted or reused, while the remainder (275 kilograms per person) went to landfill or was incinerated **(Figure 2)**. By comparison, in 1983/84, an average of 397 kilograms per person of household waste was produced, of which less than 1 per cent (3 kilograms per person) was recycled, composted or reused.

In 2009/10, around 9.4 million tonnes of household waste was collected for recycling in England. Waste for compost constituted the largest proportion collected for recycling, accounting for 40 per of the total (over 3.7 million tonnes). The next largest proportion was co-mingled materials (20 per cent), where several recyclable materials are collected in the same box or bin, for example, paper, cans and plastics. This was followed by paper and card (14 per cent). (Defra, 2011b).

Table 5   **Household waste recycling rates:[1] by region and waste disposal authority, 2009/10**

United Kingdom   Percentages

	Regional rate	Waste disposal authority			
		Lowest rate within region		Highest rate within region	
England	40	Ashford Borough Council	15	Staffordshire Moorlands District Council	62
North East	35	Middlesbrough Borough Council	23	Redcar and Cleveland Borough Council	43
North West	38	Manchester City Council MBC[2]	19	Cheshire East Council	49
Yorkshire and the Humber	37	Sheffield City Council	27	Ryedale District Council	52
East Midlands	46	Bassetlaw District Council	23	East Lindsey District Council	56
West Midlands	40	Wyre Forest District Council	26	Staffordshire Moorlands District Council	62
East	46	Great Yarmouth Borough Council	26	Rochford District Council	61
London	32	London Borough of Lewisham	17	London Borough of Bexley	51
South East	40	Ashford Borough Council	15	South Oxfordshire District Council	61
South West	43	Council of the Isles of Scilly	19	Cotswold District Council	60
Wales	40	Bridgend County Borough Council	30	Denbighshire County Council	53
Scotland[3]	35	Glasgow City Council	16	South Ayrshire	48
Northern Ireland	36	Strabane District Council	26	Magherafelt District Council	50

1 Includes composting and reused waste.

2 MBC is Metropolitan Borough Council.

3 Data for Scotland is 2008/09.

Source: Department for Environment, Food and Rural Affairs; Welsh Government; Scottish Environment Protection Agency; Department of Environment, Northern Ireland (Defra, 2010b; WAG 2010a; SEPA, 2009; DOENI, 2010)

Total household recycling as a proportion of total household waste in England was around 40 per cent in 2009/10 – the same rate as in Wales **(Table 5)**. In Northern Ireland 36 per cent of household waste was recycled, while in Scotland 35 per cent of waste was recycled in 2008/09 (the latest data available). There continued to be a wide variation in household recycling rates achieved by regions and waste disposal authorities or councils across the UK. Among the English regions, the highest recycling rate was in the East of England and the East Midlands (both 46 per cent), while London had the lowest recycling rate (32 per cent).

Across the waste disposal authorities or councils in England, recycling rates varied from 15 per cent in Ashford Borough Council, to 62 per cent in Staffordshire Moorlands District Council. The waste authority with the highest recycling rate in Wales was Denbighshire County Council, where over half (53 per cent) of all household waste was recycled, while the lowest was in Bridgend County Borough Council (30 per cent). In Northern Ireland the highest recycling rate was in Magherafelt District Council (50 per cent) and the lowest in Strabane District Council (26 per cent).

In Scotland, in 2008/09, the highest rate was in South Ayrshire (48 per cent) and the lowest in Glasgow City Council (16 per cent).

Some waste is disposed of illegally. Fly-tipping is the illegal deposit of any waste onto land or a highway that has no licence to accept it. It can cause pollution to surrounding land and waterways and damage wildlife and ecosystems. It can also damage perceptions of the local environment (see figure 10 on page 23). In 2009/10, local authorities in England dealt with nearly 947,000 incidents of fly-tipping, with nearly half (49 per cent) occurring on the highway. Nearly 6 in 10 (58 per cent) cases of fly-tipping dealt with by local authorities were recorded as being a car-boot load or less or a small van load and 63 per cent of fly-tipping cases consisting of household waste (Defra 2010b). In Wales there were 48,179 incidents of recorded fly-tipping in 2009/10. Since 2007/08 fly-tipping incidents in Wales have occurred mainly in urban local authorities, by the highway, and mostly involve household waste (WAG 2010b).

Pollution

Many everyday activities produce pollutants which can harm the environment and in turn affect human health. Pollutants can also have a detrimental impact on the quality of the local environment. Pollution can take the form of chemical substances or energy, such as noise, heat, or light and can affect air, land and water.

Figure 3   Emissions of selected air pollutants

United Kingdom
Million tonnes

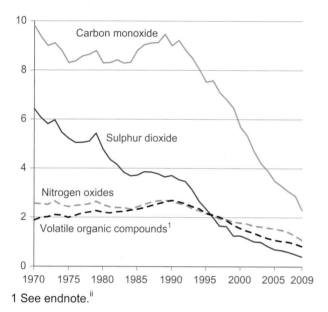

1 See endnote.[ii]

Source: Department for Environment, Food and Rural Affairs; AEA Energy and Environment (Defra, 2011c)

Emissions of the major air pollutants in the UK have been falling since the 1970s **(Figure 3)**. Carbon monoxide is formed from incomplete combustion of fuels that contain carbon. This is mostly from transport but notable contributions also come from industry and households. Release of this pollutant into the atmosphere is a health issue as it reduces the capacity of the blood to carry oxygen around the body. Between 1970 and 2009 emissions of carbon monoxide have decreased by 77 per cent from 9.8 million tonnes to 2.3 million tonnes. The reduction is due to improved engine efficiency in transport and the introduction in the early 1990s of catalytic converters in petrol-driven cars (Defra 2011d).

Sulphur dioxide and Nitrogen oxides are pollutants that irritate the airways of the lungs, increasing the symptoms of those suffering from lung diseases. Sulphur dioxide is emitted by combustion of fuels containing sulphur such as coal and heavy oils, largely by power stations and refineries. Between 1970 and 2009, emissions of sulphur dioxide decreased by 94 per cent from 6.4 million tonnes to 0.4 million tonnes. Nitrogen oxides are emitted mainly by road transport. Between 1970 and 2009, emissions of nitrogen oxides decreased by 58 per cent from 2.6 million tonnes to 1.1 million tonnes. These decreases are a largely a result of cleaner power stations, less use of coal and again the use of catalytic converters in cars (Defra 2011d).

Volatile organic compounds (VOCs)[ii] are emitted as gases from certain solids or liquids. Solvents, production processes, and the extraction and distribution of fossil fuels are the primary sources of emissions. Concentrations of many VOCs are consistently higher indoors (up to 10 times higher) than outdoors and are emitted by a wide range of products such as paints and lacquers, paint strippers, and cleaning supplies. Human health may be affected by cancer, central nervous system disorders, liver and kidney damage, reproductive disorders, and birth defects. Emissions of volatile organic compounds reached a peak in 1990 at 2.7 million tonnes and has since decreased by 69 per cent to 0.8 million tonnes in 2009. The decrease in emissions since the early 1990s reflects stricter limits on emissions from various sectors (Defra 2011d).

Figure 4 shows the number of days between 1987 and 2010 when there was moderate or higher pollution in urban and rural areas across the UK[iii]. The results are based on five pollutants, three of which have already been referred to in this chapter (carbon monoxide, nitrogen dioxide and sulphur dioxide) and ozone and particulate matter (PM_{10})[iv]. Ground level is formed from chemical reactions between precursors such as nitrogen oxides and volatile organic compounds in the presence of sunlight and can worsen the symptoms of lung diseases. PM_{10} is particulate matter that is less than 10 microns in diameter (about a seventh of the thickness of a human hair) and originates from man-made sources including vehicle exhaust emissions, coal combustion and industrial processes, and also from natural sources such as sand or sea-spray. Both these pollutants can cause breathing difficulties through long term exposure. Both these pollutants can cause breathing difficulties through long term exposure.

Figure 4   **Average number of days of moderate or higher air pollution**

United Kingdom
Number of days

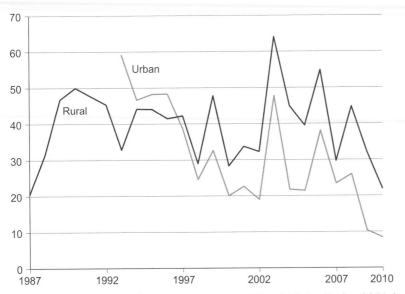

Source: Department for Environment, Food and Rural Affairs (Defra, 2011e)

The average number of days of moderate or higher air pollution for rural areas decreased between 2009 and 2010 to 22 days, the lowest since 1987. For urban areas, there was an average of 8 pollution days, down from 10 in 2009, and the lowest since records began in 1993. The rural results are mostly driven by ozone and the urban results from ozone and PM_{10}. Urban areas tend to have lower levels of ground level ozone than rural areas due to higher levels of nitric oxide, which can destroy ozone. Both ozone and PM_{10} are strongly influenced by weather and so vary over time, for example the high levels during the hot summers of 2003 and 2006.

Pollution incidents of air, water and land are monitored by the Environment Agency. In 2009 there were 770 recorded Category 1 or Category 2 pollution incidents[v] in England and Wales. The number of incidents have almost halved since 2002 when there were 1,468 serious incidents reported. Of these Category 1 or 2 incidents in 2009, 483 were water pollution, 206 land pollution and 144 air pollution (some incidents result in pollution to more than one medium).

Pollution from the land and rivers can also impact on the seas around the UK. Sewage effluent, storm water overflows and river-borne pollutants impact on the microbiological quality of bathing waters which could affect human health. The European Commission's (EC) Bathing Water Directive (76/160/EEC[vi]) gives mandatory values and guideline values for a number of physical, chemical and microbiological parameters at bathing waters, among which total and faecal coliforms are considered to be the most important. Coliforms are bacteria which inhabit the intestines of humans and other vertebrates.

Figure 5   Bathing water quality[1]

United Kingdom
Percentages

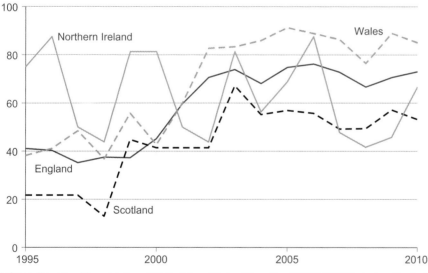

1 Compliance with guideline EC Bathing Water Directive 76/160/EEC during the bathing season. Bathing waters which are closed for a season are excluded for that year. Inland bathing waters were identified for the first time in 1998.

Source: Environment Agency; Scottish Environment Protection Agency; Northern Ireland Environment Agency (Defra, 2011f)

In 2010, 571 of the 587 coastal bathing waters in the UK met the mandatory (basic) standards of the European Bathing Water Directive, while 421 reached the guideline standard. Bathing waters complying to guideline standards in England increased from 41.1 per cent in 1995 to 73.0 per cent in 2010 **(Figure 5)**. Compliance in Scotland increased from 21.7 per cent to 53.2 per cent and in

Wales from 38.2 per cent to 85.0 per cent during the same period. Compliance in Northern Ireland was 66.7 per cent in 2010, while in 1995 it had been 75.0 per cent. Compliance in Northern Ireland is much more variable than in the other UK countries because it has only 4 per cent of the UK coastal bathing waters and just one failure will have a marked impact (Defra 2011f).

Climate change

Climate change is defined as any long-term change in the pattern of weather, temperature, wind and rainfall. Opinion on climate change is divided. According to the Defra 2010 Omnibus Survey nearly 4 in 10 (37 per cent) adults aged 16 and over in England agreed with the statement 'the effects of climate change are too far in the future to really worry me', while 46 per cent disagreed. Men were more likely to agree with this statement compared with women at 41 per cent and 34 per cent respectively (Defra, 2011a).

Climate change may result from both natural and human causes. Some studies of long-term climate change have shown a connection between the concentrations of key greenhouse gases – carbon dioxide, methane and nitrous oxide in the atmosphere and mean global temperature. The accumulation of these gases in the atmosphere may cause heat from the sun to be trapped near the Earth's surface – known as the 'greenhouse effect'.

The Kyoto Protocol is an international legally-binding agreement to reduce the emissions of greenhouse gases which was adopted in 1997 under the UN Framework Convention on Climate Change. Under the Protocol, the UK has a legally binding target to reduce its emissions of a 'basket' of six greenhouse gases by 12.5 per cent over the period 2008 to 2012. This reduction is against 1990 emission levels for carbon dioxide, methane and nitrous oxide, and 1995 levels for hydrofluorocarbons, perfluorocarbons and sulphur hexafluoride. This means that to meet the UK's Kyoto commitment, greenhouse gas emissions must be below 682.4 million tonnes of carbon dioxide (CO_2) equivalent over the first five-year commitment of the protocol (2008–2012).

The UK Climate Change Act 2008 included targets for the UK to reduce its greenhouse gases by at least 80 per cent by 2050 and at least 34 per cent by 2020. Like the Kyoto protocol it uses 1990 as its base year. It also establishes a system of five-year carbon budgets towards these targets. The first carbon budget covers 2008–12 and requires that the total UK greenhouse gas emissions do not exceed 3,018 million tonnes CO_2 equivalent[vii]. This is equivalent to 603.6 million tonnes CO_2 equivalent per year during that period. (DECC, 2008). As an additional pre 2050 target it was proposed in May 2011 that the UK would cut its emissions by 50 per cent against 1990 levels between 2023 and 2027[vii] (DECC 2011b).

Table 6   Progress towards meeting Kyoto target and 2008–2012 carbon budget target

United Kingdom   Million tonnes of carbon dioxide equivalent

	All greenhouse gases Kyoto protocol coverage[1]		All greenhouse gases UK Carbon Budgets coverage[2]	
	Actual emissions	Emissions with allowance for trading	Actual emissions	Emissions with allowance for trading
Baseline	779.9	779.9	783.1	783.1
Target (2008–12)	682.4		603.6	
1990	778.3	778.3		
2000	671.2	671.2		
2008	620.5	600.6	616.0	596.7
2009	566.3	580.0	561.8	575.3

1 The Kyoto Protocol target includes emissions from the UK, Crown Dependencies and UK Overseas Territories. The target uses a narrower definition for the Land Use, Land-Use Change and Forestry sector (LULUCF).

2 UK Carbon Budgets were introduced in 2008. Figures include emissions solely from the UK and exclude emissions from Crown Dependencies and UK Overseas Territories. Figures include a wider Land Use, Land-Use Change and Forestry sector (LULUCF).

Source: Department of Energy and Climate Change; AEA Energy and Environment (DECC, 2011a)

In 2009, UK emissions of the Kyoto basket of greenhouse gases were estimated to be 566.3 million tonnes of carbon dioxide equivalent without allowance for trading[viii] **(Table 6)**. This was 8.7 per cent lower than in 2008 (620.5 million tonnes) and 27.2 per cent lower than in 1990 (778.3 million tonnes). Carbon dioxide is the main greenhouse gas accounting for around 84 per cent of total greenhouse gas emissions in 2009, equivalent to 473.7 million tonnes. This was around 9.8 per cent lower than 2008 (525.1 million tonnes).

Table 6 also shows the UK's performance against both the Kyoto protocol and the carbon budget target. UK emissions of the basket of six greenhouse gases covered by the Kyoto Protocol (including allowances for trading) were 25.6 per cent lower in 2009 than in the base year from 779.9 to 580.0 million tonnes of carbon dioxide equivalent. For the carbon budget target, UK greenhouse gas emissions (including allowances for trading) were 26.5 per cent lower in 2009 than in the base year, down from 783.1 to 575.3 million tonnes of carbon dioxide equivalent (DECC, 2011c)

Figure 6   Source of greenhouse gas emissions[1]

United Kingdom
Index numbers (1990 = 100)

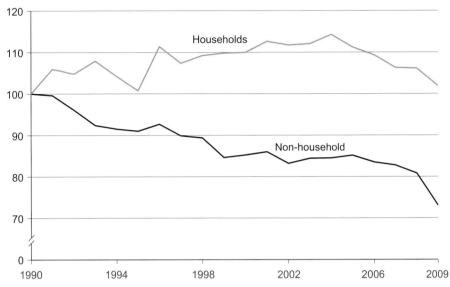

1 Carbon dioxide, methane, nitrous oxide, hydroflurocarbons, perflurocarbon and sulphur hexafluoride.
Source: Office for National Statistics; AEA Energy and Environment (ONS 2010)

According to the Office for National Statistics' Environmental Accounts[ix], between 1990 and 2009, emissions of greenhouse gases from the non-household sector (UK companies and the public sector) fell by 26.9 per cent, while the household sector rose by 1.9 per cent **(Figure 6)**. The largest proportional fall in the non-household sector was in manufacturing (47.5 per cent, equivalent to 81.8 million tonnes of CO_2 equivalent). The largest increase was in the transport and communication sector (32.1 per cent, equivalent to 21.0 million tonnes of CO_2 equivalent). Between 2008 and 2009 emissions from the non-household sector fell by 9.6 per cent, while the household sector fell by 4.0 per cent. The faster fall in greenhouse gases emissions in 2009 compared to previous years may be due to the contraction in economic activity.

Examples of the impact of climate change include changes in surface temperature, in the thermal growing season, in annual precipitation and rises in sea levels.

Figure 7   **Difference in average surface temperature: deviation from 1961–1990 average[1]**

Global and Central England[2]

Degrees Celsius

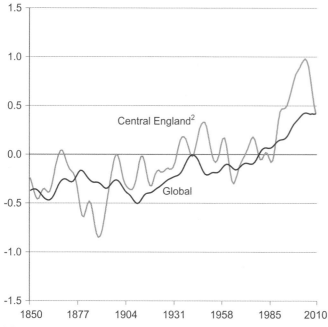

1 Data have been smoothed using a 21-point binomial filter to remove short-term variation from the time series and to get a clearer view of the underlying changes.

2 Central England temperature is representative of a roughly triangular area of the UK enclosed by Bristol, Lancashire and London.

Source: Hadley Centre for Climate Prediction and Research (DECC, 2010e)

Global thirty-year average surface temperatures[x] have risen by around 0.7°C since the end of the 19th century. Since 1979 temperatures have been consistently above the 1961–1990 average temperature, increasing from 0.02°C above average in 1979 to 0.42°C above average in 2010 **(Figure 7)**.

Average surface temperature in 'Central England' (a triangular area of the UK enclosed by Bristol, Lancashire and London) has risen by about 0.7°C since the mid 19th century. Since 1987 yearly average temperature has been consistently above the 1961–1990 average reaching a high of 0.98°C above in 2004 before decreasing to 0.42°C above in 2010. However, 2010 was the coldest year since 1986, mainly due to cold weather in January, February and December. The cold weather experienced in December made it one of the coldest calendar months since 1890.

The warmer temperatures over 'Central England' have resulted in the thermal growing season (a period of time each year during which plants can grow) generally becoming longer. The thermal growing season is defined as beginning when the temperature exceeds 5°C on five consecutive days and ending when the temperature is below 5°C for five consecutive days. There has been an increase in growing season length since 1980, largely due to the earlier onset of spring. The earliest start of the thermal growing season was in 2002 when it began on 13 January. The longest growing season in the 239-year series occurred in 2000 with 330 days. The shortest growing season was 181 days in 1782 and 1859. In 2010 the thermal growing was 255 days (DECC, 2010e).

Higher temperatures and higher sea-surface temperatures caused by the increased emissions of greenhouse gases in turn increase the water holding capacity of the atmosphere resulting in more precipitation. Across the UK, average annual rainfall varies from around 5,000 millimetres in parts of the western highlands of Scotland to around 500 millimetres in parts of East Anglia and on the borders of the Thames estuary.

Figure 8   Winter and summer precipitation[1]

England & Wales

Percentage change from 1961–1990 average

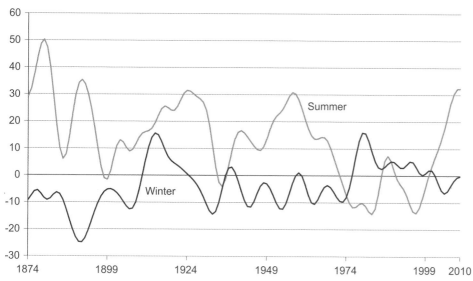

1 Winter is December to March, summer is July to August. Data have been smoothed using a 21-point binomial filter to remove short-term variation from the time series and to get a clearer view of the underlying changes.

Source: Hadley Centre for Climate Prediction and Research (DECC, 2010e)

The past decade has seen a considerable rise in the amount of summer rainfall (July to August) in England and Wales and since 1996 it has increased year on year **(Figure 8)**. Summer rainfall since 2006 has been at least 22 per cent higher than the 1961–1990 average and in 2010 was higher than it has been since 1892, at 32.3 per cent higher than the 1961–1990 average. There have been less rapid changes in winter rainfall (December to March). Since 2004 winter rainfall has been from 0.2 per cent to 6.5 per cent lower than the 1961–1990 average.

Since the mid-19th century, sea level around the world has been rising. Sea level change is a serious impact of climate change as so many people around the world live near or next to the sea. The three main reasons for this are thermal expansion[xi], the melting of glaciers and ice caps, and the loss of ice from the Greenland and West Antarctic ice sheets. A report by the Department for Energy and Climate Change looks at the sea level records at Aberdeen, Liverpool, Newlyn, North Shields and Sheerness as they are the longest sea level records available in the UK. In the past few decades, North Shields (in Newcastle) and Sheerness (in Kent) have seen the largest rises in sea level, compared with 1920 base levels. Since 1998, an increase of at least 190mm compared with 1920 was seen at both these sites. Until the mid-1980s, sea levels in Aberdeen have varied with 1920 levels. On average, in the past two decades sea levels are more than 60 mm higher than the baseline. Between 2006 and 2008 sea levels have been on average higher than in 1920 by more than 100 mm. Sea levels in Liverpool have also increased dramatically in recent years (there is no data for 2005, 2006, 2008 or 2009). Since the 1980s, sea levels have regularly been more than 100 mm higher than 1920 levels. Two of the largest rises in sea level were in 2004 and 2007 (231 mm and 279 mm respectively) (DECC, 2010e).

Local environment, countryside and wildlife

According to the 2011 Lifestyle Omnibus Survey carried out by Defra, 85 per cent of adults aged 16 and over in England felt that being proud of their local environment was important (Defra, 2011a).

Figure 9   **Problematic local environment issues,[1] 2009**

England
Percentages

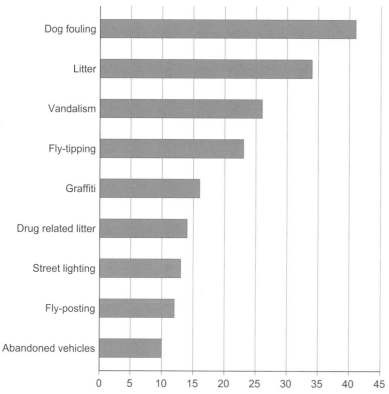

1 Respondents (1,155 on-street face-to-face interviews April 2009) were shown a show card and asked 'Thinking now about what you actually see in your local area, please indicate how much of a problem each of the following issues are? Respondents had to score each issue on a scale of 1 to 5 where 5 was a major problem and 1 was no problem. The percentages shown in the chart are those that rated the issues as 5 or 4.

Source: Keep Britain Tidy (KBT, 2009)

There are many issues that affect the local environment and people's perceptions of it. Dog fouling was considered to be the most problematic local environment quality issue to some extent to just over 4 in 10 (41 per cent) adults in England aged 16 and over in 2009 **(Figure 9)**. Just over a third (34 per cent) felt that litter was a problematic issue to some extent, while around a quarter reported that vandalism and fly-tipping was a problem to some extent (26 per cent and 23 per cent respectively). Conversely around 1 in 10 people reported that street lighting (13 per cent), fly-posting (12 per cent) and abandoned vehicles (10 per cent) were a problem to some extent. According to the same Keep Britain Tidy report, the most problematic litter types that were rated a specific problem in the respondents local environment were cigarettes (54 per cent), confectionary wrappers (45 per cent), chewing gum or cans and bottles (both 44 per cent).

With the majority of people living in an urban area in the UK green space can be an important part of people's local environment. According to Defra, over 6 in 10 (63 per cent) of adults aged 16 and over in England in 2011 reported that it was very important to have public gardens, parks, commons or other green space nearby. A further 30 per cent stated it was fairly important. Over 9 in 10 (92 per cent) visited a green space at some time, while 56 per cent did so weekly or more frequently. Just under 3 in 10 (29 per cent) stated that they visited green space one or two days a week and 15 per cent reported that they visited three to five days a week (Defra, 2011a).

Figure 10   **Reasons for spending time in green spaces,[1] 2011**

England
Percentages

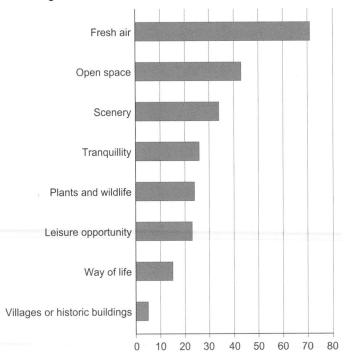

1 1,769 adults aged 16 and over were asked in March 2011 'What are the three most important reasons for spending time in public gardens, parks, commons or other green spaces'?

Source: Department for Environment, Food and Rural Affairs (Defra, 2011a)

Just over 7 in 10 (71 per cent) adults aged 16 and over in England 2011 reported that the most important reason for visiting a green space was fresh air **(Figure 10)**. Over 4 in 10 (43 per cent) felt that the open space was an important reason to visit. Over a third (34 per cent) felt that scenery was important, while around a quarter reported that tranquillity, plants and wildlife and leisure opportunities were important reasons to visit a green space (26 per cent, 24 per cent and 23 per cent respectively). People in households with children were significantly more likely than people in households without children to visit green spaces for leisure opportunities (35 per cent and 18 per cent respectively). People in households without children were significantly more likely than people in households with children to visit green spaces for the scenery (37 per cent and 27 per cent respectively).

In 2010, just over half (51 per cent) of land in the UK was either grass or rough grazing, while a fifth (20 per cent) was covered by crops or left as bare fallow. Urban land or 'land not otherwise specified' made up 15 per cent of the UK, while around 13 per cent of the UK land area was forest and woodland. Inland water covered 1 per cent of UK land area.

Table 7   Woodland area: by UK country

United Kingdom

	Thousand hectares					Percentage of total surface area[1]				
	England	Wales	Scotland	Northern Ireland[2]	United Kingdom	England	Wales	Scotland	Northern Ireland[2]	United Kingdom
1905	681	88	351	15	1,140	5.2	4.2	4.5	1.1	4.7
1924	660	103	435	13	1,211	5.1	5.0	5.6	1.0	5.0
1947	755	128	513	23	1,419	5.8	6.2	6.6	1.7	5.9
1965	886	201	656	42	1,784	6.8	9.7	8.4	3.1	7.4
1980	948	241	920	67	2,175	7.3	11.6	11.8	4.9	9.0
1995–99	1,097	287	1,281	81	2,746	8.4	13.8	16.4	6.0	11.3
2010[3]	1,294	304	1,385	88	3,070	9.9	14.6	17.8	6.5	12.7
2011[3]	1,297	304	1,390	88	3,079	10.0	14.7	17.8	6.5	12.7

1 Percentage of the total surface area excluding inland water.

2 For Northern Ireland, 1905 figure is estimate for Ulster 1908.

3 Figures for England, Wales and Scotland are based on data obtained from the National Forest Inventory.

Source: Forestry Commission, Forest Service (FC, 2010)

At the end of March 2011, the area of woodland in the UK was 3.1 million hectares **(Table 6)**. Just under half (45 per cent) was in Scotland (equivalent to 1.4 million hectares), 42 per cent in England (1.3 million hectares), 10 per cent in Wales (0.3 million hectares) and 0.1 million hectares in Northern Ireland. Since the early 1900s areas of woodland have increased in all the UK countries. Woodland in Scotland has increased by 1.0 million hectares between 1905 and 2011 and in England by 0.6 million hectares.

The Forestry Commission / Forest Service own around 28 per cent of the woodland in the UK but this proportion varies among UK countries. In Northern Ireland around 69 per cent of woodland was owned by the Forest Service, compared to 16 per cent owned by the Forestry Commission in England (FC, 2011).

Wild bird populations are a good indicator of the general state of the countryside and its associated wildlife. They occupy a range of different habitats and as they tend to be near to, or at the top of the food chain, their level of population reflects changes in insects, plants and other aspects of the environment.

Figure 11   Population of wild birds:[1] by species group

United Kingdom

Index numbers (1970=100)

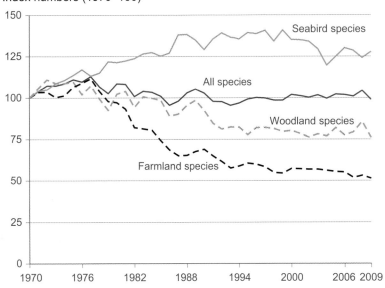

1 It was not possible to complete the Breeding Birds Survey in 2001 because of restrictions imposed during the outbreak of foot-and-mouth disease. Estimates for that year are based on the average for 2000 and 2002 for individual species. See endnote[xii] for methodology and wild bird species.

Source: British Trust for Ornithology; Royal Society for the Protection of Birds; Department for Environment, Food and Rural Affairs (Defra, 2011g)

Between 1970 and 2009 the combined population for all wild-bird species[xiii] in the UK has remained relatively stable **(Figure 11)**. However, since the 1970s breeding populations of some common farmland and woodland birds have decreased, while the seabird population has risen.

The number of farmland birds declined by 49 per cent between 1970 and 2009. The decline was mostly driven by specialist farmland birds such as the grey partridge, turtle dove, starling, tree sparrow and corn bunting populations whose populations have declined by over 70 per cent over this period. The number of woodland birds has decreased by 24 per cent between 1970 and 2009. Populations of some specialist woodland birds such as the wood warbler, willow tit and tree pipit have declined by over 70 per cent since 1970. However some specialist species such as the blackcap, great spotted woodpecker, green woodpecker and nuthatch saw their population more than double over the same period. The seabird population has increased by around 28 per cent since 1970, but different species have had mixed fortunes. For example, kittiwakes have declined by around 45 per cent since 1970 but conversely guillemots have increased by 126 per cent over the same period (Defra, 2011g).

Fish are a vital element of the ocean's ecosystem. Estimates of spawning stock biomass (the total weight of all sexually mature fish in a population) are used to determine whether the population of each stock is at a sustainable level. Historical trends in spawning stock biomass vary from species to species and fluctuate over relatively short periods depending on the success of breeding from year to year. Some stocks are at or near historical low levels as a result of both over-exploitation and natural factors, while other stocks have recovered due to reductions in fishing activity and/or more favourable environmental conditions leading to more successful spawning. Pollution of the sea has a much smaller impact on fish biomass than fishing or natural processes because concentrations of contaminants in sea water are generally low.

Figure 12   **North sea fish stocks**[1]

Thousand tonnes

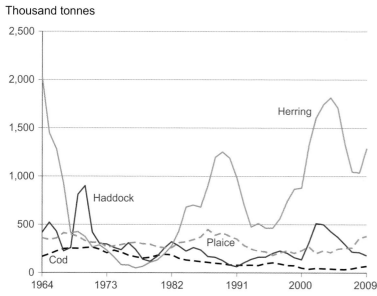

1 Spawning stock biomass (the total weight of all sexually mature fish in a population).
Source: Centre for Environment, Fisheries and Agriculture Science; International Council for the Exploration of the Sea

For fisheries to be both sustainable and productive, they must be managed in a way that minimises the risk of depleting spawning stocks so that the numbers of young fish produced each year is impaired. For example the spawning stock biomass of cod, a popular food in the UK, has declined substantially over time in waters around the UK due to a combination of overfishing and less favourable environmental conditions for spawning. The spawning stocks of cod in the North Sea and eastern English Channel declined from around 167,000 tonnes in 1964 to an all time low of 35,000 tonnes in 2006, a decrease of 79 per cent **(Figure 12)**. The cod biomass recovered slightly by 2009 to around 69,000 tonnes. The North Sea herring stock was heavily over-fished in the 1970s resulting in a 98 per cent decline in spawning stock biomass from just over 2 million tonnes in 1964 to 48,000 tonnes in 1977. A closure of the fishery between 1978 and 1982 was followed by a rapid increase in biomass to over 1 million tonnes by the late 1980s. During the 1990s a combination of increasing fishing activity and declining numbers of young fish entering the stock caused another reduction in biomass. However, management actions reduced the amount of fishing after the mid 1990s and the stock recovered again to around 1.8 million tonnes by 2004, with a more recent decline due to environmental factors.

During 2010, the International Council for the Exploration of the Sea (ICES) provided quantitative advice on spawning stock biomass and fishing mortality for 16 finfish stocks in waters around the UK in relation to reference points for sustainability. These represent a wide range of different stocks and fisheries including demersal roundfish (cod, haddock, and saithe), flatfish (sole, plaice), pelagic (mackerel, herring) and widely dispersed (blue whiting). In 2009, 38 per cent of the 16 stocks were estimated to be at full reproductive capacity and being harvested sustainably. During the period 1990 to 1999, the percentage varied around much lower values of 0 per cent to 20 per cent (ICES, 2010).

Environmental taxes

Environmental taxes include those on energy such as fossil fuel duty and climate change levy; taxes on transport such as air passenger duty and vehicle excise duty; those on pollution such as landfill tax and those on resources such as the aggregates levy. According to a survey conducted for the Green Fiscal Commission in 2007, just over half (51 per cent) of adults aged 15 and over in Great Britain supported 'green' taxes in principle, while just under a third (32 per cent) opposed them (GFC,2007).

Figure 13   Proportion of environmental taxes[1] paid: by industry sector, 2008

United Kingdom
Percentages

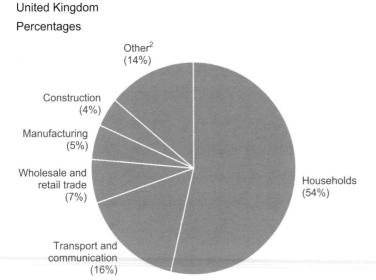

Environmental tax receipts amounted to £39.0 billion

1 See endnote [vii] on environment taxes.

2 Includes agriculture; education, health and social work; energy, gas and water supply; mining and quarrying; public administration; rest of the world; other business services and other services.

Source: Environmental Accounts, Office for National Statistics (ONS, 2010)

In 2008, environmental tax receipts amounted to £39.0 billion. UK households contributed the most towards environmental tax revenue, paying over half: £20.9 billion or 53.7 per cent **(Figure 13)**. The transport and communication industries paid £6.3 billion (16.1 per cent), while the wholesale and retail trade paid £2.6 billion (6.6 per cent). The manufacturing sector paid £2.1 billion and the construction sector £1.7 billion.

Environmental tax receipts in 2010 were £41.4 billion, 8.0 per cent of all taxation revenue. The largest proportion of the environmental taxes were from duty on hydrocarbon oils, for example, petrol and diesel (at 65.3 per cent) followed by vehicle excise duty (13.8 per cent). Environmental taxation as a proportion of Gross Domestic Product (GDP)[xiv] has fallen from 3.5 per cent in 1998 to 2.8 per cent in 2010.

References

DECC, 2008, Climate Change Act 2008, available at
www.decc.gov.uk/en/content/cms/legislation/cc_act_08/cc_act_08.aspx

DECC, 2010a, Energy consumption in the United Kingdom, available at
http://www.decc.gov.uk/en/content/cms/statistics/publications/ecuk/ecuk.aspx

DECC 2010b, The Renewable Energy Strategy (RES), available at
http://www.decc.gov.uk/en/content/cms/meeting_energy/renewable_ener/res/res.aspx

DECC, 2010c, Renewables statistics, available at
http://www.decc.gov.uk/en/content/cms/statistics/energy_stats/source/renewables/renewables.aspx

DECC, 2010d, Renewable electricity in Scotland, Wales, Northern Ireland and the regions of
England in 2009, available at
www.decc.gov.uk/assets/decc/statistics/publications/trends/articles_issue/564-trendssep10-renewable-
electricity-article.pdf

DECC 2010e, Impacts of climate change in the UK, available at
www.decc.gov.uk/en/content/cms/statistics/climate_change/impacts_cc/impacts_cc.aspx

DECC, 2011a, UK emissions statistics, available at
http://www.decc.gov.uk/en/content/cms/statistics/climate_stats/gg_emissions/uk_emissions/uk_emissions.as
px

DECC, 2011b, UK proposes Fourth Carbon Budget (Press notice), available at
http://www.decc.gov.uk/en/content/cms/news/pn11_41/pn11_41.aspx

DECC, 2011c, UK emissions statistics, 2010 provisional UK figures, available at
http://www.decc.gov.uk/en/content/cms/statistics/climate_stats/gg_emissions/uk_emissions/2010_prov/2010
_prov.aspx

Defra, 2010a, Municipal Waste Statistics 2009/10, available at
http://archive.defra.gov.uk/evidence/statistics/environment/wastats/bulletin10.htm

Defra, 2010b, Flycapture 2009-2010 data, available at
http://archive.defra.gov.uk/environment/quality/local/flytipping/flycapture-data.htm#0910

Defra, 2011a, Lifestyle Omnibus Survey: March 2011 available at
www.defra.gov.uk/statistics/environment/public-attitude/

Defra 2011b, Household waste recycling, by material, available at
http://www.defra.gov.uk/statistics/environment/waste/wrfg15-hhmaterial/

Defra, 2011c, Air Pollutant Emissions, 2009 additional results, available at
http://archive.defra.gov.uk/evidence/statistics/environment/airqual/

Defra, 2011d, What are the causes of air Pollution, available at
http://uk-air.defra.gov.uk/air-pollution/causes

Defra, 2011e, Air quality indicators – 2010 provisional UK results, available at
http://archive.defra.gov.uk/evidence/statistics/environment/airqual/

Defra, 2011f, Bathing water surveys, mandatory standards and guideline standards, available at
www.defra.gov.uk/statistics/environment/coastal-waters/cwtb01a-cwbathing/
www.defra.gov.uk/statistics/environment/coastal-waters/cwtb01b-cwbathing/

Defra, 2011g, Populations of wild birds, 1970–2009, available at,
http://archive.defra.gov.uk/evidence/statistics/environment/wildlife/kf/wdkf03.htm

DOENI, 2010, Northern Ireland Municipal Waste Management Statistics, available at
http://www.doeni.gov.uk/index/information/csrb/csrb_statistics.htm

Eurostat, 2011, Electricity generated from renewable sources, available at
epp.eurostat.ec.europa.eu/tgm/table.do?tab=table&init=1&plugin=1&language=en&pcode=tsdcc330

FC, 2011, Woodland Area, Planting & Restocking, available at
http://www.forestry.gov.uk/forestry/infd-7aqknx

GFC, 2007, Public attitudes to environmental taxation, available at
www.greenfiscalcommission.org.uk/images/uploads/Results.pdf?bcsi_scan_5099528575ce4d5c=0&bcsi_sc
an_filename=Results.pdf

ICES, 2010, Armstrong, M.J. and Holmes, I. 2011. Update of index for marine fin-fish stocks
around the UK following 2010 ICES advice. Report to Defra on PSA Delivery Agreement 28:
Secure a healthy natural environment for today and the future; Indicator 4(1): Number of fish
stocks around the UK at full reproductive capacity and harvested sustainability. March 2011.

KBT, 2009, The Word on our Street, available at
http://www.keepbritaintidy.org/Expertise/Research/ResearchReports/word_on_our_street.aspx

ONS, 2010, Environmental accounts 2010, available at
http://www.statistics.gov.uk/StatBase/Product.asp?vlnk=3698

ONS 2011, Social Trends: Household and families, available at
www.statistics.gov.uk/cci/article.asp?ID=2665

Sepa, 2009, Zero waste plan data, available at
http://www.sepa.org.uk/waste/waste_data/zero_waste_plan_data.aspx

WAG, 2010a, Municipal Waste Management Report for Wales, 2009-10, available at
http://wales.gov.uk/topics/environmentcountryside/epq/waste_recycling/bysector/municipal/annualreports/an
nualreport0910/?lang=en

WAG, 2010b, Fly-tipping, 2009–10, available at
http://wales.gov.uk/topics/statistics/headlines/environment2010/100909/?lang=en

Notes

[i] Biomass
Biomass is organic materials, such as wood by-products and agricultural wastes, which can be burned to produce energy or converted into a gas and used for fuel.

[ii] Volatile organic compounds
Volatile organic compounds (VOCs) are ozone precursors and comprise a wide range of chemical compounds including hydrocarbons, oxygenates and halogen containing species. Methane (CH_4) is an important component of VOCs but its environmental impact derives principally from its contribution to global warming. The major environmental impact of non-methane VOCs lies in their involvement in the formation of ground level ozone. Most VOCs are non-toxic or are present at levels well below guideline values. Others such as benzene and 1, 3-butadiene, are of concern because of their potential impact on human health.

[iii] Types of monitoring sites
Rural sites are in the open country away from roads, industrial areas and where people live.
Urban background sites are in urban locations (for example, parks and urban residential areas) away from emission sources.
Roadside sites are sites with sample inlets between one metre of the edge of a busy road and the back of the pavement (usually five metres from the roadside).

[iv] PM10
PM_{10} is airborne particulate matter. Specifically, it is that fraction of 'black smoke' that is thought most likely to be deposited in the lungs. It can be defined as the fraction resulting from a collection from black smoke by a size selective sampler that collects smaller particles preferentially, capturing 50 per cent of 10 micron aerodynamic diameter particles, more than 95 per cent of 5 micron particles, and less than 5 per cent of 20 micron particles.

[v] Pollution incidents
The Environment Agency defines four categories of pollution incidents:
Category 1: The most severe incidents, which involve one or more of the following:
- potential or actual persistent effect on water quality or aquatic life
- closure of potable water, industrial or agricultural abstraction necessary
- major damage to aquatic ecosystems
- major damage to agriculture and/or commerce
- serious impact on man, or
- major effect on amenity value

Category 2: Severe incidents, which involve one or more of the following:
- notification to abstractors necessary
- significant damage to aquatic ecosystems
- significant effect on water quality
- damage to agriculture and/or commerce
- impact on man, or
- impact on amenity value to public, owners or users

Category 3: Minor incidents, involving one or more of the following:
- a minimal effect on water quality
- minor damage to aquatic ecosystems
- amenity value only marginally affected, or
- minimal impact on agriculture and/or commerce

Category 4: Incidents where no impact on the environment occurred.

[vi] Bathing waters
Bathing water can be any running or still freshwater and sea water (except for water intended for therapeutic purposes and water used in swimming pools) where bathing is explicitly authorised by national authorities and where bathing is traditionally practiced by a large number of bathers. Sampling begins two weeks before the start of the bathing season and is carried out every other week at places where the daily average of

bathers is highest throughout the season. The bathing season runs from the 15 May until 30 September in England and Wales and from 1 June to 15 September in Scotland and Northern Ireland.

Coliforms are microorganisms found in the intestinal tract of animals and human beings. When found in water it indicates fecal pollution and potentially hazardous bacterial contamination. Faecal streptococci are also natural inhabitants of the gut of humans and other warm-blooded animals. However, as they have a greater ability to survive outside of the gut, they could be used as an indicator of less recent contamination by sewage.

Directive 76/160/EEC concerning the quality of bathing waters sets the following mandatory standards for the coliform parameters:
- 10,000 per 100 millilitres for total coliforms
- 2,000 per 100 millilitres for faecal coliforms

The directive requires that at least 95 per cent of samples taken for each of these parameters over the bathing season must meet the mandatory values. In practice this has been interpreted in the following manner: where 20 samples are taken only one sample for each parameter may exceed the mandatory values for the water to pass the coliform standards; where less than 20 samples are taken none may exceed the mandatory values for the water to pass the coliform standards.

The Bathing Water Directive also sets more stringent guideline microbiological standards. To comply with the tightest guideline standard, bathing waters must not exceed values of 500 total coliforms per 100 millilitres and 100 faecal coliforms per 100 millilitres in 80 per cent of water quality samples, and 100 faecal streptococci per 100 millilitres in 90 per cent of samples taken.

The Bathing Water Directive is being updated by the revised Bathing Water Directive (2006/7/EC), which will be fully implemented by 2015. The revised Directive sets tighter water quality standards based on two parameters, E.coli and intestinal enterococci. There will be four water quality classifications based on a four year data set: Excellent, Good, Sufficient and Poor, The Environment Agency will begin monitoring using the new standards in 2012 and the first classifications under the revised Directive will be issued in 2015. Until 2014, Defra will continue to report the bathing water results using the current standards.

There will be a new requirement for information about water quality and potential sources of pollution to be available at all bathing waters, with effect from 2012.

vii The UK Climate Change Act 2008
This Act includes legally binding targets for the UK to reduce its greenhouse gas emissions by at least 80 per cent by 2050, and by at least 34 per cent by 2020, both below base year levels. It also establishes a system of binding five-year carbon budgets to set the trajectory towards these targets.
Like the Kyoto Protocol, the Act uses a base year which is comprised of 1990 for carbon dioxide, methane and nitrous oxide, and 1995 for fluorinated compounds. However, this baseline figure differs from that used for reporting against the Kyoto Protocol; the baseline in the Act is revised each year to incorporate revisions made, whereas the Kyoto Protocol baseline is fixed.
The Government set the first three carbon budgets in May 2009, covering the periods 2008-12, 2013-17 and 2018-2022. The first of these budgets requires that total UK greenhouse gas emissions do not exceed 3,018 million tonnes CO2 equivalent over the five-year period 2008-12, which is about 23 per cent below the base year level on average over the period.

Summary of UK carbon Budgets, 2008-2022

	Base year (actual emissions)	Budget 1 2008-2012	Budget 2 2013-2017	Budget3 2018-2022
Budget level Metric Tonne Carbon Dioxide Equivalent (MtCO2e)		3018	2782	2544
Equivalent average annual emissions (MtCO2e)	783.1	603.6	556.4	508.8
Percentage reduction below base year levels		23	29	35

A fourth carbon budget of 1950 MtCO2e for the period 2023 to 2027 was proposed on 17th May 2011, for more information see http://www.decc.gov.uk/en/content/cms/news/pn11_41/pn11_41.aspx

[viii] **Emissions Trading**
The UK (as with all other Members States in the EU) has a cap (European Union Emissions Trading System – EU ETS) for emissions it can emit (this is mainly from power stations and heavy industry). For example, in 2009, the UK's total EU ETS emissions were less than its cap. This meant that the UK was able to either sell or carry over more emissions or allowances than they purchased or brought forward. For more detail about how the EU ETS works, see "Emissions Trading" section of the Statistics Release www.decc.gov.uk/media/viewfile.ashx?filetype=4&filepath=Statistics/climate_change/1214-stat-rel-uk-ghg-emissions-2009-final.pdf&minwidth=true

[ix] **Environmental accounts**
Environmental Accounts are satellite accounts to the National Accounts. As such they use similar concepts and classifications of industry to those employed in the National Accounts. They reflect the frameworks recommended by the European Union and United Nations for developing such accounts. For more information, please refer to the UK Environmental Accounts website.

ONS Environmental Accounts measure air emissions on a UK residents basis. This means that all emissions generated from transport at home and abroad by UK resident households and businesses are included. Emissions related to non-resident households and businesses travel and transport within the UK are excluded. Producing statistics on this basis allows for a more consistent comparison with key National Accounts indicators such as GDP and Gross Value Added.

[x] **Average temperatures and rainfall**
The World Meteorological Organisation (WMO) requires the calculation of average temperatures for consecutive periods of 30 years, with the latest covering the period 1961–90. Thirty years was chosen as a period long enough to eliminate year-to-year variations.

[xi] **Thermal expansion**
The oceans have an enormous heat storage capacity, but if global atmospheric temperatures rise, the oceans absorb heat and expand. This is called thermal expansion. A greater volume of ocean water due to thermal expansion will lead to a rise in sea level.

[xii] **Wild bird methodology**
The indices have been compiled in conjunction with the Royal Society for the Protection of Birds (RSPB), the British Trust for Ornithology (BTO) and the Joint Nature Conservation Committee (JNCC) from a wide range of sources, principally the Common Birds Census (from 1966 to 2000), the BTO/JNCC/RSPB Breeding Bird Survey (from 1994 to 2009), the BTO/Environment Agency for England and Wales (EA) Waterways Bird Survey (from 1974 to 2007), the BTO/EA Waterways Breeding Bird Survey (from 1998 to 2008), the BTO/Wildfowl & Wetland Trust/RSPB/JNCC Wetland Bird Survey counts, and the Seabird Monitoring Programme and the Periodic Seabird censuses supplied by JNCC, RSPB, the Seabird Group, SOTEAG (Shetland Oil Terminal Environmental Advisory Group) and other partners. The census sources provide an indication of the average annual rate of change between censuses for some species, and this is assumed to apply to each year between censuses.

[xiii] **Wild bird species**
Species in italics are specialists, while the remainder are generalists. A generalist species is able to thrive in a wide variety of environmental conditions and can make use of a variety of different resources. Specialist species can only thrive in a narrow range of environmental conditions and/or have a limited diet.
- **Woodland species (38):** Blackbird, *Blackcap*, Blue Tit, Bullfinch, *Capercaillie*, Chaffinch, *Chiffchaff*, *Coal Tit*, Crossbill, Dunnock, *Garden Warbler*, *Goldcrest*, *Great Spotted Woodpecker*, Great Tit, *Green Woodpecker*, *Hawfinch*, Jay, *Lesser Spotted Woodpecker*, *Lesser Redpoll*, Lesser Whitethroat, Long-tailed Tit, *Marsh Tit*, *Nightingale*, *Nuthatch*, *Pied flycatcher*, *Redstart*, Robin, *Siskin*, Song Thrush,

Sparrowhawk, Spotted Flycatcher, Tawny Owl, *Tree Pipit, Treecreeper, Willow Tit, Willow Warbler, Wood Warbler,* Wren.
- **Farmland species (19):** *Corn Bunting, Goldfinch,* Greenfinch, *Grey Partridge,* Jackdaw, Kestrel, *Lapwing, Linnet,* Reed Bunting, Rook, *Skylark, Starling, Stock Dove, Tree Sparrow, Turtle Dove, Whitethroat,* Woodpigeon, *Yellowhammer,* Yellow Wagtail.
- **Seabird species (19):** Arctic Skua, Arctic Tern, Atlantic Puffin, Black-headed Gull, Black-legged kittiwake, Common Guillemot, , Common Tern, European Shag, Great Black-backed Gull, Great Cormorant, Great Skua, Herring Gull, Lesser black-backed Gull, Little Tern, Mew Gull, Northern Fulmar, Northern Gannet, Razorbill, Sandwich Tern.

[xiv]Gross Domestic Product
Gross Domestic Product is a measure of the total economic activity occurring in the UK. It can be measured in three ways:
- Production
  Measures the Gross Domestic Product as the sum of all the Value Added by all activities which produce goods and services. (see Gross Value Added).
- Income (GDP(I))
  Measures the Gross Domestic Product as the total of incomes earned from the production of goods and services.
- Expenditure (GDP(E))
  Measures the Gross Domestic Product as the total of all expenditures made either in consuming finished goods and services or adding to wealth, less the cost of imports.